African Methodist Episcopal Church

**The African Methodist Episcopal Hymn and Tune Book**

Adapted to the Doctrine and Usages of the Church.

African Methodist Episcopal Church

**The African Methodist Episcopal Hymn and Tune Book**
*Adapted to the Doctrine and Usages of the Church.*

ISBN/EAN: 9783337119621

Printed in Europe, USA, Canada, Australia, Japan

Cover: Foto ©Thomas Meinert / pixelio.de

More available books at **www.hansebooks.com**

ADAPTED TO THE

# DOCTRINE AND USAGES OF THE CHURCH.

First Edition.

PHILADELPHIA, PA., U. S., A.:
PUBLISHED BY THE AFRICAN METHODIST EPISCOPAL BOOK CONCERN,
REV. T. W. HENDERSON, D.D., Business Manager,
No. 631 Pine Street.
1898.

## To the Ministers and Members of the African Methodist Episcopal Church.

*Greeting:*

Grace unto you, peace from God our Father and the Lord Jesus Christ. We give thanks to God the Father for the blessings he has conferred upon our church and upon the work committed to our care.

The committee appointed to compile and arrange a Hymn and Music Book for the Church has completed the work committed to it, and presents the same for your inspection, approval and use.

We are more than pleased that we have lived to see the consummation so devoutly wished for and prayed for by our fathers—a Hymn and Tune Book of our own to be used by our people.

To be convinced of the excellency of the work, one only has to examine the arrangement of the subjects, and to note the versatility of authors, words and music, embracing as they do every phase of life, from the cradle to the grave, from the Jordan to the Throne. Every condition, whether of sorrow or joy, is provided for in this book — songs for the marriage altar, communion table, festive, Easter and Endowment Days, commencement occasions, praises in the City of the living and hope for the City of the dead.

It is with great pleasure that we commend this book to all choirs in our churches and trust that since we have a book of our own that there will be uniformity in church services from the Atlantic's hesperian strand to the Golden Gates of the Pacific, and from the Northern Lakes to the everglades of Florida. Let the people praise the Lord with all their power of soul and mind; in every hamlet and in every lordly mansion, in church, school and family, let every one sing in the spirit and with an understanding, so that the earth below and the heavens above shall hear the anthem

"From all that dwell below the skies,
Let the Creator's praise arise;
Let the Redeemer's name be sung,
In every land, by every tongue"

And may it be borne on ten thousand tongues until the volume of praise and thanksgiving to God shall fill the earth and sky, and the universal praise on earth shall blend with the universal praise above, is the prayer of the superintendents of the African Methodist Episcopal Church, in the name of God our Father, Christ our Redeemer, Man our Brother.

HENRY McNEAL TURNER,
WESLEY JOHN GAINES,
BENJAMIN WILLIAM ARNETT,
BENJAMIN TUCKER TANNER,
ABRAHAM GRANT,
BENJAMIN FRANKLIN LEE,
MOSES BUCKINGHAM SALTER,
JAMES ANDERSON HANDY,
WILLIAM BENJAMIN DERRICK,
JOSIAH HAYNES ARMSTRONG.
*Bishops of the A. M. E. Church.*

## THE PUBLISHER'S WORDS.

The African Methodist Episcopal Church has been asking for a hymn and tune book for many years, and it is, therefore, with great pleasure this book is now given to the Church. Bishop Embry gave his last days on earth to its completion. To him and Prof. John T. Layton, of Washington, D. C., is due the credit for its compilation, and it is hoped that the Church will find it all that is to be desired in the way of a hymn and tune book. There will be found herein a faithful collection of the old and familiar tunes that have so long held a place in the affections of the people, and, besides, there will be found many new and inspiring tunes that will soon win a place in the hearts of all. Great care has been taken in all these selections, and it is believed that the book will compare favorably with the hymn and tune book of any other Church. We have included all the hymns of our latest book, and have added about two hundred additional ones, some of them being old standard hymns that were left out of the former book, including others that have never been published in any of our books before.

Bishop Arnett, who succeeded Bishop Embry as chairman of the committee, after consultation with numerous brethren, thought best to add a number of pieces suitable to various occasions, and it is hoped all will agree that it was a wise thing to do. No doubt some will miss a favorite hymn even from the present large collection, but since it would be impossible to put all hymns that might be desired into one book, it is believed that the collection now presented to the Church will give general satisfaction. Music for the Decalogue and the *Amens* in the sacramental service is also given, which will be of much service to our choirs. In order not to destroy the plates of the *word edition*, when we have found it necessary to add a hymn in *this*, not found in *that*, we have put the letter "*b*," after the number, which will indicate that if the hymn is wanted in the *word edition*, it will be found after that number in the supplement, which is found in the rear of the book. We give this book to the Church with the prayer that God may bless it to the edifying of the Church and to the salvation of many souls.

The space given to *Methodist Hymnody* will be found deeply interesting to all who desire to become acquainted with the important subject of the history of Methodist hymns. We hope all will read this matter with great care. Let our pastors and our choir directors everywhere see to it that our book now displaces all others, and let our people sing from their own book, which, at great labor and expense, has been prepared for them.

Praying God's blessings upon this book now given to the Church in His name,
We are faithfully yours,
T. W. HENDERSON,

PHILADELPHIA, Jan. 1, A. D. 1898.                                        Publisher.

# METHODIST HYMNODY.

The rise and progress of Methodism in the world is one of the wonders of the age. In 1739, only eight or ten persons convened in a small room in London ; now her ministers are standing guard on thousands of the outposts of Zion. The pioneer ministers were the companions of the early settlers and turned the dwelling-houses into meeting-houses and school-houses, each preacher having to be school-master as well as minister, temporal as well as spiritual adviser. The sermons, prayers and songs of the pioneers have cheered the frontiersman in his cabin and consoled him when dying.

We have great pleasure in introducing this volume to the ministers, congregations and societies of our world-wide organization, believing that it will bind the pulpit and the pew together with a golden cord, and will beget a sentiment of devotion that will strengthen the army of the living God and will encourage the young to study God in nature, Providence and Revelation—opening springs of joy and everlasting wells of salvation to the weary and thirsty pilgrim. The DICTIONARY OF HYMNOLOGY, setting forth the origin and history of Christian hymns of all ages and nations, edited by Dr. John Julian, M. A., Vicar of Wincebank, Sheffield, gives the following information :

"Methodism has made liberal contributions to the hymnody of the Christian Church. Before the first Methodist Society was formed, its founders saw the importance of singing in religious worship, and provided, out of the best available material then at command, a collection of *Psalms and Hymns* for that purpose. John Wesley made some excellent translations of German hymns, and his brother, Charles Wesley, began to write spiritual songs immediately after his conversion. His father, the Rector of Epworth, and his elder brother, S. Wesley, jun., had each written a few good hymns at a still earlier date, which remain in use at the present time. Chas. Wesley continued to write hymns for nearly fifty years and he has left over six thousand five hundred hymns and sacred poems, some of which are amongst those most frequently found in collections used in public worship. Some of the followers of John Wesley have also contributed hymns, both in the last and in this century, which have been included in many collections, and are of permanent interest.

Before dealing with the hymnody of the various Methodist bodies, it will be necessary to present some details concerning the rise and development of the principal sources from which all Methodist hymnody is derived. These sources are the *Poetical Works of John and Charles Wesley.*

i. *Poetical Works of John and Charles Wesley*—Charles Wesley pub. about *fifty* different books and tracts of hymns, from nearly all of which hymns have been selected for use in the churches. When he was a "Missioner in Georgia," John Wesley prepared and published *A collection of Psalms and Hymns*, which he described, in an enlarged edition of Wood's *Athenæ Oxoniensis*, as of the year 1736, but the imprint on the title-page is "Charles-Town, printed by Lewis Timothy, 1737." This work was the first collection of hymns published for use in the Church of England. The volume "illustrates his care to provide for the spiritual wants of those to whom he ministered; his earnest and serious temper; and his prominent ecclesiasticism." On his return to England, he prepared a new edition of that collection, and issued it in 1738. It is a 12mo. book of 84 pages. Of the American book, only one copy is known to exist; of the English reprint of 1738, three copies are known, one of which is in the Lambeth Palace library. [For details, see **England Hymnody, Church of, §1.**]

The first Methodists at Oxford sang psalms in proportion to their earnestness in religion; when they declined and shrank from the reproach of serious Godliness, the singing in their meetings was given up. After the conversion of the two Wesleys, in May, 1738, singing was resumed; and from that time to the present, frequent singing has been an essential part of Methodist worship. To encourage this form of service, John Wesley, as early as 1742, provided tune-books for the use of his followers (some of which are in use at the present time); and that all might learn to sing, he printed the melody only. We will now enumerate the original poetical works of John and Charles Wesley in detail.

1. The first collection pub. by John and Charles Wesley with their names on the title-page was entitled "Hymns and Sacred Poems," 1739, 12mo. pp. 223, and contained 139 hymns. This was reprinted the same year without the Poems, and a third ed., unabridged, is also dated 1739. In this book are given the first of Charles Wesley's compositions, and out of this volume 50 hymns were selected for the Wesley Hymn Book, 1780. A fourth edition appeared in 1743, and another in 1747.

2. Early in 1740, appeared "Hymns and Sacred Poems," an entirely new book of 209 pages, with 96 hymns, and amongst them some of the most popular now in use, including "O for a thousand tongues to sing,"—page 428, i.,—and "Jesus lover of my Soul,"—page 590, i. This volume supplied 54 hymns to the Wesley Hymn Book, 1780.

3. In 1741, the Wesleys issued "A Collection of Psalms and Hymns," a vol. of 126 pages, containing 165 compositions. This was not a reprint of the 1738 book, though containing a few of the pieces therein, but the Psalms were C. Wesley's version of various Psalms, and the Hymns were new. Only 3 of these found their way into the Wesley Hymn Book of 1780. After the death of John Wesley, Dr. Coke made additions thereto which doubled its size. It came into general use, so that the Conference of 1816 recommended it for "use in Methodist Congregations in the forenoon," from which it came to be called "The Morning Hymn Book," and such it remained till 1831, when the Supplement was added to the 1780 book.

4. In 1741, appeared "Hymns on God's Everlasting Love," in 36 pages, containing 48 new hymns, of which 19 are in the Wesley Hymn Book, 1780. The second edition contains 84 pages. The third is dated 1770.

5. In 1742, a new volume of "Hymns and Sacred Poems" appeared, with 304 pages and 155 new hymns, of which 102 were selected for the Wesley Hymn Book of 1780.

6. An enlarged edition of the collection of "Psalms and Hymns" appeared in 1743 containing 138 hymns, 17 of which are in the 1780 book.

7. In 1744, three tracts of hymns were issued, with the titles of "Hymns for the Nativity," 18 hymns. "Hymns for the Watchnight," 11. "Funeral Hymns," 16. From these three, 10 hymns are in the Wesley Hymn Book.

8. Four tracts and one volume of hymns appeared in 1745. From two only of these have selections been made. "A Short View of the Differences between the Moravians and J. and C. Wesley," contains 6 hymns, 3 of which are in the Wesley Hymn Book. The second is a most important work," "Hymns on the Lord's Supper," by Charles Wesley, a volume of 141 pages and 166 hymns, with a preface concerning the Christian Sacrament and Sacrifice, extracted from Dr. Brevint." From this work 20 hymns were selected for the Wesley Hymn Book of 1780. The hymns for "The Lord's Supper" have been often reprinted, but generally without the preface, which was never intended, as Charles Wesley has only versified portions of Dr. Brevint's remarks, in some of the hymns. In the extracts from Dr. Brevint the doctrine of the True and Real Presence is taught, and Charles Wesley embodies the teaching of the preface in his verses. In the fourth section "Concerning the Sacrament as a Means of Grace," and in paragraph 5, are these words in reference to the Efficacy of the Death of Christ: "This victim having been offered up in the fulness of times, and in the midst of the world, which is Christ's great Temple, and having been thence carried up to Heaven, which is His Sanctuary, from thence spreads Salvation all around, as the burnt-offering did its smoke. And thus His Body and Blood have everywhere, but especially at this Sacrament, a true and real presence." Catching the same inspiration, Charles Wesley expresses the same idea in at least seven of the hymns which follow:—

Hy. 33. "Drink Thy blood for sinners shed
Taste Thee in the broken Bread."

# METHODIST HYMNODY.

Hy. 57. "Who shall say how bread and wine
    God into man conveys:
    How the bread His flesh imparts,
    How the wine transmits his blood ?"

Hy. 65. Now on the sacred table laid,
    Thy flesh becomes our food."

Hy. 77. "Taste Thee in the broken Bread
    Drink Thee in the mystic wine."

Hy. 81. "We come with confidence to find
    Thy real presence here."

Hy. 116. ' To every faithful soul appear
    And show Thy real presence here."

Hy. 124. "Yet may we celebrate below
    And daily thus Thine offering show
    Exposed before Thy Father's eyes
    In this tremendous mystery,
    Present Thee bleeding on the tree
    Our Everlasting sacrifice."

It is worthy of remark, that Charles Wesley, in his "Journals," makes no mention of the publication of this volume of hymns during the year 1745, but from February to July of that year, he makes special mention of about a dozen Sacramental Services, which are described as occasions of much blessing to himself and to others, and during the octave of Easter to be communicated every day. The latter half of the year, the subject is scarcely mentioned. It seems probable, therefore, that the book was passing through the press during the months when he was so much under Sacramental influence and power. In justice to C. Wesley, it should be recorded, that the "real presence" is not alluded to in any of the six thousands hymns he wrote, apart from this 1745 book, nor did he ever allude to it in his pulpit discourses. In his "Journals," he names many instances of his baptizing adult persons, but the subject of Holy Baptism does not seem to have inspired his muse, except in "God of eternal truth and love," in the "Hymns for the use of families," 1767, and one or two others. This is the more noticeable when it is considered how strict he was generally in observing the ordinances of the Church.

9. The year 1746 was a remarkable one for the variety of subjects which occupied Charles Wesley's poetic mind; no less than nine separate tracts of hymns were issued during that year, including "Hymns for Times of Trouble," "Hymns and Prayers for Children," "On the Trinity," "On the Great Festivals," "Of Petition and Thanksgiving for the Promise of the Father," "For Our Lord's Resurrection," "For Ascension Day," "Graces before and after Meat," and for the Public Thanksgiving in October of that year. These introduced 154 new compositions, of which only 12 found their way into the Wesley Hymn Book of 1780. The Festival Hymns had Lampe's Tunes issued with them, which insured for them a long term of popularity.

10. Only one new work was issued in 1747, "Hymns for those that seek and those that have Redemption in the Blood of Jesus Christ," containing 72 pages and 52 new hymns, 25 of which were placed in the 1780 book.

11. In 1748, C. Wesley wrote a number of hymns on Marriage, the subject being then uppermost in his mind, but they were not then printed. He was married in the spring of 1749, and when the arrangements were made with his brother respecting a stipend, the question of house-furnishing was not considered. To meet the emergency, C. Wesley gathered up all his unpublished compositions, and, without consulting his brother John, issued them in two volumes. The work was sold by subscription through the preachers, was a great success, and fully accomplished the object contemplated. Those volumes extended to 668 pages, with 455 new hymns, with the old title, "Hymns and Sacred Poems." In that work will be found the largest number of the author's best hymns, and it has yielded 143 compositions to the 1780 book.

12. In 1750 only two hymn tracts appeared, "Hymns for New Year's Day" and "Hymns Occasioned by the Earthquake, March 8th." The first contained 7 new hymns, one of which has been in use in Methodist Services once at least every year since it appeared, viz., the hymn sung at the close of every watch-night Service, commencing "Come let us anew, our journey pursue." The 2 hymns selected from the "Earthquake" Tract ("Woe to the men on earth who dwell," and "By faith we find the place above") are said to be amongst the boldest of the poet's theological conceptions. In 1753 appeared "Hymns and Spiritual Songs intended for the use of Real Christians." This was followed in 1756 by an enlarged edition of the "Earthquake" Hymns, with 22 hymns and Hymns for the Year 1756, particularly for the Fast Day, Feb. 6th, with 17 new hymns, of which 57 are in the 1780 Book.

13. In 1758, was issued "Hymns of Intercession for All Mankind," but being without author's name, the popular judgment hymn given therein, "Lo! he comes with clouds descending" (p. 681, i.), was for nearly a century, attributed to Martin Madan. This tract has 34 pages and 40 new hymns, of which 8 are in the 1780 book.

14. Three new works were issued in 1759, namely, "Funeral Hys"., enlarged to 70 pages, with 43 new hymns; "Hymns for the Expected Invasion," with 8 new hymns; and "Hymns to be used on the Thanksgiving Day, November 29," and after it, 24 pages, with 15 new hymns.

15. In 1761, appeared a volume of 144 pages and 134 hymns, with the title, "Hymns for those to whom Christ is All in All." This was a selection intended for popular use; it reached a 3rd ed. During the

same year, John Wesley issued a volume of "Select Hymns for the Use of Christians of all Denomi-nations," to which was added an admirable selection of "Tunes Aunext." This useful volume was used at the Foundry ; a 2nd ed., corrected, was issued in 1765, a 3rd in 1770, and a 4th in 1773. In 1761, to encourage and improve the vocal part of Divine Service, John Wesley issued "Sacred Melody; or a Choice Collection of Psalm and Hymn Tunes ;" another book of Tunes called "Sacred Harmony," and an abridged ed. of the latter.

16. One of Charles Wesley's largest contributions to the service of song in the Church appeared in 1762, and was entitled "Short Hymns ou Select Passages of Holy Scripture," 2 vols., containing no fewer thau 2030 new compositions, out of which 99 were selected for the 1780 book. This work was rigidly revised by the author ; aud was republished in a somewhat condensed form, in 2 vols., 1794-96, after the author's death. In that work are some popular hymus, and elegant renderings of Scripture phraseology.

17. "Hymns for Children" appeared in 1763, with 100 new compositions ; and "Hymns for the use of Families" in 1767, a volume of 176 pages and 188 hymns. In the same year came "Hymns on the Trinity," with 132 pages and 182 hymns. From these three works, 51 hymns are selected for the Wes. H. Bk. Five or six other tracts of hymns followed, but out of these only one hymn found its way into the 1831 Supplement to the Wesley Hymn Book taken from "Hymns for the Nation and for the National Fast Day," February 8th, 1782.

These are the original publications from which are derived all the Wesley hymns now in use in the Hymnals of all the churches. All these volumes and tracts (except the *Ps. & Hys.* printed at Charlestown in 1736-37), with *fac similes* of title pages, are re-printed in the *Poetical Works of John and Charles Wesley*, London, 1868-72 (13 volumes), and the same are tabulated with dates, titles, pages, sizes and number of hymns, in G. J. Stevenson's *Methodist H. Bk. Notes*, 1883, p. 635.

ii. *Wesleyan Methodists.* 1. With such a variety of works, most of which were occa-sionally used by the Methodist Societies, much confusion and difficulty naturally arose, so that John Wesley did wisely when, in 1779 (soon after he had opened his chapel in the City Road, London), he prepared out of those numerous works a collection for gen-eral use in all his societies, which was issued in 1780. The necessity for such a work was felt all over the country. It extended to 504 pages, with 16 pages of contents and in-dex, and included 525 hymns. The contents were divided into the five parts and twenty sections as still retained in the revised ed. 1875. The 2nd ed., corrected, appeared in 1781; the 3rd, in 1782; the 4th, in 1784; 5th, 1786; 6th, 1788; 7th, 1791. Up to 1791 it re-mained unaltered, although, every edition having to be set up afresh, errors had crept in. These increased till 1797, when a few of the preachers presumed to prepare a new edition, which they issued with an ornamental title-page. In it, about 36 hymns were changed, and some of the favorite hymns of the people, designedly excluded by John Wesley, were included, and at the end 25 additional hymns were given, making the total 550. This edition gave so little satisfaction to the people that the Conference of 1799 appointed Dr. Coke, G. Storey, H. Moore and Adam Clarke, "to reduce the large Hymn Book to its primitive simplicity, as in the second edition, with liberty to add a note in places to explain difficult passages for the sake of the unlearned, and with dis-cretionary power in respect to the additional hymns." They rigidly revised the book, omitted 6 of the additional hymns, extended the work to 560 hymns and published it in 1800. The added hymns introduced a new and important feature into the collection which is a distinct landmark (so to speak) in the history of Methodism, by including 7 hymns by C. Wesley on *The Lord's Supper*. All the unsold copies of the 1797 book were destroyed, and the revised edition remained unaltered for thirty years.

2. The publication at Manchester, in 1825, of a piratical edition of the Collection, to-gether with copyright needs, and the desire for greater variety of hymns, led the Con-ference to appoint the Revs. Thomas Jackson and Richard Watson to make such a se-lection as would meet the wishes of the people, and in 1831 a *Supplement* was issued, ex-tending the collection from 560 to 769 hymns. These were chosen from some of Charles Wesley's original MSS.; from his *Festival Hymns* and from the collection of *Psalms and Hymns* then known as the *Morning Hymn Book*. Many from Dr. Watts were also added and a few of a popular character which were favourites with the people. The Preface is dated November 9, 1830, and in this *Dictionary* the date of this *Supplement* is given as 1830, the date of the *Preface*. Of the entire collection, including this *Supplement*, 668 hymns are by the Wesleys (father and three sons), and 101 by 20 other authors. Dr.

iv

Watts is represented by 66. Only two hymns in the book are specially adapted for Holy Baptism, one by Dr. Doddridge, commencing "See Israel's gentle Shepherd stand;" the other by C. Wesley, "God of eternal truth and love."

3. The copyright of the entire collection had for some years depended on only a few hymns, and when the right in those had run out, a new collection became a necessity. A collection was issued by a London publisher independently of the Conference in 1873. It was an improvement on the 1831 book. It was compiled by a layman at Bristol, and included 1076 hymns, amongst them being many of the best modern compositions, and 71 chants and anthems. The Wesleyan Conference, however, could not recognize the work, and the Book Committee were obliged to prepare a new collection. A large committee took the matter in hand, and devoted much time and care thereto. The edition of 1800, up to hymn 539, was retained, but each hymn was compared with the original and rigidly criticised; a few were omitted altogether; others had verses left out or added, and in this way 49 hymns were changed in the standard part of the collection. The new *Supplement* includes 487 hymns. Its contents embrace what may be designated as a poetical body of divinity. In this respect it is more complete than the book prepared by John Wesley, in that it includes hymns for Holy Baptism, the Lord's Supper and Prayers for children. It is divided into nine sections, in which the hymns are classified according to their subjects, or the season for which they are adapted, a special feature being the "Select Psalms." The authors and translators number 120. Of these, 74 contribute each one hymn, and of the rest 41 have hymns therein, numbering from two to nine each, the total ending with eleven by P. Doddridge, thirteen by J. Montgomery, fifty-eight by I. Watts and seven hundred and twenty-four by C. Wesley. For the first time the authors' names are added in the index of first lines. *The Methodist Hymn Book, illustrated with Biography, History, Incident, and Anecdote*, by George John Stevenson, M.A., 1883, deals with this collection in an exhaustive manner.

4. Taken as a whole, whilst allowing for its distinct and definite advocacy of Methodist doctrine, and admitting the otherwise great preponderance of C. Wesley's hymns, we judge this book as ranking with the best in use among Protestant Christians. It is intensely Methodistic, and it is more. It retains the Standard Hymn Book, not wrongly so-called, which John Wesley gave to his people in 1780; and it has added thereto much that is choice and valuable from most branches of the Church of Christ. The wisdom displayed by the Conference in retaining the *Standard* portion of the old collection is realized when we find that it has done more to conserve the essential doctrines of Methodism amongst the multitude than the combined prose writings of all her divines.

5. The provisions for *Children and Young Persons*, which is an important feature in modern hymnody, is not new, either in Methodism or elsewhere. For the Methodists, C. Wesley pub. his *Hymns for Children*, in 1763. Many of these compositions are far beyond the comprehension of children, but their object was attained in drawing attention to the spiritual wants and education of the young. In 1814, Joseph Benson, a preacher and divine of high repute with the Methodists, published:—

Hymns for Children and Young Persons, on the Principal Truths and Duties of Religion and Morality. Selected from various Authors and arranged in a natural and Systematic Order. London, 1806.

Joseph Benson also published, eight years afterwards:—

Hymns for Children, selected chiefly from the publications of the Revs. John and Charles Wesley, and Dr. Watts, and arranged in proper Order. London, 1814.

From the Preface to the first of these collections, (the second has no preface,) we find that it was compiled and published "to meet the wishes of many persons in different parts of the United Kingdom," but there is no indication that it (or the second collection either) had the official sanction of the Conference, although "printed at the Conference Office." The Conference, however, took up the matter at a later date, and in 1835 Thomas Jackson and Richard Watson, "compiled by the direction of the Methodist Book Committee in London":—

A Collection of Hymns for the Use of Wesleyan Methodist Sunday Schools.—London, 1835.

# METHODIST HYMNODY.

At the request of the same "Book Committee of the Wesleyan Conference," Dr. W. H. Rule compiled, and the Conference published, in 1857:—

The Wesleyan Methodist Sunday School Hymn Book.—London, 1857.

This was followed in 1870 by a "Selection of Hymns suitable for use in Day and Sunday Schools." . . "made by a number of Ministers, at the request of the Wesleyan Methodist Book Committee," which was compiled chiefly by the Rev. Samuel Lees, and published as:—

The Methodist Scholars' Hymn Book.—London, 1870.

Finally, in 1879, there was issued, after some delay, which is apologized for in the preface:

The Methodist Sunday School Hymn Book. A Collection of Hymns and Spiritual Songs for Use in Schools and Families. Compiled by Direction of the Wesleyan Methodist Conference.-London,1879.

This collection of 589 hymns, by a very large number of authors, is not only the best hymn book for children extant amongst the Methodist Societies, but it has no equal elsewhere except the Church of England *Children's Hymn Book* by Mrs. Cary Brock. Both the official Hymn Books issued by the Conference have suitable tunes published with some of the editions. (See Children's Hymns, § iv.)

iii. *Methodist New Connexion.*—1.   This branch of the Methodist family originated in 1796; the cause being the exclusion of Alexander Kilham from the ministry by the Conference of that year.   From the time of J. Wesley's death, those preachers whom he had ordained had occasionally administered the sacrament of the Lord's Supper. One of the old preachers who had done so, was much blamed for his conduct.   Mr. Kilham wrote a defence of his conduct in *An Address to the Members and friends of the Newcastle Society*, in which he also discussed the question of the right of the people to have the sacrament from their own preachers.   That address in pamphlet form, was much commended by many of the old preachers, including Dr. Coke, H. Moore, J. Pawson, T. Taylor, W. Bramwell, S. Bradburn, and others, some of whom freely distributed the Address in their circuits.   They also, by letters, encouraged Kilham to continue his advocacy of the rights of the people to the privileges asked for by them. Kilham wrote and spoke freely on the subject for a few years, and for so doing he was at the desire of Mr. Mather, censured by the Conference of 1793.   Other preachers, including Mr. Taylor and Mr. Bradburn, had also published their opinions in support of Kilham's views, but they were not censured.   For this act of partiality, the Conference was blamed, and Kilham was encouraged by many preachers who desired to conciliate the Societies rather than the Conference.   At the Conference of 1795, some steps were taken to reconcile the contending parties, under the name of the "Plan of Pacification," but it did not fully meet the case.   Soon afterwards Kilham published a pamphlet entitled *The Progress of Liberty*, in which he pointed out the defects in the Plan of 1795, and sketched the *Outline of a Constitution*.   This *Outline* included the following principles :

1st.   That the power to admit and expel members should be the act of the preachers with the consent of the people. 2.  The members to have advice in choosing their leaders. 3. That local preachers be examined and admitted by preachers and lay officers conjointly.  4.  That Quarterly Meetings should have a voice in recommending young men as preachers.  5.  That the people have the right to representation in all the Church Courts, including the Annual Conference.  6.  That religious worship be held in such hours as were most convenient for the people.  7.  That the Societies receive the sacraments of Baptism and the Lord's Supper from the hands of their own Ministers.

For publishing this pamphlet, and advocating the principles it contained, Kilham was tried and expelled from the ministry, in 1796.   Those principles became the basis of the Methodist New Connexion, which took permanent form at a Conference held in August 1797, in Ebenezer Chapel, Leeds.   Kilham's chief opponent was Alexander Mather, whom J. Wesley had ordained as a bishop to exercise authority in his Societies.   The New Connexion was commenced with 9 circuits, 7 itinerant preachers (5 of whom had belonged to the parent Society), and over 5,000 members.   It was in defense of the principles advocated by Kilham that the new Society was formed; and the preachers and lay-officers have exercised equal rights in the government of the Society throughout its history.

2. At the first, the New Connexion adopted the use of the Wes. H. Bk., but a few years later a *Supplement* was prepared by order of the Conference, and was designated *The Small Hymn Book*. It consisted of 276 hymns. This *Supplement* reached a 5th edition in 1810, and was used till the new hymn-book of 1835 was issued.

3. Soon after the Wesleyans issued their *Supplement* in 1831, the New Connexion Conference appointed a committee to prepare a revised and enlarged collection for use in their Societies. The Revs. Thomas Mills and William Shuttleworth were the acting members. The Preface says that they took from the Wes. H. Bk. and from its *Supplement*, the best hymns "for poetic merit, happy Scriptural illustration, and those which most clearly expressed breathings after peace and holiness. With these were combined a number of other hymns from various authors, and a few by pious persons of poetic genius, composed for the work." Such hymns only were admitted as "gave prominence to those doctrinal and experimental truths which are the chief glory of Methodism." This work was divided into seven parts, and forty-one sections. All the copyright hymns in the *Wes. H. Bk.* were omitted, and, as far as the Committee knew them, the names of authors were added to the hymns. This was the first official Methodist Collection with authors' names. The total number of hymns was 664, and of these nearly 50 were new, and by 27 authors not found in the *Wes. H. Bk.* This book was in use for over a quarter of a century, when it was superseded by the Collection published in 1863.

4. This *New Collection* was undertaken by a Committee, with the Rev. Henry Piggin as chief acting member. It was first issued in May, 1863, and included 1024 hymns by 130 authors. A collection of suitable tunes for each hymn, prepared by the Rev. James Ogden, has since been published.

5. Whilst Mr. Piggin and his coadjutors were preparing a new collection for congregational use, the Rev. John Stokoe, then a New Connexion minister, now a clergyman in the Irish Church, was preparing a smaller collection for use in their Sunday schools and homes, which was pub. in December, 1862, with the title *The Juvenile Hymn Book*. It contains 315 hymns, classified under seventeen sections, with authors' names added to each, where known.

iv. *Primitive Methodists.*—1. This branch of the Methodist family originated in 1810 by the expulsion from the Methodist Society of Hugh Bourne (q.v.). Previous to this, H. Bourne had compiled a small hymn book, which he published in 1809. What was long known amongst the Primitives as *The Small Book* was issued in 1821, and consisted of 154 hymns, most of which were by Charles Wesley and William Sanders, a few by Dr. Watts, and 16 by Bourne. This *Small Book* was widely known in all parts of the land by the first couplet in the book—

> "Christ he sits on Zion's hill,
> He receives poor sinners still,"

with the chorus:

> "I a soldier sure shall be
> Happy in Eternity."

2. With the growth of the Society, a larger number of hymns was required, and in 1824–25, Bourne prepared and issued what he called the *Large Hymn Book*, which included 536 hymns. Of these, 16 were by William Sanders, and 146 were the joint production of William Sanders and Hugh Bourne ; a few were by Dr. Watts, Cowper and Dr. Doddridge; 225 by Charles Wesley; and 20 new hymns by Bourne. A lengthy preface describes the Service of Song as set forth in the Old and New Testaments, and deals with Private Prayer, Preaching, Prayer M-etings, Class Meetings, Love Feasts, Camp Meetings and Musical Instruments. Bourne says of the new hymns that they are "of a superior cast, and they lead into the mystery of faith."

3. As the Societies increased, a still greater variety of hymns was desired, and the Conference appointed the Rev. John Flesher to prepare an enlarged book. He acknowledges his own inability for performing the duty, but collected 852 hymns "from numerous popular authors, living and deceased, and enriched with original hymns and

selected ones, altered or re-made." Mr. Flesher adds: "I had thought my lack of sufficient poetic genius and taste would save me from such an appointment, but when chosen, I was surprised, afraid, and humbled, and durst not disobey." This unqualified editor proceeded to correct and mangle over 225 hymns. It need not be added, that few but himself have approved of his work. In his preface he remarks:—

"Knowing that Providence had not stereotyped the productions of any poet, I have freely altered or re-made hymns from authors of different grades of talent and reputation—an important item in strengthening the copyright."

This book, issued in 1854, may be safely described as the worst edited and most severely mutilated collection of hymns ever published.

4. The Conference of 1882 appointed a committee to prepare an entirely new collection. This was published in 1887, as *The Primitive Methodist Hymnal, compiled by a committee appointed by the Conference of 1882.* It contains 1052 hymns by over 300 known authors and translators [besides hymns by several that are unknown], ranging from the earliest ages of hymnody to the present, and from the Unitarians on the one hand, to the Latin and Greek Churches on the other. It is divided into twelve sections, which are again subdivided: but the arrangement of subjects is more often after the manner of the Congregationalists than that usually adopted in Methodist collections, and is the arrangement of Flesher's book simplified. It is supplied with the usual Indices of first lines of "verses" of "texts," of "subjects," &c., and a table of "authors and translators," with the numbers of their hymns. This last is in addition to the names of the authors being added to the hymns throughout the book. It is purely and intensely Methodistic, whilst in the number of its authors, in the comprehensiveness of its subjects, in the richness of its poetry, in the care and accuracy displayed in its text, and in the designations of authorship, it has no equal in Methodist hymnody.

5. Provision for the children in the Sunday schools has been made by the publication of the *Primitive Methodist Sunday School Hymn Book*, in 1879. It was edited by G. Booth, M. D., and William Beckworth. It is an admirable collection, is well edited, and is set to suitable music. Its use is extensive.

v. *United Methodist Free Churches.*—1. These Churches were formed by the amalgamation, in 1857, of several separate Societies, the members of which had formerly belonged to the Wesleyan Methodist Society. The first of these was that known as the *Protestant Methodists*, who, in 1827-28, came out on the Organ Question at Leeds. Another section was formed in 1834-35, when Dr. Samuel Warren was expelled, the proceedings against him arising chiefly out of the formation at that time of a Theological Institution. These two sections united to form the *Wesleyan-Methodist Association.* They used the *Wes. H. Bk.* with a small *Supplement* added. In 1849-50, owing to the expulsion of the Revs. James Everett, Samuel Dunn, and William Griffith from the Wesleyan Conference, another division resulted, and a Society designated the *Wesleyan Reformers* was established, which soon had fifty thousand adherents. Mr. Everett was expelled on suspicion of having written *The Fly Sheets* and *Wesleyan Takings*, and published them anonymously; Mr. Dunn, for publishing *The Wesley Banner*, a monthly magazine, and for declining to discontinue the work as desired by the Conference; Mr. Griffith for reporting the proceedings of the Conference in *The Wesleyan Times.* The body then formed by those who adhered to these ministers, at their Annual Delegate Meeting held in Sheffield, in August, 1852, appointed the Rev. James Everett to prepare a new edition of the *Wes. H. Bk.*, with the addition of such new hymns as would replace the copyright hymns which could not be used. The preface to that book is dated July 1st, 1853. The *Supplement* contained 243 hymns in addition to the hymns in the *Wes. H. Bk.* In these were included the compositions of 15 authors not then in the *Supplement* to the *Wes. H. Bk.* At the end of this collection there is an index which gives the source whence every hymn in the book is derived, together with the author's name. The collection contains 804 hymns.

2. When the *Wesleyan Methodist Association* and the *Wesleyan Reformers*, who

united in 1857 to form the *Methodist Free Churches*, held their annual assembly in Sheffield, in 1859, they resolved to have a new hymn book, and appointed the Revs. James Everett and Matthew Baxter to prepare the same. They were to retain all the original Wes. H. Bk. of 1780, and add "A Supplement of 250 hymns, and also hymns suitable for a Sunday School." The preface is dated October, 1860. Changes were made in 53 hymns, but none of the new hymns were by authors other than those who had already contributed. From No. 778 to 821 the hymns were all new. Five doxologies and two graces closed the collection of 828 hymns. The Supplement was issued in 1861 as a separate book, with the sub-title *Miscellaneous Hymns*. Their *Sunday School Hymns*, 1860, is a fairly good collection.

3. The *Methodist Free Churches* are compiling a new collection of hymns, which may appear in 1889. A committee of ministers have been employed for a long time in its preparation. The *Sunday S. H. Bk.* appeared in 1888.

vi. *Bible Christians.* 1.—The founder of this Society was William O'Bryan, a Cornishman, born February 6th, 1778, at Gunwen, Luxillian. His father owned a farm and was a Cornish miner. Both his parents were Methodists, and had heard John Wesley preach. They had preaching services in their own dwelling-house. William had a fair education, and the curate of the parish offered to prepare him for college. He was converted under the Methodists in May 1789, was apprenticed to the drapery business, became worldly, lost his religion, and again gave his heart to God, November 5th, 1795. He heard J. Wesley preach twice, and received his blessing. He began to preach in 1801, was married in 1803, and made a local preacher in 1809. For preaching in villages beyond his own parish, where there was no Methodist preaching, he was expelled from the Methodist Society. Being urged to continue his preaching, he found in North Devon fourteen villages without any places of worship, and in November, 1814, he left his home to itinerate and preach in those places. In October, 1815, he preached in the house of Mr. Thorne, at Shebbear, and, being urged to do so, he then formed those present into a religious Society. This Society was at first known by the name *Arminian Bible Christians:* afterwards the initial word was dropped, and they have since been known as *Bible Christians*, and sometimes locally, *Brianites*. Their chief Societies are in Cornwall and Devonshire, but they have a few elsewhere. O'Bryan compiled their first hymn-book, about 1819, when their first Conference was held. In 1829, a separation took place. O'Bryan left the body in 1831, and went to America, where he died, January 8th, 1868. For his share in the copyright of the hymn-book, and for other claims, the Conference allowed him twenty pounds a year till he died. The hymn book is divided into six parts and twenty-eight sections. The hymns are mostly those in use in the *Wes. H. Bk.*, but they are rearranged throughout, and several by 18 other authors were added. In July, 1862, a fourth edition was issued, with nine hymns changed; the names of authors added as far as known, the index of Scripture texts enlarged, and an index of verses. The sixth edition is dated 1882. The Conference of 1885 appointed a committee to prepare a new and more comprehensive collection, to be published in due course.

2. In 1832, a Sunday School Union for the Bible Christians was formed at Shebbear, in Devonshire, and they published *The Child's Hymn Book* for use in their schools. In 1863, a new ed. was prepared and published, containing 272 hymns, more than 66 of which were new. That book has served the Connexion nearly a quarter of a century, and is still in favour. The hymns are carefully classified, but no authors' names are given.

vii. *Conclusion.*—When the Methodist Ecumenical Conference was held in City Road Chapel, in September, 1881, a suggestion was made to have one comprehensive hymn-book for all the branches of Methodism throughout the world. This course, however, has not been adopted.

Translations of English hymns into various European and other languages have been made for use by the various branches of the Methodist Societies on the Continent of Europe and on Mission Stations. In several instances these translations have been supplemented by original hymns in the vernacular, and composed chiefly by the resident missionaries. [See **Missions, Foreign.**]

# METHODIST HYMNODY.

The Methodist hymn-writers are very limited in number. The provision made by Jno. and Chas. Wesley for every aspect of Methodism, the stereotyped character of each book when issued, the great number of years it had to run before any omissions or additions could be made, and the intense affection of Methodists for their old hymns, have had much to do in producing this result. When at rare intervals outlets for pent-up poetic life were made in new editions of old books, and in collections for children and the young, W. M. Bunting, W. M. Punshon, B. Gough, J. Lyth, G. S. Rowe, J. Briggs, E. E. Jenkins, M. G. Pears, and a few others have produced lyrics of merit and usefulness; but no great singer has appeared in Methodism since Charles Wesley was gathered to his father.

# HYMN BOOK OF 1818.

The following statements in relation to the Hymnology of the African Methodist Episcopal Church will give some idea of the progress the Church has made. The Fathers of the Church were aware that every denomination, to be successful, must provide for the needs of its members. They first provided the Law and Doctrine in the Discipline in 1817, and in 1818, the first Hymn-book was printed by Richard Allen, Daniel Coker, James Chapman and Jacob Tapsico. It contained 314 Hymns and Spiritual Songs, each of them full of doctrine and spiritual food. The Book was divided on general subjects as follows: Invitations to Sinners, 10; Penitential, 24; Rejoicing and Praise, 35; Trusting in Grace and God's Providence, 18; Christian Warfare, 6; Divine Goodness, 18; Redemption, 8; Christian Fellowship, 14; Parting with Christian Friends, 6; Backsliding, 5; Death and Judgment, 22; New Year's and Christmas. 6; Pastoral Duties, 5; Baptismal and Sacramental-10; Morning and Evening Hymns, 6; Birthdays, Marriages, Parents — Master and Servant, Consolation for the Sick, all had appropriate words. This was the table spread by the Founders of our Church.

This was the first Book of song published by the Children of Oppression, the very first to give expression in their own selected language, of the Christian hope of the race. It had a very wide circulation in the North and a few of them went to the South among the freedman of the race. Rev. George Hogarth, a deacon of the New York Annual Conference, was General Book Steward from 1836 to 1848. He printed an edition of the Hymn Book and secured the copyright in his own name. When Rev. A. R. Green succeeded him in 1848, he had no control of the Hymn Book. The matter was brought before the Philadelphia Conference, a committee was appointed to adjust the difficulty between the ex-General Book Steward and the Acting General Book Steward. The committee did not make any report at the next Conference, for Rev. George Hogarth had departed this life and appeared before the judge of all the earth. The Rev. A. R. Green, in a report to the Ohio Conference, states that it was impossible for him to furnish Hymn Books to the trade as fast as demanded. In 1852. Rev. M. M. Clark was elected Editor and General Book Steward and continued until 1855, when he resigned; he published one edition of the Hymn Book. Rev. J. P. Campbell was appointed to fill the vacancy and was elected in 1856, in Cincinnati, Ohio. During his administration, he got out an edition of the Hymn Book. There were editions printed between 1860 and 1864, 1864 and 1868, 1868 and 1872, by the several Business Managers. There were small changes in every edition, but no general changes.

# HYMN BOOK OF 1876.

The Bishops in their address to the Church use the following language :

BELOVED BRETHREN :—The General Conference of 1868 appointed Rev. H. M. Turner to revise our old hymn book, which was equivalent to authorizing him to compile a new one. He entered heartily upon his work, and at the end of eight years has given us a compilation, which, in many respects is excellent, inasmuch as it is more varied, comprehensive and useful than that which we have been using for the last forty years, because it has a larger collection of Wesleyan hymns, and is therefore richer in Wesleyan Christian ideas expressed in lyrical form. Considered as a compilation, it is certainly a great improvement upon the whole book as it existed from 1836 to the present time. The Divisions, entitled "Birthdays," "Fast and Thanksgivings." "Morning and Evening," the "Seasons," "Baptisms," are enriched by additional hymns from the pens of other evangelical lyrists. New divisions have been created, embracing hymns and spiritual songs suited to the progressive spirit of these modern times, such as the sections, entitled "Missions," "Dedication of Churches and Laying of Corner Stones," "On Reading the Holy Scriptures," "Revivals," "Patriotic Songs," "Farewell." The whole compilation ends with twelve sweetly solemn chants, and seventeen doxologies suited to all known metres.

The usefulness of this edition is enhanced by having annexed to it : (a) Our Ritual. (b) The General Rules, which, not only our Pastors, but every one of our members, also, ought to be able to repeat from memory. (c) The Reception of Members, which all *ought* to read, at least once a quarter, in order that they may be reminded of their sacred obligations. We recommend the whole book to you, dear brethren and sisters, as one well adapted to intensify the flames of private personal devotion, as well as to promote the cause of Religion in the public worship of the living God.

But, beloved, forget not that hymns, spiritual songs—lyrics of the most elevated poetry, breathing the noblest sentiments—avail us nothing, unless we sing with the spirit and the understanding; therefore, in the language of the Apostle, we exhort you to be filled with the Spirit. speaking to yourselves in psalms and hymns and spiritual songs, singing and making melody in your hearts to the Lord And with David, "Praise ye the Lord, for it is good to sing praises unto our God. for it is pleasant and praise is comely." "Serve the Lord with gladness, com; into his presence with singing." "I will sing of mercy and judgment, unto thee, O Lord, will I sing."

Daniel A. Payne, A. W. Wayman, Jabez P. Campbell, James A. Shorter, T. M. D. Ward, J. M. Brown, Bishops of the African Methodist Episcopal Church
*September 1st, 1876.*

The Book was published by the Publication Department, and there were 958 pages and 1115 Hymns, Chants and Doxologies. It was the authorized Hymn Book from 1876 to 1892. In the organization of the Church after the war, many thousand were sold and much good was done. The old hymns gave way to the new, and the children of freedom sang a new song from their own Church Book.

The General Conference held in Baltimore, Md., passed the following resolutions :

WHEREAS, A long felt want in our Sunday Schools has been filled by the introduction of a Sunday School *Song Book* by one of *our own race*, Rev. J. W. Randolph, Therefore,

*Resolved*, That we adopt for use in our Sunday Schools, the book entitled "Everlasting Joy."

This Book was in use for some time but was not a general favorite.

# 1888.

The subject of a Hymnal was before the General Conference at Indianapolis, in 1888. The Bishop appointed a committee to whom was referred the whole subject:

The said committee made the following report, May 28th, which was adopted; viz:

The Committee on Hymnal reported as follows:

Your Committee to whom the subject of a new Hymnal for the A. M. E. Church was referred, is of the opinion

I. That the growing intelligence of our church demands more uniformity in our song worship.

II. That there are those who are fully able to do the work of getting out the book or Hymnal aforesaid.

III. That our Hymn Book should be revised and a Hymnal compiled.

IV. That the bench of Bishops be the Committee to whom the new Hymnal shall be submitted, and when the Bishops approve the work of the Committee on Revision, they have power to submit the same to the church as the Hymnal of the A. M. E. Church.

V. That the Committee on Revision be allowed actual expenses in going to and from the sittings of the Committee; also while engaged in the work of compilation.

VI. That the prepared work of the Hymnal, after receiving the approval of the Bishops, be turned over to the publication department for publication.

VII. That the money coming in from the sale of the Hymnal should go into the treasury of the publishing department.

I. Your Committee would recommend that our present hymn book be cut down to nine hundred hymns.

II. That the ceremonies now in the hymn book be retained.

Your Committee would also recommend that the business manager and editor of the *Christian Recorder* be added to the Committee on Hymnal, from the church at large.

III. That the Hymnal be separate and apart from our church hymn book.

B. F. Watson, *Chairman,*  
Evans Tyree,  
J. A. Johnson,  
F. Savage,  
Jno. H. C. Austin,  *Committee*  
L. J. Coppin,  *on*  
J. W. Beckett,  *Hymnal.*  
S. H. Jefferson,  
B. A. J. Nixon, *Sec'y.*

Report was adopted.

# THE HYMN BOOK OF 1892.

This collection of hymns and sacred songs was gathered and arranged by REV. J. C. EMBRY, under the supervision of the REV. BISHOPS T. M. D WARD, D. D., and B. T. TANNER, D D., who were appointed by the Episcopal Council to execute the work, at their meeting held in Macon, Ga , January, 1892

Concerning the work itself, we observe : 1. It is done in response to an almost universal demand. 2. This demand was for a cheaper book, and one of better arrangment than the old, in order that a music edition might be made. These requirements necessitated,—(a) a smaller book to meet the demand for price; (b) a grouping of the hymns metrically, so as to easily supply music for the same. 3. The collection is made chiefly from our own book and that of the M. E. Church. A few are from the Presbyterian, a few are from the Baptist Hymnal, and still a few others from miscellaneous sources. Finally, there are eighteen selections from the Psalmody of the U. P. Church, all of which have been reduced to popular metre.

The Wesleyan hymns prevail largely, and the whole collection will be found breathing a pure, orthodox and evangelical spirit. Original compositions by our own clergy are : Bishops Payne, Turner, Handy, Tanner and the Revs. H. T Johnson, J. R Scott, and J. C. Embry. The Church Hymnal is the standard by which we are gauged ; it is doctrinal, core and centre, around which we all build our denominational loyalty and Christian devotion.

# METHODIST HYMNODY.

The following is the arrangement of the subjects of the book:

## TABLE OF SUBJECTS.

The Bishops in their address to the Church, in their Council, June 15, 1892, used the following language :

The chants of the former editions have been dropped, because impracticable for use, and the liturgy of Baptism and the Lord's Supper restored. The index- ing has been executed with neatness and taste, and the whole work, typograph- ically, is a gem. We pronounce it, therefore, highly creditable to the Church, and to those who have done the work. We commend the work to the whole Church until the General Conference of 1896 shall utter a final verdict. After all, the best test of any work is the test of usefulness. May these hymns and sacred songs, issuing as a stream from the pure fountain of the Divine oracles, commend themselves in sweet satisfaction to the thousands of our Zion.

Daniel A. Payne, A. W. Wayman, T. M. D. Ward, H. M. Turner, W. J. Gaines, B. W. Arnett, Benj. T. Tanner, A. Grant, B. F. Lee, M. B. Salter, James A. Handy.—Bishops of the A. M. E. Church.

## MUSIC HYMNAL 1897.

The present volume of Hymns and Music is the crystallization of the needs of the Church, and the recommendation of the committee of 1888, at India- napolis. The Bishops appointed a committee to compile and edit an edition of a Hymnal for the use of our congregation, and after several meetings the committee failed to agree. The Bishops' Council at Macon, Ga., January, 1892, appointed Bishops T. M. D. Ward and B. T. Tanner, a committee to make arrangements for its compilation and publication. They made arrange- ments with Rev. J. C. Embry to compile the same under their supervision. Dr. Embry pursued his labors for several years; finally, the matter was presented to the Bishops' Council. In June, 1895, Prof. J. T. Layton, of Washington, D. C., sent a letter to the Bishops' Council at Wilberforce, Ohio, proposing to publish a Hymnal for the Church. The proposition was accepted and Bishop B. T. Tanner was appointed Editor in behalf of the Bishops. Com- mittee – B. T. Tanner, J. C. Embry and John T. Layton.

In 1896, at the Bishops' Council, Dr. J. C. Embry made a report on his work and that of Prof. J. T. Layton, on the Hymnal. Bishops B. W. Arnett and W. J. Gaines were added to the committee and ordered to have the Book ready for the General Conference of 1896 In 1897, Rev. J C. Embry made a statement in relation to the Hymnal; he had arranged for its publica- tion, but the Bishops decided that it must be done under the authority of the Publication Department and Rev. T. W. Henderson B. M., was added to the committee, and the Department given authority to finish and publish the Book. The work of arranging the Hymns and Music was done by Bishop J. C. Embry and Prof. J. T. Layton, and presented to the other members of the committee. The publication of the Historical Facts, in relation to the Hymnody of Meth- odism was thought to be wise, for it would give the ministers of the Church a general knowledge of the rise and progress of the Hymnody. This volume will stand as a memorial to the work of the Rev. J. C. Embry, who worked on it until the last hours of his life. His last work, his last word, and last thoughts were his Hymnal. He spent his last days working for the Church and well has he done his work, as the Book we introduce to the public will tell. After the death of Bishop Embry, the committee decided to nave some Hymns for Anniversaries and Festival Occasions, such as may be used at commencement exercises, Children's Day, Easter Day and Endowment Day.

The Committee on Compilation has finished the work where Bishop Embry left it, and performed the duty assigned by the General Conference, through the Council of Bishops and present the result of their labors to the ministers and members of the African Methodist Episcopal Church and through it to the Commonwealth of Christianity. We pray that God the Father, will approve the work dedicated to the triumphs of his Son, and that the Holy Spirit will sanctify each Hymn. The Church has long called for a Hymnal, the children and choirs wanted a tune book, the age demanded a denominational collection of sacred songs and music to be sung in our Fathers' and Mothers' Church.

We pray the God of David, the sweet singer of Israel, to bless these songs at the family altar, in the Church and schoolhouses, giving inspiration in the conflict of life and victory in death.

Committee on Compilation and Publication.

BENJ. WILLIAM ARNETT,
BENJ. TUCKER TANNER,
WESLEY JOHN GAINES,
JNO. T. LAYTON,
T. WELLINGTON HENDERSON,
JAMES CRAWFORD EMBRY (deceased Aug. '97)

# TABLE OF SUBJECTS.

# WORSHIP.

**1 AZMON. C. M.**    GLASER.

1. O for a thous-and tongues to sing My great Re-deem-er's praise!

The glo-ries of my God and King, The triumphs of his grace!

---

*Opening worship.*    C. M.

1 O For a thousand tongues to sing
My great Redeemer's praise!
The glories of my God and King,
The triumphs of his grace!

2 My gracious Master and my God,
Assist me to proclaim,—
To spread through all the earth abroad
The honors of thy Name.

3 Jesus! the Name that charms our fears,
That bids our sorrows cease:
'Tis music in the sinner's ears,
'Tis life, and health, and peace.

4 He breaks the power of cancelled sin,
He sets the pris'ner free:
His blood can make the foulest clean;
His blood availed for me.

5 He speaks—and, listening to his voice,
New life the dead receive;
The mournful, broken hearts rejoice;
The humble poor believe.

6 Hear him, ye deaf; his praise, ye dumb,
Your loosened tongues employ;
Ye blind, behold your Saviour come,
And leap, ye lame, for joy.
*C. Wesley.*

---

**2** *Psalm lviii. Morning service.*    C. M.

1 Early, my God, without delay,
I haste to seek thy face:
My thirsty spirit faints away,
Without thy cheering grace.

2 So pilgrims, on the scorching sand,
Beneath a burning sky,
Long for a cooling stream at hand;
And they must drink or die.

3 I've seen thy glory and thy power
Through all thy temple shine:
My God, repeat that heavenly hour,
That vision so divine.

4 Not all the blessings of a feast
Can please my soul so well,
As when thy richer grace I taste,
And in thy presence dwell.

5 Not life itself, with all its joys,
Can my best passions move,
Or raise so high my cheerful voice,
As thy forgiving love.

6 Thus, till my last expiring day,
I'll bless my God and King!
Thus will I lift my hands to pray,
And tune my lips to sing.
*Watts.*

7

WORSHIP.

3 METROPOLITAN. C. M.                                J. T. LAYTON.

1. The truth of God shall still en-dure, And firm his prom-ise stand;

Be-liev-ing souls may rest se-cure In his al-might-y hand.

*Faithfulness of God.*        C. M.

1 The truth of God shall still endure,
   And firm his promise stand;
   Believing souls may rest secure
   In his almighty hand.

2 Should earth and hell their forces join,
   He would contemn their rage,
   And render fruitless their design
   Against his heritage.

3 The rainbow round about his throne
   Proclaims his faithfulness;
   He will his purposes perform,
   His promises of grace.

4 The hills and mountains melt away,
   But he is still the same:
   Let saints to him their homage pay,
   And magnify his name.
                              *Beddome.*

4        *Divine Guidance, and Rest.*   C. M.

1 Before thy mercy-seat, O Lord,
   Behold, thy servants stand,
   To ask the knowledge of thy word,
   The guidance of thy hand.

2 Let thy eternal truths, we pray,
   Dwell richly in each heart;
   That from the safe and narrow way
   We never may depart.

3 Lord, from thy word remove the seal,
   Unfold its hidden store;
   And, as we read, O may we feel
   Its value more and more.

4 Help us to see the Saviour's love
   Beaming from every page;
   And let the thoughts of joys above
   Our inmost souls engage.

5 Thus while thy word our footsteps guides
   Shall we be truly blest;
   And safe arrive where love provides
   An everlasting rest.
                        *William H. Bathurst.*

5         *Joy of public worship.*    L. M.
          [ Tune, Federal Street. ]

1 Great God, attend, while Zion sings
   The joy that from thy presence springs:
   To spend one day with thee on earth
   Exceeds a thousand days of mirth.

2 Might I enjoy the meanest place
   Within thy house, O God of grace,
   Not tents of ease, nor thrones of power,
   Should tempt my feet to leave thy door.

3 God is our sun, he makes our day;
   God is our shield, he guards our way
   From all assaults of hell and sin,
   From foes without, and foes within.

4 All needful grace will God bestow,
   And crown that grace with glory too;
   He gives us all things, and withholds
   No real good from upright souls.

5 O God, our King, whose sovereign sway
   The glorious hosts of heaven obey,
   And devils at thy presence flee;
   Blest is the man that trusts in thee.
                              *Isaac Watts.*

8

**6 FEDERAL STREET. L. M.** HENRY K. OLIVER.

1. Awake, my soul, in joy - ful lays, And sing thy great Redeemer's praise;

He just-ly claims a song from thee: His lov-ing-kind-ness, O! how free!

---

*Praise for Loving-kindness.* L. M.

1 Awake my soul, in joyful lays,
And sing thy great Redeemer's praise;
He justly claims a song from thee:
His loving kindness, O! how free!

2 He saw me ruined in the fall,
Yet loved me notwithstanding all;
He saved me from my lost estate;
His loving-kindness, O! how great!

3 Though numerous hosts of mighty foes,
Though earth and hell my way oppose,
He safely leads my soul along;
His loving-kindness, O! how strong!

4 When trouble, like a gloomy cloud,
Has gathered thick, and thundered loud,
He near my soul has always stood;
His loving-kindness, O! how good!

5 Soon shall I pass the gloomy vale,
Soon all my mortal powers shall fail;
Oh! may my last expiring breath
His loving-kindness sing in death!
*Medley.*

**7** *God Worthy of all Praise.* L. M.

1 Be thou exalted, O my God,
Above the heavens, where angels dwell
Thy power on earth be known abroad,
And land to land thy wonders tell.

2 My heart is fixed; my song shall raise
Immortal honors to his name;
Awake, my tongue, to sound his praise,
His wondrous goodness to proclaim.

3 High o'er the earth his mercy reigns,
And reaches to the utmost sky;
His truth to endless years remains,
When lower worlds dissolve and die.

4 Be thou exalted, O my God,
Above the heavens, where angels dwell;
Thy power on earth be known abroad,
And land to land thy wonders tell.
*Watts.*

**8** *The Sovereign Jehovah.* L. M.

1 Before Jehovah's awful throne,
Ye nations bow with sacred joy;
Know that the Lord is God alone;
He can create, and he destroy.

2 His sovereign power, without our aid,
Made us of clay, and formed us men;
And when, like wandering sheep, we stray'd,
He brought us to his fold again.

3 We are his people: we his care;
Our souls, and all our mortal frame;
What lasting honors shall we rear,
Almighty Father, to thy name?

4 We'll crowd thy gates with thankful songs;
High as the heaven our voices raise;
And earth, with her ten thousand tongues,
Shall fill thy courts with sounding praise.

5 Wide as the world is thy command,
Vast as eternity thy love;
Firm as a rock thy truth shall stand,
When rolling years shall cease to move.
*Watts.*

**9 WOODWORTH. L. M.**   WILLIAM B. BRADBURY, 1849.

1. Come, O my soul, in sa - cred lays At - tempt thy great Cre - a - tor's praise: But, O! what tongue can speak his fame, What verse can reach the loft - y theme?

*Majesty and Dominion of God.* L. M.

1 Come, O my soul in sacred lays
Attempt thy great Creator's praise:
But, O! what tongue can speak his fame,
What verse can reach the lofty theme?

2 Enthroned amid the radiant spheres,
He glory like a garment wears;
To form a robe of light divine,
Ten thousand suns around him shine.

3 In all our Maker's grand designs,
Almighty power, with wisdom, shines;
His works, through all this wondrous frame,
Declare the glories of his name.

4 Raised on devotion's lofty wing,
Do thou, my soul, his glories sing;
And let his praise employ thy tongue
Till listening worlds shall join the song.
*Blacklock.*

**10** *Praise Offered to God. Psalm* cxvii. L. M.

1 From all that dwell below the skies,
Let the Creator's praise arise:
Let the Redeemer's name be sung,
Through ev'ry land, by ev'ry tongue.
Eternal are thy mercies, Lord,
Eternal truth attends thy word:
Thy praise shall sound from shore to shore,
Till suns shall rise and set no more.

2 Your lofty themes, ye mortals, bring,
In songs of praise divinely sing;

The great salvation loud proclaim,
And shout for joy the Saviour's name!
In every land begin the song;
To every land the strains belong:
In cheerful sounds all voices raise
And fill the world with loudest praise.
*Watts.*

**11** *Take up thy Cross.* L. M.

1 "Take up thy cross," the Saviour said,
"If thou wouldst my disciple be:
Deny thyself, the world forsake,
And humbly follow after me."

2 Take up thy cross; let not its weight
Fill thy weak spirit with alarm;
His strength shall bear thy spirit up,
And brace thy heart and nerve thine arm.

3 Take up thy cross, nor heed the shame;
Nor let thy foolish pride rebel;
Thy Lord for thee the cross endured,
To save thy soul from death and hell.

4 Take up thy cross, then, in his strength,
And calmly every danger brave;
'Twill guide thee to a better home,
And lead to victory o'er the grave.

5 Take up thy cross, and follow Christ;
Nor think till death to lay it down;
For only he who bears the cross
May hope to wear the glorious crown.
*Charles W. Everest.*

**12 ST. THOMAS. S. M.**

A charge to keep I have, A God to glo-ri-fy;

A nev-er dy-ing soul to save, And fit it for the sky;

*Keeping the charge of the Lord.*

A CHARGE to keep I have, S. M.
  A God to glorify :
A never dying soul to save,
  And fit it for the sky ;

2 To serve the present age,
  My calling to fulfill :
O may it all my powers engage,
  To do my Master's will !

3 Arm me with jealous care,
  As in thy sight to live ;
And O, thy servant, Lord, prepare,
  A strict account to give !

4 Help me to watch and pray,
  And on thyself rely,
Assur'd, if I my trust betray,
  I shall for ever die.
                              *C. Wesley.*

**13** *"Sing praises to God."* **S. M.**

AWAKE, and sing the song
  Of Moses and the Lamb ;
Tune every heart and every tongue,
  To praise the Saviour's name.

2 Sing of his dying love ;
  Sing of his rising power ;
Sing how he intercedes above
  For those whose sins he bore.

3 Tell, in seraphic strains,
  What he has done for you ;
How he has taken off your chains,
  And formed your hearts anew.

4 His faithfulness proclaim
  While life to you is given ;
Join hands and hearts to praise his
    name,
  Till we all meet in heaven.
                              *Hammond.*

**14** *Met in his name.* **S. M.**

JESUS, we look to thee,
  Thy promised presence claim,
Thou in the midst of us shalt be,
  Assembled in thy name.

2 Thy name salvation is,
  Which here we come to prove ;
Thy name is life, and health, and
    peace,
  And everlasting love.

3 Not in the name of pride
  Or selfishness we meet ;
From nature's paths we turn aside,
  And worldly thoughts forget.

4 We meet the grace to take,
  Which thou hast freely given ;
We meet on earth for thy dear sake,
  That we may meet in heaven.

5 Present we know thou art,
  But O thyself reveal !
Now, Lord, let every bounding
    heart
  The mighty comfort feel.

6 O may thy quickening voice
  The death of sin remove ;
And bid our inmost souls rejoice,
  In hope of perfect love.
                              *Charles Wesley.*

11

## 15 ITALIAN HYMN. 6s & 4s.

Come, thou Al- might- y King. Help us thy name to sing. Help us to praise; Father all

glo - ri-ous, O'er all vic - to - ri - ous. Come and reign ov- er us, An-cient of Days.

*Praise to the Trinity.* 6s & 4s.

COME, thou Almighty King.
Help us thy name to sing,
Help us to praise;
Father all glorious,
O'er all victorious.
Come and and reign over us,
Ancient of Days.

2 Jesus, our Lord, descend:
From all our foes defend
Nor let us fall :
Let thine almighty aid
Our sure defence be made,
Our souls on thee be stayed ;
Lord, hear our call.

3 Come, thou incarnate Word,
Gird on thy mighty sword ;
Our prayer attend ;
Come, and thy people bless :
Come, give thy word success;
Spirit of holiness,
On us descend.

4 Come, holy Comforter,
Thy sacred witness bear,
In this glad hour ; .
Thou, who almighty art,
Now rule in every heart,
And ne'er from us depart,
Spirit of power.

*Dobell's Col.*

## OLIVET. 6s & 4s. (Second Tune.)

**16 RATHBUN. 8s & 7s.**  ITHAMAR CONKEY.

1. Praise to thee, thou great Cre - a - tor; Praise be thine from ev - 'ry tongue; Join, my soul, with ev - 'ry crea-ture, Join the u - ni - ver - sal song.

*God of our Salvation.*    8s & 7s.

1 Praise to thee, thou great Creator;
Praise be thine from every tongue;
Join, my soul, with every creature,
Join the universal song.

2 Father, source of all compassion,
Free, unbounded grace is thine:
Hail the God of our salvation;
Praise him for his love divine.

3 For ten thousand blessings given,
For the hope of future joy,
Sound his praise through earth and heaven,
Sound Jehovah's praise on high.

4 Joyfully on earth adore him,
Till in heaven our song we raise;
There, enraptured, fall before him,
Lost in wonder, love and praise.
*Fawcett.*

**16 b.**    *"Make a Joyful Noise."*    8s & 7s.
[Words Ed.]

1 Music! bring thy sweetest treasures,
Dulcet melody and chord,
Link the notes with loveliest measures,
To the glory of the Lord.

2 Wing the praise from every nation,
Sweetest instruments employ,
Raise the chorus of Creation,
Swell the universal joy.

3 Far away be gloom and sadness;
Spirits with seraphic fire!
Tongues with hymns, and hearts with glad-
ness!
Higher sound the chords, and higher.

4 To the Father, to the Saviour,
To the Spirit, Source of light,
As it was, is now, and ever,
Praise in heaven's supremest height.
*James Edmeston.*

**16 c.**    [Words Ed.    8s & 7s.

1 Holy Father, thou hast taught me
I should live to thee alone;
Year by year, thy hand hath brought me
On through dangers oft unknown.

2 When I wandered, thou hast found me;
When I doubted, sent me light,
Still thine arm has been around me,
All my paths were in thy sight.

3 In the world will foes assail me,
Craftier, stronger far than I;
And the strife will never fail me,
Well I know, before I die.

4 Therefore, Lord, I come, believing
Thou canst give the power I need;
Through the prayer of faith receiving
Strength—the Spirit's strength, indeed.

5 I would trust in thy protecting,
Wholly rest upon thine arm;
Follow wholly thy directing,
Thou, mine only guard from harm!

6 Keep me from mine own undoing,
Help me turn to thee when tried,
Still my footsteps, Father, viewing,
Keep me ever at thy side.
*Unknown.*

## 17 LIFE. 8s & 7s. 6 lines.

THOMAS HASTINGS, 1831.

1. Hark! ten thous-and harps and voic - es Sound the note of
2. Je - sus, hail! whose glo - ry bright-ens All a - bove, and
3. King of glo - ry, reign for - ev - er; Thine an ev - er -
4. Sav - iour, hast - en thine ap - pear - ing; Bring, O, bring the

praise a - bove; Je - sus reigns, and heav'n re - joic - es;
gives it worth; Lord of life, thy smile en - light - ens,
last - ing crown: Noth - ing from thy love shall sev - er
glo - rious day, When, the aw - ful sum - mons hear - ing,

Je - sus reigns, the God of love: See, he sits on yon - der throne;
Cheers, and charms, thy saints on earth: When we think of love like thine,
Those whom thou hast made thine own. Hap - py ob - jects of thy grace,
Heav'n and earth shall pass a - way: Then, with gold - en harps, we'll sing,

Je - sus rules the world a - lone, Je - sus rules the world a - lone.
Lord, we own it love di - vine, Lord, we own it love di - vine.
Des - tined to be - hold thy face, Des - tined to be - hold thy face.
"Glo - ry, glo - ry to our King." Glo - ry, glo - ry to our King."

KELLY.

14

**18 MANOAH. C. M.**

From ROSSINI, 1792-1868.

1. When all the mer-cies of my God, My ris-ing soul sur-veys;

Why, my cold heart, art thou not lost In won-der, love, and praise?

---

*An Act of Thanksgiving.*  C. M.

*Psalm* lxxxix. 26–37.

1 When all the mercies of my God,
  My rising soul surveys;
  Why, my cold heart, art thou not lost
  In wonder, love, and praise?

2 To all my weak complaints and cries
  Thy mercy lent an ear;
  Ere yet my feeble thoughts had learn'd
  To form themselves in pray'r.

3 When in the slipp'ry paths of youth,
  With heedless steps I ran,
  Thine arm, unseen, conveyed me safe,
  And led me up to man.

4 Through hidden dangers, toils and death,
  It gently clear'd my way,
  And through the pleasing snares of vice,
  More to be feared than they.

5 Through every period of my life,
  Thy goodness I'll pursue;
  And after death, in distant worlds,
  The pleasing theme renew.

6 Through all eternity to thee
  A grateful song I'll raise;
  But O! eternity's too short
  To utter all thy praise.

*Addison.*

**19** *My meditation of him shall be sweet.* C. M.

*Psalm* civ. 34.

1 While thee I seek, protecting Power!
  Be my vain wishes still'd;
  And may this consecrated hour
  With better hopes be filled.

2 Thy love the power of thought bestow'd,
  To thee my thoughts would soar;
  Thy mercy o'er my life has flow'd,
  That mercy I adore.

3 In each event of life, how clear
  Thy ruling hand I see;
  Each blessing to my soul most dear,
  Because conferr'd by thee.

4 In every joy that crowns my days,
  In every pain I bear,
  My heart shall find delight in praise,
  Or seek relief in pray'r.

5 When gladness wings the favor'd hour,
  Thy love my thoughts shall fill:
  Resign'd, when storms of sorrow lower,
  My soul shall meet thy will.

6 My lifted eye, without a tear,
  The gath'ring storm shall see;
  My steadfast heart shall know no fear—
  That heart will rest on thee.

*Williams.*

## 20 WARWICK. C. M.

SAMUEL STANLEY, cir. 1810.

1. Come, thou De - sire of all thy saints, Our hum-ble strains at - tend,
While with our prais - es and complaints, Low at thy feet we bend.

*The Desire of all nations.*    C. M.

1 Come, thou Desire of all thy saints,
  Our humble strains attend,
While with our praises and complaints,
  Low at thy feet we bend.

2 How should our songs, like those above
  With warm devotion rise!
How should our souls on wings of love,
  Mount upward to the skies!

3 Come, Lord, thy love alone can raise
  In us the heavenly flame;
Then shall our lips resound thy praise,
  Our hearts adore thy name.

4 Now, Saviour, let thy glory shine,
  And fill thy dwellings here,
Till life, and love, and joy divine,
  A heaven on earth appear.

5 Then shall our hearts, enraptured, say,
  "Come, great Redeemer, come,
And bring the bright, the glorious day,
  That calls thy children home."
*Anne Steele.*

## 21 *Psalm* cxlviii.    C. M.

1 Praise ye the Lord, y' immortal choirs
  That fill the worlds above;
Praise him who formed you of his fires,
  And feeds you with his love.

2 Shine to his praise, ye crystal skies,
  The floor of his abode;
Or veil in shades your thousand eyes,
  Before your brighter God.

3 Thou restless globe of golden light,
  Whose beams create our days,
Join with the silver queen of night
  To own your borrowed rays.

4 Let the shrill birds his honors raise,
  And climb the morning sky:
While grov'ling beasts attempt his praise
  In hoarser harmony.

5 Thus while the meaner creatures sing,
  Ye mortals take the sound:
Echo the glories of your King
  Through all the nations round.
*Watts.*

## 22 *Watchfulness and Prayer.*    C. M.

1 Alas! what hourly dangers rise,
  What snares beset my way;
To heav'n I fain would lift mine eyes,
  And hourly watch and pray.

2 How oft my mournful thoughts complain,
  And melt in flowing tears!
Striving against my foes in vain,
  I sink amid my fears.

3 O gracious God, in whom I live,
  My feeble efforts aid:
Help me to watch, and pray, and strive,
  Nor let me be dismay'd.

4 O keep me in thy heav'nly way,
  And bid the tempter flee:
And never, never let me stray
  From happiness and thee.
*Steele.*

16

**23 LENOX. H. M.** LEWIS EDSON.

1. A - rise, my soul, a - rise, Shake off thy guilty fears, The bleeding sac - ri - fice

In my be - half ap - pears; Be - fore the throne my Sure - ty stands,

My name is writ-ten on his hands, My name is writ-ten on his hands.

*Intercession of Christ.* H. M.
*Rom.* viii. 15; *Heb.* vii. 25.

1 Arise, my soul, arise,
　Shake off thy guilty fears,
　The bleeding sacrifice
　　In my behalf appears;
　Before the throne my Surety stands,
　My name is written on his hands.

2 He ever lives above,
　For me to intercede,
　His all-redeeming love,
　　His precious blood to plead:
　His blood atoned for all our race,
　And sprinkles now the throne of grace.

3 Five bleeding wounds he bears,
　Received on Calvary;
　They pour effectual pray'rs,
　　They strongly speak for me:
　Forgive him, O forgive, they cry!
　Nor let that ransom'd sinner die.

4 The Father hears him pray,
　His dear annointed One;
　He cannot turn away
　　The presence of his Son;
　His Spirit answers to the blood,
　And tells me I am born of God.

5 My God is reconciled;
　His pardoning voice I hear:
　He owns me for his child;

I can no longer fear:
With confidence I now draw nigh,
And, "Father, Abba, Father," cry.
*Charles Wesley.*

**24** *Exhortation to Praise.* H. M.

1 Ye tribes of Adam, join
　With heaven, and earth, and seas,
　And offer notes divine
　　To your Creator's praise.
　　Ye holy throng
　　Of angels bright,
　　In worlds of light
　　Begin the song.

2 The shining worlds above
　In glorious order stand,
　Or in swift courses move,
　　By his supreme command:
　　He spake the word,
　　And all their frame
　　From nothing came
　　To praise the Lord.

3 Let all the nations fear
　The God that rules above;
　He brings his people near,
　　And makes them taste his love:
　　While earth and sky
　　Attempt his praise,
　　His saints shall raise
　　His honors high.
　　*Watts.*

17

## 25 CONWAY. C. M.

ENGLISH MELODY.

I Come, let us use the grace di - vine, And all with one ac - cord,

In a per - pet - - ual cov - - 'nant join

In a per - pet - ual cov-'nant join Our-selves to Christ the Lord.

*Renewing of a Covenant. Jer.* i. 4. C. M.

1 Come, let us use the grace divine,
 And all, with one accord,
 In a perpetual cov'nant join
 Ourselves to Christ the Lord.

2 Give up ourselves through Jesus' pow'r
 His name to glorify;
 And promise in this sacred hour,
 For God to live and die.

3 The cov'nant we this moment make
 Be ever kept in mind;
 We will no more our God forsake,
 Or cast his words behind.

4 We never will throw off his fear,
 Who hears our solemn vow;
 And if thou art well pleas'd to hear,
 Come down and meet us now!

5 Thee, Father, Son and Holy Ghost,
 Let all our hearts receive;
 Present with the celestial host,
 The peaceful answer give.

6 To each the cov'nant blood apply,
 Which takes our sins away;
 And register our names on high,
 And keep us to that day.    *C. Wesley.*

## 26    *Opening Worship.*    C. M.

1 Once more we come before our God;
 Once more his blessings ask :
 O may not duty seem a load
 Nor worship prove a task !

2 Father, thy quick'ning Spirit send
 From heaven in Jesus' name,
 To make our waiting minds attend,
 And put our souls in frame.

3 May we receive the word we hear,
 Each in an honest heart :
 And keep the precious treasure there,
 And never with it part.

4 To seek thee all our hearts dispose,
 To each thy blessings suit,
 And let the seed thy servant sows
 Produce abundant fruit.    *Hart.*

## 27    *Love of Christ celebrated.*    C. M.

1 To our Redeemer's glorious name
 Awake the sacred song!
 O, may his love—immortal flame—
 Tune every heart and tongue.

2 His love what mortal thought can reach!
 What mortal tongue display!
 Imagination's utmost stretch
 In wonder dies away

3 Dear Lord, while we, adoring, pay
 Our humble thanks to thee,
 May every heart with rapture say,
 "The Saviour died for me."

4 O, may the sweet, the blissful theme
 Fill every heart and tongue,
 Till strangers love thy charming name,
 And join the sacred song.
    *Annie Steele.*

18

**28 DEVIZES. C. M.**  ISAAC TUCKER, 1800.

1. God moves in a mys - teri - ous way His won - ders
to per - form: He plants his foot - steps in the sea,
And rides up - on the storm, And rides up - on the storm.

*"Wonderful in Counsel."* C. M.

1 God moves in a mysterious way
  His wonders to perform:
  He plants his footsteps in the sea,
  And rides upon the storm.

2 Deep in unfathomable mines
  Of never-failing skill,
  He treasures up his bright designs,
  And works his sovereign will.

3 Ye fearful saints, fresh courage take:
  The clouds ye so much dread
  Are big with mercy, and shall break
  In blessings on your head.

4 Judge not the Lord by feeble sense,
  But trust him for his grace;
  Behind a frowning providence,
  He hides a smiling face.

5 His purposes will ripen fast,
  Unfolding every hour;
  The bud may have a bitter taste,
  But sweet will be the flower.

6 Blind unbelief is sure to err,
  And scan his work in vain;
  God is his own interpreter,
  And he will make it plain.
  *Cowper.*

**29** *Praise to the Son.* C. M.

1 O for a thousand seraph tongues
  To bless th' incarnate Word!

O for a thousand thankful songs
  In honor of my Lord!

2 Come, tune afresh your golden lyres,
  Ye angels round the throne;
  Ye saints, in all your sacred choirs,
  Adore th' eternal Son.
  *C. Wesley.*

**30** *Psalm* ciii. 8-12. C. M.

1 My soul repeat his praise
  Whose mercies are so great;
  Whose anger is so slow to rise,
  So ready to abate.

2 God will not always chide;
  And when his strokes are felt,
  His strokes are fewer than our crimes,
  And lighter than our guilt.

3 High as the heavens are raised
  Above the ground we tread,
  So far the riches of his grace
  Our highest thoughts exceed.

4 His power subdues our sins;
  And his forgiving love,
  Far as the east is from the west,
  Doth all our guilt remove.

5 While all his wondrous works,
  Through his vast kingdom, show
  Their Maker's glory, thou, my soul,
  Shalt sing his graces too.
  *Watts.*

19

# WORSHIP.

## 31 GREENWOOD. S. M.

JOSEPH E. SWEETSER, 1849.

1. A - rise, and bless the Lord, Ye peo - ple of his choice;

A - rise, and bless the Lord your God, With heart, and soul, and voice.

---

*Exhortation to Praise.* S. M.

1 Arise, and bless the Lord,
  Ye people of his choice;
  Arise, and bless the Lord your God,
  With heart, and soul, and voice.

2 Though high above all praise,
  Above all blessing high,
  Who would not fear his holy name,
  And laud and magnify?

3 O for the living flame
  From his own altar brought,
  To touch our lips, our souls inspire,
  And wing to heaven our thought.

4 God is our strength and song,
  And his salvation ours;
  Then be his love in Christ proclaimed
  With all our ransomed powers.

5 Arise and bless the Lord:
  The Lord your God adore;
  Arise, and bless his glorious name,
  Henceforth, forevermore.
                              *Montgomery.*

## 32    *Happiness of Heaven.*    S. M.

### Psalm xlvii.

1 Come ye that love the Lord,
  And let your joys be known:
  Join in a song with sweet accord,
  While ye surround his throne:

2 Let those refuse to sing
  Who never knew our God;
  But servants of the heav'nly King
  May speak their joys abroad.

3 The God that rules on high,
  That all the earth surveys,
  That rides upon the stormy sky,
  And calms the roaring seas:

4 This awful God is ours,
  Our Father and our love.
  He will send down his heav'nly pow'rs
  To carry us above.

5 There we shall see his face,
  And never, never sin!
  There from the river of his grace,
  Drink endless pleasures in:

6 Yea, and before we rise
  To that immortal state,
  The thoughts of such amazing bliss
  Should constant joys create.
                              *Watts.*

## 33    *The Song of Heaven.*    L. M.

[Tune, Ward. L. M.]

1 The countless multitude on high,
  Who tune their songs to Jesus' name
  All merit of their own deny,
  And Jesus' worth alone proclaim.

2 Firm on the ground of sovereign grace
  They stand before Jehovah's throne;
  The only song in that blest place
  Is, "Thou art worthy, thou alone."

3 With spotless robes of purest white,
  And branches of triumphal palm,
  They shout, with transports of delight,
  The ceaseless, universal psalm,—

4 "Salvation's glory all be paid
  To him who sits upon the throne,
  And to the Lamb, whose blood was shed,
  Thou, thou art worthy, thou alone."
                              *Percy Chapel Col.*

# INVOCATION AND PRAISE.

SCOTCH. ARR. BY LOWELL MASON, 1830.

1. God of my life, thro' all my days I'll tune the grate-ful notes of praise;

The song shall wake with opening light, And war-ble to the si-lent night.

**34** *Song of Gratitude and Praise.* L. M.

1 God of my life, through all my days
I'll tune the grateful notes of praise;
The song shall wake with opening light,
And warble to the silent night.

2 When anxious care would break my rest,
And grief would tear my throbbing breast,
The notes of praise ascending high,
Shall check the murmur and the sigh.

3 When death o'er nature shall prevail,
And all the powers of language fail,
Joy through my swimming eyes shall break,
And mean the thanks I cannot speak.

4 But, O, when that last conflict's o'er,
And I am chained to earth no more,
With what glad accents shall I rise,
To join the music of the skies!

5 Then shall I learn th' exalted strains
That echo through the heavenly plains,
And emulate with joy unknown,
The glowing seraphs 'round thy throne.
*Doddridge.*

**35** *Praise and Holy Fear.* L. M.

1 Come, let our voices join to raise
A sacred song of solemn praise:
God is a sovereign King: rehearse
His honor in exalted verse.

2 Come, let our souls address the Lord,
Who framed our natures by his word;
He is our Shepherd: we, the sheep
His mercy chose, his pastures keep.

3 Come, let us turn with holy fear,
To him who now invites us near;
Accept the offered grace to-day,
Nor lose the blessing by delay.

4 Come, seize the promise while it waits,
And march to Zion's heavenly gates;
Believe, and take the promised rest;
Obey, and be forever blest.
*Watts.*

**36** *For Zion's Peace.* L. M.

1 O thou, our Saviour, Brother, Friend,
Behold a cloud of incense rise;
The prayers of saints to heaven ascend,
Grateful, accepted sacrifice.

2 Regard our prayers for Zion's peace;
Shed in our hearts thy love abroad;
Thy gifts abundantly increase;
Enlarge, and fill us all with God.

3 Before thy sheep, great Shepherd, go,
And guide into thy perfect will;
Cause us thy hallowed name to know;
The work of faith in us fulfill.

4 Help us to make our calling sure;
O let us all be saints indeed,
And pure, as thou thyself art pure,
Conformed in all things to our Head.

5 Take the dear purchase of thy blood:
Thy blood shall wash us white as snow;
Present us sanctified to God,
And perfected in love below.
*Chas. Wesley.*

21

# WORSHIP.

SYLVANUS B. POND, 1835.

1. Come, let us lift our joy-ful eyes Up to the courts a - bove, And
smile to see our Fa - ther there, Up - on a throne of love.

---

***Access to God by a Mediator.*** C. M.

1 Come, let us lift our joyful eyes
  Up to the courts above,
  And smile to see our Father there,
  Upon a throne of love.

2 Come, let us bow before his feet,
  And venture near the Lord;
  No fiery cherub guards his seat,
  Nor double-flaming sword.

3 The peaceful gates of heavenly bliss
  Are opened by the Son;
  High let us raise our notes of praise,
  And reach th' almighty throne.

4 To thee ten thousand thanks we bring,
  Great Advocate on high,
  And glory to th' eternal King,
  Who lays his anger by.
                              *Watts.*

**38** *The Hope of Heaven. Col.* iii. 1. C. M.

1 How happy ev'ry child of grace,
  Who knows his sins forgiv'n!
  This earth, he cries, is not my place,
  I seek my place in heav'n:

2 A country far from mortal sight;
  Yet, O! by faith I see
  The land of rest, the saints' delight,
  The heav'n prepared for me.

3 O what a blessed hope is ours!
  While here on earth we stay,
  We more than taste the heav'nly pow'rs,
  And antedate that day;

4 We feel the resurrection near,
  Our life in Christ conceal'd.
  And with his glorious presence here
  Our earthen vessels fill'd.

5 O would he more of heav'n bestow!
  And when the vessels break,
  Our ransom'd spirits then shall go,
  To grasp the God we seek:

6 In rapt'rous awe on him I'll gaze,
  Who bought the sight for me.
  And shout and wonder at his grace
  Through all eternity.
                              *C. Wesley.*

**39** *Walking in the ways of Christ.* C. M.
                    *Deut.* v. 30–33.

1 Happy the souls to Jesus join'd,
  And sav'd by grace alone:
  Walking in all his ways, they find
  Their heaven on earth begun.

2 The church triumphant in thy love,
  Their mighty joys we know;
  They sing the Lamb in hymns above,
  And we in hymns below.

3 Thee, in thy glorious realm, they praise
  And bow before thy throne!
  We in the kingdom of thy grace,
  The kingdoms are but one.

4 The holy to the holiest leads,
  From thence our spirits rise;
  And he that in thy statutes treads,
  Shall meet thee in the skies.
                              *C. Wesley.*

**40 CAMBRIDGE. C. M.**

RANDALL.

1. Praise waits in Zi - on, Lord, for thee; There shall our vows be paid;

Thou hast an ear when sinners pray; All flesh shall seek thine aid, All flesh shall seek thine aid.

*Worship of God in His Temple.* C. M.

1 Praise waits in Zion, Lord, for thee;
  There shall our vows be paid;
  Thou hast an ear when sinners pray;
  All flesh shall seek thine aid.

2 O Lord, our guilt and fears prevail;
  But pardoning grace is thine,
  And thou wilt grant us power and skill
  To conquer every sin.

3 Blest are the men whom thou wilt choose
  To bring them near thy face;

Give them a dwelling in thy house,
  To feast upon thy grace.

4 In answering what thy church requests,
  Thy truth and terror shine;
  And works of dreadful righteousness
  Fulfil thy kind design.

5 Thus shall the wondering nations see
  The Lord is good and just;
  And distant islands fly to thee,
  And make thy name their trust.

*Watts.*

**ST. STEPHEN. C. M. (Hymn, No. 133.)**

1. Come, Ho - ly Spir - it, heav'n-ly Dove! With all thy quick'ning pow'rs,

Kin - dle a flame of sa - cred love, In these cold hearts of ours.

# WORSHIP.

## 41 WOODWORTH. L. M.

WM. B. BRADBURY.

1. Blest hour, when mor-tal man re-tires To hold communion with his God;

To send to heav'n his warm de-sires, And list-en to the sa - cred word.

---

*Blest Hour of Prayer.*    L. M.

1 Blest hour, when mortal man retires
  To hold communion with his God;
To send to heaven his warm desires,
  And listen to the sacred word.

2 Blest hour, when God himself draws nigh,
  Well pleased his people's voice to hear;
To hush the penitential sigh,
  And wipe away the mourner's tear.

3 Blest hour, for, where the Lord resorts,
  Foretastes of future bliss are given ;
And mortals find his earthly courts
  The house of God, the gate of heaven.

4 Hail, peaceful hour! supremely blest
  Amid the hours of worldly care ;
The hour that yields the spirit rest,
  That sacred hour, the hour of prayer.

5 And when my hours of prayer are past,
  And this frail tenement decays,
Then may I spend in heaven at last
  A never-ending hour of praise.

*Thomas Raffles.*

## 42    *Acts.* i. 9.    L. M.

1 The mighty Conqueror leaves the dead,—
  Jesus the Lord ascends on high;
The powers of hell are captive led,
  Dragged to the portals of the sky.

2 There his triumphal chariot waits,
  And angels chant the solemn lay:
" Lift up your heads, ye heavenly gates ;
  Ye everlasting doors, give way.

3 Loose all your bars of massy light,
  And wide unfold the radiant scene ;
He claims these mansions as his right,
  Receive the King of glory in."

4 " Who is the King of Glory, who? "
  " The Lord, that all our foes o'ercame;
The world, sin, death, and hell o'erthrew,
  Jesus is the conqueror's name."

5 Lo! his triumphal chariot waits,
  And angels chant the solemn lay :
" Lift up your heads, ye heavenly gates ;
  Ye everlasting doors, give way."

6 " Who is the King of Glory, who? "
  " The Lord, of boundless power possessed,
The King of saints and angels too,
  God over all, for ever blessed."

*C. Wesley.*

## 43    *Psalm* xix.    L. M.

1 The heavens declare thy glory, Lord,
  In every star thy wisdom shines;
But when our eyes behold thy word,
  We read thy name in fairer lines.

2 The rolling sun, the changing light,
  And night and day thy power confess;
But the blest volume thou hast writ,
  Reveals thy justice and thy grace.

3 Sun, moon, and stars, convey thy praise
  Round the whole earth, and never stand;
So when thy truth began its race,
  It touch'd and glanc'd on every land.

4 Nor shall thy spreading gospel rest,
  Till through the earth thy truth has run ;
Till Christ has all the nations bless'd,
  That see the light, or feel the sun.

5 Great Sun of righteousness, arise !
  Bless the dark world with heavn'ly light :
The gospel makes the simple wise;
  Thy laws are pure, thy judgments right.

*Watts.*

# Section 2.

# THE HOLY SCRIPTURES.

**44 GERMANY. L. M.**  FROM LUDWIG VON BEETHOVEN, 1770-1827.

1. Now let my soul, e - ter - nal King, To thee in grate-ful trib - ute bring;

My knee with hum - ble hom-age bow; My tongue per - form its sol - emn vow.

*The Saviour seen in the Scriptures.* L. M.

1 Now let my soul, eternal King,
To thee its grateful tribute bring;
My knee with humble homage bow;
My tongue perform its solemn vow.

2 All nature sings thy boundless love,
In worlds below and worlds above;
But in thy blessed word I trace
Diviner wonders of thy grace.

3 There, what delightful truths I read;
There, I behold the Saviour bleed:
His name salutes my listening ear,
Revives my heart and checks my fear.

4 There Jesus bids my sorrows cease,
And gives my laboring conscience peace;
He lifts my grateful thoughts on high,
And points to mansions in the sky.

5 For love like this, O let my song,
Through endless years, thy praise prolong;
Let distant climes thy name adore,
Till time and nature are no more.
*Ottiwell Heginbotham.*

**44 b**      *Micah* vi. 6-8.      L. M.
[Words Ed.]

1 Wherewith, O Lord, shall I draw near,
And bow myself before thy face?

How in thy purer eyes appear?
What shall I bring to gain thy grace?

2 Will gifts delight the Lord most high?
Will multiplied oblations please?
Thousands of rams his favors buy?
Or slaughtered hecatombs appease?

3 Can these avert the wrath of God?
Can these wash out my guilty stain?
Rivers of oil, and seas of blood,
Alas, they all must flow in vain.

4 Whoe'er to thee themselves approve,
Must take the path thyself hath showed:
Justice pursue, and mercy love,
And humbly walk by faith with God.

5 But though my life henceforth be thine,
Present for past can ne'er atone:
Though I to thee the whole resign,
I only give thee back thine own.

6 What have I then wherein to trust?
I nothing have, I nothing am;
Excluded is my every boast;
My glory swallowed up in shame.

7 Guilty I stand before thy face;
On me I feel thy wrath abide;
'Tis just the sentence should take place,
'Tis just,—but O, thy Son hath died.

25

# THE HOLY SCRIPTURES.

**45  WOODSTOCK. C. M.**

DEODATUS DUTTON, JR., 1829.

1. What glo - ry gilds the sa-cred page! Ma - jes - tic, like the sun,

It gives a light to ev - er - y age; It gives, but bor - rows none.

---

*Light and Glory of the Sacred Page.* C. M.

1 What glory gilds the sacred page!
  Majestic, like the sun,
  It gives a light to every age;
  It gives, but borrows none.

2 The power that gave it still supplies
  The gracious light and heat;
  Its truths upon the nations rise:
  They rise, but never set.

3 Lord! everlasting thanks be thine
  For such a bright display,
  As makes a world of darkness shine
  With beams of heavenly day.

4 Our souls rejoicingly pursue
  The steps of him we love,
  Till glory break upon our view,
  In brighter worlds above.
  *Cowper*

**46**      *Before Sermon.*      C. M.

1 Father of all, in whom alone
  We live, and move, and breathe,
  One bright, celestial ray dart down,
  And cheer thy sons beneath.

2 While in thy word we search for thee,
  ( We search with trembling awe ! )
  Open our eyes and let us see
  The wonders of thy law.

3 Now let our darkness comprehend
  The light that shines so clear;
  Now the revealing Spirit send,
  And give us ears to hear.

4 Before us make thy goodness pass,
  Which here by faith we know ;
  Let us in Jesus see thy face.
  And die to all below.
  *C. Wesley.*

**47**    *Search the Scriptures. John* v. 39. C. M.

1 The counsels of redeeming grace
  The sacred leaves unfold ;
  And here the Saviour's lovely face
  Our raptur'd eyes behold.

2 Here light descending from above
  Directs our doubtful feet;
  Here promises of heavenly love
  Our ardent wishes meet.

3 Our numerous griefs are here redress'd,
  And all our wants supplied ;
  Naught we can ask to make us bless'd
  Is in this book denied.

4 For these inestimable gains.
  That so enrich the mind,
  O may we search with eager pains,
  Assured that we shall find !
  *S. Stennett.*

26

**48  ST. MARTINS. C. M.**　　　　　　　　　WM. TANSUR, 1735.

1. Fa - ther of mer - cies in thy word, What
end - less glo - ry shines! For - ev - er be thy
name a - dored For these ce - les - tial lines.

*Delighting in the Word.*　　C. M.

1 Father of mercies in thy word,
　What endless glory shines!
　Forever be thy name adored
　For these celestial lines.

2 Here may the wretched sons of want
　Exhaustless riches find,
　Riches above what earth can grant,
　And lasting as the mind.

3 Here the fair tree of knowledge grows
　And yields a free repast,
　Sublimer sweets than nature knows
　Invite the longing taste.

4 Here the Redeemer's welcome voice
　Spreads heavenly peace around;
　And life, and everlasting joys,
　Attend the blissful sound.

5 O may these heavenly pages be
　My ever dear delight;
　And still new beauties may I see,
　And still increasing light!

6 Divine Instructor, gracious Lord,
　Be thou for ever near;

Teach me to love thy sacred word,
　And view my Saviour there.　*Steele.*

**49**　*The Excellence of the Scriptures.* C. M.

1 Laden with guilt and full of fears,
　I fly to thee, O Lord;
　And not a glimpse of hope appears,
　But in thy written word.

2 The volume of my Father's grace
　Does all my grief assuage:
　Here I behold my Saviour's face,
　Almost in every page.

3 This is the field where hidden lies
　The pearl of price unknown;
　That merchant is divinely wise
　Who makes the pearl his own.

4 Here consecrated water flows
　To quench my thirst of sin;
　Here the fair tree of knowledge grows,
　Nor danger dwells therein.

5 O may thy counsels, mighty God,
　My roving feet command:
　Nor I forsake the happy road
　That leads to thy right hand. *Watts.*

27

## 50 RATHBUN. 8s & 7s.

ITHAMAR CONKEY.

1. Pre-cious vol - ume! what thou do - est, Oth - er books at - tempt in vain.

Plain - est, full - est, sweet - est, tru - est, All our good from thee we gain!

*"My tongue shall speak of thy word."* 8s & 7s.
*Psalm* cxix. 172.

1 Precious volume! what thou doest,
   Other books attempt in vain.
   Plainest, fullest, sweetest, truest,
   All our good from thee we gain!

2 How thy living words refresh us!
   Words of truth and grace they are;
   Than the finest gold more precious,
   Than the honey sweeter far.

3 What lay hid from ancient sages,
   What they sought, but fail'd to find,
   This, unfolded in thy pages,
   Now appears to all mankind.

4 Far too high for man to reach it,
   'Tis reveal'd from heav'n above;
   God himself alone can teach it:
   'Tis the mystery of love.

5 Precious volume! all revealing,
   All that we have need to know:
   Nothing from our view concealing,
   That can profit here below.

6 Hope we have: this hope is cheering,
   That the things we know not now,
   In the day of his appearing,
   Christ will to his people show.
                                    *Kelly's Hymns.*

## WILMOT. 8s & 7s. (*Doxology.*)

{ May the grace of Christ our Sav-iour, And the Fa - ther's boundless love,
{ Thus may we a - bide in un - ion With each oth - er in the Lord;

With the Ho - ly Spir - it's fav - or, Rest up - on us from a - bove! }
And pos - sess, in sweet com - mun - ion, Joys which earth cannot af - ford. }

# BEING AND ATTRIBUTES OF GOD.

**51 DUNDEE. C. M.**

SCOTCH PSALTER.

1. Hail, Fa-ther, Son, and Ho-ly Ghost, One God in per-sons three:

Of thee we make our joy-ful boast, Our songs we make of thee!

*Divine Excellence.*     C. M.

1 Hail, Father, Son, and Holy Ghost,
  One God in persons three:
Of thee we make our joyful boast,
  Our songs we make of thee!

2 Thou neither canst be felt nor seen:
  Thou art a spirit pure:
Thou from eternity hast been,
  And always shalt endure.

3 Present alike in every place,
  Thy Godhead we adore:
Beyond the bounds of time and space
  Thou dwell'st for evermore.

4 In wisdom infinite thou art,
  Thine eye doth all things see;
And every thought of every heart
  Is fully known to thee.

5 Whate'er thou wilt, in earth below
  Thou dost in heaven above;
But chiefly we rejoice to know
  Th' almighty God of love.
             *C. Wesley.*

**52**      *The Trinity.*     C. M.

1 Hail, holy, holy, holy Lord!
  Whom one in three we know:
By all thy heavenly host adored,
  By all thy Church below.

2 One undivided Trinity
  With triumph we proclaim:

Thy universe is full of thee,
  And speaks thy glorious name.

3 Thee, holy Father, we confess:
  Thee, holy Son, adore:
Spirit of truth and holiness,
  We praise thee evermore.

4 The incommunicable right,
  Almighty God, receive!
Which angel-choirs ere long shall join
  To sing thy praise above.

5 Hail, holy, holy, holy Lord,
  (Our heavenly song shall be,)
Supreme, essential One, adored
  In coëternal Three!
             *C. Wesley.*

**52 b**      *Spirituality.*     7s, 6 lines.
[ Words Ed. Tune, Toplady, page 65.]

1 Abba, Father, hear thy child,
  Late in Jesus reconciled;
Hear, and all the graces shower,
All the joy, and peace, and power;
All my Saviour asks above,
All the life and heaven of love.

2 Holy Ghost, no more delay;
  Come, and in thy temple stay:
Now, thine inward witness bear,
Strong, and permanent, and clear:
Spring of life, thyself impart;
Rise eternal in my heart.
             *C. Wesley.*

# BEING AND ATTRIBUTES OF GOD.

53 DEVIZES. C. M.

ISAAC TUCKER.

1. Fre - quent the day of God re - turns To shed its quick - 'ning beams; And yet how slow de - vo - tion burns; How lan - guid are its flames! How lan - guid are its flames!

---

*Grateful Praise. Lev.* xix. 30.   C. M.

1 Frequent the day of God returns
  To shed its quickening beams;
  And yet how slow devotion burns;
  How languid are its flames!

2 Accept our faint attempts to love,
  Our frailties, Lord, forgive;
  We would be like thy saints above,
  And praise thee while we live.

3 Increase, O Lord, our faith and hope,
  And fit us to ascend
  Where the assembly ne'er breaks up,
  The Sabbath ne'er shall end:—

4 Where we shall breathe in heavenly air,
  With heavenly lustre shine,
  Before the throne of God appear,
  And feast on love divine:—

5 Where we in high seraphic strains,
  Shall all our powers employ;
  Delighted range the ethereal plains,
  And take our fill of joy.

6 To Father, Son and Holy Ghost,
  One God whom we adore,
  Be glory as it was, is now,
  And shall be evermore.
  *Browne.*

54   1 *Chron.* xxix. 10-13.   C. M.

1 Bless'd be our everlasting Lord,
  Our Father, God, and King!
  Thy sovereign goodness we record,
  Thy glorious power we sing.

2 Thy goodness and thy truth to see,
  To every soul abound:
  A vast unfathomable sea
  Where all our thoughts are drowned.

3 Its streams the whole creation reach,
  So plenteous is the store,
  Enough for all, enough for each,
  Enough for evermore.

4 Faithful, O Lord, thy mercies are!
  A rock that cannot move:
  A thousand promises declare
  Thy constancy of love.   *C. Wesley.*

  *Doxology.*   L. M.

The peace which God alone reveals,
  And by his word of grace imparts,
Which only the believer feels,
  Direct, and keep, and cheer our hearts;
And may the holy Three in One.
  The Father, Word, and Comforter,
Pour an abundant blessing down
  On every soul assembled here.

30

55 OAKVILLE. C. M.      J. ALBERT JOHNSON.

1. Fa - ther a - bove the con-cave sky, En-throned in light pro-found,

At thy com-mand, the light-nings fly, And thun-ders roar a - round.

*God seen in his works.*     C. M.

1 Father above the concave sky,
  Enthroned in light profound,
At thy command, the lightnings fly,
  And thunders roar around.

2 O who can see the beaming sun,
  The smiling moon at night,
The snowy clouds, the countless stars,
  Enrob'd with dazzling light.

3 And yet refuse to sing thy praise,
  In sweetest notes of love?
Or echo to angelic lays,
  Which fill the worlds above?

4 Whene'er I tread the blooming plains
  And pluck the fragrant flower,
The luscious fruits, the yellow grains,
  I see thy matchless power.

5 What moves on earth, or wings the air,
  Or swims the swelling sea,
Is but a ray of life to point
  Immortal man to thee.
          *Bishop Payne.*

56    *Psalm* cxxxix. 1-6.    C. M.

1 Lord, all I am is known to thee:
  In vain my soul would try
To shun thy presence, or to flee
  The notice of thine eye.

2 Thy all-surrounding sight surveys
  My rising and my rest,
My public walks, my private ways,
  The secrets of my breast.

3 My thoughts lie open to thee, Lord,
  Before they're formed within,
And ere my lips pronounce the word,
  Thou know'st the sense I mean.

4 O wondrous knowledge! deep and high:
  Where can a creature hide?
Within thy circling arms I lie,
  Beset on every side.

5 So let thy grace surround me still,
  And like a bulwark prove,
To guard my soul from every ill,
  Secured by sovereign love.
          *Watts.*

56b    *Praise to God.*    C. M.
     [Words Ed.]

1 The Lord of Sabbath let us praise,
  In concert with the blest,
Who, joyful in harmonious lays,
  Employ an endless rest.

2 Thus, Lord, while we remember thee,
  We blest and pious grow;
By hymns of praise we learn to be
  Triumphant here below.

3 On this glad day a brighter scene
  Of glory was display'd,
By the eternal Word, than when
  This universe was made.

4 He rises, who mankind has bought,
  With grief and pain extreme:
'Twas great to speak the world from naught;
  'Twas greater to redeem.
          *S. Wesley.*

31

# BEING AND ATTRIBUTES OF GOD.

**57  WARD. L. M.**  SCOTCH. ARR. BY LOWELL MASON, 1830.

1. E - ternal, depth of love di - vine, In Je - sus, God with us, dis - played,

How bright thy beaming glo - ries shine! How wide thy heal-ing streams are spread!

### The God of all Grace.  L. M.
[From the German.]

1 Eternal depth of love divine,
In Jesus, God with us, displayed,
How bright thy beaming glories shine!
How wide thy healing streams are spread!

2 With whom dost thou delight to dwell?
Sinners, a vile and thankless race:
O God! what tongue aright can tell
How vast thy love, how great thy grace?

3 The dictates of thy sovereign will
With joy our grateful hearts receive:
All thy delight in us fulfill:
Lo! all we are to thee we give.

4 To thy sure love, thy tender care,
Our flesh, soul, spirit, we resign:
O fix thy sacred presence there,
And seal th' abode for ever thine!

*Trans. by J. Wesley.*

**58**  *Psalm* xxxvi. 5–9.  L. M.

1 High in the heavens, eternal God,
Thy goodness in full glory shines:
Thy truth shall break through every cloud
That veils and darkens thy designs.

2 Forever firm thy justice stands,
. As mountains their foundations keep:
Wise are the wonders of thy hands:
Thy judgments are a mighty deep.

3 Thy providence is kind and large,
Both man and beast thy bounty share:
The whole creation is thy charge,
But saints are thy peculiar care.

4 My God! how excellent thy grace!
Whence all our hope and comfort springs:
The sons of Adam in distress
Fly to the shadow of thy wings.

5 Life, like a fountain, rich and free,
Springs from the presence of the Lord;
And in thy light our souls shall see
The glories promised in thy word.

*Watts.*

**58 b**  *The Divine Comforter.*  L. M.
[Words Ed.]

1 Come, O Creator Spirit blest!
And in our souls take up thy rest!
Come, with thy grace and heavenly aid,
To fill the hearts which thou hast made.

2 Great Comforter! to thee we cry;
O highest Gift of God most high!
O fount of life! O fire of love!
Send sweet anointing from above!

3 Kindle our senses from above,
And make our hearts o'erflow with love;
With patience firm, and virtue high,
The weakness of our flesh supply.

4 Far from us drive the foe we dread,
And grant us thy true peace instead;
So shall we not, with thee for guide,
Turn from the path of life aside

5 Oh, may thy grace on us bestow
The Father and the Son to know,
And thee through endless times confessed
Of both th' eternal Spirit blest.

**59 HURSLEY. L. M.**  ADAPTED FROM FRANCIS JOSEPH HAYDN, 1732-1809.

1. Praise ye the Lord! 'tis good to raise Your hearts and
voi - ces in his praise: His na - ture and his
works in - vite To make this du - ty our de - light.

---

*Psalm cxlvii. 1-11.*  L. M.

1 Praise ye the Lord! 'tis good to raise
Your hearts and voices in his praise:
His nature and his works invite
To make this duty our delight.

2 He formed the stars, those heavenly flames;
He counts their numbers, calls their names;
His wisdom's vast, and knows no bound,
A deep where all our thoughts are drowned.

3 Sing to the Lord, exalt him high,
Who spreads his clouds along the sky;
There he prepares the fruitful rain,
Nor lets the drops descend in vain.

4 He makes the grass the hills adorn;
He clothes the smiling fields with corn:
The beasts with food his hands supply,
And the young ravens when they cry.

5 What is the creature's skill or force,
The sprightly man, or warlike horse,
The piercing wit, the active limb?
All are too mean delights for him.

6 But saints are lovely in his sight;
He views his children with delight;
He sees their hope, he knows their fear;
He looks, and loves his image there.

*Watts.*

---

**60**  *Opening Worship.*  L. M.

1 O thou, whom all thy saints adore,
We now with all thy saints agree,
And bow our inmost souls before
Thy glorious, awful majesty.

2 The King of nations we proclaim:
Who would not our great Sovereign fear?
We long t' experience all thy name,
And now we come to meet thee here.

3 We come, great God, to seek thy face,
And for thy loving-kindness wait;
And O, how dreadful is this place!
'Tis God's own house, 'tis heaven's gate!

4 Tremble our hearts to find thee nigh,
To thee our trembling hearts aspire;
And, lo! we see descend from high
The pillar and the flame of fire.

5 Still let it on th' assembly stay,
And all the house with glory fill;
To Canaan's bounds point out the way,
And lead us to thy holy hill.

6 There let us all with Jesus stand,
And join the general Church above;
And take our seats at thy right hand,
And sing thine everlasting love.

*C. Wesley.*

33

## 61 ROTHWELL. L. M.

*Firm and Spirited.*

ROTHWELL.

1. O God, thou bot - tom - less a - byss! Thee to per - fec - tion
who can know? O height im-mense! What words suf - fice Thy count - less
at - tri - butes to show? Thy count - less at - tri - butes to show?

---

*The Glory of God.*  L. M.

[From the German of Dr. Breithaupt.]

1 O God, thou bottomless abyss!
  Thee to perfection who can know?
  O height immense! What words suffice
  Thy countless attributes to show?

2 Unfathomable depths thou art!
  O plunge me in thy mercy's sea!
  Void of true wisdom is my heart:
  With love embrace and cover me!

3 While thee, all infinite, I set,
  By faith, before my ravished eye,
  My weakness bends beneath the weight:
  O'erpowered, I sink, I faint, I die.

4 Eternity thy fountain was,
  Which, like thee, no beginning knew:
  Thou wast ere time began his race,
  Ere glowed with stars th' ethereal blue.

5 Greatness unspeakable is thine—
  Greatness, whose undiminished ray,
  When short-lived worlds are lost, shall shine
  When earth and heaven are fled away.

*Translated by J. Wesley*

---

## 62  *Divine Majesty.*  L. M.

1 Eternal Power, whose high abode
  Becomes the grandeur of a God:
  Infinite lengths beyond the bounds
  Where stars revolve their little rounds.

2 Thee while the first archangel sings,
  He hides his face behind his wings;
  And ranks of shining thrones around
  Fall worshipping, and spread the ground.

3 Lord, what shall earth and ashes do?
  We would adore our Maker too!
  From sin and dust to thee we cry,
  The Great, the Holy and the High!

4 Earth from afar hath heard thy fame,
  And worms have learned to lisp thy name;
  But, O! the glories of thy mind
  Leave all our soaring thoughts behind!

5 God is in heaven, and men below:
  Be short our tunes; our words be few!
  A solemn rev'rence checks our songs,
  And praise sits silent on our tongues.

*Watts.*

34

# BEING AND ATTRIBUTES OF GOD.

**63  ST. PETERSBURGH. L. M.**                    BORTNIANSKY.

1. Thou art, O God, the life and light Of all this wondrous world we see;
Its glow by day, its smile by night, Are but reflections caught from thee;

Wher-e'er we turn, thy glo-ries shine, And all things fair and bright are thine.

---

*All things are of God.*  L. M. 6 lines.

1 Thou art, O God, the life and light
   Of all this wondrous world we see;
   Its glow by day, its smile by night,
   Are but reflections caught from thee;
   Where'er we turn, thy glories shine,
   And all things fair and bright are thine.

2 When day, with farewell beam, delays
   Among the opening clouds of even,
   And we can almost think we gaze,
   Through opening vistas, into heaven,—
   Those hues, that mark the sun's decline,
   So soft, so radiant, Lord, are thine.

3 When night, with wings of starry gloom,
   O'ershadows all the earth and skies,
   Like some dark, beauteous bird,whose plume
   Is sparkling with unnumbered eyes,—
   That sacred gloom, whose fires divine
   So grand, so countless, Lord, are thine.

4 When youthful Spring around us breathes,
   Thy Spirit warms her fragrant sigh;
   And every flower that Summer wreathes
   Is born beneath thy kindling eye:
   Where'er we turn, thy glories shine,
   And all things fair and bright are thine.

                                    *Moore.*

---

**64**              *Psalm* xxiii.       L. M. 6 lines.

1 The Lord my pasture shall prepare,
   And feed me with a shepherd's care:
   His presence shall my wants supply,
   And guard me with a watchful eye:
   My noonday walks he shall attend,
   And all my midnight hours defend.

2 When in the sultry glebe I faint,
   Or on the thirsty mountain pant,
   To fertile vales and dewy meads
   My weary, wandering steps he leads,
   Where peaceful rivers, soft and slow,
   Amid the verdant landscape flow.

3 Though in the path of death I tread,
   With gloomy horrors overspread,
   My steadfast heart shall fear no ill,
   For thou, O Lord, art with me still:
   Thy friendly crook shall give me aid,
   And guide me through the dreadful shade.

4 Though in a bare and rugged way,
   Through devious, lonely wilds I stray,
   Thy bounty shall my pains beguile,
   The barren wilderness shall smile,
   With sudden greens and herbage crowned,
   And streams shall murmur all around.

                                   *Addison.*

35

**65  BROOKLYN.  H. M.**  J. ZUNDEL.

1. The Lord Je ho-vah reigns. His throne is built on high; The gar-ments he as-

sumes  Are light and maj-es-ty:  His glo-ries shine with beams so bright

No mor-tal eye can bear the sight. No mor-tal eye can bear the sight.

*Wondrous Condescension.*  H. M.

1 The Lord Jehovah reigns,
  His throne is built on high;
The garments he assumes
  Are light and majesty:
His glories shine with beams so bright
No mortal eye can bear the sight.

2 The thunders of his hand
  Keep the wide world in awe;
His wrath and justice stand
  To guard his holy law:
And where his love resolves to bless,
His truth confirms and seals the grace.

3 Through all his mighty works
  Amazing wisdom shines;
Confounds the powers of hell,
  And all their dark designs:
Strong is his arm, and shall fulfill
His great decrees and sovereign will.

4 And will this sovereign King
  Of glory condescend,
And will he write his name,
  My Father and my Friend?
I love his name, I love his word;
Join all my powers to praise the Lord.

*Isaac Watts.*

**66**  *Psalm* xlvii. 5-9.  H. M.

1 God is gone up on high
  With a triumphant noise;
The clarions of the sky
  Proclaim th' angelic joys!
Join all on earth, rejoice and sing;
Glory ascribe to glory's King.

2 God in the flesh below,
  For us he reigns above:
Let all the nations know
  Our Jesus' conqu'ring love!
Join all on earth, rejoice and sing;
Glory ascribe to glory's King.

3 All power to our great Lord
  Is by the Father given;
By angel-hosts adored,
  He reigns supreme in heaven:
Join all on earth, rejoice and sing;
Glory ascribe to glory's King.

4 Till all the earth, renewed
  In righteousness divine,
With all the hosts of God
  In one great chorus join.
Join all on earth, rejoice and sing;
Glory ascribe to glory's King.

*C. Wesley.*

**67 STATE STREET. S. M.**

1. My God, my life, my love, To thee, to thee I call:

I can-not live if thou re-move, For thou art all in all.

*All-sufficiency.*      S. M.

1 My God, my life, my love,
  To thee, to thee I call:
I cannot live if thou remove,
  For thou art all in all.

2 Thy shining grace can cheer
  This dungeon where I dwell:
'Tis paradise when thou art here—
  If thou depart, 'tis hell.

3 The smilings of thy face,
  How amiable they are!
'Tis heaven to rest in thine embrace,
  And nowhere else but there.

4 To thee, and thee alone,
  The angels owe their bliss:
They sit around thy gracious throne,
  And dwell where Jesus is.

5 Thou art the sea of love,
  Where all my pleasures roll!
The circle where my passions move,
  And centre of my soul.

6 To thee my spirits fly,
  With infinite desire:
And yet how far from thee I lie,
  O Jesus, raise me higher!
                  *Watts.*

**GREENWOOD. S. M.**    (Second Tune.)

1. My God, my life, my love, To thee, to thee I call:

I cannot live if thou re-move, For thou art all in all.

37

BEING AND ATTRIBUTES OF GOD.

**68  IMMORTALITY. S. M.**                    W. H. H. BUTLER.

1. Come, sound his praise a - broad, And hymns of glo - ry sing:

Je - ho - vah is the sovereign God, The u - ni - ver - sal King.

*Opening worship.    Psalm xcv.    S. M.*

1 Come, sound his praise abroad,
   And hymns of glory sing:
Jehovah is the sovereign God,
   The universal King.

2 He formed the deeps unknown,
   He gave the seas their bound:
The wat'ry worlds are all his own,
   And all the solid ground.

3 Come, worship at his throne:
   Come, bow before the Lord:
We are his work, and not our own,
   He formed us by his word.

4 To-day attend his voice,
   Nor dare provoke his rod:
Come, like the people of his choice,
   And own your gracious God.
                        *Watts.*

**69**        *Psalm xxiii.*        S. M.

1 The Lord my Shepherd is,
   I shall be well supplied;
Since he is mine, and I am his,
   What can I want beside?

2 He leads me to the place
   Where heavenly pasture grows,
Where living waters gently pass,
   And full salvation flows.

3 If e'er I go astray,
   He doth my soul reclaim,
And guide me in his own right way,
   For his most holy name.

4 While he affords his aid,
   I cannot yield to fear:
Though I should walk through death's
      dark shade,
My Shepherd's with me there.

5 In spite of all my foes,
   Thou dost my table spread.
My cup with blessings overflows,
   And joy exalts my head.
                        *Watts.*

**70**        *Psalm ciii. 1–7.*        S. M.

1 O bless the Lord, my soul;
   Let all within me join,
And aid my tongue to bless his name,
   Whose favors are divine.

2 O bless the Lord, my soul;
   Nor let his mercies lie
Forgotten in unthankfulness,
   And without praises die.

3 'Tis he forgives thy sins;
   'Tis he relieves thy pain;
'Tis he who heals thy sicknesses,
   And makes thee young again.

4 He crowns thy life with love,
   When ransomed from the grave;
He, who redeemed my soul from hell,
   Hath sovereign power to save.

5 He fills the poor with good:
   He gives the sufferers rest:
The Lord hath judgment for the proud,
   And justice for th' opprest.
                        *Watts.*

38

**71 MELODY. C. M.** CHAPIN. 1823.

1. Fa - ther, how wide thy glo - ry shines, How high thy won - ders rise!

Known thro' the earth by thou - sand signs, By thou-sands through the skies.

### Glory, Mercy, Grace. C. M.

1 Father, how wide thy glory shines,
   How high thy wonders rise!
Known through the earth by thousand signs,
   By thousands through the skies.

2 Those mighty orbs proclaim thy power;
   Their motions speak thy skill:
And on the wings of every hour
   We read thy patience still.

3 Part of thy name divinely stands
   On all thy creatures writ;
They show the labor of thy hands,
   Or impress of thy feet:

4 But when we view thy strange design
   To save rebellious worms,
Where vengeance and compassion join
   In their divinest forms;

5 Here the whole Deity is known,
   Nor dares a creature guess
Which of the glories brighter shone,
   The justice or the grace.

6 Now the full glories of the Lamb
   Adorn the heavenly plains;
Bright seraphs learn Immanuel's name,
   And try their choicest strains.

7 O may I bear some humble part
   In that immortal song!
Wonder and joy shall tune my heart,
   And love command my tongue.
                                    *Isaac Watts.*

### 72 Psalm cxlv. C. M.

1 Let every tongue thy goodness speak,
   Thou sovereign Lord of all;
Thy strength'ning hands uphold the weak
   And raise the poor that fall.

2 When sorrows bow the spirit down,
   When virtue lies distressed,
Beneath the proud oppressor's frown,
   Thou giv'st the mourner rest.

3 Thou know'st the pains thy servants feel,
   Thou hear'st thy children's cry;
And their best wishes to fulfill,
   Thy grace is ever nigh.

4 Thy mercy never shall remove
   From men of heart sincere:
Thou sav'st the souls whose humble love
   Is joined with holy fear.

5 My lips shall dwell upon thy praise,
   And spread thy fame abroad;
Let all the sons of Adam raise
   The honors of their God.
                                    *Watts.*

# BEING AND ATTRIBUTES OF GOD.

**73** *God's Condescension.* C. M.

[ Tune Dundee, page 29.]

1 O thou, to whom all creatures bow
　Within this earthly frame,
　Through all the world, how great art thou!
　How glorious is thy name!

2 When heaven, thy glorious work on high,
　Employs my wondering sight,—
　The moon, that nightly rules the sky,
　With stars of feebler light.—

3 Lord, what is man, that thou shouldst choose
　To keep him in thy mind?
　Or what his race, that thou shouldst prove
　To them so wondrous kind?

4 O thou, to whom all creatures bow
　Within this earthly frame,
　Through all the world, how great art thou!
　How glorious is thy name!

*Tate & Brady.*

**74 WARREN. L. M.** V. C. TAYLOR.

1. Fa-ther of spir-its, na-ture's God, Our in-most thoughts are known to thee;

Thou, Lord, canst hear each i-dle word, And ev-ery pri-vate ac-tion see.

*Omnipresence of God.* L. M.

1 Father of spirits, nature's God,
　Our inmost thoughts are known to thee;
　Thou, Lord, canst hear each idle word,
　And every private action see.

2 Could we, on morning's swiftest wings,
　Pursue our flight through trackless air,
　Or dive beneath deep ocean's springs,
　Thy presence still would meet us there.

3 In vain may guilt attempt to fly,
　Concealed beneath the pall of night;
　One glance from thy all-piercing eye
　Can kindle darkness into light.

4 Search thou our hearts, and there destroy
　Each evil thought, each secret sin,
　And fit us for those realms of joy,
　Where nought impure shall enter in.

*Spirit of the Psalms*

**75** *Wisdom and Knowledge of God.* L. M.

1 Awake, my tongue; thy tribute bring
　To him who gave thee power to sing;
　Praise him who has all praise above,
　The source of wisdom and of love.

2 How vast his knowledge! how profound!
　A depth where all our thoughts are drown'd;
　The stars he numbers, and their names
　He gives to all those heavenly flames.

3 Through each bright world above, behold
　Ten thousand thousand charms unfold;
　Earth, air and mighty seas combine
　To speak his wisdom all divine.

4 But in redemption, O, what grace!
　Its wonders, O, what thought can trace!
　Here wisdom shines forever bright;
　Praise him, my soul, with sweet delight!

*Needham.*

40

## BEING AND ATTRIBUTES OF GOD.

**76  STEWARD. L. M.**                                          J. T. LAYTON.

1. Fa - ther of all, whose power - ful voice Called forth this
u - ni - ver - sal frame! Whose mer - cies o - ver
all re - joice, Through end - less a - ges still the same.

---

*The Lord's Prayer.*        **L. M. | 77**        *God is Love.*        8s & 7s.

[ Tune Wilmot, page 28.]

1  Father of all, whose powerful voice
   Called forth this universal frame !
   Whose mercies over all rejoice,
   Through endless ages still the same:

2  Thou by thy word upholdest all ;
   Thy bounteous love to all is showed :
   Thou hear'st thy every creature's call ;
   And fillest every mouth with good.

3  In heaven thou reign'st enthroned in light,
   Nature's expanse before thee spread ;
   Earth, air and sea before thy sight,
   And hell's deep gloom, are open laid :

4  Wisdom, and might, and love, are thine ;
   Prostrate before thy face we fall,
   Confess thine attributes divine,
   And hail thee sovereign Lord of all.

5  Thee, sovereign Lord, let all confess,
   That move in earth, or air, or sky ;
   Revere thy power, thy goodness bless,
   Tremble before thy piercing eye.

6  All ye who owe to him your birth,
   In praise your every hour employ :
   Jehovah reigns : be glad, O earth,
   And shout, ye morning stars, for joy!

*J. Wesley.*

1  God is love ; his mercy brightens
   All the path in which we rove ;
   Bliss he wakes, and woe he lightens ;
   God is wisdom, God is love.

2  Chance and change are busy ever ;
   Man decays, and ages move ;
   But his mercy waneth never ;
   God is wisdom, God is love.

3  E'en the hour that darkest seemeth
   Will his changeless goodness prove ;
   From the gloom his brightness streameth,
   God is wisdom, God is love.

4  He with earthly cares entwineth
   Hope and comfort from above :
   Everywhere his glory shineth ;
   God is wisdom, God is love.

*Bowring.*

**77 b**    *The Aged Disciple's Prayer.*  L. M.
[ Words Ed.]

1  Forewarn'd by my Redeemer's love,
   I soon shall lay this body down ;
   But ere my soul from earth remove,
   O may I put thine image on.

2  Saviour! thy meek and lowly mind
   Be to thine aged servant given ;
   And glad I'll drop this tent, to find
   My everlasting home in heaven.

41

# BEING AND ATTRIBUTES OF GOD.

**78  ARIEL.  C. P. M.**                                        LOWELL MASON, 1836.

1. Be - gin my soul, th'ex - alt - ed lay, Let each enraptured tho't obey, And praise th'Almighty's name: Lo! heaven and earth, and seas and skies, In one me - lo-dious concert rise, To swell th'inspiring theme. To swell th'inspir - ing theme.

*Psalm* cxlviii.     C. P. M.

1 Begin, my soul, th' exalted lay,
Let each enraptured thought obey,
  And praise th' Almighty's name :
Lo! heaven and earth, and seas and skies,
In one melodious concert rise,
  ||: To swell the inspiring theme. :||

2 Ye fields of light, celestial plains,
Where gay, transporting beauty reigns,
  Ye scenes divinely fair :
Your Maker's wondrous power proclaim,
Tell how he formed your shining frame,
  ||: And breathed the fluid air. :||

3 Ye angels, catch the thrilling sound;
While all the adoring thrones around
  His boundless mercy sing;
Let every list'ning saint above
Wake all the tuneful soul of love,
  ||: And touch the sweetest string. :||

4 Let saints, redeemed from death and hell,
In louder, loftier numbers, tell
  The wonders of his grace :
Beyond creation's utmost bounds,
Above her noblest, sweetest sounds,
  ||: Declare Jehovah's praise. :||
                              *Ogilvie.*

**78 b.**      *Second Part.*     C. P. M.
               [ Words Ed. ]

1 Ye fields of light, celestial plains,
Where pure, serene effulgence reigns,
  Ye scenes divinely fair,
Your Maker's wondrous power proclaim,
Tell how he formed your shining frame,
  ||: And breathed the fluid air. :||

2 Join all ye stars, the vocal choir;
'Thou dazzling orb of liquid fire,
  The mighty chorus aid ;
And, soon as evening vails the plain,
Thou moon, prolong the hallowed strain,
  ||: And praise him in the shade. :||

3 Thou heaven of heavens, his vast abode,
Proclaim the glories of thy God ;
  Ye worlds declare his might ;
He spake the word, and ye were made,
Darkness and dismal chaos fled,
  ||: And nature sprung to light. :||

4 Let every element rejoice ;
Ye thunders, burst with awful voice
  To him who bids you roll ;
His praise in softer notes declare,
Each whispering breeze of yielding air,
  ||: And breathe it to the soul. :||"
                              *Ogilvie.*

42

# Section 4.

# OF CHRIST.

**79** ANTIOCH. C. M.        HANDEL. ARR BY L. MASON.

1. Joy to the world—the Lord is come! Let earth re - ceive her King; Let

ev - ery heart pre - pare him room, And heav'n and nature sing, And

And heav'n and na-ture

heav'n and na - ture sing,.................... And heav-en and na - ture sing.

sing,........................

*Psalm* xcviii.     C. M.

1 Joy to the world—the Lord is come!
   Let earth receive her King:
   Let every heart prepare him room,
   And heaven and nature sing.

2 Joy to the earth—the Saviour reigns!
   Let men their songs employ;
   While fields and floods, rocks, hills and plains,
   Repeat the sounding joy.

3 No more let sins and sorrows grow,
   Nor thorns infest the ground:
   He comes to make his blessings flow,
   Far as the curse is found.

4 He rules the world with truth and grace;
   And makes the nations prove
   The glories of his righteousness,
   And wonders of his love.

*Watts.*

**80**     *The Prince of Peace.*     C. M.

1 To us a Child of hope is born,
   To us a Son is given:
   Him shall the tribes of earth obey,
   Him, all the hosts of heaven.

2 His name shall be the Prince of peace,
   For evermore adored,—
   The Wonderful, the Counsellor,
   The great and mighty Lord.

3 His power, increasing, still shall spread:
   His reign no end shall know;
   Justice shall guard his throne above,
   And peace abound below.

4 To us a Child of hope is born;
   To us a Son is given;—
   The Wonderful, the Counsellor,
   The mighty Lord of heaven.

*J. Morrison.*

43

**81**     *The Inauguration.*    C. M.

1 See, from on high, a light divine
On Jesus' head descend;
And hear the sacred voice from heaven,
    That bids us all attend : —

2 " This is my well-beloved Son,"
Proclaimed the voice Divine :
" Hear him." his Heavenly Father said,
    " For all his words are mine."

3 His mission thus confirmed from heaven,
    The great Messiah came,

And heavenly wisdom taught to man,
    In God, the Father's name.

4 The path of heavenly peace he showed,
    That leads to bliss on high,
Where all his faithful foll'wers here
    Shall live, no more to die.

5 O may we then, who own him Lord,
    And his loved name profess,
By all our words and actions prove
    That we his mind possess.

*Unknown*

**82**   RETURN. C. M.          HASTINGS.

1. Mortals, a-wake, with an-gels join, And chant the sol - emn lay;

Joy, love, and grat - i - tude, com - bine To hail th'au - spic - ious day.

*The Incarnation.*    C. M.

1 Mortals, awake, with angels join,
And chant the solemn lay :
Joy, love, and gratitude, combine
To hail th' auspicious day.

2 In heaven the rapt'rous song began,
And sweet seraphic fire
Through all the shining legions ran,
And strung and tuned the lyre.

3 Swift through the vast expanse it flew,
And loud the echo rolled :
The theme, the song, the joy was new,
'Twas more than heaven could hold.

4 Down through the portals of the sky
Th' impetuous torrent ran ;
And angels flew with eager joy
To bear the news to man.

5 With joy the chorus we'll repeat,
Glory to God on high !

Good-will and peace are now complete :
Jesus was born to die."

*Medler.*

**83**     *The Guiding Star.*     C. M.

1 Bright was the guiding star. that led,
With mild, benignant ray,
The Gentiles to the lowly bed
Where our Redeemer lay.

2 But, lo ! a brighter, clearer light
Now points to his abode :
It shines through sin and sorrow's night,
To guide us to our Lord.

3 O, haste, to follow where it leads ;
The gracious call obey,
Be rugged wilds. or flow'ry meads,
The Christian's destined way.

4 O, gladly tread the narrow path,
While light and grace are giv'n :
Who meekly follow Christ on earth,
Shall reign with him in heav'n.

*Spir. of the Ps.*

4

OF CHRIST.

**84 DENNIS. S. M.**

FROM HANS G. NÄGELI, 1773-1836.
ADAPTED BY LOWELL MASON, 1849.

1. To God, the on - ly wise, Our Sav - iour and our King,

Let all the saints be - low the skies Their hum - ble prais - es bring.

*Jude* 24, 25.　　　　　　S. M.

1 To God, the only wise,
　Our Saviour and our King,
　Let all the saints below the skies
　Their humble praises bring.

2 'Tis his almighty love,
　His counsel and his care,
　Preserves us safe from sin and death,
　And every hurtful snare.

3 He will present our souls,
　Unblemished and complete,
　Before the glory of his face,
　With joys divinely great.

4 Then all the chosen seed
　Shall meet around the throne;
　Shall bless the conduct of his grace,
　And make his wonders known.

5 To our Redeemer, God,
　Wisdom with power belongs,
　Immortal crowns of majesty,
　And everlasting songs.
　　　　　　　　*Watts.*

**85**　　*The Victory of the Cross.*　　S. M.

1 Jesus, the Conqueror, reigns,
　In glorious strength arrayed;
　His kingdom over all maintains,
　And bids the earth be glad:

2 Ye sons of men, rejoice
　In Jesus' mighty love;
　Lift up your heart, lift up your voice,
　To him who rules above.

3 Extol his kingly power;
　Kiss the exalted Son,
　Who died, and lives to die no more,
　High on his Father's throne:

4 Our Advocate with God,
　He undertakes our cause,
　And spreads through all the earth abroad
　The victory of his cross.
　　　　　　　*Charles Wesley.*

**86**　　*Atoning Sacrifice.*　　S. M.

1 Not all the blood of beasts,
　On Jewish altars slain,
　Could give the guilty conscience peace,
　Or wash away the stain.

2 But Christ, the heavenly Lamb,
　Takes all our sins away:
　A sacrifice of nobler name,
　And richer blood than they.

3 My faith would lay her hand
　On that dear head of thine,—
　While like a penitent I stand,
　And there confess my sin,
　　　　　　　　*Watts.*

45

# OF CHRIST.

## 87  ALL SAINTS. L. M.

1. To us a child of roy-al birth, Heir of the prom-is-es, is giv'n!

Th' In-vis-i-ble ap-pears on earth, The Son of man, the God of heav'n.

*"Unto us a Son is given."* L. M.

1 To us a child of royal birth,
  Heir of the promises, is given!
  Th' Invisible appears on earth,
  The Son of man, the God of heaven.

2 A Saviour born, in love supreme
  He comes, our fallen souls to raise:
  He comes, his people to redeem,
  With all his plenitude of grace.

3 The Christ, by raptured seers foretold,
  Filled with th' eternal Spirit's power,
  Prophet, and Priest, and King, behold,
  And Lord of all the worlds adore.

4 The Lord of hosts, the God most high,
  Who quits his throne on earth to live,
  With joy we welcome from the sky,
  With faith into our hearts receive.
                            *C. Wesley.*

## 88  *"Unto us a Child is Born."* S. M.

[ Tune, Greenwood, page 20. S. M. ]

1 Father, our hearts we lift
  Up to thy gracious throne,
  And thank thee for the precious gift
  Of thine incarnate Son!

2 The gift unspeakable
  We thankfully receive,
  And to the world thy goodness tell,
  And to thy glory live.

3 Jesus, the holy child,
  Doth, by his birth, declare
  That God and man are reconciled,
  And one in him we are.

4 A peace on earth he brings,
  Which never more shall end:
  The Lord of hosts, the King of kings,
  Declares himself our friend.

5 His kingdom from above
  He doth to us impart,
  And pure benevolence and love
  O'erflow the faithful heart.
                            *C. Wesley.*

## 89  *Gal.* vi. 14.  L. M.

1 When I survey the wondrous cross
  On which the Prince of glory died,
  My richest gain I count but loss,
  And pour contempt on all my pride.

2 Forbid it, Lord, that I should boast,
  Save in the death of Christ my God:
  All the vain things that charm me most,
  I sacrifice them to his blood.

3 See, from his head, his hands, his feet,
  Sorrow and love flow mingled down!
  Did e'er such love and sorrow meet?
  Or thorns compose so rich a crown?

4 Were the whole realm of nature mine,
  That were a present far too small;
  Love so amazing, so Divine,
  Demands my soul, my life, my all.
                            *Watts.*

46

# OF CHRIST.

**90**     *His exemplary Life.*    L . M.

[ Tune, Missionary Chant 48.]

1 My dear Redeemer, and my Lord,
I read my duty in thy word;
But in thy life the law appears,
Drawn out in living characters.

2 Such was thy truth, and such thy zeal,
Such def'rence to thy Father's will,
Such love, and meekness so divine,
I would transcribe, and make them mine.

3 Cold mountains, and the midnight air,
Witness the fervor of thy prayer;
The desert thy temptations knew,
Thy conflict, and thy vict'ry too.

4 Be thou my pattern; make me bear
More of thy gracious image here :
Then God, the Judge, shall own my name
Among the foll'wers of the Lamb.

*Watts.*

**91**   ALETTA. 7s.            W. B. BRADBURY.

Hark! the her - ald an - gels sing, "Glo - ry to the new-born King!
Joy - ful all ye na - tions rise, Join the tri -umphs of the skies;

Peace on earth, and mer - cy mild; God and sin-ners rec - on - ciled! }
With th'an - gel - ic hosts pro - claim, "Christ is born in Beth - le -hem!" }

### The Incarnation.     7s.

1 Hark! the herald angels sing,
"Glory to the new-born King!
Peace on earth, and mercy mild;
God and sinners reconciled!"
Joyful all ye nations rise,
Join the triumphs of the skies;
With th' angelic hosts proclaim,
"Christ is born in Bethlehem!"

2 Christ, by highest heaven adored,
Christ, the everlasting Lord ;
Late in time behold him come,
Offspring of a virgin's womb ;
Veiled in flesh the Godhead see,
Hail th' incarnate Deity !
Pleased as man with men t' appear,
Jesus our Immanuel here.

3 Come, Desire of nations, come !
Fix in us thy humble home ;
Rise, the woman's conqu'ring seed,
Bruise in us the serpent's head;

Adam's likeness now efface,
Stamp thine image in its place :
Second Adam from above,
Reinstate us in thy love.

*C. Wesley.*

**92**      *Brazen Serpent.*     7s.

1 O that I could look to thee,
Jesus, lifted up for me,
Me, a wounded Israelite,
Me, expiring in thy sight !

2 Guilt, the serpent's sting, I feel,
Anguish inconceivable,
Bleeding, gasping on the ground,
Dying of the pois'nous wound,

3 But, with a believing eye,
If I can my Lord espy,
Hanging on the sacred pole,
I, e'en I, shall be made whole.

4 Give me now to find thee near,
Now as crucified appear :
Life is through thy wounds alone;
Mine to heal, display thy own.

*C. Wesley.*

OF CHRIST.

## 93 MISSIONARY CHANT. L. M.

ZUENER.

1. When, marshall'd on the night-ly plain, The glitt'ring hosts be-stud the sky,

One star a-lone, of all the train, Can fix the sin-ner's wand'ring eye.

*The Star of Bethlehem.* L. M.

1 When, marshall'd on the nightly plain,
The glitt'ring hosts bestud the sky,
One star alone, of all the train,
Can fix the sinner's wandering eye.

2 Hark! hark! to God the chorus breaks,
From every host, from every gem;
But one alone the Saviour's speaks—
It is the Star of Bethlehem!

3 Once on the raging seas I rode;
The storm was loud, the night was dark;
The ocean yawned, and rudely blow'd
The wind that tossed my foundering bark.

4 Deep horror then my vitals froze;
Death-struck, I ceas'd the tide to stem;
When suddenly a star arose—
It was the Star of Bethlehem!

5 It was my guide, my light, mine all;
It bade my dark forebodings cease;
And, through the storm and danger's thrall,
It led me to the port of peace.

6 Now, safely moor'd, my perils o'er,
I'll sing, first in night's diadem,
Forever, and for evermore—
The Star—the Star of Bethlehem!
*H. K. White.*

## 94  *Believe and be saved.*  L. M.

*John iii. 16, 17, 18.*

1 Not to condemn the sons of men,
Did Christ, the Son of God, appear:—
No weapons in his hands are seen,
No flaming sword, nor thunder there.

2 Such was the pity of our God,—
He lov'd the race of man so well,—
He sent his Son, to bear our load
Of sins, and save our souls from hell.

3 Sinners, believe the Saviour's word;
Trust in his mighty name, and live:
A thousand joys his lips afford;
His hands a thousand blessings give.

4 But vengeance and damnation lies
On rebels who refuse his grace;
Who God's eternal Son despise,
The hottest hell shall be their place.
*Watts.*

## 94 b  [ Words Ed. ]  L. M.

1 Eternal Spirit, we confess
And sing the wonders of thy grace;
Thy power conveys our blessings down
From God the Father and the Son.

2 Enlightened by thine heavenly ray,
Our shades and darkness turn to-day;
Thine inward teachings make us know
Our danger and our refuge too,

3 Thy power and glory work within,
And break the chains of reigning sin;
Our wild, imperious lusts subdue,
And form our wretched hearts anew.

4 The troubled conscience knows thy voice,
Thy cheering words awake our joys;
Thy words allay the stormy wind,
And calm the surges of the mind.
*Watts.*

48

# OF CHRIST.

**95  STONEFIELD.  L. M.**   STANLEY.

1. Ye that pass by, be - hold the Man! The man of griefs condemned for you,

The Lamb of God, for sin - ners slain, Weeping to Cal-va - ry pursue!

---

*The Suffering and Crucifixion of Christ.* L. M.
*Matt.* xxvii. 26-53.

1 Ye that pass by, behold the Man!
  The man of griefs condemned for you,
  The Lamb of God, for sinners slain,
  Weeping to Calvary pursue!

2 See! how his back the scourges tear,
  While to the bloody pillar bound!
  The ploughers made long furrows there,
  Till all his body is one wound.

3 Nor can he thus their hate assuage;
  His innocence to death pursued,
  Must fully glut their utmost rage:
  Hark! how they clamor for his blood!

4 His sacred limbs they stretch, they tear,
  With nails they fasten to the wood!
  His sacred limbs, exposed and bare,
  Or only cover'd with his blood!

5 See, there! his temples crown'd with thorns,
  His bleeding hands extended wide!
  His streaming feet transfixt and torn!
  The fountain gushing from his side!

6 Where is the King of Glory now?
  The everlasting Son of God!
  The Immortal hangs his languid brow:
  The Almighty faints beneath his load!
                                  *C. Wesley.*

**96**   *Dying, Rising, Reigning.*   L. M.
            [Orwell, page 50.]

1 He dies! the Friend of sinners dies!
  Lo! Salem's daughters weep around;
  A solemn darkness veils the skies:
  A sudden trembling shakes the ground:

2 Come, saints, and drop a tear or two
  For him who groaned beneath your load:
  He shed a thousand drops for you,
  A thousand drops of richer blood.

3 Here's love and grief beyond degree:
  The Lord of glory dies for man!
  But lo! what sudden joys we see!
  Jesus, the dead, revives again!

4 The rising God forsakes the tomb;
  Up to his Father's courts he flies;
  Cherubic legions guard him home,
  And shout him welcome to the skies!

5 Break off your tears, ye saints, and tell
  How high your great Deliv'rer reigns:
  Sing how he spoiled the hosts of hell,
  And led the monster death in chains!

6 Say, " Live for ever, wondrous King!
  Born to redeem, and strong to save!"
  Then ask the monster, " Where's thy sting?"
  And, "Where's thy vict'ry, boasting grave."
                                  *Watts.*

49

96 ORWELL. L. M.                                        L. MASON.

1. He dies! the Friend of sin-ners dies! Lo! Sa-lem's daughters weep a-round;

A sol-emn dark-ness veils the skies; A sud-den trembling shakes the ground.

*"It is finished."*                    L. M.

1 'Tis finished! The Messiah dies,
   Cut off for sins, but not his own!
   Accomplished is the sacrifice,
   The great redeeming work is done.

2 'Tis finished! All the debt is paid:
   Justice Divine is satisfied:
   The grand and full atonement made:
   God for a guilty world hath died.

3 The veil is rent in Christ alone:
   The living way to heaven is seen:

   The middle wall is broken down,
   And all mankind may enter in.

4 The types and figures are fulfilled:
   Exacted is the legal pain:
   The precious promises are sealed:
   The spotless Lamb of God is slain.

5 Saved from the legal curse I am:
   My Saviour hangs on yonder tree:
   See there the meek, expiring Lamb!
   'Tis finished! He expires for me.
                              *Charles Wesley.*

97 BERA. L. M.                                        J. E. GOULD.

1. 'Tis finish'd! The Mes-si-ah dies, Cut off for sins, but not his own!

Accomplish'd is the sac-ri-fice, The great re-deem-ing work is done.

# OF CHRIST.

**98 LISCHER. H. M.** DR. L. MASON.

Re - joice, the Lord is King! Your Lord and King a - dore;
Mor - tals, give thanks and sing, And tri - umph ev - er - more;

Lift up your hearts, lift up your voice, Re-joice, a - gain I say, re-joice,

Re - joice, a - gain I say, re - joice.

Cho. Rejoice, a - gain I say, re - joice.

*Rejoice evermore.* H. M.

1 Rejoice, the Lord is King!
Your Lord and King adore;
Mortals, give thanks and sing,
And triumph evermore;
Lift up your hearts, lift up your voice;
Rejoice, again I say, rejoice.

2 Jesus, the Saviour, reigns,
The God of truth and love;
When he had purged our stains,
He took his seat above;
Lift up your hearts, lift up your voice;
Rejoice, again I say, rejoice.

3 His kingdom cannot fail,
He rules o'er earth and heaven;
The keys of death and hell
Are to our Jesus given:
Lift up your hearts, lift up your voice;
Rejoice, again I say, rejoice.

4 He sits at God's right hand
Till all his foes submit,
And bow to his command,
And fall beneath his feet;
Lift up your hearts, lift up your voice;
Rejoice, again I say, rejoice.

5 He all his foes shall quell,
And all our sins destroy;
Let every bosom swell
With pure seraphic joy;
Lift up your hearts, lift up your voice;
Rejoice, again I say, rejoice.

6 Rejoice in glorious hope;
Jesus the Judge shall come,
And take his servants up
To their eternal home;
We soon shall hear the archangel's voice;
The trump of God shall sound,—Rejoice!
*Charles Wesley.*

51

OF CHRIST.

**99 CLAREMONT. H. M.**  ARR. W. B. BRADBURY.

1. Join all the glorious names Of wis-dom, love, and power, That ev - er mor-tals knew, That an - gels ev - er bore: All are too mean to speak his worth, Too mean to set speak his worth, Too mean to set my Sav - iour forth.

*Various Offices of Christ.* H. M.

1 Join all the glorious names
  Of wisdom, love. and power,
That ever mortals knew,
  That angels ever bore:
All are too mean to speak his worth,
Too mean to set my Saviour forth.

2 But O! what gentle terms,
  What conde-cending ways,
Doth our *Redeemer* use
  To teach his heavenly grace!
Mine eyes with joy and wonder see
What forms of love he bears for me.

3 Arrayed in mortal flesh.
  The *Covenant-Angel* stands,
And hold- the promises
  And pardons in his hands:
Commissioned from his Father's throne
To make his grace to mortals known.

4 Great *Prophet* of my God,
  My tongue would bless thy name:
By thee the joyful news
  Of our salvation came.—
The joyful news of sins forgiven,
Of hell subdued, and peace with Heaven.

*Watts.*

**100** *High Priest.* H. M.

1 Jesus. my great *High Priest*,
  Offered his blood and died:
My guilty conscience seeks
  No sacrifice beside:
His powerful blood did once atone,
And now it pleads before the throne.

2 My *Advocate* appears
  For my defence on high:
The Father bows his ears,
  And lays his thunder by:
Not all that earth or hell can say
Shall turn his heart. his love away.

3 O thou almighty *Lord*,
  My *Conq'ror* and my *King*,
Thy sceptre. and thy sword,
  Thy reigning grace I sing
Thine is the power: behold I sit
In willing bonds beneath thy feet.

4 Now let my soul arise,
  And tread the tempter down;
My *Captain* leads me forth
  To conquest and a crown:
A feeble saint shall win the day,
Though death and hell obstruct the way.

*Watts.*

52

**101 SEGUR.** 8s, 7s & 4s.  J. P. HOLBROOK.

1. Hark! the voice of love and mer-cy Sounds a-loud from Cal-va-ry;

See! it rends the rocks a-sun-der, Shakes the earth, and veils the sky;

"It is fin-ished" "It is fin-ished" Hear the dy-ing Sav-iour cry.

*It is Finished.*  8s, 7s & 4s.

1 Hark! the voice of love and mercy
Sounds aloud from Calvary;
See! it rends the rocks asunder,
Shakes the earth, and veils the sky;
" It is finished: "
Hear the dying Saviour cry.

2 " It is finished! " O what pleasure
Do these precious words afford!
Heavenly blessings, without measure,
Flow to us from Christ the Lord:
" It is finished: "
Saints, the dying words record.

3 Tune your harps anew, ye seraphs;
Join to sing the pleasing theme;
All on earth, and all in heaven,
Join to praise Immanuel's name;
Hallelujah!
Glory to the bleeding Lamb.
*Jonathan Evans.*

**101 b** *Coronation of the King of Kings.*

[Words Ed.]  8s, 7s & 4s.

1 Look, ye saints, the sight is glorious,
See the Man of sorrows now;

From the fight returned victorious,
Every knee to him shall bow :
Crown him, crown him ;
Crowns become the Victor's brow.

2 Crown the Saviour, angels, crown him ;
Rich the trophies Jesus brings ;
In the seat of power enthrone him,
While the heavenly concave rings :
Crown him, crown him ;
Crown the Saviour King of kings.

3 Sinners in derision crowned him,
Mocking thus the Saviour's claim ;
Saints and angels crowd around him,
Own his title, praise his name :
Crown him, crown him ;
Spread abroad the Victor's fame.

4 Hark! those bursts of acclamation !
Hark! those loud triumphant chords !
Jesus takes the highest station ;
Oh, what joy the sight affords !
Crown him, crown him,
King of kings and Lord of lords.
*Thos. Kelley.*

53

# OF CHRIST.

**102** RODMAN. 11s & 10s.

DR. L. MASON.

*Animated.*

1. Bright - est and best of the sons of the morn - ing.
2. Cold, on his cra - dle, the dew - drops are shin - ing,
3. Say, shall we yield him, in cost - ly de - vo - tion,
4. Vain - ly we of - fer each am - ple ob - la - tion;

Dawn on our dark - ness, and lend us thine aid;
Low lies his bed with the beasts of the stall;
O - dors of E - den and oft' - rings di - vine?
Vain - ly with gifts would his fa - vor se - cure;

Star of the East, the ho - ri - zon a - dorn - ing,
An - gels a - dore him, in slum - ber re - clin - ing,—
Gems of the mount - ain, and pearls of the o - cean,
Rich - er by far is the heart's ad - o - ra - tion;

Guide where the in - fant Re - deem - er is laid.
Mak - er, and Mon - arch, and Sa - viour of all.
Myrrh from the for - est, and gold from the mine?
Dear - er to God are the pray'rs of the poor.

HEBER.

54

# OF CHRIST.

*The Birth of Christ. Luke ii. 11-16.*

**103  ANNIE.  11s & 10s.**

J. C. EMBRY, 1897.

1. Hith - er, ye faith - ful, haste with songs of tri - umph,
2. O, Je - sus! for such won - drous con - de - scen - sion,
3. Shout his al - might - y name, ye choirs of an - gels,

To Bethlehem go, the Lord of Life to meet; To you this day, is
Our praise and rev - 'rence are an off-'ring meet, Now is the Word made
Let the ce - les - tial courts his praise re - peat; Un - to our God be

*rit.*

born a Prince and Sa - viour, O, come and let us wor-ship at his feet.
flesh, and dwells a - mong us, O, come and let us wor-ship at his feet.
glo - ry in the high - est, O, come and let us wor-ship at his feet.

**103 b.**

*" We would see Jesus."*
[Words Ed.]

11s & 10s

1 We would see Jesus—for the shadows lengthen,
Across this little landscape of our life;
We would see Jesus our weak faith to strengthen,
For the last weariness—the final strife.

2 We would see Jesus—the great Rock Foundation,
Whereon our feet were set by sovereign grace;
Not life, nor death, with all their agitation,
Can thence remove us, if we see his face.

3 We would see Jesus—other lights are fading,
Which for long years we have rejoiced to see;
The blessings of our pilgrimage are failing,
We would not mourn them, for we go to thee.

4 We would see Jesus—this is all we're needing,
Strength, joy and willingness come with the sight;
We would see Jesus, dying, risen, pleading,
Then welcome day, and farewell mortal night!

*Anon.*

55

**104** **BAVARIA.** **8s & 7s.**

1. Hark! what mean those ho-ly voi-ces Sweet-ly sound-ing thro' the skies?
Lo! th' an-gelic host re-joi-ces, Heav'nly hal-le-lu-jahs rise.

Lis-ten to the wondrous sto-ry Which they chant in hymns of joy:

Glo-ry in the high-est, glo-ry! Glo-ry be to God most high!

*The Incarnation.* 8, 7, 8, 7.

1 Hark! what mean those holy voices
    Sweetly sounding through the skies?
Lo! th' angelic host rejoices,
    Heavenly hallelujahs rise.
Listen to the wondrous story
    Which they chant in hymns of joy:
Glory in the highest, glory!
    Glory be to God most high!

2 Peace on earth, good-will from heaven,
    Reaching far as man is found:
Souls redeem'd and sins forgiven,
    Loud our golden harps shall sound.
Christ is born, the great Anointed,
    Heaven and earth his praises sing:
O! receive whom God appointed
    For your Prophet, Priest and King.

3 Hasten, mortals, to adore him,
    Learn his name and taste his joy:
Till in heaven ye sing before him,
    Glory be to God most high!
Let us learn the wondrous story
    Of our great Redeemer's birth:

Spread the brightness of his glory
    Till it cover all the earth.
                                        *Cawood.*

**105**  *Luke* ii. 8-14.  **C. M.**
              [ Tune Heber, page 57.]

1 While shepherds watch'd their flocks by
        night,
    All seated on the ground,
The angel of the Lord came down,
    And glory shone around.
" Fear not," said he, ( for mighty dread
    Had seiz'd their troubled mind,)
"Glad tidings of great joy I bring
    To you and all mankind.

2 "To you, in David's town, this day,
    Is born of David's line,
The Saviour, who is Christ the Lord;
    And this shall be the sign:
"The heavenly babe you there shall find
    To human view display'd,
All meanly wrapp'd in swathing bands,
    And in a manger laid."
                                        *Patrick.*

# OF CHRIST.

## 106  HEBER.  C. M.

GEORGE KINGSLEY.

1. Hark, the glad sound! the Sav-iour comes—The Sav-iour, prom - is'd long;
Let ev - 'ry heart pre - pare a throne, And ev - 'ry voice a song.

*Design and Object of his Advent.*  C. M.

2 He comes, the pris'ner to release,
  In Satan's bondage held;
The gates of brass before him burst,
  The iron fetters yield.

3 He comes, from thickest films of vice,
  To clear the mental ray,
And on the eyes oppress'd by night
  To pour celestial day.

4 He comes, the broken heart to bind,
  The wounded soul to cure,
And, with the treasures of his grace,
  T' enrich the humble poor.

5 Our glad hosannas, Prince of peace,
  Thy welcome shall proclaim,
And heaven's eternal arches ring
  With thy beloved name.
                        *Doddridge.*

**107**    *Stupenduous Love.*    C. M.

1 Plunged in a gulf of dark despair,
  We wretched sinners lay,
Without one cheering beam of hope,
  Or spark of glimm'ring day.

2 With pitying eyes the Prince of grace
  Beheld our helpless grief;
He saw, and ( O amazing love )!
  He ran to our relief.

3 Down from the shining seats above
  With joyful haste he fled,
Entered the grave in mortal flesh,
  And dwelt among the dead.

4 O for this love let rocks and hills
  Their lasting silence break!
And all harmonious human tongues
  The Saviour's praises speak.

5 Angels, assist our mighty joys,
  Strike all your harps of gold;
But when you raise your highest notes,
  His love can ne'er be told!
                        *Watts.*

**108**    *The Fountain of Atonement.*    C. M.

1 There is a fountain filled with blood,
  Drawn from Immanuel's veins;
And sinners, plunged beneath that flood,
  Lose all their guilty stains.

2 The dying thief rejoiced to see
  That fountain in his day;
And there may I, though vile as he,
  Wash all my sins away.

3 Dear dying Lamb, thy precious blood
  Shall never lose its power,
Till all the ransomed Church of God
  Be saved to sin no more.

4 E'er since, by faith, I saw the stream
  Thy flowing wounds supply,
Redeeming love has been my theme,
  And shall be till I die.

5 Then, in a nobler, sweeter song,
  I'll sing thy power to save,
When this poor lisping, stamm'ring tongue
  Lies silent in the grave.
                        *Cowper.*

OF CHRIST.

109 CORONATION. C. M.                                    OLIVER HOLDEN.

1. Be - hold the Sav - iour of man - kind Nailed to the shame - ful tree!

How vast the love that him in - clined To bleed and die for thee!

How vast the love that him in - clined To bleed and die for thee!

2 Hark, how he groans! while nature shakes,
And earth's strong pillars bend!
The temple's veil in sunder breaks,
The solid marbles rend.

3 'Tis done! the precious ransom's paid!
"Receive my soul!" he cries:
See where he bows his sacred head!
He bows his head, and dies!
                                        *S. Wesley, Sr.*

**110**     *Coronation of Christ*     C. M.

1 All hail the power of Jesus' name!
Let angels prostrate fall:
Bring forth the royal diadem,
And crown him Lord of all!

2 Ye chosen seed of Israel's race,—
A remnant weak and small,—
Hail him who saves you by his grace,
And crown him Lord of all.

3 Ye Gentile sinners, ne'er forget
The wormwood and the gall:
Go, spread your trophies at his feet,
And crown him Lord of all.

4 Let every kindred, every tribe
On this terrestrial ball,
To him all majesty ascribe,
And crown him Lord of all.

5 O that, with yonder sacred throng,
We at his feet may fall!
We'll join the everlasting song,
And crown him Lord of all.
                                        *Perronet.*

**111**     *"I am the Way."*     L. M.
[Tune, Rest, page 59. L. M.]

1 Jesus, my all, to heaven is gone,
He whom I fix my hopes upon;
His track I see, and I'll pursue
The narrow way, till him I view.

2 The way the holy scriptures went,
The road that leads from banishment,
The King's highway of holiness,
I'll go, for all his paths are peace.

3 This is the way I long have sought,
And mourned because I found it not:
My grief a burden long has been,
Because I was not saved from sin.

4 The more I strove against its power,
I felt its weight and guilt the more;
Till late I heard my Saviour say,
"Come hither, soul, I AM THE WAY."

5 Lo! glad I come, and thou, blest Lamb,
Shalt take me to thee as I am:
Nothing but sin have I to give,
Nothing but love shall I receive.
                                        *Cennick.*

58

**112** REST. L. M.
*Tenderly.*

1. The day of Christ, the day of God, We hum-bly hope with joy to see,

Wash'd in the sanc-ti-fy-ing blood Of an ex-pir-ing De-i-ty.—

---

*" Over all, God blessed forever."* L. M.

1 The day of Christ, the day of God,
    We humbly hope with joy to see,
Washed in the sanctifying blood
    Of an expiring Deity—

2 Who did for us his life resign:
    There is no other God but one;
For all the plentitude divine
    Resides in the eternal Son.

3 Spotless, sincere, without offence,
    O may we to his day remain!
Who trust the blood of Christ to cleanse
    Our souls from every sinful stain.

4 Lord, we believe the promise sure!
    The purchased Comforter impart!
Apply thy blood to make us pure—
    To keep us pure in life and heart!

5 Then let us see that day supreme,
    When none thy Godhead shall deny!
Thy sovereign majesty blaspheme,
    Or count thee less than the Most High.
                                    *C. Wesley.*

**113** L. M.
*Praise to God for his Perfections and Providence.*

1 Praise ye the Lord : my heart shall join
    In work so pleasant, so divine:
My days of praise shall ne'er be past,
    While life, and thought, and being, last.

2 Happy the man whose hopes rely
    On Israel's God : he made the sky,
And earth, and seas, with all their train;
    And none shall find his promise vain.

3 His truth forever stands secure ;
    He saves th' oppressed, he feeds the poor,
He helps the stranger in distress,
    The widow and the fatherless.

4 He loves the saints : he knows them well,
    But turns the wicked down to hell :
Thy God, O Zion, ever reigns;
    Praise him in everlasting strains.
                                    *Watts.*

**114** *The Grace of Christ.* L. M.

1 Now to the Lord a noble song!
    Awake, my soul : awake, my tongue ;
Hosanna to th' Eternal Name,
    And all his boundless love proclaim.

2 See, where it shines in Jesus' face,
    The brightest image of his grace :
God, in the person of his Son,
    Has all his mightiest works outdone.

3 The spacious earth and spreading flood
    Proclaim the wise, the powerful God ;
And thy rich glories from afar,
    Sparkle in every rolling star:

4 But in his looks a glory stands,
    The noblest labor of thy hands;
The pleasing lustre of his eyes
    Outshines the wonders of the skies.
                                    *Watts.*

*Doxology.* L. M.

Praise God from whom all blessings flow ;
Praise him all creatures here below;
Praise him above, ye heavenly host;
Praise Father, Son, and Holy Ghost.

OF CHRIST.

## 115 ARLINGTON. C. M.

DR. ARNE.

1. The Sun of Right-eous-ness ap-pears, To set in blood no more;

A - dore the Scatt'-rer of your fears, Your ris - ing Sun a - dore.

### Resurrection. C. M.

1 The Sun of Righteousness appears,
   To set in blood no more :
   Adore the Scatt'rer of your fears,
   Your rising Sun adore.

2 The saints, when he resigned his breath;
   Unclosed their sleeping eyes;
   He breaks again the bands of death,
   Again the dead arise.

3 Alone the dreadful race he ran,
   Alone the wine-press trod :
   He dies and suffers as a man ;
   He rises as a God.

4 In vain the stone, the watch, the seal,
   Forbid an early rise
   To him who breaks the gates of hell,
   And opens paradise.
                        S. Wesley, Jr.

### 116 Rejoicing in the Risen Christ. C. M.

1 Awake, glad soul! awake! awake!
   Thy Lord has risen long;
   Go to his grave and with thee take,
   Both tuneful heart and song.

2 Where life is waking all around,
   Where love's sweet voices sing,
   The first bright blossom may be found
   Of an eternal spring.

3 The shade and gloom of life are fled
   This resurrection day ;
   Henceforth in Christ are no more dead,
   The grave hath no more prey.

4 In Christ we live, in Christ we sleep,
   In Christ we wake and rise,
   And the sad tears death makes us weep,
   He wipes from all our eyes.

5 Then wake, glad heart! awake! awake!
   And seek thy risen Lord!
   Joy in his resurrection take,
   And comfort in his word!
                        S. B. Monsell.

### 116 b My Portion. C. M.
[Words Ed.]

1 Thou art my portion, O my God!
   Soon as I know thy way,
   My heart makes haste t' obey thy word,
   And suffers no delay.

2 I choose the path of heavenly truth,
   And glory in my choice ;
   Not all the riches of the earth
   Could make me so rejoice,

3 The testimonies of thy grace
   I set before mine eyes ;
   Thence I derive my daily strength,
   And there my comfort lies.

4 If once I wander from thy path,
   I think upon my ways ;
   Then turn my feet to thy commands,
   And trust thy pard'ning grace.

5 Now I am thine, for ever thine,
   Oh, save thy servant, Lord!
   Thou art my shield, my hiding-place,
   My hope is in thy word.
                        Watts.

OF CHRIST.

117 FULTON. 7s.                                    WM. B. BRADBURY.

1. Hail, the day that sees him rise, Rav - ished from our wist - ful eyes!

Christ, a - while to mor - tals given, Re - as - cends his na - tive heaven.

*Ascension Day.*        7s.

1 Hail the day that sees him rise,
  Ravished from our wistful eyes!
  Christ, awhile to mortals given,
  Re-ascends his native heaven.

2 There the pompous triumph waits :
  Lift your heads, eternal gates!
  Wide unfold the radiant scene ;
  Take the King of glory in !

3 Circled round with angel powers,
  Their triumphant Lord and ours,
  Conqueror over death and sin,—
  Take the King of glory in !

4 Him through highest heaven receives,
  Still he loves the earth he leaves ;
  Though returning to his throne,
  Still he calls mankind his own.

5 See, he lifts his hands above !
  See, he shows the prints of love !
  Hark, his gracious lips bestow
  Blessings on his Church below !

6 Saviour, parted from our sight,
  High above yon azure height,
  Grant our hearts may hither rise,
  Following thee beyond the skies.
                      *Charles Wesley.*

**117 b**        *Psalm ii.*

[Words Ed.]

1 Wherefore do the nations wage
  War against the King of kings ?

Whence the people's madd'ning rage,
  Fraught with vain imaginings ?

2 Haughty chiefs, and rulers proud,
  Forth in banded fury run,
  Braving with defiance loud
  God and his anointed Son.

3 " Let us break their bonds in twain !
  Let us cast their cords away ! "—
  But the Highest with disdain
  Sees and mocks their vain array.

4 " High on Zion I prepare,"
  Thus he speaks, " a regal throne :
  Thou, my Prince, my chosen heir,
  Rise to claim it as thine own ! "

5 " Son of God, with God the same,
  Enter thine imperial dome !
  Lo ! the shaking heavens proclaim,
  Mightiest Lord, thy kingdom come.

6 " Pomp or state dost thou demand ?
  In thy Father's glory shine !
  Dost thou ask for high command ?
  Lo ! the universe is thine ! "

7 Ye who spurn his righteous sway,
  Yet, ah yet, he spares your breath :
  Yet his hand, averse to slay,
  Balances the bolt of death.

8 Ere that dreadful bolt descends,
  Haste before his feet to fall,
  Kiss the sceptre he extends,
  And adore him, Lord of all !
                      *C. Wesley.*

61

**118   ESSEX.   7s, 5 lines.**                                THOMAS CLARK. 1775-1859.

1. Christ, the Lord, is risen a - gain, Christ hath bro - ken ev - 'ry chain; Hark! an-gel - ic voi - ces cry, Sing - ing ev - er - more on high, Hal - le - lu - jah! Praise the Lord!

*The Lord is Risen.*   7s, 5 lines.

1 Christ, the Lord, is risen again,
Christ hath broken every chain;
Hark! angelic voices cry,
Singing evermore on high,
Hallelujah! Praise the Lord!

2 He who gave for us his life,
Who for us endured the strife,
Is our Paschal Lamb to-day!
We, too, sing for joy, and say,
Hallelujah! Praise the Lord!

3 He who bore all pain and loss,
Comfortless, upon the cross,
Lives in glory now on high,
Pleads for us, and hears our cry:
Hallelujah! Praise the Lord!

4 Now he bids us tell abroad
How the lost may be restored,
How the penitent forgiven,
How we, too, may enter heaven!
Hallelujah! Praise the Lord!

[*Michael Weisse, Tr. by Miss C. Winkworth.*]

**118 b**      *The Crucifixion.*      L. M.
[ Tune, Barnby, page 63. L. M.]
[ Words Ed.]

1 Extended on a cursed tree,
Besmeared with dust, and sweat, and blood,
See there, the King of glory see!
Sinks, and expires, the Son of God!

2 Who, who, my Saviour, this hath done?
Who could thy sacred body wound?
No guilt thy spotless heart hath known,
No guile hath in thy lips been found.

3 I,—I alone have done the deed!
'Tis I thy sacred flesh have torn:
My sins have caused thee, Lord, to bleed,
Pointed the nail, and fixed the thorn.

4 For me, the burden, to sustain
Too great, on thee, my Lord, was laid:
To heal me, thou hast borne the pain;
To bless me, thou a curse wast made.

5 In the devouring lion's teeth,
Torn, and forsook of all, I lay:
Thou sprang'st into the jaws of death,
From death to save the helpless prey?

6 My Saviour, how shall I proclaim,
How pay the mighty debt I owe?
Let all I have, and all I am,
Ceaseless to all thy glory show.

7 Too much to thee I cannot give;
Too much I cannot do for thee:
Let all thy love, and all thy grief,
Grav'n on my heart for ever be!

8 Still let thy tears, thy groans, thy sighs,
O'erflow my eyes, and heave my breast;
Till loose from flesh and earth I rise,
And ever in thy bosom rest.

*From the German of Dessler, J. Wesley.*

**119 BARNBY. L. M.**

1. Of him who did sal - va - tion bring I could for - ev - er think and sing;

A - rise, ye need - y, he'll re-lieve; A - rise, ye guilt - y, he'll forgive.

*Love which passeth Knowledge.* L. M.

[From the Latin of St. Bernard.]

1 Of him who did salvation bring
I could forever think and sing:
Arise, ye needy, he'll relieve;
Arise, ye guilty, he'll forgive.

2 Ask but his grace, and lo, 'tis given!
Ask, and he turns your hell to heaven:
Though sin and sorrow wound my soul,
Jesus, thy balm will make it whole.

3 To shame our sins he blushed in blood,
He closed his eyes to show us God:
Let all the world fall down and know
That none but God such love can show.

4 'Tis thee I love, for thou alone
I shed my tears and make my moan!
Where'er I am, where'er I move,
I meet the object of thy love.

5 Insatiate to this spring I fly:
I drink, and yet am ever dry:
Ah! who against thy charms is proof?
Ah! who that loves can love enough?

**120** *The Lord is Risen.* 7s.

[Tune, Pleyel's Hymn, page 85. 7s.]

1 Christ, the Lord, is risen to-day,
Sons of men and angels say;
Raise your joys and triumphs high;
Sing, ye heavens,—and earth, reply.

2 Love's redeeming work is done;
Fought the fight, the battle won:
Lo! the sun's eclipse is o'er;
Lo! he sets in blood no more.

3 Vain the stone, the watch, the seal,
Christ has burst the gates of hell;
Death in vain forbids his rise;
Christ hath opened paradise.

4 Lives again our glorious King;
Where, O Death, is now thy sting?
Once he died our souls to save:
Where's thy victory, boasting Grave?

5 Soar we now where Christ has led,
Following our exalted Head:
Made like him, like him we rise:
Ours the cross, the grave, the skies.

*Charles Wesley.*

**121** *Rev.* v. 12–14. L. M.

1 What equal honors shall we bring
To thee, O Lord our God, the Lamb,
When all the notes that angels sing
Are far inferior to thy name?

2 Worthy is he that once was slain,
The Prince of life, that groaned and died:
Worthy to rise, and live, and reign
At his almighty Father's side.

3 Power and dominion are his due
Who stood condemned at Pilate's bar:
Wisdom belongs to Jesus too,
Though he was charged with madness
here.

4 All riches are his native right,
Yet he sustained amazing loss:
To him ascribe eternal might,
Who left his weakness on the cross.

*Watts.*

## 122 ELIZABETHTOWN. C. M.

GEORGE KINGSLEY.

1. Come, let us join our cheer - ful songs With an - gels round the throne:

Ten thousand thousand are their tongues, But all their joys are one.

*Rev.* v. 11-13.  C. M.

1 Come, let us join our cheerful songs
  With angels round the throne:
  Ten thousand thousand are their tongues,
  But all their joys are one.

2 Worthy the Lamb that died, they cry,
  To be exalted thus:
  Worthy the Lamb, our hearts reply,
  For he was slain for us.

3 Jesus is worthy to receive
  Honor and power divine;
  And blessings, more than we can give,
  Be, Lord, forever thine.

4 The whole creation join in one
  To bless the sacred name
  Of him that sits upon the throne,
  And to adore the Lamb.
                        *Watts.*

## 123  The Name of Jesus.  C. M.

1 How sweet the name of Jesus sounds
  In a believers' ear!
  It soothes his sorrows, heals his wounds,
  And drives away his fear.

2 It makes the wounded spirit whole,
  And calms the troubled breast;
  'Tis manna to the hungry soul,
  And to the weary, rest.

3 Dear Name, the rock on which I build,
  My shield and hiding-place;
  My never-failing treasury, filled
  With boundless stores of grace.

4 Jesus, my Shepherd, Brother, Friend,
  My Prophet, Priest, and King;
  My Lord, my Life, my Way, my End,
  Accept the praise I bring.

5 Weak is the effort of my heart,
  And cold my warmest thought;
  But when I see thee as thou art,
  I'll praise thee as I ought.
                        *Newton.*

## 123 b  His regal state.  C. M.
  [Words Ed.]

1 Rejoice and sing, the Lord is King,
  And make a cheerful noise:
  To God your ceaseless praises bring,
  Again I say, Rejoice!

2 The great I AM!—from heaven he came,
  To make that heaven our own:
  Bow every knee to Jesus' name,
  And kiss th' incarnate Son.

3 The Son of God poured out his blood
  And soul in sacrifice;
  Plunge all in that mysterious flood
  That bears you to the skies.

4 The Victim slain arose again,
  Returning from the dead:
  Ye saints, essay your choicest strain,
  And shout your living Head.

5 His glorious reign He shall maintain;—
  Your crowns from him receive;
  And live, redeemed from death and pain,
  As long as God shall live.
                        *C. Wesley.*

OF CHRIST.

**124  TOPLADY. 7s, 6 lines.**

*FINE.*

1. Rock of a - ges, cleft for me, Let me hide my - self in thee;

*D. C.* Be of sin the dou - ble cure, Save from wrath and make me pure.

*D. C.*

Let the wa - ter and the blood, From thy wound - ed side which flowed,

---

*Rock of Ages.* 7s, 6 lines.

1 Rock of ages, cleft for me,
Let me hide myself in thee:
Let the water and the blood,
From thy wounded side which flowed,
Be of sin the double cure,
Save from wrath and make me pure.

2 Could my tears forever flow,
Could my zeal no languor know,
These for sin could not atone;
Thou must save, and thou alone:
In my hand no price I bring,
Simply to thy cross I cling.

3 While I draw this fleeting breath,
When my eyes shall close in death,
When I rise to worlds unknown,
And behold thee on thy throne,
Rock of ages, cleft for me,
Let me hide myself in thee.

*Toplady.*

**125**  *The True light.* 7s, 6 lines.

1 Christ, whose glory fills the skies,
Christ, the true, the only Light,
Sun of righteousness, arise,
Triumph o'er the shades of night;
Day-spring from on high, be near,
Day-star, in my heart appear.

2 Dark and cheerless is the morn,
Unaccompanied by thee;
Joyless is the day's return,
Till thy mercy's beams I see;
Till thou inward life impart,
Glad my eyes, and warm my heart.

3 Visit then this soul of mine;
Pierce the gloom of sin and grief;
Fill me, Radiancy divine;
Scatter all my unbelief:
More and more thyself display,
Shining to the perfect day.

*Charles Wesley.*

**125 b**  *Here at thy Cross.* L. M.
[ Words Ed.  Tune, Germany, page 25.]

1 Here at thy cross, incarnate God,
I lay my soul beneath thy love;
Beneath the droppings of thy blood,
Jesus, nor shall it e'er remove.

2 Not all that tyrants think or say,
With rage and lightning in their eyes,
Nor hell shall fright my heart away,
Should hell with all its legions rise.

3 Yes, I'm secure beneath thy blood,
And all my foes shall lose their aim;
Hosanna to my Saviour God,
And my best honors to his name.

65

# 𝕿HE 𝕳OLY SPIRIT.

**126** SILVER STREET. S. M.

I. Come, Ho - ly Spir it, come, Let thy bright beams a - rise;

Dis - pel the sor - row from our minds, The dark - ness from our eyes.

---

*Sanctifying Influence.*    S. M.

1 Come, Holy Spirit, come,
   Let thy bright beams arise;
Dispel the sorrow from our minds,
   The darkness from our eyes.

2 Convince us all of sin ;
   Then lead to Jesus' blood,
And to our wondering view reveal
   The mercies of our God.

3 Revive our drooping faith,
   Our doubts and fears remove,
And kindle in our breasts the flame
   Of never-dying love.

4 'Tis thine to cleanse the heart,
   To sanctify the soul,
To pour fresh life in every part,
   And new-create the whole.

5 Dwell, Spirit, in our hearts,
   Our minds from bondage free ;
Then shall we know, and praise, and love,
   The Father, Son, and Thee.
                *Hart.*

**127**    *His Influences Sought.*    S. M.

1 Come. Holy Spirit. come,
   With energy Divine.
And on this poor, benighted soul,
   With beams of mercy shine.

2 O melt this frozen heart ;
   This stubborn will subdue ;
Each evil passion overcome,
   And form me all anew !

3 The profit will be mine,
   But thine shall be the praise;
And unto thee will I devote
   The remnant of my days.
             *Beddome.*

**128**    *Spirit of Faith.*    S. M.

1 Spirit of faith come down,
   Reveal the things of God ;
And make to us the Godhead known,
   And witness with the blood.

2 'Tis thine the blood t' apply,
   And give us eyes to see.
Who did for every sinner die,
   Hath surely died for me.

3 No man can truly say
   That Jesus is the Lord,
Unless thou take the veil away,
   And breathe the living word :

4 Then, only then. we feel
   Our int'rest in his blood ;
And cry with joy unspeakable,
   "Thou art my Lord. my God ! "

5 O that the world might know
   That all-atoning Lamb !
Spirit of faith, descend and show
   The virtue of his name :

6 The grace which all may find,
   The saving power, impart ;
And testify to all mankind,
   And speak in every heart.
            *C. Wesley.*

# THE HOLY SPIRIT.

## 129 CHATHAM. C. M.

*Slowly.*

1. Spir - it Di - vine, at - tend our pray'r, And make our hearts thy home;

De - scend with all thy gracious pow'r: Come, Ho - ly Spir - it, come!

---

*Revelations of the Spirit.*     C. M.

1 Spirit Divine, attend our prayer,
  And make our hearts thy home;
Descend with all thy gracious power:
Come, Holy Spirit, come!

2 Come as the light: to us reveal
  Our sinfulness and woe;
And lead us in those paths of life
  Where all the righteous go.

3 Come as the fire, and purge our hearts,
  Like sacrificial flame:
Let our whole soul an offering be
  To our Redeemer's name.

4 Come as the wind, with rushing sound,
  With pentecostal grace;
And make the great salvation known
  To all the human race.

5 Spirit Divine, attend our prayer,
  And make our hearts thy home;
Descend with all thy gracious power:
Come, Holy Spirit, come!
                              *Andrew Reed.*

## 130     *The Enlightening Spirit.*     C. M.

1 Come, Holy Ghost, our hearts inspire;
  Let us thine influence prove;
Source of the old prophetic fire,
  Fountain of life and love.

2 Come, Holy Ghost, for moved by thee
  The prophets wrote and spoke;
Unlock the truth, thyself the key;
  Unseal the sacred book.

3 Expand thy wings, celestial Dove,
  Brood o'er our nature's night;
On our disordered spirits move,
  And let there now be light.

4 God, through himself, we then shall know
  If thou within us shine;
And sound, with all thy saints below,
  The depths of love divine.
                              *Charles Wesley.*

## 131     *Regeneration by the Spirit.*     C. M.

1 Not all the outward forms on earth,
  Nor rites that God has given,
Nor will of man, nor blood, nor birth,
  Can raise a soul to heaven.

2 The sovereign will of God alone
  Creates us heirs of grace,
Born in the image of his Son,
  A new, peculiar race.

3 The Spirit, like some heavenly wind,
  Breathes on the sons of flesh,
Creates anew the carnal mind,
  And forms the man afresh.

4 Our quickened souls awake and rise
  From their long sleep of death,
On heavenly things we fix our eyes,
  And praise employs our breath.
                              *Watts.*

# THE HOLY SPIRIT.

1. E - ter - nal Spir - it, God of truth, Our con - trite hearts in - spire;

Re - vive the flame of heav'n - ly love, And feed the pure de - sire.

*Reviving Spirit.*  C. M.

1 Eternal Spirit, God of truth,
Our contrite hearts inspire;
Revive the flame of heavenly love,
And feed the pure desire.

2 'Tis thine to soothe the sorrowing mind,
With guilt and fear oppressed;
'Tis thine to bid the dying live,
And give the weary rest.

3 Subdue the power of every sin,
Whate'er that sin may be,
That we, with humble, holy heart,
May worship only thee.

4 Then with our spirits witness bear
That we are sons of God,
Redeemed from sin, from death and hell,
Through Christ's atoning blood.
*Pratt's Col.*

**133**  *His Quickenings Implored.*  C. M.

1 Come, Holy Spirit, Heavenly Dove,
With all thy quick'ning powers,
Kindle a flame of sacred love
In these cold hearts of ours.

2 Look how we grovel here below,
Fond of these earthly toys;
Our souls, how heavily they go,
To reach eternal joys!

3 In vain we tune our formal songs,
In vain we strive to rise:
Hosannas languish on our tongues,
And our devotion dies.

4 And shall we then forever live
At this poor dying rate?
Our love so faint, so cold to thee,
And thine to us so great?

5 Come, Holy Spirit, Heavenly Dove,
With all thy quick'ning powers;
Come, shed abroad a Saviour's love,
And that shall kindle ours.
*Watts.*

**134**  *The Interpreter. After Sermon.*  C. M.

1 The Spirit breathes upon the word,
And brings the truth to sight:
Precepts and promises afford
A sanctifying light.

2 A glory gilds the sacred page,
Majestic like the sun;
It gives a light to every age,
It gives—but borrows none.

3 The Hand that gave it still supplies
The gracious light and heat;
His truths upon the nations rise,—
They rise, but never set.

4 Let everlasting thanks be thine
For such a bright display,
As makes a world of darkness shine
With beams of heavenly day.
*Cowper.*

**135 PORTUGAL. L. M.**

1. Je - sus, we on the words de - pend, Spo-ken by thee while pres-ent here,

"The Fa - ther in my name shall send The Ho - ly Ghost, the Com - fort - er."

---

*The Promised Comforter.*   L. M.

1 Jesus, we on the words depend,
   Spoken by thee while present here,
   "The Father in my name shall send
   The Holy Ghost, the Comforter."

2 That heavenly Teacher of mankind,
   That Guide, infallible, impart,
   To bring thy sayings to our mind,
   And write them on our faithful heart.

3 That peace of God, that peace of thine,
   O might he now to us bring in,
   And fill our souls with power divine,
   And make an end of fear and sin!

4 The length and breadth of love reveal,
   The height and depth of Deity!
   And all the sons of glory seal,
   And change and make us all like thee.
                                    *C. Wesley.*

**136**        *Our Guide.*        L. M.

1 Come, gracious Spirit, heavenly Dove,
   With light and comfort from above;
   Be thou our Guardian, thou our Guide;
   O'er every thought and step preside.

2 To us the light of truth display,
   And make us know and choose thy way;

---

   Plant holy fear in every heart,
   That we from God may ne'er depart.

3 Lead us to holiness—the road
   Which we must take to dwell with God;
   Lead us to Christ—the living way;
   Nor let us from his pastures stray;—

4 Lead us to God.—our final rest,—
   To be with him forever blest;
   Lead us to heaven, its bliss to share—
   Fullness of joy forever there.
                                    *Browne.*

**136 b**        *Spirit of Grace.*        L. M.
                 [ Words Ed.]

1 Come, sacred Spirit, from above,
   And fill the coldest heart with love:
   Oh, turn to flesh the flinty stone,
   And let thy sovereign power be known.

2 Speak thou, and from the haughtiest eyes
   Shall floods of contrite sorrow rise;
   While all their glowing souls are borne
   To seek that grace which now they scorn.

3 Oh, let a holy flock await
   In crowds around thy temple-gate!
   Each pressing on with zeal to be
   A living sacrifice to thee.
                                    *P. Doddridge.*

69

**137 SEYMOUR. 7s.**  ARRANGED FROM WEBER.

1. Ho-ly Ghost, with light di-vine, Shine up-on this heart of mine;

Chase the shades of night a-way, Turn my dark-ness in-to day.

*The work of the Holy Spirit.*  7s.

1 Holy Ghost, with light divine,
  Shine upon this heart of mine;
  Chase the shades of night away,
  Turn my darkness into day.

2 Holy Ghost, with power divine,
  Cleanse this guilty heart of mine;
  Long hath sin, without control,
  Held dominion o'er my soul.

3 Holy Ghost, with joy divine,
  Cheer this saddened heart of mine;
  Bid my many woes depart,
  Heal my wounded, bleeding heart.

4 Holy Spirit, all divine,
  Dwell within this heart of mine;
  Cast down every idol-throne,
  Reign supreme—and reign alone.
                              *Andrew Reed.*

**138**   *Earnest of Endless Rest.*   7s.

1 Gracious Spirit, love divine,
  Let thy light within me shine!
  All my guilty fears remove;
  Fill me with thy heavenly love.

2 Speak thy pardoning grace to me;
  Set the burdened sinner free;
  Lead me to the Lamb of God;
  Wash me in his precious blood.

3 Life and peace to me impart;
  Seal salvation on my heart;

Breathe thyself into my breast,
Earnest of immortal rest.

4 Let me never from thee stray;
  Keep me in the narrow way;
  Fill my soul with joy divine;
  Keep me, Lord, forever thine.
                              *John Stocker.*

**139** *Receive ye the Holy Ghost.* L. M. 6 lines.

*John 20. 22.*

1 Come, Holy Ghost, our souls inspire,
  And lighten with celestial fire;
  Thou the anointed Spirit art,
  Who dost thy sevenfold gifts impart:
  Thy blessed unction from above
  Is comfort, life, and fire of love.

2 Enable with perpetual light
  The dullness of our blinded sight;
  Anoint and cheer our soiled face
  With the abundance of thy grace;
  Keep far our foes, give peace at home;
  Where thou art guide, no ill can come.

3 Teach us to know the Father, Son,
  And thee, of both, to be but one;
  That through the ages all along,
  This may be our endless song:
  Praise to thy eternal merit,
  Father, Son, and Holy Spirit.
                *Gregorian Chant.—Tr. by J. Cosin.*

# GOSPEL INVITATIONS AND WARNING

**140 HEBRON. L. M.**

1. Come, sinners, to the gos-pel feast, Let ev-'ry soul be Je-sus' guest,

Ye need not one be left be-hind, For God hath bid-den all mankind.

---

*The hearty welcome.*　　L. M.

1 Come, sinners, to the gospel feast;
Let every soul be Jesus' guest;
Ye need not one be left behind,
For God hath bidden all mankind.

2 Sent by my Lord, on you I call;
The invitation is to all:
Come, all the world! come, sinner, thou;
All things in Christ are ready now.

3 Come, all ye souls by sin oppressed,
Ye restless wand'rers after rest,
Ye poor, and maimed, and halt, and blind,
In Christ a hearty welcome find.

4 My message as from God receive:
Ye all may come to Christ and live:
O let his love your hearts constrain,
Nor suffer him to die in vain.

5 See him set forth before your eyes,
That precious, bleeding sacrifice!
His offered benefits embrace,
And freely now be saved by grace!
　　　　　　　　　　*C. Wesley.*

**141**　*The Gospel Supper.*　L. M.

1 Sinners, obey the gospel word!
Haste to the supper of my Lord!
Be wise to know your gracious day;
All things are ready; come away.

2 Ready the Father is to own,
And kiss his late-returning son:
Ready your loving Saviour stands,
And spreads for you his bleeding hands.

3 Ready the Spirit of his love
Just now your hardness to remove;
T' apply and witness with the blood,
And wash and seal the sons of God.

4 Ready for you the angels wait,
To triumph in your blest estate:
Tuning their harps, they long to praise
The wonders of redeeming grace.

5 The Father, Son, and Holy Ghost,
Are ready with their shining host:
All heaven is ready to resound,
"The dead's alive! the lost is found!"
　　　　　　　　　　*C. Wesley.*

**142**　*Invitation and Warning.*　S. M.
[Tune, Greenwood, page 72. S. M.]

1 The Lord declares his will,
And keeps the world in awe;
Amidst the smoke on Sinai's hill
Breaks out his fiery law.

2 The Lord reveals his face,
And, smiling from above,
Sends down the gospel of his grace,
Th' epistles of his love.

3 These sacred words impart
Our Maker's just commands;
The pity of his melting heart,
And vengeance of his hands.

4 We read the heavenly word,
We take the offered grace,
Obey the statutes of the Lord,
And trust his promises.
　　　　　　　　　　*Watts.*

**143  GREENWOOD. S. M.**                          *"ROOT AND SWEETZER COLL."*

1 The Spir it, in our hearts, Is whispering, "Sin - ner, come;"

The bride,the church of Christ, proclaims To all his chil - dren, "Come!"

---

### The Spirit Inviting.          S. M.

1 The Spirit, in our hearts,
  Is whispering, "Sinner, come;"
  The bride, the church of Christ, proclaims
  To all his children, "Come!"

2 Let him that heareth say
  To all about him, "Come;"
  Let him that thirsts for righteousness
  To Christ, the fountain, come.

3 Yes, whosoever will,
  O, let him freely come,
  And freely drink the stream of life;
  'Tis Jesus bids him come.

4 Lo! Jesus, who invites,
  Declares, "I quickly come;"
  Lord, even so; we wait thy hour;
  O blest Redeemer, come.

                          *Epis. Col.*

**144      The Warning.          S. M.**

1 And will the Judge descend?
  And must the dead arise?
  And not a single soul escape
  His all-discerning eyes?—

2 And from his righteous lips
  Shall this dread sentence sound,
  And through the millions of the damned
  Spread black despair around?—

3 "Depart from me, accursed,
  To everlasting flame,
  For rebel-angels first prepared,
  Where mercy never came."

4 How will my heart endure
  The terrors of that day,
  When earth and heaven before his face,
  Astonished, shrink away?

5 But ere that trumpet shakes
  The mansions of the dead,
  Hark, from the gospel's gentle voice
  What joyful tidings spread!

6 Ye sinners, seek his grace,
  Whose wrath ye cannot bear;
  Fly to the shelter of his cross,
  And find salvation there.
                          *Doddridge.*

**145      Living temples.          S. M.**

1 And will the mighty God,
  Whom heaven cannot contain,
  Make me his temple and abode,
  And in me live and reign?

2 Come, Spirit of the Lord,
  Teacher and heavenly Guide!
  Be it according to thy word,
  And in my heart reside.

3 O Holy, Holy Ghost!
  Pervade this soul of mine:
  In me renew thy Pentecost,
  Reveal thy power divine!

4 Make it my highest bliss
  Thy blessed fruits to know;
  Thy joy, and peace, and gentleness,
  Goodness and faith to show.
                          *George Rawson.*

72

**146** EVAN. C. M. HAVERGAL.

*Moderato.*

1. Let ev - ery mor - tal ear at - tend, And ev - ery heart re - joice;

The trum - pet of the gos - pel sounds With an in - vit - ing voice.

*Isaiah* lv. 1-3.     C. M.

1 Let every mortal ear attend,
   And every heart rejoice ;
The trumpet of the gospel sounds
   With an inviting voice.

2 Ho ! all ye hungry, starving souls,
   That feed upon the wind,
And vainly strive with earthly toys
   To fill an empty mind.

3 Eternal wisdom hath prepared
   A soul-reviving feast,
And bids your longing appetites
   The rich provision taste.

4 Ho ! ye that pant for living streams,
   And pine away and die,
Here you may quench your raging thirst
   With springs that never dry.

5 Rivers of love and mercy here,
   In a rich ocean, join;
Salvation, in abundance, flows
   Like floods of milk and wine.

6 The happy gates of gospel grace
   Stand open night and day :
Lord, we are come to seek supplies,
   And drive our wants away.
                      *Watts.*

**147**     *Come to Jesus.*     C. M.

1 Come, humble sinner, in whose breast
   A thousand thoughts revolve,

Come, with your guilt and fear oppressed,
   And make this last resolve :

2 I'll go to Jesus, though my sin
   Hath like a mountain rose,
I know his courts, I'll enter in,
   Whatever may oppose :

3 Prostrate I'll lie before his throne,
   And there my guilt confess;
I'll tell him I'm a wretch undone,
   Without his sovereign grace.

4 I'll to the gracious King approach,
   Whose sceptre pardon gives ;
Perhaps he may command my touch,
   And then the suppliant lives.

5 Perhaps he may admit my plea,
   Perhaps he'll hear my prayer ;
But if I perish, I will pray
   And perish only there.

6 I can but perish if I go,
   I am resolved to try ;
For if I stay away, I know
   I must forever die.

7 But if I die with mercy sought,
   When I the King have tried,
This were to die ( delightful thought ! )
   As sinner never died.
                      *E. Jones.*

**148  AVON. C. M.**

1. The Sav-iour calls,—let ev-ery ear At-tend the heaven-ly sound; Ye doubt-ing souls, dis-miss your fear, Hope smiles re-viv-ing round.

---

**The Free Invitation.**     C. M.

1 The Saviour calls,—let every ear
  Attend the heavenly sound;
  Ye doubting souls, dismiss your fear,
  Hope smiles reviving round.

2 For every thirsty, longing heart,
  Here streams of bounty flow;
  And life, and health, and bliss, impart
  To banish mortal woe.

3 Here springs of sacred pleasure rise
  To ease your every pain;
  ( Immortal fountain! full supplies! )
  Nor shall you thirst in vain.

4 Ye sinners, come; 'tis mercy's voice;
  The gracious call obey:
  Mercy invites to heavenly joys,—
  And can you yet delay?

5 Dear Saviour! draw reluctant hearts;
  To thee let sinners fly,
  And take the bliss thy love imparts;
  And drink, and never die.
                              *Steele.*

**149**     *Revelation* iii. 20.     C. M.

1 Come, let us who in Christ believe,
  Our common Saviour praise:
  To him, with joyful voices, give
  The glory of his grace.

2 He now stands knocking at the door
  Of every sinner's heart;
  The worst need keep him out no more,
  Or force him to depart.

3 Through grace we hearken to thy voice,
  Yield to be saved from sin;

In sure and certain hope rejoice
That thou wilt enter in.

4 Come quickly in, thou heavenly Guest,
  Nor ever hence remove;
  But sup with us, and let the feast
  Be everlasting love.
                              *C. Wesley.*

**150**     *The Year of Jubilee.*     H. M.
        [Tune Lenox, page 75.  H. M.]

1 Blow ye the trumpet, blow,
  The gladly solemn sound!
  Let all the nations know,
  To earth's remotest bound,
  The year of jubilee is come!
  Return, ye ransomed sinners, home.

2 Jesus, our great High Priest,
  Hath full atonement made:
  Ye weary spirits, rest;
  Ye mournful souls, be glad:
  The year of jubilee is come!
  Return, ye ransomed sinners, home.

3 Extol the Lamb of God,
  The all-atoning Lamb;
  Redemption in his blood
  Throughout the world proclaim:
  The year of jubilee is come!
  Return, ye ransomed sinners, home.

4 Ye slaves of sin and hell,
  Your liberty receive.
  And safe in Jesus dwell,
  And blest in Jesus live:
  The year of jubilee is come!
  Return, ye ransomed sinners, home.

5 Ye who have sold for naught
    Your heritage above,
  Shall have it back unbought,
    The gift of Jesus' love :
  The year of jubilee is come!
  Return, ye ransomed sinners, home.

6 The gospel trumpet hear,
    The news of heavenly grace :
  And, saved from earth, appear
    Before your Saviour's face;
  The year of jubilee is come!
  Return, ye ransomed sinners, home.

*C. Wesley.*

**150  LENOX. H. M.**  EDSON.

1. Blow ye the trumpet, blow; The glad-ly sol-emn sound! Let all the nations know,
The year of ju - bi - lee is come; Re-
To earth's re-mot-est bound, The
The year of ju - bi -
The year of ju - bi - lee is come; Re-turn, ye ransomed
turn, ye ransomed sin-ners, home.
year of ju - bi - lee is come; Re - turn, ye ransomed sin - ners, home.
lee is come; Re - turn, ye ran - - somed sin - ners, home.
sinners, home.

**151  *Jesus, the all-atoning Lamb.*  H. M.**

1 Let earth and heaven agree,
    Angels and men be joined,
  To celebrate with me
    The Saviour of mankind :
  To adore the all-atoning Lamb,
  And bless the sound of Jesus' name.

2 Jesus! transporting sound!
    The joy of earth and heaven ;
  No other help is found,
    No other name is given,
  By which we can salvation have ;
  But Jesus came the world to save.

3 Jesus! harmonious name !
    It charms the hosts above;
  They evermore proclaim

And wonder at his love:
  'Tis all their happiness to gaze,—
  'Tis heaven to see our Jesus' face.

4 His name the sinner hears,
    And is from sin set free;
  'Tis music in his ears ;
    'Tis life and victory;
  New songs do now his lips employ,
  And dances his glad heart for joy.

5 O unexampled love !
    O all-redeeming grace !
  How swiftly didst thou move
    To save a fallen race !
  What shall I do to make it known,
  What thou for all mankind hast done?

*C. Wesley.*

**152 DOVER. S. M.** WILLIAMS.

1. Grace! 'tis a charm - ing sound! Har - mo - nious to my ear!

Heav'n with the ech - o shall resound, And all the earth shall hear.

---

*Transcendent Grace.* **S. M.**

1 Grace! 'tis a charming sound!
  Harmonious to my ear!
  Heaven with the echo shall resound,
  And all the earth shall hear.

2 Grace first contrived the way
  To save rebellious man;
  And all the steps *that* grace display
  Which drew the wondrous plan.

3 Grace taught my wand'ring feet
  To tread the heavenly road;
  And new supplies each hour I meet
  While pressing on to God.

4 Grace all the work shall crown,
  Through everlasting days:
  It lays in heaven the topmost stone,
  And well deserves the praise.
        *Doddridge.*

**153** *Our debt paid upon the Cross.* **S. M.**

1 What majesty and grace
  Through all the gospel shine!
  'Tis God that speaks, and we confess
  The doctrine most divine.

2 Down from his throne on high,
  The mighty Saviour comes;
  Lays his bright robes of glory by,
  And feeble flesh assumes.

3 The debt that sinners owed,
  Upon the cross he pays:
  Then through the clouds ascends to God,
  'Midst shouts of loftiest praise.

---

4 There our High Priest appears
  Before his Father's throne;
  Mingles his merits with our tears,
  And pours salvation down.

5 Great Sovereign, we adore
  Thy justice and thy grace,
  And on thy faithfulness and power
  Our firm dependence place.
        *Samuel Stennett.*

**154** *The gift unspeakable.* **L. M.**

[*Tune, Federal Street,* page 77. L. M.]

1 Happy the man who finds the grace,
  The blessing of God's chosen race,
  The wisdom coming from above,
  The faith that sweetly works by love.

2 Wisdom divine! who tells the price
  Of wisdom's costly merchandise?
  Wisdom to silver we prefer,
  And gold is dross compared to her.

3 Her hands are filled with length of days,
  True riches and immortal praise:
  Her ways are ways of pleasantness,
  And all her flowery paths are peace.

4 Happy the man who wisdom gains;
  Thrice happy, who his guest retains:
  He owns, and shall forever own,
  Wisdom, and Christ, and heaven, are one.
        *Charles Wesley.*

# GOSPEL INVITATIONS AND WARNING.

**155  FEDERAL STREET. L. M.**   H. K. OLIVER.

1. How sweetly flowed the gos-pel's sound From lips of gen - tle - ness and grace,

While list'ning thousands gath - ered round, And joy and rev'rence filled the place.

### The Divine Teacher.  L. M.

1 How sweetly flowed the gospel's sound
From lips of gentleness and grace,
While listening thousands gathered round,
And joy and reverence filled the place.

2 From heaven he came, of heaven he spoke,
To heaven he led his followers' way:
Dark clouds of gloomy night he broke,
Unveiling an immortal day.

3 "Come, wanderers, to my Father's home;
Come, all ye weary ones, and rest."
Yes, sacred Teacher, we will come,
Obey, and be forever blest.

4 Decay, then, tenements of dust!
Pillars of earthly pride, decay!
A nobler mansion waits the just,
And Jesus has prepared the way.

*Sir John Bowring.*

**156**  *Before Preaching to the Young.*  C. M.

[Tune, Arlington, page 60.  C. M.]

1 Grace is a plant, where'er it grows,
Of pure and heavenly root;
But fairest in the youngest shows,
And yields the sweetest fruit.

2 Ye careless ones, O hear betimes
The voice of sovereign love!
Your youth is stained with many crimes,
But mercy reigns above.

3 True, you are young, but there's a stone
Within the youngest breast,
Or half the crimes which you have done
Would rob you of your rest.

4 For you the public prayer is made;
O join the public prayer!
For you the secret tear is shed;
O shed yourselves a tear!

5 We pray that you may early prove
The Spirit's power to teach:
You cannot be too young to love
That Jesus whom we preach.

*Cowper.*

**157**  *Before an Inviting Sermon.*  C. M.

[Tune, Maitland, page 68.  C. M.]

1 Jesus, Redeemer of mankind,
Display thy saving power;
Thy mercy let these outcasts find,
And know their gracious hour.

2 Ah! give them, Lord, a longer space,
Nor suddenly consume;
But let them take the proffered grace,
And flee the wrath to come.

3 O wouldst thou cast a pitying look,
On every stony heart,
Like that which faithless Peter broke,
All goodness as thou art.

4 Who thee beneath their feet have trod,
And crucified afresh,
Touch with thine all-victorious blood,
And turn the stone to flesh.

5 Open their eyes thy cross to see,
Their ears to hear thy cries:
Sinner, thy Saviour weeps for thee,
For thee he weeps and dies.

*C. Wesley.*

77

# GOSPEL INVITATIONS AND WARNING.

**158** AMES. L. M.

*Poco Adagio.*

1. A - rise, my tend'rest thoughts, a - rise; To torrents melt, my streaming eyes;

And thou, my heart, with anguish feel Those evils which thou canst not heal.

*Grieving for the transgressors.* L. M.

1 Arise, my tend'rest thoughts, arise;
To torrents melt, my streaming eyes;
And thou, my heart, with anguish feel
Those evils which thou canst not heal.

2 See human nature sunk in shame:
See scandals poured on Jesus' name;
The Father wounded through the Son,
The world abused, the soul undone.

3 See the short course of vain delight
Closing in everlasting night—
In flames, that no abatement know,
Though briny tears for ever flow.

4 My God, I feel the mournful scene;
My bowels yearn o'er dying man;
And fain my pity would reclaim,
And snatch the firebrands from the flame.

5 But feeble my compassion proves,
And can but weep where most it loves;
Thy own all-saving arm employ,
And turn these drops of grief to joy.
*Doddridge.*

**159** *Before an Inviting Sermon.* L. M.

1 Shepherd of souls, with pitying eye,
The thousands of our Israel see;
To thee, in their behalf, we cry;
Ourselves but newly found in thee.

2 See where o'er desert wastes they err,
And neither food nor feeder have;
Nor fold nor place of refuge near;
For no man cares their souls to save.

3 Thy people, Lord, are sold for naught;
Nor know they their Redeemer nigh:
They perish whom thyself hath bought;
Their souls for lack of knowledge die.

4 Why should the foe thy purchase seize?
Remember, Lord, thy dying groans:
The need of all thy suff'rings these:
O claim them for thy ransomed ones!
*C Wesley.*

**160** *All Things are Ready.* S. M.

*Matt.* 22. 4.

[ Tune, Thatcher, page 79. S. M.]

1 " All things are ready," come,
Come to the supper spread;
Come, rich and poor, come, old and young,
Come, and be richly fed.

2 " All things are ready," come,
The invitation's given,
Through Him who now in glory sits
At God's right hand in heaven.

3 " All things are ready," come,
The door is open wide;
O feast upon the love of God,
For Christ, his Son, has died.

4 " All things are ready," come,
To-morrow may not be;
O sinner, come, the Saviour waits
This hour to welcome thee.
*Albert Midlane.*

78

**160 THATCHER. S. M.** HANDEL.

1. "All things are read - y," come, Come to the sup - per spread; Come, rich, and poor, come, old and young, Come, and be rich - ly fed.

**161**

*Seek him while he may be found.* S. M.

1 My son, know thou the Lord,
  Thy father's God obey;
  Seek his protecting care by night,
  His guardian hand by day.

2 Call, while he may be found;
  Seek him while he is near;
  Serve him with all thy heart and mind,
  And worship him with fear.

3 If thou wilt seek his face,
  His ear will hear thy cry;
  Then shalt thou find his mercy sure,
  His grace forever nigh.

4 But if thou leave thy God,
  Nor choose the path to heaven,
  Then shalt thou perish in thy sins,
  And never be forgiven.
  *Robert C. Brackenbury.*

**161 LULU. S. M.**

1. My son, know thou the Lord, Thy fa-ther's God o - bey;
Seek his pro-tect - ing care by night, His guardian hand by day.

*Doxology.* 10 s.

To Father, Son and Spirit ever blest,
Eternal praise and worship be addressed,
From age to age, ye saints, his name adore,
And spread his fame, 'till time shall be no more.
*S. Brown.*

**162  COME, YE DISCONSOLATE.  11s & 10s.**  WEBBE.

1. Come, ye dis - con - so - late, wher - e'er ye lan - guish,
2. Joy of the des - o - late, Light of the stray - ing,
3. Go, ask the in - fi - del what boon he brings us—
4. Here see the bread of life; see wa - ters flow - ing,

Come, and at God's al - tar fer - vent - ly kneel:
Hope of the pen - i - tent, fade - less and pure,
What charm for ach - ing hearts, he can re - veal,
Forth from the throne of God, bound - less in love;

Here bring your wound - ed hearts, here tell your an - guish;
Here speaks the Com - fort - er, in God's name say - ing,
Sweet as the heav - en - ly prom - ise hope sings us,
Come to the feast pre-pared; come, ev - er know - ing.

Earth has no sor - row that Heav'n can - not heal.
Earth has no sor - row that Heav'n can - not cure.
Earth has no sor - row that God can - not heal.
Earth has no sor - rows, but Heav'n can re - move.

MOORE.

## GOSPEL INVITATIONS AND WARNING.

**163 REGENT SQUARE.** 8s, 7s & 7s.    HENRY SMART, LONDON.

1. Come to Cal - vary's ho - ly mount-ain, Sin - ners ruin ed by the fall;

Here a pure and heal - ing fount-ain, Flows to you, to me, to all,

In a full per - pet - ual tide, O - pened when our Sav-iour died.

*The Healing Fountain.* 8s 7s & 7s.

1 Come to Calvary's holy mountain,
    Sinners ruined by the fall;
Here a pure and healing fountain,
    Flows to you, to me, to all,
In a full perpetual tide,
Opened when our Saviour died.

2 Come, in sorrow and contrition,
    Wounded, impotent, and blind;
Here the guilty, free remission,
    Here the lost a refuge find.
Health this fountain will restore;
He that drinks need thirst no more.

3 Come, ye dying, live forever,
    'Tis a soul-reviving flood;
God is faithful; he will never
    Break this covenant sealed in blood;
Signed when our Redeemer died,
Sealed when he was glorified.
                    *James Montgomery.*

**163 b**    *"Jesus Wept."*    8s, 7s & 7s
        [ Words Ed.]

1 Jesus wept! those tears are over,
    But his heart is still the same;

Kinsman, Friend, and elder Brother,
    Is his everlasting name.
Saviour, who can love like thee,
Gracious One of Bethany?

2 When the pangs of trial seize us,
    When the waves of sorrow roll,
I will lay my head on Jesus,
    Pillow of the troubled soul.
Surely, none can feel like thee,
Weeping One of Bethany!

3 Jesus wept! and still in glory,
    He can mark each mourner's tear;
Living to retrace the story
    Of the hearts he solaced here.
Lord, when I am called to die,
Let me think of Bethany.

4 Jesus wept! that tear of sorrow
    Is a legacy of love;
Yesterday, to-day, to-morrow,
    He the same doth ever prove.
Thou art all in all to me,
Living One of Bethany!
                    *E. Denny.*

81

## GOSPEL INVITATIONS AND WARNING.

**164** GREENVILLE. 8s, 7s & 4s.

1. Sin-ners, will you scorn the mes-sage Sent in mer-cy from a-bove?

D. C.—Lis-ten to it; lis-ten to it; Ev-ery line is full of love.

D. C.

Ev-ery sen-tence, O how ten-der! Ev-ery line is full of love.

---

*Hear, and Live.* 8s, 7s & 4s.

1 Sinners, will you scorn the message
  Sent in mercy from above?
  Every sentence, O how tender!
  Every line is full of love:
      Listen to it;
  Every line is full of love.

2 Hear the heralds of the gospel
  News from Zion's King proclaim:
  "Pardon to each rebel sinner,
  Free forgiveness in his name:"
      How important!
  "Free forgiveness in his name."

3 Tempted souls they bring you succor;
  Fearful hearts, they quell your fears,
  And, with news of consolation,
  Chase away the falling tears:
      Tender heralds!
  Chase away the falling tears.

4 O ye angels, hovering round us,
  Waiting spirits, speed your way;
  Haste ye to the court of heaven,
  Tidings bear without delay,
      Rebel sinners
  Glad the message will obey.
          *Jonathan Allen.*

**165** *The Desire of Nations.* 8, 7.

[Tune, Rathbun, page 28. 8, 7.]

1 Come, thou long-expected Jesus,
  Born to set thy people free:
  From our fears and sins release us
  Let us find our rest in thee.

2 Israel's Strength and Consolation,
  Hope of all the earth thou art;
  Dear Desire of every nation,
  Joy of every longing heart.

3 Born thy people to deliver,
  Born a child, and yet a King,
  Born to reign in us forever,
  Now thy gracious kingdom bring.

4 By thine own eternal Spirit,
  Rule in all our hearts alone;
  By thine all-sufficient merit,
  Raise us to thy glorious throne.
          *Charles Wesley.*

*Doxology.* 8s, 7s & 4s.

Great Jehovah! we adore thee,
God, the Father, God, the Son,
God, the Spirit, joined in glory
  On the same eternal throne;
      Endless praises
  To Jehovah, Three in One.

**166** EVEN ME. 8s, 7s & 3s. (ZOAR.) , W. B. BRADBURY.

1. { Lord, I hear of show'rs of bless- ing Thou art scatter-ing full and free; }
   { Show'rs, the thirs-ty land re-fresh -ing : Let some drops fall now on me, }

E - ven me, E - ven me, Let some drops now fall on me.

---

*Even Me.* 8s, 7s & 3s.

1 Lord, I hear of showers of blessing
  Thou art scattering full and free :
Showers, the thirsty land refreshing :
  Let some drops now fall on me,
    Even me.

2 Pass me not, O God, my Father,
  Sinful though my heart may be ;
Thou mightst leave me, but the rather
  Let thy mercy light on me,
    Even me.

3 Pass me not, O gracious Saviour,
  Let me live and cling to thee ;
I am longing for thy favor ;
  Whilst thou'rt calling, O call me,
    Even me.

4 Pass me not, O mighty Spirit,
  Thou canst make the blind to see ;
Witnesser of Jesus' merit,
  Speak the word of power to me,
    Even me.

5 Love of God, so pure and changeless,
  Blood of Christ, so rich, so free,
Grace of God, so strong and boundless,
  Magnify them all in me.
    Even me.

*Mrs. Elizabeth Codner.*

**167** *The Issues of Life and Death.* S. M.

[Tune, Dover, 76. S. M.]

1 O where shall rest be found,
    Rest for the weary soul ?
  'Twere vain the ocean depths to sound,
    Or pierce to either pole :

2 The world can never give
    The bliss for which we sigh :
  'Tis not the whole of life to live,
    Nor all of death to die.

3 Beyond this vale of tears
    There is a life above,
  Unmeasur'd by the flight of years ;
    And all that life is love.

4 There is a death whose pang
    Outlasts the fleeting breath ;
  O! what eternal horrors hang
    Around "the second death !"

5 Lord God of truth and grace,
    Teach us that death to shun,
  Lest we be banish'd from thy face,
    And evermore undone.

6 Here would we end our quest :
    Alone are found in thee
  The life of perfect love—the rest
    Of immortality.

*Montgomery.*

GOSPEL INVITATIONS AND WARNING.

168 SALEM. L. M.          "PSALMODIST."

1. Say, sin - ner, hath a voice with - in Oft whispered to thy se - cret soul,

Urged thee to leave the ways of sin, And yield thy heart to God's con-trol?

*Quench not the Spirit.*    L. M.
1 *Thess.* v. 19.

1 Say, sinner, hath a voice within
Oft whispered to thy secret soul,
Urged thee to leave the ways of sin,
And yield thy heart to God's control?

2 Sinner, it was a heavenly voice,
It was the Spirit's gracious call;
It bade thee make the better choice,
And haste to seek in Christ thine all.

3 Spurn not the call to life and light;
Regard in time the warning kind:
That call thou mayst not always slight,
And yet the gate of mercy find.

4 God's Spirit will not always strive
With hardened, self-destroying man;
Ye, who persist his love to grieve,
May never hear his voice again.

5 Sinner, perhaps this very day
Thy last accepted time may be;
O shouldst thou grieve him now away,
Then hope may never beam on thee.
*Mrs. Ann B. Hyde.*

169 *Haste, Traveler, haste!* L. M.

1 Haste, traveler, haste! the night comes on,
And many a shining hour is gone;
The storm is gathering in the west,
And thou art far from home and rest.

2 O far from home thy footsteps stray;
Christ is the life, and Christ the Way,
And Christ the Light; thy setting sun
Sinks ere thy morning is begun.

3 The rising tempest sweeps the sky;
The rains descend, the winds are high:
The waters swell, and death and fear
Beset thy path, nor refuge near.

4 Then linger not in all the plain,
Flee for thy life, the mountain gain;
Look not behind, make no delay,
O speed thee, speed thee on thy way.
*William B. Collyer.*

170 *The Invitation.* 8, 7, 8, 7, 4, 7.
[Tune, Harwell, page 135.]

1 Come, ye sinners, poor and needy,
Weak and wounded, sick and sore,
Jesus ready stands to save you,
Full of pity, love and power:
He is able,
He is willing, doubt no more.

2 Now, ye needy, come and welcome,
God's free bounty glorify;
True belief and true repentance,
Every grace that brings you nigh,
Without money,
Come to Jesus Christ and buy.

3 Let not conscience make you linger;
Nor of fitness fondly dream;
All the fitness he requireth
Is to feel your need of him:
This he gives you,
'Tis the Spirit's glimm'ring beam.

4 Come, ye weary, heavy-laden,
Bruised and mangled by the fall;
If you tarry till you're better,
You will never come at all:
Not the righteous,
Sinners Jesus came to call.

5 Agonizing in the garden,
Lo! your Maker prostrate lies!
On the bloody tree behold him!
Hear him cry before he dies,
"It is finished!"
Sinners, will not this suffice? *Hart.*

84

GOSPEL INVITATIONS AND WARNING.

**171 PLEYEL'S HYMN. 7s.** *PLEYEL.*

1. Pil - grim bur - dened with thy sin, Haste to Zi - on's gate to - day;

There, till mer - cy let thee in, Knock and weep and watch and pray.

*The Christian Pilgrim.* 7 s.

1 Pilgrim burdened with thy sin,
  Haste to Zion's gate to-day;
  There, till mercy let thee in,
  Knock and weep and watch and pray.

2 Knock—for mercy lends an ear;
  Weep—she marks the sinner's sigh;
  Watch—till heavenly light appear;
  Pray—she hears the mourner's cry.

3 Mourning pilgrim! what for thee
  In this world can now remain?
  Seek that world from which shall flee,
  Sorrow, shame, and tears, and pain.

4 Sorrow shall forever fly;
  Shame shall never enter there;
  Tears be wiped from every eye—
  Pain in endless bliss expire.

**172** *Exhorting to Turn to God.* 7 s.
*Why Will Ye Die? O House of Israel.*
*Ezek.* xviii. 31.

1 Sinners, turn, why will ye die?
  God, your Maker, asks you why:
  God, who did your being give,
  Made you with himself to live.

2 He the fatal cause demands,
  Asks the work of his own hands;
  Why, ye thankless creatures, why,
  Will ye cross his love and die?

3 Sinners, turn, why will ye die?
  God, your Saviour, asks you why;
  God, who did your souls retrieve,
  Died himself, that you might live.

4 Will you let him die in vain?
  Crucify your Lord again?
  Why, ye ransom'd sinners, why,
  Will ye slight his grace and die?

5 Sinners, turn, why will ye die?
  God, the Spirit, asks you why;
  He, who all your lives hath strove,
  Woo'd you to embrace his love:

6 Will you not the grace receive?
  Will you still refuse to live?
  Why, ye long-sought sinners, why,
  Will ye grieve your God, and die?
                              *C. Wesley.*

**173** *The Works of Sin.* 7, 6 lines.
  [ Tune, Toplady, page 65.]

1 Hearts of stone, relent, relent!
  Break, by Jesus' cross subdued;
  See his body mangling, rent,
  Covered with his flowing blood!
  Sinful soul, what hast thou done?
  Crucified the Eternal Son?

2 Yes, thy sins have done the deed,
  Driven the nails that fixed him there,
  Crowned with thorns his sacred head,
  Pierced him with a soldier's spear,
  Made his soul a sacrifice:
  For a sinful world he dies.

3 Wilt thou let him die in vain?
  Still to death pursue our God?
  Open all his wounds again?
  Trample on his precious blood?
  No; with all my sins I'll part;
  Saviour, take my broken heart. *C. Wesley.*

85

GOSPEL INVITATIONS AND WARNING.

## 174 BURTON. L. M.

1. This is the word of truth and love, Sent to the na-tions from a-bove;

Je-ho-vah here re-solves to show What his al-might-y grace can do.

---

*The Power of Truth.* L. M.

1 This is the word of truth and love,
Sent to the nations from above;
Jehovah here resolves to show
What his almighty grace can do.

2 This remedy did wisdom find,
To heal diseases of the mind—
This sovereign balm, whose virtues can
Restore the ruined creature, man.

3 The gospel bids the dead revive :
Sinners obey the voice, and live :
Dry bones are raised and clothed afresh ;
And hearts of stone are turned to flesh.

4 May but this grace my soul renew,
Let sinners gaze and hate me too ;
The word that saves me does engage
A sure defence from all their rage.
*Watts.*

## 175 *Gospel Liberty Proclaimed.* L. M.
*Isaiah* lii. 1–15.

1 Awake, Jerusalem, awake !
No longer in thy sins lie down ;
The garment of salvation take,
Thy beauty and thy strength put on.

2 Shake off the dust that blinds thy sight,
And hides the promise from thine eyes ;
Arise, and struggle into light,
Thy great Deliv'rer calls, arise !

3 Shake off the bands of sad despair,
Sion, assert thy liberty ;

Look up, thy broken heart prepare,
And God shall set the captive free.

4 Vessels of mercy, sons of grace,
Be purged from every sinful stain ;
Be like your Lord, his word embrace,
Nor bear his hallow'd name in vain.

5 The Lord shall in your front appear,
And lead the pompous triumph on ;
His glory shall bring up the rear,
And perfect what his grace begun.
*C. Wesley*

## 176 *Returning to Christ.* C. M
[Tune, Heber, page 97. C. M.]

1 My head is low, my heart is sad,
My feet with travel torn,
Yet, O my Saviour, thou art glad
To see thy child return !

2 It was thy love that homeward led,
Thy arm that upward stayed ;
It is thy hand which on my head
Is now in mercy laid.

3 O Saviour, in this broken heart
Confirm the trembling will,
Which longs to reach thee where thou art,
Rest in thee and be still.

4 Within that bosom which hath shed
Both tears and blood for me,
O let me hide this aching head,
Once pressed and blessed by thee.
*John S. B. Monsell.*

**177  JUBILEE.  8s, 7s & 4s.**                                        MOZART.

1. Day of judgment, day of wonders! Hark! the trumpet's aw - ful sound,
2. See the Judge our na - ture wear-ing, Clothed in ma - jes - ty di - vine!
3. At his call the dead a - wak - en,—Rise to life from earth and sea;

Loud-er than a thous-and thund-ers, Shakes the vast cre - a - tion round!
You who long for his ap - pear - ing Then shall say, " This God is mine."
All the pow'rs of na - ture, shak - en By his looks, pre - pare to flee :

How the summons, How the sum-mons Will the sin - ner's heart con-found!
Gra - cious Sa-viour, Gra-cious Sa-viour, Own me in that day for thine!
Care - less sin - ner, Care-less sin - ner, What will then be-come of thee?

NEWTON.

**178** *Come ye to the waters. Isaiah* lv. 1 - 3. L. M.
[ Tune, Burton, page 86. L. M.]

1 Ho ! every one that thirsts, draw nigh ;
  'Tis God invites the fallen race :
  Mercy and free salvation buy;
  Buy wine, and milk, and gospel grace.

2 Come to the living waters, come !
  Sinners, obey your Maker's call ;
  Return, ye weary wanderers, home,
  And find my grace is free for all.

3 See from the rock a fountain rise ;
  For you in healing streams it rolls ;
  Money ye need not bring, nor price,
  Ye lab'ring, burdened, sin-sick souls.

4 Nothing ye in exchange shall give :
  Leave all you have, and are, behind ;
  Frankly the gift of God receive,
  Pardon and peace in Jesus find.

5 I bid you all my goodness prove ;
  My promises for all are free :
  Come, taste the manna of my love,
  And let your souls delight in me.
                                    *Wesley.*

**179**              *Revelation* iii. 20.              L. M.
               [ Tune, Burton, page 86. L. M. ]

1 Behold a Stranger at the door !
  He gently knocks, has knocked before ;
  Has waited long—is waiting still :
  You treat no other friend so ill.

2 O lovely attitude ! He stands
  With melting heart and bleeding hands :
  O matchless kindness ! and he shows
  This matchless kindness to his foes !

3 But will he prove a Friend indeed ?
  He will : the very Friend you need ;
  The Friend of sinners—yes, 'tis he,
  With garments dyed on Calvary.

4 Rise, touched with gratitude Divine ;
  Turn out his enemy and thine,
  That soul-destroying monster, sin,
  And let the heavenly Stranger in.

5 Admit him, ere his anger burn ;
  His feet departed, ne'er return ;
  Admit him, or the hour's at hand
  You'll at his door rejected stand.
                                    *Grigg.*

**180  TELEMANN'S CHANT. 7s.**                                    ZEUNER.

1. Has-ten, sin-ner, to be wise: Stay not for the mor-row's sun;

Wis-dom, if thou still de-spise, Hard-er is she to be won.

---

*"Escape for thy life."*          7s.

1 Hasten, sinner, to be wise :
  Stay not for the morrow's sun ;
  Wisdom, if thou still despise,
  Harder is she to be won.

2 Hasten, mercy to implore :
  Stay not for the morrow's sun ;
  Lest thy season should be o'er
  Ere this evening's stage be run.

3 Hasten, sinner, to return ;
  Stay not for the morrow's sun ;
  Lest thy lamp should cease to burn
  Ere salvation's work is done.

4 Hasten, sinner, to be blest ;
  Stay not for the morrow's sun :
  Lest the curse should thee arrest
  Ere the morrow is begun.
                              *T. Scott.*

**181**  *Psalm* l. 16, 17, 20, 21.  S, 7, S, 7, 4, 7.
  [ Tune, Jubilee, page 87.  8s. 7s & 4s.]

1 Why, O sinner, me profaning,
  Why, says God, my statutes name ?
  Why, my cov'nant grace disdaining,
  Still my cov'nant grace proclaim ?
    Hating counsel ;
  All my laws exposed to shame.

2 Long in silence I have waited,
  Long thy guilt in secret grown ;
  Till thy heart, with pride elated,
  Thought my counsels like thy own :
    I'll reprove thee,
  Till thy crimes exact are known.

3 Sinners, hear Jehovah speaking !
    Ye who, thoughtless, God despise !
  Hear, lest, in his wrath awaking,
  Vengeance rend you as it flies ;
    None can save you,
  If his arm to judgment rise.
                              *Goode.*

**181 b**    *The Invitation Accepted.*          7s.
            [ Words Ed.]

1 Come, ye weary sinners, come,
    All who groan beneath your load ;
  Jesus calls his wand'rers home :
    Hasten to your pard'ning God.

2 Come, ye guilty souls, oppressed,
    Answer to the Saviour's call.—
  "Come, and I will give you rest,
    Come, and I will save you all."

3 Jesus, full of truth and love,
    We thy kindest word obey ;
  Faithful let thy mercies prove ;
    Take our load of guilt away :

4 Fain we would on thee rely,
    Cast on thee our every care,
  To thine arms of mercy fly,
    Find our lasting quiet there.

5 Lo ! we come to thee for ease,
    True and gracious as thou art ,
  Now our groaning souls release,
    Write forgiveness on our heart.
                              *Wesley.*

# REPENTANCE AND CONVERSION.

**182  HURSLEY.  L. M.**  ADAPTED FROM FRANCIS JOSEPH HAYDN, 1732-1809.

1. O for a glance of heaven - ly day, To take this stub - born heart a - way,
And thaw with beams of love Di - vine, This heart, this froz - en heart of mine!

---

*Hardness of Heart Lamented.*  L. M.

1 O for a glance of heavenly day,
To take this stubborn heart away,
And thaw with beams of love Divine,
This heart, this frozen heart of mine!

2 The rocks can rend; the earth can quake;
The seas can roar; the mountains shake:
Of feeling, all things show some sign,
But this unfeeling heart of mine.

3 To hear the sorrows thou hast felt,
O Lord, an adamant would melt!
But I can read each moving line,
And nothing moves this heart of mine.

4 Thy judgment, too, unmoved I hear,
(Amazing thought!) which devils fear:
Goodness and wrath in vain combine
To stir this stupid heart of mine.

5 But something yet can do the deed;
And that blest something much I need:
Thy Spirit can from dross refine,
And melt and change this heart of mine.
*Hart.*

**183**  *Psalm* li. 13-19.  L. M.

1 A broken heart, my God, my King,
To thee a sacrifice I bring:
The God of grace will ne'er despise
A broken heart for sacrifice.

2 My soul lies humbled in the dust,
And owns thy dreadful sentence just:
Look down, O Lord, with pitying eye,
And save the soul condemned to die.

3 Then will I teach the world thy ways,
Sinners shall learn thy sovereign grace;
I'll lead them to my Saviour's blood,
And they shall praise a pard'ning God.

4 O may thy love inspire my tongue!
Salvation shall be all my song;
And all my powers shall join to bless
The Lord, my strength and righteousness.
*Watts.*

**184**  *Psalm* li. 1-4.  L. M.

1 Show pity, Lord, O Lord, forgive,
Let a repenting rebel live;
Are not thy mercies large and free?
May not a sinner trust in thee?

2 My crimes are great, but don't surpass
The power and glory of thy grace:
Great God, thy nature hath no bound,
So let thy pard'ning love be found.

3 O wash my soul from every sin,
And make my guilty conscience clean!
Here on my heart the burden lies,
And past offences pain mine eyes.

4 My lips with shame my sins confess,
Against thy law, against thy grace;
Lord, should thy judgments grow severe,
I am condemned, but thou art clear.

5 Yet save a trembling sinner, Lord,
Whose hope, still hov'ring round thy word,
Would light on some sweet promise there,
Some sure support against despair.
*Watts.*

**185 GRATITUDE. L. M.**  HASTINGS

1. O that my load of sin were gone! O that I could at last sub-mit

At Je-sus' feet to lay it down! To lay my soul at Je-sus' feet!

---

*Seeking Perfect Rest in Christ.* L. M.

1 O that my load of sin were gone!
   O that I could at last submit
At Jesus' feet to lay it down!
   To lay my soul at Jesus' feet!

2 Rest for my soul I long to find:
   Saviour of all, if mine thou art,
Give me thy meek and lowly mind,
   And stamp thine image on my heart.

3 Break off the yoke of inbred sin,
   And fully set my spirit free;
I cannot rest till pure within,
   Till I am wholly lost in thee.

4 Fain would I learn of thee, my God,
   Thy light and easy burden prove,
The cross, all stained with hallowed blood,
   The labor of thy dying love.

5 I would, but thou must give the power:
   My heart from every sin release;
Bring near, bring near the joyful hour,
   And fill me with thy perfect peace.

6 Come, Lord, the drooping sinner cheer,
   Nor let thy chariot wheels delay:
Appear, in my poor heart appear!
   My God, my Saviour, come away!

*C. Wesley.*

---

**186**  *Struggling after Christ.*  S. M.

[Tune, Dunbar, page 91. S. M.]

1 Ah! whither should I go,
   Burdened, and sick, and faint!
To whom should I my troubles show,
   And pour out my complaint?

2 My Saviour bids me come;
   Ah! why do I delay?
He calls the weary sinner home,
   And yet from him I stay!

3 What is it keeps me back,
   From which I cannot part?
Which will not let the Saviour take
   Possession of my heart!

4 Some cursed thing unknown
   Must surely lurk within;
Some idol which I will not own,
   Some secret bosom-sin.

5 I now believe in thee
   Compassion reigns alone;
According to my faith, to me
   O let it, Lord, be done!

6 In me is all the bar,
   Which thou wouldst fain remove;
Remove it, and I shall declare
   That God is only love.

*C. Wesley.*

# REPENTANCE AND CONVERSION.

**186 DUNBAR. S. M.**  
E. W. DUNBAR, 1854.

1. Ah! whith - er should I go, Bur - dened, and sick, and faint!
To whom should I my trou - bles show, And pour out my com-plaint?

---

**187** *Giving All for Christ.*    S. M.

1 And can I yet delay
  My little all to give?
To tear my soul from earth away
For Jesus to receive?

2 Nay, but I yield, I yield!
  I can hold out no more:
I sink, by dying love compelled,
And own thee, conqueror!

3 Though late, I all forsake;
  My friends, my all resign;

Gracious Redeemer, take, O take,
And seal me ever thine!

4 Come, and possess me whole,
  Nor hence again remove:
Settle and fix my wav'ring soul
With all thy weight of love.

5 My one desire be this,
  Thy only love to know;
To seek and taste no other bliss,
No other good below.

*C. Wesley.*

---

**187 HUDSON. S. M.**  
R. HARRISON.

1. And can I yet de - lay My lit - tle all to give? To
tear my soul from earth a - way For Je - sus to re - ceive?

91

**188 CHELMSFORD. C. M.**    OLD ENGLISH MELODY.

1. Fa-ther, I stretch my hands to thee, No oth-er help I know;

If thou with-draw thy-self from me, Ah! whith-er shall I go?

*Praying for Faith.*    C. M.

1 Father, I stretch my hands to thee,
  No other help I know;
  If thou withdraw thyself from me,
  Ah! whither shall I go?

2 What did thine only Son endure,
  Before I drew my breath!
  What pain, what labor, to secure
  My soul from endless death!

3 O Jesus, could I this believe,
  I now should feel thy power!
  Now my poor soul thou wouldst retrieve,
  Nor let me wait one hour.

4 Author of faith, to thee I lift
  My weary, longing eyes:
  O let me now receive that gift,
  My soul without it dies!

5 Surely thou canst not let me die;
  O speak, and I shall live;
  And here I will unwearied lie,
  Till thou thy Spirit give.

6 The worst of sinners would rejoice,
  Could they but see thy face;
  O let me hear thy quick'ning voice,
  And taste thy pard'ning grace!
                          *C. Wesley.*

**189**    *Surrendering at the Cross.*    C. M.

1 Alas! and did my Saviour bleed?
  And did my Sovereign die?
  Would he devote that sacred head
  For such a worm as I?

2 Was it for crimes that I have done
  He groaned upon the tree?
  Amazing pity! grace unknown!
  And love beyond degree!

3 Well might the sun in darkness hide,
  And shut his glories in,
  When Christ, the mighty Maker, died
  For man, the creature's sin!

4 Thus might I hide my blushing face,
  While his dear cross appears;
  Dissolve my heart in thankfulness,
  And melt mine eyes to tears.

5 But drops of grief can ne'er repay
  The debt of love I owe:
  Here, Lord, I give myself away,
  'Tis all that I can do.
                          *Watts.*

*Gloria Patri.*

Glory be to the Father, and to the Son,
  And to the Holy Ghost,—
As it was in the beginning, is now, and
  ever shall be.
World without end.—Amen.

REPENTANCE AND CONVERSION.

## 190 WARWICK. C. M.

*Flowing Style.*

1. Still, for thy lov-ing-kind-ness, Lord, I in thy tem-ple wait: I look to find thee in thy word, Or at thy ta-ble meet.

---

*Seeking the Power.*    C. M.

1 Still, for thy loving-kindness, Lord,
  I in thy temple wait;
  I look to find thee in thy word,
  Or at thy table meet.

2 Here in thine own appointed ways,
  I wait to learn thy will;
  Silent I stand before thy face,
  And hear thee say, " Be still!"

3 " Be still! and know that I am God!"—
  'Tis all I live to know;
  To feel the virtue of thy blood,
  And spread its praise below!

4 I wait my vigor to renew,
  Thine image to retrieve!
  The veil of outward things pass through,
  And gasp in thee to live.

5 I work; and own the labor vain,
  And thus from works I cease:
  I strive; and see my fruitless pain,
  Till God create my peace.
         *C. Wesley.*

## 191        C. M.

" *O that I knew where I might find him.*"
       Job xxiii. 3.

*Sins and Sorrows laid before God.*

1 O that I knew the secret place
  Where I might find my God!

  I'd spread my wants before his face,
  And pour my woes abroad.

2 I'd tell him how my sins arise;
  What sorrows I sustain;
  How grace decays, and comfort dies
  And leaves my heart in pain.

3 He knows what arguments I'd take
  To wrestle with my God;
  I'd plead for his own mercy's sake,
  And for my Saviour's blood.

4 My God will pity my complaints,
  And heal my broken bones;
  He takes the meaning of his saints,
  The language of their groans.

5 Arise, my soul, from deep distress,
  And banish ev'ry fear;
  He calls thee to his throne of grace,
  To spread thy sorrows there.
         *Watts.*

*Doxology.*      8s & 7s.
*Communion of saints.*

1 May the grace of Christ our Saviour,
  And the Father's boundless love,
  With the Holy Spirit's favor,
  Rest upon us from above.

2 Let us thus abide in union
  With each other and the Lord,
  And possess in sweet communion,
  Joys which earth cannot afford.

93

**192** ZERAH. C. M.  L. MASON.

1. O for a clos-er walk with God, A calm and heav-enly frame;

A light to shine up-on the road That leads me to the Lamb.

A light to shine up-on the road That leads me to the Lamb.

*The Backslider's Prayer.* C. M.

1 O for a closer walk with God,
A calm and heavenly frame;
": A light to shine upon the road
That leads me to the Lamb. :||

2 Where is the blessedness I knew
When first I saw the Lord?
||: Where is the soul-refreshing view
Of Jesus and his word? :||

3 What peaceful hours I once enjoyed!
How sweet their mem'ry still!
||: But they have left an aching void
The world can never fill. :||

4 Return, O holy Dove, return,
Sweet messenger of rest!
||: I hate the sins that made thee mourn,
And drove thee from my breast. :||

5 The dearest idol I have known,
Whate'er that idol be,
||: Help me to tear it from thy throne,
And worship only thee. :||

6 So shall my walk be close with God,
Calm and serene my frame;
||: So purer light shall mark the road
That leads me to the Lamb. :||

*Cowper.*

**193** *The Backslider's Plea.* 7s.

[ Tune, Seymour, page 70.]

1 Depth of mercy! can there be
Mercy still reserved for me?
Can my God his wrath forbear?
Me, the chief of sinners, spare?

2 I have long withstood his grace,
Long provoked him to his face;
Would not hearken to his calls;
Grieved him by a thousand falls.

3 Lo! I cumber still the ground:
Lo! an Advocate is found!
" Hasten not to cut him down :
Let this barren soul alone! "

4 Jesus speaks, and pleads his blood:
He disarms the wrath of God!
Now my Father's bowels move;
Justice lingers into love.

5 Kindled his relentings are:
Me he now delights to spare;
Cries "How shall I give thee up?"
Lets the lifted thunder drop.

6 There for me the Saviour stands,
Shows his wounds, and spreads his hands;
God is love! I know, I feel;
Jesus weeps, and loves me still.

*C. Wesley.*

# REPENTANCE AND CONVERSION.

**194  RICHMOND.  S. M.**                                   ANON.

1. O Je-sus! full of grace, To thee I make my moan: Let me a-gain be-hold thy face, Call home thy ban-ished one.

---

*The Backslider's Return.*      S. M.

1  O Jesus! full of grace,
   To thee I make my moan:
   Let me again behold thy face,
   Call home thy banished one.

2  Again my pardon seal,
   Again my soul restore,
   And freely my backslidings heal,
   And bid me sin no more.

3  Wilt thou not bid me rise?
   Speak, and my soul shall live:
   Forgive, my gasping spirit cries,
   Abundantly forgive.

4  For thine own mercy's sake,
   Relieve my wretchedness:
   And O, my pardon give me back,
   And give me back my peace!
                                 *C. Wesley.*

**195**      *The Plea.*      S. M.

1  Jesus, my Lord, attend
   Thy feeble creature's cry;
   And show thyself the sinner's Friend,
   And set me up on high.

2  From hell's oppressive power
   My struggling soul release,
   And to thy Father's grace restore,
   And to thy perfect peace.

3  Rivers of life divine
   From thee, their fountain, flow;
   And all who know that love of thine,
   The joy of angels know.

4  That thou cans't here forgive
   Grant me to testify;
   And justified by faith to love,
   And in that faith to die.
                                 *C. Wesley.*

**195 b**   *Surrendering the heart.*   S. M.
            [ Words Ed.]

1  When shall thy love constrain,
   And force me to thy breast?
   When shall my soul return again
   To her eternal rest?

2  Ah! what avails my strife,
   My wand'ring to and fro?
   Thou last words of endless life:
   Ah! whither should I go?

3  Thy condescending grace
   To me did freely move:
   It calls me still to seek thy face,
   And stoops to ask my love.

4  Lord, at thy feet I fall,
   I groan to be set free:
   I fain would now obey the call,
   And give up all for thee.

5  To rescue me from woe,
   Thou didst with all things part,
   Didst lead a suff'ring life below,
   To gain my worthless heart.

6  My worthless heart to gain,
   The God of all that breathe
   Was found in fashion as a man,
   And died a cursed death.
                                 *C. Wesley.*

**196 PETERBOROUGH. C. M.**

L. MASON.

1. How sad our state by na-ture is! Our sin how deep it stains!

And Sa-tan binds our cap-tive souls Fast in his slav-ish chains.

*"Help thou my unbelief."*  C. M.

1 How sad our state by nature is!
  Our sin how deep it stains!
  And Satan binds our captive souls
  Fast in his slavish chains.

2 But there's a voice of sovereign grace
  Sounds from the sacred word:
  Ho! ye despairing sinners, come,
  And trust a faithful Lord.

3 My soul obeys the gracious call,
  And runs to this relief;
  I would believe thy promise, Lord,
  O help my unbelief!

4 To the blest fountain of thy blood,
  Incarnate God, I fly;
  Here let me wash my spotted soul
  From crimes of deepest dye.

5 A guilty, weak and helpless worm,
  Into thy arms I fall:
  Be thou my strength and righteousness,
  My Jesus and my all.
                                        *Watts.*

**197**  *Before an Inviting Sermon.*  C. M.

1 Jesus, thou all-redeeming Lord,
  Thy blessings we implore;
  Open the door to preach the word,
  The great effectual door.

2 Gather the outcasts in, and save
  From sin and Satan's power;
  And let them now acceptance have,
  And know their gracious hour.

3 Lover of souls! thou know'st to prize
  What thou hast bought so dear:
  Come, then, and in thy people's eyes,
  With all thy wounds appear!

4 Appear, as when of old confessed,
  The suff'ring Son of God;
  And let them see thee in thy vest,
  But newly dipped in blood.
                                        *C. Wesley.*

**198**  *Divine Excellence.*  C. M.

1 What grace, O Lord, and beauty shone
  Around thy steps below;
  What patient love was seen in all
  Thy life and death of woe!

2 For, ever on thy burdened heart
  A weight of sorrow hung;
  Yet no ungentle, murmuring word
  Escaped thy silent tongue.

3 Thy foes might hate, despise, revile,
  Thy friends unfaithful prove;
  Unwearied in forgiveness still,
  Thy heart could only love.

4 Oh, give us hearts to love like thee!
  Like thee, O Lord, to grieve
  Far more for others' sins than all
  The wrongs that we receive.

5 One with thyself, may every eye,
  In us, thy brethren, see
  The gentleness and grace that spring
  From union, Lord, with thee.
                                        *Sir Edw. Denny.*

**199  HEBER. C. M.**                    GEORGE KINGSLEY.

*1. Come, hap - py souls, ap - proach your God  With new me - lo - dious songs:*

*Come, ren - der to  Al - might - y grace  The trib - ute of  your tongues.*

**199**          *Call to Praise.*          C. M.

1 Come, happy souls, approach your God
　With new melodious songs:
　Come, render to Almighty grace
　The tribute of your tongues.

2 So strange, so boundless was the love
　That pitied dying men,
　The Father sent his equal Son
　To give them life again.

3 Thy hands, dear Jesus, were not arm'd
　With a revenging rod,
　No hard commission to perform
　The vengeance of a God.

4 But all was mercy, all was mild,
　And wrath forsook the throne,
　When Christ on the kind errand came,
　And brought salvation down.

5 Here, sinners, you may heal your wounds,
　And wipe your sorrows dry:
　Trust in the mighty Saviour's name.
　And you shall never die.  *Watts.*

**200**          *The Joyful Sound.*          C. M.

1 Salvation! O the joyful sound!
　What pleasure to our ears!
　A sovereign balm for every wound,
　A cordial for our fears.

2 Salvation! let the echo fly
　The spacious earth around,
　While all the armies of the sky
　Conspire to raise the sound.

3 Salvation! O thou bleeding Lamb!
　To thee the praise belongs:
　Salvation shall inspire our hearts,
　And dwell upon our tongues.
　　　　　　　　　*Isaac Watts.*

**200  ST. PETER. C. M.**                 W. B. BRADBURY.

*1. Sal - va - tion! O  the  joy - ful sound! What pleas - ure  to  our ears!*

*A  sovereign balm for ev - 'ry wound, A  cor - dial for  our fears.*

97

## 201 MARTYN. 7s. D.

1. { Je-sus, lov-er, of my soul, Let me to thy bo-som fly,
   { While the near-er wa-ters roll, While the tem-pest still is high;

Hide me, O my Sav-iour, hide, Till the storm of life is past;

Safe in-to the ha-ven guide, O re-ceive my soul at last.

*Refuge in Christ.*     7s.

1 Jesus, lover of my soul,
  Let me to thy bosom fly,
While the nearer waters roll,
  While the tempest still is high:

2 Hide me, O my Saviour, hide,
  Till the storm of life is past;
Safe into the haven guide,
  O receive my soul at last!

3 Other refuge have I none,
  Hangs my helpless soul on thee:
Leave, ah! leave me not alone,
  Still support and comfort me!

4 All my trust on thee is stayed,
  All my help from thee I bring.
Cover my defenceless head
  With the shadow of thy wing.

5 Thou, O Christ, art all I want;
  More than all in thee I find:
Raise the fallen, cheer the faint,
  Heal the sick, and lead the blind.

6 Just and holy is thy name;
  I am all unrighteousness:
False, and full of sin, I am,
  Thou art full of truth and grace.

7 Plenteous grace with thee is found,
  Grace to cover all my sin:
Let the healing streams abound,
  Make and keep me pure within:

8 Thou of life the fountain art;
  Freely let me take of thee:
Spring thou up within my heart.
  Rise to all eternity!

*C. Wesley.*

**202 DOWNS. C. M.**

1. I ask the gift of right-eous-ness, The sin-sub-du-ing pow'r,—

Pow'r to be-lieve, and go in peace, And nev-er grieve thee more.

*Vehement Desires.*  C. M.

1 I ask the gift of righteousness,
  The sin-subduing power,—
  Power to believe, and go in peace,
  And never grieve thee more.

2 I ask the blood-bought pardon sealed,
  The liberty from sin,
  The grace infused, the love revealed,
  The kingdom fixed within.

3 Thou hear'st me for salvation pray;
  Thou seest my heart's desire:
  Made ready in thy powerful day,
  The fulness I require.

4 Art thou not able to convert?
  Art thou not willing too?
  To change this old rebellious heart,
  To conquer and renew?
                                  *C. Wesley.*

**203**                          L. M.
*An Advocate with the Father.*  1 *John*, 2: 1.

[Tune, Portugal, page 69. L. M.]

1 Jesus, my Advocate above,
  My Friend before the throne of love,
  If now for me prevails thy prayer,
  If now I find thee pleading there,—

2 If thou the secret wish convey,
  And sweetly prompt my heart to pray,
  Hear, and my weak petitions join,
  Almighty Advocate, to thine.

3 Jesus, my heart's desire obtain:
  My earnest suit present, and gain:

My fullness of corruption show;
  The knowledge of myself bestow.

4 O sovereign Love, to thee I cry,
  Give me thyself, or else I die!
  Save me from death, from hell set free;
  Death, hell, are but the want of thee.
                                  *Charles Wesley.*

**204**       *The Voice of Jesus.*    C. M.

1 I heard the voice of Jesus say,
  "Come unto me and rest;
  Lay down, thou weary one, lay down
  Thy head upon my breast!"
  I came to Jesus as I was,
  Weary, and worn, and sad;
  I found in him a resting-place,
  And he hath made me glad.

2 I heard the voice of Jesus say,
  "Behold, I freely give
  The living water; thirsty one,
  Stoop down, and drink, and live!"
  I came to Jesus, and I drank
  Of that life-giving stream;
  My thirst was quenched, my soul revived,
  And now I live in him.

3 I heard the voice of Jesus say,
  "I am this dark world's Light;
  Look unto me, thy morn shall rise
  And all thy day be bright!"
  I looked to Jesus, and I found
  In him my Star, my Sun;
  And in that light of life I'll walk,
  Till all my journey's done.
                                  *Horatius Bonar.*

## 205 MOUNT AUBURN. C. M.

GEO. KINGSLEY.

1. Come, O thou all - vic - to-rious Lord, Thy pow'r to us make known;

Strike with the ham - mer of the word, And break these hearts of stone.

*Prayer for Conversion.* C. M.

1 Come, O thou all-victorious Lord,
  Thy power to us make known ;
  Strike with the hammer of the word,
  And break these hearts of stone.

2 O that we all might now begin
  Our foolishness to mourn !
  And turn at once from every sin,
  And to the Saviour turn.

3 Give us ourselves and thee to know
  In this our gracious day :
  Repentance unto life bestow,
  And take our sins away.

4 Convince us first of unbelief,
  And freely then release ;
  Fill every soul with sacred grief,
  And then with sacred peace.

*C. Wesley.*

### MORN. C. M. (Second Tune.)

1. Come, O thou all - vic - to-rious Lord, Thy pow'r to us make known;

Strike with the ham - mer of the word, And break these hearts of stone.

# JUSTIFICATION AND ADOPTION.

**206** GERAR. S. M.

L. MASON.

1. How can a sin - ner know His sins on earth for - giv'n

How can my gra - cious Sa - viour show My name in-scrib'd in heav'n?

*Internal Religion.* 1 *John* i. 3-11. S. M.

1 How can a sinner know
His sins on earth forgiven?
How can my gracious Saviour show
My name inscribed in heaven?

2 What we have felt and seen
With confidence we tell;
And publish to the sons of men
The signs infallible.

3 We who in Christ believe
That he for us hath died,
We all his unknown peace receive,
And feel his blood applied.

4 Exults our rising soul,
Disburden'd of her load,
And swells unutterably full
Of glory and of God.

5 His love surpassing far
The love of all beneath,
We find within our hearts, and dare
The pointless darts of death.

6 Stronger than death or hell
The sacred power we prove;
And conqu'rors of the world we dwell
In heaven, who dwell in love.
*C. Wesley.*

**207** *Filial Trust.* S. M.
[ Tune, Shirland, page 102. S. M.]

1 I lift my soul to God,
My trust is in his name;
Let not my foes that seek my blood
Still triumph in my shame.

2 From the first dawning light
Till the dark evening rise,
For thy salvation, Lord! I wait
With ever-longing eyes.

3 Remember all thy grace,
And lead me in thy truth;
Forgive the sins of riper days,
And follies of my youth.

4 The Lord is just and kind;
The meek shall learn his ways,
And every humble sinner find
The methods of his grace.

5 For his own goodness' sake
He saves my soul from shame;
He pardons, though my guilt be great,
Through my Redeemer's name.
*Watts.*

**207 b** *The sure foundation.* S. M
[ Words Ed.]

1 In every trying hour
My soul to Jesus flies;
I trust in his almighty power
When swelling billows rise.

2 His comforts bear me up;
I trust a faithful God;
The sure foundation of my hope
Is in my Saviour's blood.

3 Loud hallelujahs sing
To our Redeemer's name,
In joy or sorrow—life or death
His love is still the same.
*Coombs.*

## 207 SHIRLAND. S. M.
STANLEY.

1. I lift my soul to God, My trust is in his name;

Let not my foes that seek my blood Still tri - umph in my shame.

**208** *Adoption.* S. M.

1 Behold! what wondrous grace
The Father hath bestowed
On sinners of a mortal race,—
To call them sons of God!

2 'Tis no surprising thing
That we should be unknown:
The Jewish world knew not their King,
God's everlasting Son.

3 Nor does it yet appear
How great we must be made;

But when we see our Saviour here,
We shall be like our Head.

4 A hope so much divine,
May trials well endure,
May purge our souls from sense and sin,
As Christ, the Lord is pure.

5 If in my Father's love
I share a filial part,
Send down thy Spirit, like a dove,
To rest upon my heart.

*Watts.*

## 208 EDINBORO'. S. M.
DR. EDWARD MILLER.

1. Be - hold! what wond-rous grace The Fa - ther hath be - stowed

On sin - ners of a mor - tal race,— To call them sons of God!

102

JUSTIFICATION AND ADOPTION.

## 209 MELMORE. L. M.
W. MARTIN.

*Slowly.*

1. I thirst, thou wounded Lamb of God, To wash me in thy cleansing blood;

To dwell with-in thy wounds; then pain Is sweet, and life or death is gain.

---

*Love and Joy.*    L. M.
[From the German.]

1 I thirst, thou wounded Lamb of God,
To wash me in thy cleansing blood;
To dwell within thy wounds; then pain
Is sweet, and life or death is gain.

2 Take my poor heart, and let it be
Forever closed to all but thee!
Seal thou my breast, and let me wear
That pledge of love forever there.

3 How blest are they who still abide
Close sheltered in thy bleeding side!
Who life and strength from thence derive,
And by thee move, and in thee live.

4 What are our works but sin and death,
Till thou thy quick'ning Spirit breathe?
Thou giv'st the power thy grace to move:
O wondrous grace! O boundless love!

5 How can it be, thou heavenly King,
That thou shouldst us to glory bring?
Make slaves the partners of thy throne,
Decked with a never-fading crown!

6 Hence our hearts melt, our eyes o'erflow,
Our words are lost, nor will we know
Nor will we think of aught beside,
"My Lord, my Love is crucified."

7 Ah! Lord, enlarge our scanty thought,
To know the wonders thou hast wrought,
Unloose our stamm'ring tongues to tell
Thy love immense, unsearchable!

8 First-born of many brethren thou,
To thee, lo, all our souls we bow:
To thee our hearts and hands we give;
Thine may we die, thine may we live.
*J. Wesley.*

## 210 *Receiving the Atonement.* L. M.
[From the German of Zinzendorf.]

1. Jesus, thy blood and righteousness
My beauty are, my glorious dress:
'Midst flaming worlds, in these arrayed,
What joy shall I lift up my head.

2 Bold shall I stand in thy great day,
For who aught to my charge shall lay?
Fully absolved through these I am,
From sin, and fear, from guilt and shame.

3 The holy, meek, unspotted Lamb,
Who from the Father's bosom came,
Who died for me, e'en me, t' atone,
Now for my Lord and God I own.

4 Lord, I believe thy precious blood,
Which, at the mercy-seat of God,
Forever doth for sinners plead,
For me, e'en for my soul, was shed.

5 Lord, I believe were sinners more
Than sands upon the ocean shore,
Thou hast for ALL a ransom paid,
For ALL a full atonement made.
*J. Wesley.*

103

# JUSTIFICATION AND ADOPTION.

**211** *Ezekiel* xxxvi. 23–25. L. M.
[ Tune Woodworth, page 24. L. M.]

1 God of all power, and truth, and grace,
Which shall from age to age endure;
Whose word, when heaven and earth shall
Remains, and stands forever sure : [pass,

2 Calmly to thee my soul looks up,
And waits thy promises to prove,
The object of my steadfast hope,
The seal of thy eternal love.

3 That I thy mercy may proclaim,
That all mankind thy truth may see,
Hallow thy great and glorious name,
And perfect holiness in me.

4 Thy sanctifying Spirit pour,
To quench my thirst, and make me
clean ;
Now, Father, let the gracious shower
Descend, and make me pure from sin.

*C. Wesley.*

**212** GRIGGS. C. M.

J. GRIGGS.

1. My God, the spring of all my joys, The life of my de-lights,

The glo - ry of my bright - est days, And com - fort of my nights!

*God the source of joy.* C. M.

1 My God, the spring of all my joys,
The life of my delights,
The glory of my brightest days,
And comfort of my nights.

2 In darkest shades if thou appear,
My dawning is begun ;
Thou art my soul's bright morning star,
And thou my rising sun.

3 The opening heavens around me shine
With beams of sacred bliss,
If Jesus show his mercy mine,
And whisper I am his.

4 My soul would leave this heavy clay
At that transporting word,
Run up with joy the shining way,
To see and praise my Lord.

5 Fearless of hell and ghastly death,
I'd break through every foe ;

The wings of love and arms of faith
Would bear me conqu'ror through.

*Watts.*

**213** *Looking to Christ.* C. M.

1 Look unto him, ye nations; own
Your God, ye fallen race ;
Look, and be saved through faith alone,
Be justified by grace.

2 See all your sins on Jesus laid :
The Lamb of God was slain ;
His soul was once an off'ring made
For every soul of man.

3 Awake from guilty nature's sleep,
And Christ shall give you light :
Cast all your sins into the deep,
And wash the crimson white.

4 With me, your Chief, ye then shall know,
Shall feel, your sins forgiven ;
Anticipate your heaven below,
And own that love is heaven.

*C. Wesley.*

**214 BOLLEY. 7s.**

FROM HAYDN.

1. Je - sus is our com - mon Lord, He our lov - ing Sav - iour is:

By his death to life re - stored, Mis - 'ry we ex-change for bliss.

*Bliss.* 7s.

1 Jesus is our common Lord,
He our loving Saviour is:
By his death to life restored,
Mis'ry we exchange for bliss,—

2 Bliss to carnal minds unknown:
O 'tis more than tongue can tell!
Only to believers shown,
Glorious and unspeakable.

3 Christ, our Brother and our Friend,
Shows us his eternal love:
Never shall our triumphs end,
Till we take our seats above.

4 Let us walk with him in white;
For our bridal day prepare,
For our partnership in light,
For our glorious meeting there!

C. Wesley.

**215 SICILY. 8s & 7s.**

1. Je - sus, I my cross have tak - en, All to leave and fol - low thee;

Nak - ed, poor, de - spised, for - sak - en, Thou, from hence, my all shalt be:

*Forsaking all to follow Christ.* 8s & 7s.

1 Jesus, I my cross have taken,
All to leave and follow thee;
Naked, poor, despised, forsaken,
Thou, from hence, my all shalt be:

2 And while thou shalt smile upon me,
God of wisdom, love, and might,
Foes may hate and friends disown me;
Show thy face, and all is bright.

3 Man may trouble and distress me;
'Twill but drive me to thy breast;
Life with trials hard may press me;
Heaven will bring me sweeter rest;

4 O, 'tis not in grief to harm me,
While thy love is left to me;
O, 'twere not in joy to charm me,
Were that joy unmixed with thee.

Grant.

# JUSTIFICATION AND ADOPTION.

**216  ROWLEY.  6s & 9s.**

1. O how hap-py are they, Who the Sav-iour o-bey, And have laid up their treas-ure a-bove! Tongue can nev-er ex-press The sweet comfort and peace Of a soul in its ear-li-est love, Of a soul in its ear-li-est love.

*The Joys of Conversion.*    6s & 9s.

1  O how happy are they,
    Who the Saviour obey,
And have laid up their treasure above!
    Tongue can never express
    The sweet comfort and peace
Of a soul in its earliest love.

2  That sweet comfort was mine,
    When the favor divine
I received through the blood of the Lamb!
    When my heart first believed,
    What a joy I received,
What a heaven in Jesus's name!

3  'Twas a heaven below
    My dear Redeemer to know,
And the angels could do nothing more,
    Than to fall at his feet,
    And the story repeat,
And the Lover of sinners adore.

4  Jesus all the day long
    Was my joy and my song:
O that all his salvation might see!
    "He hath loved me," I cried,
    "He hath suffered and died,
To redeem even rebels like me."

5  O the rapturous height
    Of that holy delight
Which I felt in the life-giving blood!
    Of my Saviour possessed,
    I was perfectly blest,
As if filled with the fullness of God.

6  Now my remnant of days,
    Will I spend in his praise,
Who hath died my poor soul to redeem.
    Whether many or few,
    All my days are his due,
May they all be devoted to him.
                    *Charles Wesley.*

106

# JUSTIFICATION AND ADOPTION.

**217  WAYMAN. L. M.**                                        H. F. GRANT.

1. Just as I am, with-out one plea, But that thy blood was shed for

me, And that thou bidst me come to thee, O Lamb of God, I come! I come!

---

*Just as I am.*                     L. M.

1 Just as I am, without one plea,
  But that my blood was shed for me,
  And that thou bidst me come to thee,
    O Lamb of God, I come! I come!

2 Just as I am, and waiting not
  To rid my soul of one dark blot,
  To thee, whose blood can cleanse each spot,
    O Lamb of God, I come! I come!

3 Just as I am, though tossed about
  With many a conflict, many a doubt,
  Fightings and fears, within, without,
    O Lamb of God, I come! I come!

4 Just as I am, poor, wretched, blind,
  Sight, riches, healing of the mind,
  Yea, all I need, in thee, to find,
    O Lamb of God! I come! I come!

5 Just as I am, thou wilt receive,
  Wilt welcome, pardon, cleanse, relieve;
  Because thy promise I believe,
    O Lamb of God, I come! I come!

6 Just as I am, thy love unknown
  Hath broken every barrier down;
  Now to be thine, yea, thine alone,
    O Lamb of God, I come! I come!
                              *Miss Elliott.*

**218**        *The Well of Life.*        C. M.

[Tune, Mount Auburn, page 100. C. M.]

1 Fountain of life, to all below
  Let thy salvation roll;
  Water, replenish, and o'erflow
  Every believing soul.

2 Into that happy number, Lord,
    Us weary sinners take;
  Jesus, fulfill thy gracious word,
    For thine own mercy's sake.

3 Turn back our nature's rapid tide,
    And we shall flow to thee,
  While down the stream of time we glide
    To our eternity.

4 The well of life to us thou art,
    Of joy the swelling flood,
  Wafted by thee, with willing heart,
    We swift return to God.

5 We soon shall reach the boundless sea;
    Into thy fullness fall;
  Be lost and swallowed up in thee,
    Our God, our all in all.
                        *Charles Wesley.*

**218 b**                            C. M.

*Living by Faith in the Son of God.*

[Tune, Morn, page 100. C. M.]

1 Blest Jesus, while in mortal flesh
    I hold my frail abode,
  Still would my spirit rest on thee,
    My Saviour and my God.

2 On thy dear cross I fix my eyes,
    Then raise them to thy seat;
  Till love dissolves my inmost soul,
    At my Redeemer's feet.

3 Be dead, my heart, to worldly charms
    Be dead to every sin;
  And tell the boldest foe without,
    That Jesus reigns within.
                            *Doddridge.*

107

**219 CHRIST, THE SOLID ROCK. L. M. 6 lines.** WM. B. BRADBURY.

1. My hope is built on noth - ing else Than Je-sus' blood and righteousness;
2. When darkness veils his love - ly face, I rest on his un-chang-ing grace;
3. His oath, his cov - en - ant, his blood, Sup - port me in the whelming flood;
4. When he shall come with trum-pet sound, O, may I then in him be found ·

I dare not trust the sweet-est frame, But whol - ly lean on Je - sus' name.
In ev - ery high and storm - y gale, My an-chor holds with - in the vale.
When all a-round my soul gives way, He then is all my hope and stay.
Drest in his right-eous - ness a - lone, Fault-less to stand be - fore his throne!

CHORUS.

On Christ, the Sol - id Rock I stand; All oth - er ground is

sink - ing sand, All oth - er ground is sink - ing sand.

REV. EDWARD MOTE, 1825.

108

JUSTIFICATION AND ADOPTION.

**220 EFFINGHAM. L. M.**                    ENGLISH.

1. We have no out-ward right-eous-ness, No mer-its or good works to plead;

We on-ly can be saved by grace; Thy grace, O Lord, is free in-deed.

*Salvation by Grace.*     L. M.

1 We have no outward righteousness,
No merits or good works to plead ;
We only can be saved by grace ;
Thy grace, O Lord, is free indeed.

2 Save us by grace, through faith alone.
A faith thou must thyself impart;
A faith that would by works be shown,
A faith that purifies the heart :

3 A faith that doth the mountains move,
A faith that shows our sins forgiven,
A faith that sweetly works by love,
And ascertains our claim to heaven.

4 This is the faith we humbly seek,
The faith in thy all-cleansing blood,
That blood which doth for sinners speak ;
O let it speak us up to God !

*Charles Wesley.*

**221**     *Following the Saviour.*     L. M.

1 O thou, to whose all-searching sight
The darkness shineth as the light,
Search, prove my heart, it pants for thee ;
O burst these bonds, and set it free.

2 Wash out its stains, refine its dross,
Nail my affections to the cross ;
Hallow each thought ; let all within
Be clean, as thou, my Lord, art clean.

3 If in this darksome wild I stray,
Be thou my light, be thou my way ;

No foes, no violence I fear,
No fraud, while thou, my God, art near.

4 When rising floods my soul o'erflow,
When sinks my heart in waves of woe,
Jesus, thy timely aid impart,
And raise my head, and cheer my heart.

5 Saviour, where'er thy steps I see,
Dauntless, untired, I follow thee ;
O let thy hand support me still,
And lead me to thy holy hill.

6 If rough and thorny be the way,
My strength proportion to my day ;
Till toil, and grief, and pain shall cease,
Where all is calm, and joy, and peace.

*Tr. by J. Wesley*

**221 b**     *Luke* xv. 10.     L. M.

1 Who can describe the joys that rise
Through all the courts of paradise,
To see a prodigal return,
To see an heir of glory born !

2 With joy the Father doth approve
The fruit of his eternal love :
The Son with joy looks down and sees
The purchase of his agonies.

3 The Spirit takes delight to view
The holy soul he formed anew ;
And saints and angels join to sing
The growing empire of their King.

*Watts.*

109

## JUSTIFICATION AND ADOPTION.

222 HAPPY DAY. L. M.

:S: CHORUS.

1. { Oh, hap-py day that fixed my choice On thee, my Sav-iour and my God! }
{ Well may this glowing heart re-joice, And tell its rap-ture all a-broad. } Hap-py

FINE. D. S.

day, Hap-py day, When Jesus wash'd my sins away! { He taught me how to watch and pray, }
{ And live re-joic-ing every day; }

### O Happy Day!     L. M.

1 O happy day that fixed my choice
On thee, my Saviour and my God !
Well may this glowing heart rejoice,
And tell its raptures all abroad.

Cho.—Happy day, happy day,
When Jesus washed my sins away!
He taught me how to watch and pray,
And live rejoicing every day;
Happy day, happy day,
When Jesus washed my sins away!

2 O happy bond, that seals my vows
To him who merits all my love!
Let cheerful anthems fill his house,
While to that sacred shrine I move.

Cho.—Happy day, happy day,
When Jesus washed my sins away!
He taught me how to watch and pray,
And live rejoicing every day;
Happy day, happy day,
When Jesus washed my sins away!

3 'Tis done, the great transaction's done:
I am my Lord's, and he is mine;
He drew me, and I followed on,
Charmed to confess the voice divine.

Cho.—Happy day, happy day,
When Jesus washed my sins away!
He taught me how to watch and pray,
And live rejoicing every day;
Happy day, happy day,
When Jesus washed my sins away!

4 Now rest, my long-divided heart :
Fixed on this blissful center, rest :
Nor ever from thy Lord depart,
With him of every good possessed.

Cho.—Happy day, happy day,
When Jesus washed my sins away!
He taught me how to watch and pray,
And live rejoicing every day;
Happy day, happy day,
When Jesus washed my sins away!

5 High heaven, that heard the solemn vow,
That vow renewed shall daily hear,
Till in life's latest hour I bow,
And bless in death a bond so dear.

Cho.—Happy day, happy day,
When Jesus washed my sins away!
He taught me how to watch and pray,
And live rejoicing every day;
Happy day, happy day,
When Jesus washed my sins away!

*Philip Doddridge.*

110

**223 HEBER. C. M.**                                    GEORGE KINGSLEY.

1. A - maz - ing grace! how sweet the sound That saved a wretch like me!

I once was lost, but now am found, Was blind, but now I see.

*Amazing grace.*          C. M.

1 Amazing grace! how sweet the sound
   That saved a wretch like me!
   I once was lost, but now am found,
   Was blind, but now I see.

2 'Twas grace that taught my heart to fear,
   And grace my fears relieved;
   How precious did that grace appear
   The hour I first believed!

3 Through many dangers, toils, and snares
   I have already come;
   'Tis grace has brought me safe thus far,
   And grace will lead me home.

4 The Lord has promised good to me,
   His word my hope secures;
   He will my shield and portion be
   As long as life endures.

5 Yes, when this flesh and heart shall fail,
   And mortal life shall cease,
   I shall possess, within the veil,
   A life of joy and peace.

6 The earth shall soon dissolve like snow,
   The sun forbear to shine;
   But God, who called me here below,
   Will be forever mine.
                              *John Newton.*

**224**          *Rom. iv. 16–25.*          C. M.

1 Father of Jesus Christ, my Lord,
   My Saviour and my Head,
   I trust in thee, whose powerful word
   Hath raised him from the dead.

2 Thou know'st for my offence he died,
   And rose again for me;
   Fully and freely justified,
   That I might live to thee.

3 Eternal life to all mankind
   Thou hast in Jesus given;
   And all who seek, in him shall find
   The happiness of heaven.

4 All nations of the earth are blest
   In him, who would restore,
   And take them all into his rest,
   And bid them sin no more.

5 O God, thy record I believe,
   In Abrah'm's footsteps tread;
   And wait, expecting to receive
   The Christ, the promised Seed!
                              *C. Wesley.*

*Doxology.*          C. M.

Let God the Father, and the Son,
   And Spirit be adored,
Where there are works to make him known,
   Or saints to love the Lord.

111

# Section 9.

# Consecration and Holiness Implored.

## 225 AZMON. C. M.

1. My God, my God, to thee I cry; Thee on - ly would I know;
Thy pur - i - fy - ing blood ap - ply, And wash me white as snow.

---

*" Purge me—and I shall be clean."* C. M.
*Psalm* li. 7.

1 My God, my God, to thee I cry;
  Thee only would I know;
  Thy purifying blood apply,
  And wash me white as snow.

2 Touch me, and make the leper clean;
  Purge my iniquity:
  Unless thou wash my soul from sin,
  I have no part in thee.

3 But art thou not already mine?
  Answer, if mine thou art!
  Whisper within, thou Love Divine,
  And cheer our drooping heart.

4 Behold for me the Victim bleeds,
  His wounds are open wide;
  For me the blood of sprinkling pleads,
  And speaks me justified.
                        *C. Wesley.*

## 226    *A perfect heart.*    C. M.

1 O for a heart to praise my God,
  A heart from sin set free!
  A heart that always feels thy blood,
  So freely spilt for me!

2 A heart resigned, submissive meek,
  My great Redeemer's throne;
  Where only Christ is heard to speak,
  Where Jesus reigns alone.

3 O for a lowly, contrite heart,
  Believing, true, and clean,
  Which neither life nor death can part
  From him that dwells within!

4 A heart in every thought renewed,
  And full of love divine;
  Perfect, and right, and pure, and good,
  A copy, Lord, of thine.

5 Thy nature, gracious Lord, impart;
  Come quickly from above;
  Write thy new name upon my heart,
  Thy new, best name of Love.
                        *Charles Wesley.*

## 227    *The paradise of love*    C. M.
  [ Tune, Burlin, page 113. C. M. ]

1 O Jesus! at thy feet we wait,
  Till thou shalt bid us rise.
  Restored to our unsinning state
  To love's sweet paradise.

2 Saviour from sin, we thee receive;
  From all indwelling sin,
  Thy blood, we steadfastly believe,
  Shall make us thoroughly clean.

3 Since thou wouldst have us free from sin
  And pure as those above,
  Make haste to bring thy nature in,
  And perfect us in love!

4 The counsel of thy love fulfil;
  Come quickly, gracious Lord!
  Be it according to thy will,
  According to thy word.

5 O that the perfect grace were given,
  Thy love diffused abroad!
  O that our hearts were all a heaven,
  For ever filled with God!
                        *C. Wesley.*

CONSECRATION AND HOLINESS IMPLORED.

**227 BURLIN. C. M.**  WOODBURY.
*With Firmness.*

1. O Jesus! at thy feet we wait, Till thou shalt bid us rise,

Re-stored to our un-sinning state To love's sweet par-a-dise.

**228 *Perfect Love.* C. M.**

1 When Christ doth in my heart appear,
And love erects its throne,
I then enjoy salvation here,
And heaven on earth begun.

2 When God is mine, and I am his,
Of paradise possessed,
I taste unutterable bliss,
And everlasting rest.

3 The bliss of those that fully dwell,
Fully in thee believe,

'Tis more than angel tongues can tell,
Or angel-minds conceive.

4 Thou only know'st who did obtain,
And die to make it known:
The great salvation now explain,
And perfect us in one.

5 May I, may all who humbly wait,
The glorious joy receive,—
Joy above all conception great,
Worthy of God to give.
*C. Wesley.*

**228 CHRISTMAS. C. M.**  ARR. FROM HANDEL.

1. When Christ doth in my heart ap-pear, And love e-rects its throne, I

then enjoy sal-vation here, And heav'n on earth begun, And heav'n on earth begun.

113

**229 VALELAND. C. M.**

*Slow and Solemnly.*

1. For-ev-er here my rest shall be, Close to thy bleed-ing side;

This all my hope, and all my plea, For me the Sav - iour died.

*Perfect Purification.* C. M.

1 Forever here my soul shall be,
   Close to thy bleeding side;
   This all my hope, and all my plea,
   For me the Saviour died.

2 My dying Saviour, and my God,
   Fountain for guilt and sin,
   Sprinkle me ever with thy blood,
   And cleanse and keep me clean.

3 Wash me, and make me thus thine own;
   Wash me, and mine thou art:
   Wash me, but not my feet alone,
   My hands, my head, my heart.

4 Th' atonement of thy blood apply,
   Till faith to sight improve,
   Till hope in full fruition die,
   And all my soul be love.
                              *C. Wesley.*

**230**   *My All-sufficient Good.*   C. M.

1 I would be thine, thou know'st I would,
   And have thee all my own:
   Thee, O my all-sufficient Good!
   I want, and thee alone.

2 Thy name to me, thy nature grant!
   This, only this, be given:
   Nothing beside my God I want:
   Nothing in earth or heaven.

3 Come, O my Saviour, come away!
   Into my soul descend!
   No longer from thy creature stay,
   My Author and my End!

4 Come, Father, Son and Holy Ghost,
   And seal me thine abode!
   Let all I am in thee be lost;
   Let all be lost in God!
                              *C. Wesley.*

**231**   *The Rapture of Love.*   C. M.

1 I know that my Redeemer lives,
   And ever prays for me:
   A token of his love he gives,
   A pledge of liberty.

2 I find him lifting up my head,
   He brings salvation near:
   His presence makes me free indeed,
   And he will soon appear.

3 He wills that I should holy be!
   What can withstand his will?
   The counsel of his grace in me
   He surely shall fulfill.

4 Jesus, I hang upon thy word;
   I steadfastly believe
   Thou wilt return, and claim me, Lord,
   And to thyself receive.

5 Joyful in hope, my spirit soars
   To meet thee from above,
   Thy goodness thankfully adores;
   And sure I taste thy love.
                              *C. Wesley.*

**232  AHIRA. S. M.**                    GREATOREX.

1. Fa - ther, I dare be - lieve Thee mer - ci - ful and true:

Thou wilt my guilt - y soul for - give, My fall - en soul re - new.

*Waiting at the Cross.*    S. M.

1 Father, I dare believe
  Thee merciful and true :
  Thou wilt my guilty soul forgive,
  My fallen soul renew.

2 Come then, for Jesus' sake,
  And bid my heart be clean :
  An end of all my troubles make,
  An end of all my sin.

3 I cannot wash my heart,
  But by believing thee,
  And waiting for thy blood t' impart
  The spotless purity.

4 While at thy cross I lie,
  Jesus, the grace bestow ;
  Now thy all-cleansing blood apply,
  And I am white as snow.
                         *C. Wesley*

**233  INVERNESS. S. M.**              DR. L. MASON.

1. Je - sus, my truth, my way, My sure, un - er - ing light,

On thee my feeb - le steps I stay, Which thou wilt guide a - right.

*Depending on Christ.*    S. M.

1 Jesus, my truth, my way,
  My sure, unerring light,
  On thee my feeble steps I stay,
  Which thou wilt guide aright.

2 My wisdom and my guide,
  My counsellor thou art :
  O never let me leave thy side,
  Or from thy paths depart.

3 I lift mine eyes to thee,
  Thou gracious, bleeding Lamb,

That I may now enlighten'd be,
  And never put to shame.

4 Never will I remove
  Out of thy hands my cause ;
  But rest in thy redeeming love,
  And hang upon thy cross.

5 Teach me the happy art,
  In all things to depend
  On thee : O never, Lord, depart,
  But love me to the end.
                         *C. Wesley.*

115

# CONSECRATION AND HOLINESS IMPLORED.

## 234 UPTON. L. M.

DR. L. MASON.

1. Come, Sav-iour, Je-sus, from a-bove! As-sist me with thy heav'nly grace; Emp-ty my heart of earth-ly love, And for thy-self pre-pare the place.

---

*The Act of Consecration.* L. M.

[ From the French.]

1 Come, Saviour, Jesus, from above!
Assist me with thy heavenly grace;
Empty my heart of earthly love,
And for thyself prepare the place.

2 O let thy sacred presence fill,
And set my longing spirit free,
Which pants to have no other will,
But day and night to feast on thee.

3 While in this region here below,
No other good will I pursue;
I'll bid this world of noise and show,
With all its glitt'ring snares, adieu!

4 That path with humble speed I'll seek
In which my Saviour's footsteps shine,
Nor will I hear nor will I speak
Of any other love but thine.

5 Henceforth may no profane delight
Divide this consecrated soul;
Possess it, thou, who hast the right,
As Lord and Master of the whole.

*J. Wesley.*

## 235 L. M.

*There Remaineth therefore a Rest to the People of God. Heb. iv. 9.*

1 Come, O thou greater than our heart,
And make thy faithful mercies known;
The mind which was in thee impart;
Thy constant mind in us be shown.

---

2 O let us by thy cross abide,
Thee, only thee, resolved to know,
The Lamb for sinners crucified,
A world to save from endless woe.

3 Take us into thy people's rest,
And we from our own works shall cease;
With thy meek Spirit arm our breast,
And keep our minds in perfect peace.

4 Jesus, for this we calmly wait;
O let our eyes behold thee near!
Hasten to make our heaven complete:
Appear, our glorious God, appear!

*Charles Wesley.*

## 236 *Christ All in All.* L. M.

1 Holy, and true, and righteous Lord,
I wait to prove thy perfect will:
Be mindful of thy gracious word,
And stamp me with thy Spirit's seal.

2 Open my faith's interior eye:
Display thy glory from above;
And all I am shall sink and die,
Lost in astonishment and love.

3 Confound, o'erpower me by thy grace,
I would be by myself abhorred;
All might, all majesty, all praise,
All glory, be to Christ my Lord.

4 Now let me gain perfection's height;
Now let me into nothing fall,
As less than nothing in thy sight,
And feel that Christ is all in all.

*Charles Wesley.*

116

CONSECRATION AND HOLINESS IMPLORED.

**237 OLIVET. L. M.** L. MASON.

1. O Je-sus, full of truth and grace, O all - a - ton - ing Lamb of God,

I wait to see thy glo - rious face; I seek re - demp-tion through thy blood.

*Waiting for the Promise.* L. M.

1 O Jesus, full of truth and grace,
O all-atoning Lamb of God,
I wait to see thy glorious face;
I seek redemption through thy blood.

2 Thou art the anchor of my hope;
The faithful promise I receive:
Surely thy death shall raise me up,
For thou hast died that I might live.

3 Satan, with all his arts, no more
Me from the gospel hope can move;
I shall receive the gracious power,
And find the pearl of perfect love.

4 My flesh which cries, "It cannot be,"
Shall silence keep before the Lord;
And earth, and hell, and sin shall flee
At Jesus' everlasting word.
*Charles Wesley.*

**238** *For Lowliness and Purity.* L. M.

1 Jesus, in whom the Godhead's rays
Beam forth with mildest majesty
I see thee full of truth and grace,
And come for all I want to thee.

2 Save me from pride—the plague expel;
Jesus, thine humble self impart:
O let thy mind within me dwell;
O give me lowliness of heart.

3 Enter thyself, and cast out sin;
Thy spotless purity bestow:
Touch me, and make the leper clean;
Wash me, and I am white as snow.

4 Sprinkle me, Saviour, with thy blood,
And all thy gentleness is mine;
And plunge me in the purple flood,
Till all I am is lost in thine.
*Charles Wesley.*

**239** *The promised land of perfect love.* L. M.

1 If, Lord, I have acceptance found
With thee, or favor in thy sight,
Still with thy grace and truth surround,
And arm me with thy Spirit's might.

2 O may I hear thy warning voice,
And timely fly from danger near,
With rev'rence unto thee rejoice,
And love thee with a filial fear!

3 Still hold my soul in second life,
And suffer not my feet to slide:
Support me in the glorious strife,
And comfort me on every side.

4 O give me faith, and faith's increase;
Finish the work begun in me,
Preserve my soul in perfect peace,
And let me always rest on thee!
*C. Wesley.*

117

**240 LUTON. L. M.** S. BURDER.

1. He wills that I should ho-ly be; That ho-li-ness I long to feel; That full di-vine con-form-i-ty To all my Sav-iour's right-eous will.

*The Will of God.* L. M.

1 He wills that I should holy be;
That holiness I long to feel;
That full divine conformity
To all my Saviour's righteous will.

2 See, Lord, the travail of thy soul
Accomplished in the change of mine;
And plunge me, every whit made whole,
In all the depths of love divine.

3 On thee, O God, my soul is stayed,
And waits to prove thine utmost will;
The promise by thy mercy made,
Thou canst, thou wilt, in me fulfil.

4 No more I stagger at thy power,
Or doubt thy truth, which cannot move:
Hasten the long expected hour,
And bless me with thy perfect love.
*Charles Wesley.*

**241** *Heavenly bliss in Prospect.* L. M.

1 Arise, my soul, on wings sublime,
Above the vanities of time;
Let faith, now pierce the veil and see
The glories of eternity.

2 Born by a new, celestial birth,
Why should I grovel here on earth?
Why grasp at vain and fleeting toys,
So near to heaven's eternal joys?

3 Shall aught beguile me on the road,
The narrow road that leads to God?

Or can I love this earth so well,
As not to long with God to dwell?

4 To dwell with God, to taste his love,
Is the full heaven enjoyed above:
The glorious expectation now
Is heavenly bliss begun below.
*Thomas Gibbons.*

**242** *The New Covenant.* L. M.

1 O God, most merciful and true,
Thy nature to my soul impart;
'Stablish with me the covenant new,
And stamp thine image on my heart.

2 To real holiness restored,
O let me gain my Saviour's mind;
And in the knowledge of my Lord,
Fullness of life eternal find.

3 Remember, Lord, my sins no more,
That them I may no more forget;
But, sunk in guiltless shame, adore,
With speechless wonder at thy feet.

4 O'erwhelmed with thy stupendous grace,
I shall not in thy presence move;
But breathe unutterable praise,
And rapturous awe and silent love.

5 Then every murmuring thought, and vain,
Expires, in sweet confusion lost:
I cannot of my cross complain,
I cannot of my goodness boast.
*C. Wesley.*

# CHRISTIAN PERFECTION.

**243 MERIBAH. C. P. M.**  DR. L. MASON.

1. O glo-rious hope of per-fect love, It lifts me up to things a-bove;

It bears on ea-gles' wings; It gives my ravished soul a taste,

And makes me for some moments feast With Je-sus' priests and kings.

---

*Rejoice in Hope.* C. P. M.

1 O glorious hope of perfect love,
It lifts me up to things above;
It bears on eagles' wings;
It gives my ravished soul a taste,
And makes me for some moments feast
With Jesus' priests and kings.

2 Rejoicing now in earnest hope,
I stand, and, from the mountain top,
See all the land below:
Rivers of milk and honey rise,
And all the fruits of paradise
In endless piety grow.

3 A land of corn, and wine, and oil,
Favored with God's peculiar smile,
With every blessing blessed:
There dwells the Lord our Righteousness,
And keeps his own in perfect peace,
And everlasting rest.

4 Now, O my Joshua, bring me in!
Cast out thy foes; the inbred sin,
The carnal mind, remove:
The purchase of thy death divide;
And, O! with all the sanctified,
Give me a lot of love!

*C. Wesley.*

---

**244** *Panting for fullness of Love.* C. P. M.

1 O love divine, how sweet thou art!
When shall I find my willing heart
All taken up by thee?
I thirst, I faint, I die to prove
The greatness of redeeming love,
The love of Christ to me.

2 Stronger his love than death or hell;
Its riches are unsearchable:
The first-born sons of light
Desire in vain its depths to see;
They cannot reach the mystery,
The length, the breadth, the height.

3 God only knows the love of God;
O that it now were shed abroad
In this poor stony heart!
For love I sigh, for love I pine:
This only portion, Lord, be mine;
Be mine this better part.

4 O that I could forever sit
With Mary at the Master's feet!
Be this my happy choice:
My only care, delight, and bliss,
My joy, my heaven on earth, be this,
To hear the Bridegroom's voice.

*Charles Wesley.*

# CHRISTIAN PERFECTION.

**245 BREMEN. C. P. M.**  THOS. HASTINGS.

1. Saviour, on me the grace be-stow, That, with thy chil - dren, I may know My sins on earth for - giv'n; Give me to prove the king-dom mine, And taste, in ho - li - ness di - vine, The hap - pi - ness of heaven.

*The pure in heart shall see God.* C. P. M.

1 Saviour, on me the grace bestow,
That, with thy children, I may know
My sins on earth forgiven;
Give me to prove the kingdom mine,
And taste, in holiness divine,
The happiness of heaven.

2 Me with that restless thirst inspire,
That sacred, infinite desire,
And feast my hungry heart:
Less than thyself cannot suffice;
My soul for all thy fullness cries,
For all thou hast and art.

3 Jesus, the crowning grace impart;
Bless me with purity of heart,
That, now beholding thee,
I soon may view thy open face,
On all thy glorious beauties gaze,
And God forever see.
*Charles Wesley.*

*Doxology.* C. P. M.

To Father, Son, and Holy Ghost,
Be praise amid the heavenly host,
And in the church below;
From whom all creatures draw their breath,
By whom redemption blessed the earth,
From whom all comforts flow

**246** *Power over Temptation.* C. P. M.

1 Help, Lord, to whom for help I fly,
And still my tempted soul stand by
Throughout the evil day;
The sacred watchfulness impart,
And keep the issues of my heart,
And stir me up to pray.

2 My soul with thy whole armor arm;
In each approach of sin alarm,
And show the danger near:
Surround, sustain, and strengthen me,
And fill with godly jealousy
And sanctifying fear.

3 Whene'er my careless hands hang down,
O let me see thy gathering frown,
And feel thy warning eye;
And, starting, cry from ruin's brink
"Save, Jesus, or I yield, I sink;
O save me, or I die."

4 If near the pit I rashly stray.
Before I wholly fall away,
The keen conviction dart:
Recall me by that pitying look,
That kind, upbraiding glance, which broke
Unfaithful Peter's heart.
*C. Wesley.*

120

## CHRISTIAN PERFECTION.

**247 OLMSTED. C. M.**

1. O Joy - ful sound of gos - pel grace! Christ shall in me ap - pear!

Christ shall in me ap - pear: I, e - ven I, shall see his face;

I shall be ho - ly here, I shall be ho - ly here.

---

*Rejoicing in Hope.*　　　　C. M.

1 O joyful sound of gospel grace!
　Christ shall in me appear;
　I, even I, shall see his face;
　I shall be holy here.

2 The glorious crown of righteousness
　To me reached out I view;
　Conqu'ror through him, I soon shall seize,
　And wear it as my due.

3 The promised land from Pisgah's top
　I now exult to see:
　My hope is full ( O glorious hope ! )
　Of immortality.

4 He visits now the house of clay;
　He shakes his future home;
　O wouldst thou, Lord, on this glad day,
　Into thy temple come!

5 With me, I know, I feel, thou art;
　But this cannot suffice,
　Unless thou plantest in my heart
　A constant paradise.

*C. Wesley.*

---

**248** *The heart dissolving in Love.* C. M.

1 Jesus hath died that I might live,
　Might live to God alone;
　In him eternal life receive,
　And be in spirit one.

2 Saviour, I thank thee for the grace,
　The gift unspeakable:
　And wait with arms of faith t' embrace,
　And all thy love to feel.

3 My soul breaks out in strong desire
　The perfect bliss to prove;
　My longing heart is all on fire
　To be dissolved in love.

4 Give me thyself; from every boast,
　From every wish set free:
　Let all I am in thee be lost;
　But give thyself to me.

5 Thy gifts, alas! cannot suffice,
　Unless thyself be given;
　Thy presence makes my paradise,
　And where thou art is heaven.

*C. Wesley.*

121

# CHRISTIAN PERFECTION.

1. Be - ing of be - ings, God of love, To thee our hearts we raise;

Thy all - sus - tain - ing pow'r we prove, And glad - ly sing thy praise.

---

*The fulness of God.*    C. M.

1 Being of beings, God of love,
   To thee our hearts we raise;
   Thy all-sustaining power we prove,
   And gladly sing thy praise.

2 Thine, wholly thine. we pant to be,
   Our sacrifice receive:
   Made, and preserved, and saved by thee,
   To thee ourselves we give.

3 Heavenward our every wish aspires,
   For all thy mercy's store;
   The sole return thy love requires,
   Is that we ask for more.

4 For more we ask; we open then
   Our hearts to embrace thy will;
   Turn, and revive us, Lord, again;
   With all thy fullness fill.
                            *C. Wesley.*

250    *The thought of God.*    C. M.

1 O how the thought of God attracts
   And draws the heart from earth,
   And sickens it of passing shows
   And dissipating mirth!

2 'Tis not enough to save our souls,
   To shun the eternal fires;
   The thought of God will rouse the heart
   To more sublime desires.

3 God only is the creature's home,
   Though rough and strait the road,
   Yet nothing less can satisfy
   The love that longs for God.

4 O utter but the name of God
   Down in your heart of hearts,
   And see how from the world at once
   All tempting light departs!

5 A trusting heart, a yearning eye.
   Can win their way above;
   If mountains can be moved by faith,
   Is there less power in love?
                    *Frederick W. Faber.*

251    *Walk in the light.*    C. M.

1 Walk in the light! so shalt thou know
   That fellowship of love,
   His Spirit only can bestow
   Who reigns in light above.

2 Walk in the light! and thou shalt find
   Thy heart made truly his.
   Who dwells in cloudless light enshrined,
   In whom no darkness is.

3 Walk in the light! and thou shalt own
   Thy darkness passed away.
   Because that light hath on thee shone
   In which is perfect day.

4 Walk in the light! and e'en the tomb
   No fearful shade shall wear;
   Glory shall chase away its gloom,
   For Christ hath conquered there.

5 Walk in the light! thy path shall be
   Peaceful, serene, and bright;
   For God, by grace, shall dwell in thee,
   And God himself is light.
                    *Bernard Barton.*

# CHRISTIAN PERFECTION.

**252 HENRY. C. M.**

SYLVANUS B. POND. 1835.

1. Spir - it of peace, ce - les - tial Dove, How ex - cel - lent thy praise! No rich - er gift than Chris - tian love Thy gra - cious pow'r dis - plays.

---

C. M.

*Excellence of Christain unanimity and Love.*

1 Spirit of peace, celestial Dove,
  How excellent thy praise !
No richer gift than Christian love
  Thy gracious power displays.

2 Sweet as the dew on herb and flower,
  That silently distills,
At evening's soft and balmy hour,
  On Zion's fruitful hills,—

3 So, with mild influence from above,
  Shall promis'd grace descend,
Till universal peace and love
  O'er all the earth extend.
  *Spirit of the Psalms.*

**253** *" Thy will be done."* C. M.

1 Jesus, the life, the truth, the way,
  In whom I now believe,
As taught by thee, in faith I pray,
  Expecting to receive.

2 Thy will by me on earth be done,
  As by the powers above,
Who always see thee on thy throne,
  And glory in thy love.

3 I ask in confidence the grace,
  That I may do thy will,
As angels who behold thy face,
  And all thy words fulfil.

4 Surely I shall, the sinner I,
  Shall serve thee without fear,
If thou my nature sanctify
  In answer to my prayer.
  *C. Wesley.*

**254** *A holy heart the Saviour's home.* C. M.

1 What is our calling's glorious hope
  But inward holiness !
For this to Jesus I look up,
  I calmly wait for this.

2 I wait, till he shall touch me clean,
  Shall life and power impart,
Give me the faith that casts out sin,
  And purifies the heart.

3 This is the dear redeeming grace,
  For every sinner free ;
Surely it shall on me take place,
  The chief of sinners, me.

4 From all iniquity, from all,
  He shall my soul redeem !
In Jesus I believe, and shall
  Believe myself to him.

5 When Jesus makes my heart his home,
  My sin shall all depart ;
And, lo he saith : " I quickly come,
  To fill and rule thy heart ! "
  *C. Wesley.*

CHRISTIAN PERFECTION.

**255 PLEYEL'S HYMN. 7s.**   PLEYEL.

1. Hark, my soul, it is the Lord! 'Tis thy Sav-iour, hear his word!

Je - sus speaks, he speaks to thee: "Say, poor sin - ner, lov'st thou me?"

*Love to the Saviour.*   7s.

1 Hark, my soul, it is the Lord!
'Tis thy Saviour, hear his word!
Jesus speaks, he speaks to thee:
"Say, poor sinner, lov'st thou me?"

2 I delivered thee when bound,
And, when bleeding, healed thy wound;
Sought thee wand'ring, set thee right,
Turned thy darkness into light.

3 Can a mother's tender care
Cease toward the child she bare?
Yes, she may forgetful be,
Yet will I remember thee.

4 Mine is an unchanging love,
Higher than the heights above,
Deeper than the depths beneath,
Free and faithful, strong as death.

5 Thou shalt see my glory soon,
When the work of faith is done.
Partner of my throne shalt be:
"Say, poor sinner, lov'st thou me?"

6 Lord, it is my chief complaint
That my love is still so faint;
Yet I love thee and adore:
O for grace to love thee more!
*Cowper.*

**256**   *Humble Aspirations.*   7s.

1 When, my Saviour, shall I be
Perfectly resigned to thee?
Poor and vile in my own eyes,
Only in thy wisdom wise?

2 Only thee content to know;
Ignorant of all below?
Only guided by thy light;
Only mighty in thy might?

3 So I may the Spirit know,
Let him as he listeth blow;
Let the manner be unknown.
So I may with thee be one.

4 Fully in my life express
All the heights of holiness;
Sweetly let my spirit prove
All the depths of humble love.
*C. Wesley.*

**256 b**   7s.
*Longing to be complete in Christ.*
[Words Ed.]

1 Saviour of the sin-sick soul,
Give me faith to make me whole;
Finish thy great work of grace;
Cut it short in righteousness.

2 Speak the second time, "Be clean!"
Take away my inbred sin;
Every stumbling-block remove;
Cast it out by perfect love.

3 Nothing less will I require,
Nothing more can I desire:
None but Christ to me be given;
None but Christ in earth or heaven.

4 O that I might now decrease!
O that all I am might cease!
Let me into nothing fall!
Let my Lord be all in all.

124

# CHRISTIAN PERFECTION.

## 257 FENBURN. S. M.

Je - sus, my strength, my hope, On thee I cast my care;
Give me on thee to wait, Till I can all things do;

With hum-ble con - fi - dence look up, And know thou hear'st my prayer.
On thee, al-might - y to cre - ate, Al - might-y to re - new.

---

*For Entire Consecration.*  S. M.

1 Jesus, my strength, my hope,
  On thee I cast my care,
With humble confidence look up,
  And know thou hear'st my prayer.
Give me on thee to wait,
  Till I can all things do;
On thee, almighty to create,
  Almighty to renew.

2 I want a sober mind,
  A self-renouncing will,
That tramples down, and casts behind,
  The baits of pleasing ill:
A soul inured to pain,
  To hardship, grief, and loss;
Bold to take up, firm to sustain,
  The consecrated cross.

3 I want a godly fear,
  A quick discerning eye,
That looks to thee when sin is near,
  And sees the tempter fly:
A spirit still prepared,
  And armed with jealous care;
Forever standing on its guard,
  And watching unto prayer.

*C. Wesley.*

**258**  *For Perfect Submission.*  S. M.

1 I want a heart to pray,
  To pray, and never cease;
Never to murmur at thy stay,
  Or wish my suffering less.
This blessing, above all,
  Always to pray, I want;
Out of the deep on thee to call,
  And never, never faint.

2 I want a true regard,
  A single, steady aim,
Unmoved by threatening or reward,
  To thee and thy great name;
A jealous, just concern
  For thine immortal praise;
A pure desire that all may learn
  And glorify thy grace.

3 I rest upon thy word;
  The promise is for me;
My succor and salvation, Lord,
  Shall surely come from thee:
But let me still abide,
  Nor from my hope remove,
Till thou my patient spirit guide
  Into thy perfect love.

*Charles Wesley.*

125

# CHRISTIAN PERFECTION.

259 MEAR. C. M.

1. Wit-ness, ye men and an-gels, now, Be-fore the Lord we speak;

To him we make our sol-emn vow, A vow we dare not break:

---

*The Solemn Vow.*  C. M.

1 Witness, ye men and angels now,
  Before the Lord we speak;
  To him we make our solemn vow,
  A vow we dare not break:

2 That long as life itself shall last,
  Ourselves to Christ we yield;
  Nor from his cause will we depart,
  Or ever quit the field.

3 We trust not in our native strength,
  But on his grace rely,
  That, with returning wants, the Lord
  Will all our need supply.

4 Lord, guide our doubtful feet aright,
  And keep us in thy ways;
  And, while we turn our vows to prayers,
  Turn thou our prayers to praise.
  *Benjamin Beddome.*

260 *"I will take the cup of salvation."* C. M.
    *Psalm cxvi. 13.*

1 What shall I render to my God
  For all his mercy's store?
  I'll take the gifts he hath bestowed,
  And humbly ask for more.

2 My vows I will to his great name
  Before his people pay,
  And all I have, and all I am,
  Upon his altar lay.

3 Thy lawful servant, Lord, I owe
  To thee whate'er is mine,
  Born in thy family below,
  And by redemption thine.

4 The God of all-redeeming grace
  My God I will proclaim,
  Offer the sacrifice of praise,
  And call upon his name.

5 Praise him, ye saints, the God of love,
  Who hath my sins forgiven,
  Till, gathered to the Church above,
  We sing the songs of heaven.
  *Samuel Wesley.*

261    *Accept my Heart.*    C. M.

1 My God, accept my heart this day,
  And make it always thine;
  That I from thee no more may stray,
  No more from thee decline.

2 Before the cross of him who died,
  Behold, I prostrate fall;
  Let every sin be crucified,
  Let Christ be all in all.

3 Let every thought, and work, and word,
  To thee be ever given;
  Then life shall be thy service, Lord,
  And death the gate of heaven!
  *Matthew Bridges.*

# CHRISTIAN PERFECTION.

**262**          C. M.

*Soul and body dedicated to the Lord.*

[Tune, Mear, page 126. C. M.]

1 Let him to whom we now belong,
  His sovereign right assert;
And take up every thankful song,
  And every loving heart.

2 He justly claims us for his own,
  Who bought us with a price:

The Christian lives to Christ alone;
  To Christ alone he dies.

3 Jesus, thine own at last receive;
  Fulfil our heart's desire;
And let us to thy glory live,
  And in thy cause expire.

4 Our souls and bodies we resign;
  With joy we render thee
Our all,—no longer ours, but thine
  To all eternity.   *Charles Wesley.*

**263** ADMAH. L. M. 6 lines.

1 O God, what off - 'ring shall I give To thee, the Lord of earth and skies?
2 Now then, my God, thou hast my soul: No lon - ger mine, but thine I am:
3 Thou hast my flesh, thy hal-lowed shrine, De - vo - ted sole - ly to thy will:

My spir-it, soul, and flesh re - ceive, A ho - ly, liv - ing sac - ri - fice:
Guard thou thine own, pos - sess it whole; Cheer it with hope, with love in-flame.
Here let thy light for - ev - er shine: This house still let thy pres-ence fill:

Small as it is, 'tis all my store; More shouldst thou have, if I had more.
Thou hast my spir - it; there dis - play Thy glo - ry to the per-fect day.
O Source of life! live, dwell, and move In me, till all my life be love.

JOACHIM LANGE. TR. BY J. WESLEY.

**264**     *The Single Eye.*    L. M.   6 lines.

1 Behold the servant of the Lord!
  I wait thy guiding hand to feel;
To hear and keep thy every word,
  To prove and do thy perfect will:
Joyful from my own works to cease,
Glad to fulfil all righteousness.

2 My every weak, though good design,
  O'errule or change, as seems thee meet:
Jesus, let all my work be thine!

Thy work, O Lord, is all complete,
  And pleasing in thy Father's sight;
Thou only hast done all things right.

3 Here, then, to thee thine own I leave;
  Mold as thou wilt thy passive clay;
But let me all thy stamp receive.
But let me all thy words obey;
Serve with a single heart and eye,
And to thy glory live and die
                *Charles Wesley.*

# CHRISTIAN PERFECTION.

**265 BROWNELL. L. M. 6 lines.**

1 I thank thee, un-cre-a-ted Sun, That thy bright beams on me have shined,

I thank thee, who hast o-ver-thrown My foes, and healed my wounded mind;

I thank thee, whose en-liven-ing voice Bids my freed heart in thee re-joice.

---

*Pressing toward the Mark.* L. M. 6 lines.

1 I thank thee, uncreated Sun,
　That thy bright beams on me have shined;
　I thank thee, who hast overthrown
　My foes, and healed my wounded mind;
　I thank thee, whose enlivening voice
　Bids my freed heart in thee rejoice.

2 Uphold me in the doubtful race,
　Nor suffer me again to stray,
　Strengthen my feet, with steady pace
　Still to press forward in thy way;
　My soul and flesh, O Lord of might,
　Fill, satiate, with thy heavenly light.

3 Give to mine eyes refreshing tears;
　Give to my heart chaste, hallowed fires;
　Give to my soul, with filial fears,
　The love that all heaven's host inspires;
　That all my powers, with all their might,
　In thy sole glory may unite.

4 Thee will I love, my joy, my crown:
　Thee will I love, my Lord, my God;
　Thee will I love, beneath thy frown
　Or smile, thy scepter or thy rod.
　What though my flesh and heart decay?
　Thee shall I love in endless day!

*Johann A. Scheffler. Tr. by J. Wesley.*

**266** L. M. 6 lines.

*The Prize of our High Calling.*

1 Jesus, thy boundless love to me
　No thought can reach, no tongue declare;
　O knit my thankful heart to thee,
　And reign without a rival there:
　Thine wholly, thine alone, I am:
　Be thou alone my constant flame.

2 O grant that nothing in my soul
　May dwell, but thy pure love alone:
　O may thy love possess me whole,
　My joy, my treasure, and my crown:
　Strange flames far from my heart remove;
　My every act, word, thought, be love.

3 Unwearied may I this pursue;
　Dauntless to the high prize aspire;
　Hourly within my soul renew
　This holy flame, this heavenly fire:
　And day and night, be all my care
　To guard the sacred treasure there.

4 In suffering be thy love my peace;
　In weakness be thy love my power;
　And when the storms of life shall cease,
　Jesus, in that important hour,
　In death as life be thou my guide,
　And save me, who for me hast died.

*Paul Gerhardt. Tr. by J. Wesley.*

# THE CHURCH COMFORTED AND ENCOURAGED.

**267 EUCHARIST. L. M.**                                     I. B. WOODBURY.

1. Je-sus, from whom all blessings flow, Great Build - er of thy Church be - low,

If now thy Spir - it move my breast, Hear, and ful - fil thine own re - quest.

L. M.

1 Jesus, from whom all blessings flow,
Great Builder of thy Church below,
If now thy Spirit move my breast,
Hear, and fulfil thine own request.

2 The few that truly call thee Lord,
And wait thy sanctifying word,
And thee their utmost Saviour own,—
Unite, and perfect them in one.

3 O let them all thy mind express!
Stand forth thy chosen witnesses;
Thy power unto salvation show,
And perfect holiness below.

4 In them let all mankind behold
How Christians lived in days of old;
Mighty their envious foes to move,
A proverb of reproach—and love.

5 Call them into thy wondrous light,
Worthy to walk with thee in white!
Make up thy jewels, Lord, and show
Thy glorious, spotless Church below.
                              *C. Wesley.*

**268**         *Psalm lxxxiv. 1-7.*         L. M.

1 How pleasant, how divinely fair,
O Lord of hosts, thy dwellings are!
With strong desire my spirit faints
To meet th' assemblies of thy saints.

2 Blest are the saints that sit on high,
Around thy throne of majesty;
Thy brightest glories shine above,
And all their work is praise and love.

3 Blest are the souls that find a place
Within the temple of thy grace:
Here they behold thy gentler rays,
And seek thy face, and learn thy praise.

4 Blest are the men whose hearts are set
To find the way to Zion's gate;
God is their strength, and through the road
They lean upon their helper, God.

5 Cheerful they walk with growing strength,
Till all shall meet in heaven at length,
Till all before thy face appear,
And join in nobler worship there.
                              *Watts.*

**269**         *Psalm lxv. 1-5.*         L. M.

1 The praise of Zion waits for thee,
My God; and praise becomes thy house;
There shall thy saints thy glory see,
And there perform their public vows.

3 O thou whose mercy bends the skies,
To save when humble sinners pray,
All lands to thee shall lift their eyes,
And grateful isles of every sea,
                              *Watts.*

# THE CHURCH COMFORTED AND ENCOURAGED.

**270 DODGE. L. M.**

J. P. HOLBROOK.

1. God is the ref-uge of his saints, When storms of sharp dis-tress in - vade;

Ere we can of - fer our com-plaints, Be - hold him present with his aid.

---

*Psalm* xlvi. 1-5.  L. M.

1 God is the refuge of his saints,
   When storms of sharp distress invade;
   Ere we can offer our complaints,
   Behold him present with his aid.

2 Let mountains from their seats be hurled
   Down to the deep, and buried there—
   Convulsions shake the solid world—
   Our faith shall never yield to fear.

3 Loud may the troubled ocean roar—
   In sacred peace our souls abide;
   While every nation, every shore,
   Trembles and dreads the swelling tide.

4 There is a stream, whose gentle flow
   Supplies the city of our God;
   Life, love, and joy, still gliding through,
   And wat'ring our divine abode.

5 That sacred stream, thy holy word,
   Our grief allays, our fear controls,
   Sweet peace thy promises afford,
   And give new strength to fainting souls.
                                    *Watts.*

**271**  *The ministry instituted.*  L. M.

1 The Saviour, when to heaven he rose,
   In splendid triumph o'er his foes,
   Scattered his gifts on men below,
   And still his royal bounties flow.

2 Hence sprang the apostles' honored name,
   Sacred beyond heroic fame:
   In humbler forms, before our eyes,
   Pastors and teachers hence arise.

3 From Christ they all their gifts derive,
   And, fed by Christ, their graces live;
   While guarded by his mighty hand,
   'Midst all the rage of hell they stand.

4 So shall the bright succession run
   Through all the courses of the sun;
   While unborn churches, by their care,
   Shall rise and flourish large and fair.

5 Jesus, now teach our hearts to know
   The spring whence all these blessings flow,
   Pastors and people shout thy praise,
   Through the long round of endless days.
                                *Philip Doddridge.*

**271 b**  L. M.

1 Fountain of grace, rich, full, and free,
   What need I that is not in thee?
   Full pardon, strength to meet the day,
   And peace which none can take away.

2 Doth sickness fill the heart with fear,
   'Tis sweet to know that thou art near.
   Am I with dread of justice tried?
   'Tis sweet to feel that Christ hath died.

3 In life, thy promises of aid
   Forbid my heart to be afraid:
   In death, peace gently vails the eyes;
   Christ rose, and I shall surely rise.

4 O all-sufficient Saviour! be
   This all-sufficiency to me;
   Nor pain, nor sin, nor death can harm
   The weakest shielded by thine arm.
                           *James Edmeston,* 1844.

130

**272 REST. L. M.**

WM. B. BRADBURY.

1. Comfort, ye min - is - ters of grace, Comfort the peo - ple of your Lord,

O lift ye up the fal - len race, And cheer them by the gos - pel word.

---

*Isaiah* xl 1-5.  L. M.

1 Comfort, ye ministers of grace,
  Comfort the people of your Lord,
O lift ye up the fallen race,
And cheer them by the gospel word.

2 Go into every nation. go,
  Speak to their trembling hearts, and cry
Glad tidings unto all we show:
Jerusalem, thy God is nigh.

3 Hark! in the wilderness a cry,
  A voice that loudly calls, Prepare!
Prepare your hearts, for God is nigh.
And means to make his entrance there!

4 The Lord your God shall quickly come:
  Sinners, repent, the call obey;
Open your hearts to make him room;
Ye desert souls, prepare his way.

5 The Lord shall clear his way through all:
  Whate'er obstructs, obstructs in vain;
The vale shall rise, the mountain fall,
Crooked be straight, and rugged plain.

6 The glory of the Lord displayed
  Shall all mankind together view,
And what his mouth in truth hath said,
His own almighty hand shall do.
                              *C. Wesley.*

---

**273**  *Angels of the Church.*  L. M.

1 Draw near, O Son of God, draw near!
  Us with thy flaming eye behold;
Still in thy Church vouchsafe t' appear,
And let our candlestick be gold.

2 Still hold the stars in thy right hand,
  And let them in thy lustre glow,
The lights of a benighted land,
The angels of thy Church below.

3 Make good their apostolic boast,
  Their high commission let them prove,
Be temples of the Holy Ghost,
And filled with faith, and hope, and love.

4 Their hearts from things of earth remove,
  Sprinkle them, Lord, from sin and fear,
Fix their affections all above,
And lay up all their treasures there.

5 Give them an ear to hear thy word;
  Thou speakest to the Churches now;
And let all tongues confess their Lord,
Let every knee to Jesus bow.
                              *C. Wesley.*

*Doxology.*  L. M.

Praise God, from whom all blessings flow;
Praise him, all creatures here below;
Praise him above, ye heavenly host;
Praise Father, Son, and Holy Ghost.

**274 MOUNT EPHRAIM. S. M.** MILGROVE.

1. Far as thy name is known The world de - clares thy praise · Thy saints, O Lord, be - fore thy throne Their songs of hon - or raise.

*Psalm* xlviii. 10–14. S. M.

1 Far as thy name is known
The world declares thy praise:
Thy saints, O Lord, before thy throne
Their songs of honor raise.

2 With joy let Judah stand
On Zion's chosen hill,
Proclaim the wonders of thy hand,
And counsels of thy will.

3 Let strangers walk around
The city where we dwell;
Compass and view the holy ground,
And mark the building well—

4 The order of thy house,
The worship of thy court,
The cheerful songs, the solemn vows,
And make a fair report.

5 How decent and how wise!
How glorious to behold!
Beyond the pomp that charms the eyes,
And rites adorned with gold.
*Watts.*

**275** *For an increase of laborers.* S. M.

1 Lord of the harvest, hear
Thy needy servants' cry;
Answer our faith's effectual prayer,
And all our wants supply.

2 On thee we humbly wait,
Our wants are in thy view:
The harvest, truly, Lord, is great,
The laborers are few.

3 Convert, and send forth more
Into thy Church abroad,
And let them speak the word of power,
As workers with their God.

4 O let them spread thy name,
Their mission fully prove;
Thy universal grace proclaim,
Thine all-redeeming love!
*C. Wesley.*

**276** *The Reunion.* S. M.

1 O happy, happy place,
Where saints and angels meet!
There we shall see each other's face,
And all our brethren greet.

2 With joy we shall behold,
In yonder blest abode,
The patriarchs and prophets old,
And all the saints of God.

3 Abrah'm and Isaac there,
And Jacob shall receive
The foll'wers of their faith and prayer
Who now in bodies live.

4 We shall our time beneath
Live out in cheerful hope,
And fearless pass the vale of death,
And gain the mountain-top.

5 To gather home his own,
God shall his angels send,
And bid our bliss, on earth begun,
In glorious triumph end.
*Wesley.*

# THE CHURCH COMFORTED AND ENCOURAGED.

**277  VARINA. C. M. Double**  ARRANGED BY G. F. ROOT.

1. { Je - sus, the name high o - ver all, In hell, or earth, or sky! }
   { An - gels and men be - fore it fall, And dev - ils fear and fly. }

Je - sus, the name to sin - ners dear, The name to sin - ners giv'n;

It scat - ters all their guilt - y fear; It turns their hell to heav'n.

*The minister's theme.*  C. M.

1 Jesus, the name high over all,
    In hell, or earth, or sky!
  Angels and men before it fall,
    And devils fear and fly.

2 Jesus, the name to sinners dear,
    The name to sinners giv'n;
  It scatters all their guilty fear;
    It turns their hell to heav'n.

3 Jesus the pris'ner's fetters breaks,
    And bruises Satan's head;
  Power into strengthless souls it speaks,
    And life into the dead.

4 O that the world might taste and see
    The riches of his grace;
  The arms of love that compass me
    Would all mankind embrace.

5 His only righteousness I show,
    His saving truth proclaim;
  'Tis all my business here below,
    To cry, "Behold the lamb!"

6 Happy, if with my latest breath
    I may but gasp his name!

Preach him to all, and cry in death,
    "Behold, behold the Lamb!"
        *C. Wesley.*

**278**                              C. M.
*"For I am not ashamed of the Gospel of
    Christ." Romans* i: 16.

1 I'm not asham'd to own the Lord,
    Or to defend his cause,
  Maintain the honor of his word,
    The glory of his cross.

2 Jesus, my God, I know his name,
    His name is all my trust,
  Nor will he put my soul to shame,
    Nor let my hope be lost.

3 Firm as his throne his promise stands,
    And he can well secure
  What I've committed to his hands
    Till the decisive hour.

4 Then will he own my worthless name
    Before his Father's face,
  And in the New Jerusalem
    Appoint my soul a place.
        *Watts.*

133

# THE CHURCH COMFORTED AND ENCOURAGED.

**279 BARBY. C. M.** TANSUR.

*1. How did my heart re-joice to hear My friends de-vout-ly say,*

*"In Zi-on let us all ap-pear, And keep the sol-emn day!*

*Let us go into the house of the Lord.* C. M.
*Psalm* cxxii.

1 How did my heart rejoice to hear
  My friends devoutly say,
  " In Zion let us all appear,
    And keep the solemn day ! "

2 I love her gates, I love the road.
  The Church adorned with grace,
  Stands like a palace built for God,
    To show his milder face.

3 Up to her courts, with joys unknown,
  The holy tribes repair;
  The Son of David holds his throne
  And sits in judgment there.

4 He hears our praises and complaints;
  And, while his awful voice
  Divides the sinners from the saints,
  We tremble and rejoice !

5 Peace be within this sacred place,
  And joy a constant guest !
  With holy gifts and heavenly grace
  Be her attendants blest.

6 My soul shall pray for Zion still,
  While life or breath remains;
  There my best friends, my kindred dwell,
  There God, my Saviour, reigns.

*Watts.*

**279 b BERNARD. C. M.** HOLBROOK.

*1. Fa-ther, I wait be-fore thy throne; Call me a child of thine;*
*2. There shed thy prom-is-ed love a-broad, And make my com fort strong:*

*Send down the spir-it of thy Son, To form my heart di-vine.*
*Then shall I say, "My Fa-ther, God!" With an un-wav 'ring tongue.*

134

# THE CHURCH COMFORTED AND ENCOURAGED.

**280   HARWELL.   8s & 7s.   D.**

Glo-rious things of thee are spok - en, Zi - on, cit - y of our God!
He whose word can ne'er be brok - en, Formed thee for his own a - bode.

On the rock of a - ges founded, What can shake thy sure re-pose?
On the Rock of a - ges founded, What can shake thy sure re - pose?

With sal - va - tion's walls sur - round-ed, Thou may'st smile at all thy foes.

*Supplies of the Church.*   8s & 7s.   D.

1 Glorious things of thee are spoken,
   Zion, city of our God!
   He, whose word can ne'er be broken,
   Formed thee for his own abode.
   On the Rock of Ages founded,
   What can shake thy sure repose?
   With salvation's walls surrounded,
   Thou may'st smile at all thy foes.

2 See! the streams of living waters
   Springing from eternal love,
   Well supply thy sons and daughters,
   And all fear of want remove.
   Who can faint while such a river
   Ever flows their thirst t' assuage?
   Grace which like the Lord, the giver,
   Never fails from age to age.

3 Round each habitation hov'ring,
   See the cloud and fire appear,
   For a glory and a cov'ring—
   Showing that the Lord is near.
   Glorious things of thee are spoken,
   Zion, city of our God!
   He, whose word can ne'er be broken,
   Chose thee for his own abode.

*Newton.*

**281**   8s & 7s.   D.

*God Her Everlasting Light.*

1 Hear what God the Lord hath spoken:
   O my people, faint and few,
   Comfortless, afflicted, broken,
   Fair abodes I build for you.
   Scenes of heartfelt tribulation
   Shall no more preplex your ways:
   You shall name your walls "Salvation,"
   And your gates shall all be "Praise."

2 There, like streams that feed the garden,
   Pleasures without end shall flow,
   For the Lord, your faith rewarding,
   All his bounty shall bestow.
   Still in undisturbed possession,
   Peace and righteousness shall reign;
   Never shall you feel oppression,
   Hear the voice of war again.

3 Ye, no more your suns descending,
   Waning moons no more shall see;
   But, your griefs forever ending,
   Find eternal noon in me:
   God shall rise, and, shining o'er you,
   Change to day the gloom of night;
   He, the Lord, shall be your glory,
   God your everlasting light.

*William Cowper.*

135

## 282 ZION. 8s, 7s, 4.

T. HASTINGS.

1. On the mountain's top ap - pear-ing, Lo! the sa - cred her - ald stands,

Wel-come news to Zi - on bear-ing, Zi - on, long in hos - tile lands: Mourning

captive! God himself shall loose thy bands, Mourning captive! God himself shall loose thy bands.

*Good News for Zion.*     Ss, 7s & 4s.

1 On the mountain's top appearing,
Lo! the sacred herald stands,
Welcome news to Zion bearing,
Zion, long in hostile lands:
‖: Mourning captive!
God himself shall loose thy bands. :‖

2 Has thy night been long and mournful?
Have thy friends unfaithful proved?
Have thy foes been proud and scornful,
By thy sighs and tears unmoved?
‖: Cease thy mourning;
Zion still is well beloved. :‖

3 God, thy God, will now restore thee;
He himself appears thy Friend;
All thy foes shall flee before thee:
Here their boasts and triumphs end:
‖: Great deliverance
Zion's King will surely send. :‖

4 Peace and joy shall now attend thee:
All thy warfare now is past;
God thy Saviour will defend thee:
Victory is thine at last:

‖: All thy conflicts
End in everlasting rest. :‖
*Thomas Kelly.*

## 283

8s, 7s & 4s.

*Jehovah, the Defense of Zion.*

1 Zion stands with hills surrounded,
Zion, kept by power divine:
All her foes shall be confounded,
Though the world in arms combine:
‖: Happy Zion,
What a favored lot is thine. :‖

2 Every human tie may perish;
Friend to friend unfaithful prove;
Mothers cease their own to cherish;
Heaven and earth at last remove;
‖: But no changes
Can attend Jehovah's love. :‖

3 In the furnace God may prove thee,
Thence to bring thee forth more bright,
But can never cease to love thee,
Thou art precious in his sight:
‖: God is with thee,
God, thine everlasting light. :‖
*Thomas Kelly.*

# THE CHURCH COMFORTED AND ENCOURAGED.

## 284 DAYSPRING. S. M.

C. BRYAN.

1. I love thy king-dom, Lord, The house of thine a-bode,

The Church our blest Re-deem-er saved With his own pre-cious blood.

*Love for Zion.*     S. M.

1 I love thy kingdom, Lord,
 The house of thine abode.
 The Church our blest Redeemer saved
 With his own precious blood.

2 I love thy Church, O God!
 Her walls before thee stand,
 Dear as the apple of thine eye,
 And graven on thy hand.

3 For her my tears shall fall,
 For her my prayers ascend;
 To her my cares and toils be given,
 Till toils and cares shall end.

4 Beyond my highest joy
 I prize her heavenly ways,
 Her sweet communion, solemn vows,
 Her hymns of love and praise.

5 Sure as thy truth shall last,
 To Zion shall be given
 The brightest glories earth can yield,
 And brighter bliss of heaven.
 *Timothy Dwight.*

## 285     S. M.
*The Church's Confidence and Security.*

1 Who in the Lord confide,
 And feel his sprinkled blood,
 In storms and hurricanes abide
 Firm as the mount of God:

2 Steadfast, and fixed, and sure,
 His Zion cannot move;
 His faithful people stand secure
 In Jesus' guardian love.

3 As round Jerusalem
 The hilly bulwarks rise,
 So God protects and covers them
 From all their enemies.

4 On every side he stands,
 And for his Israel cares;

And safe in his almighty hands
 Their souls forever bears.
 *Charles Wesley.*

## 286     *The Trinity Invoked.*     S. M.

1 O Lord our God! arise,
 The cause of truth maintain,
 And wide o'er all the peopled world
 Extend her blessed reign.

2 Thou Prince of life! arise,
 Nor let thy glory cease;
 Far spread the conquests of thy grace,
 And bless the earth with peace.

3 Thou Holy Ghost! arise,
 Extend thy quickening wing,
 And o'er a dark and ruined world
 Let light and order spring.

4 All on the earth arise,
 To God the Saviour sing,
 From shore to shore, from earth to heaven,
 Let echoing anthems ring.
 *Ralph Wardlaw from the Presbyterian Coll.*

## 287     *The throne of grace.*     S. M.

1 Behold the throne of grace;
 The promise calls us near;
 There Jesus shows a smiling face,
 And waits to answer prayer.

2 My soul, ask what thou wilt,
 Thou canst not be too bold;
 Since his own blood for thee he spilt,
 What else can he withhold?

3 Thine image, Lord, bestow,
 Thy presence and thy love,
 That we may serve thee here below,
 And reign with thee above.

4 Teach us to live by faith,
 Conform our wills to thine;
 Let us victorious be in death,
 And then in glory shine. *John Newton.*

137

# MINISTERIAL COMMISSION.

**288** DUKE STREET. L. M.    J. HATTON.

1. Go forth, ye her - alds, in my name, Sweet-ly the gos - pel trum-pet sound;

The glorious ju - bi - lee pro-claim, Where'er the hu - man race is found.

L. M.

*Christ's Commission to Preach the Gospel.*
*Matt.* x. 7-16.

1 Go forth, ye heralds, in my name,
   Sweetly the gospel trumpet sound;
   The glorious jubilee proclaim,
   Where'er the human race is found.

2 The joyful news to all impart,
   And teach them where salvation lies,
   With care bind up the broken heart
   And wipe the tears from weeping eyes.

3 Be wise as serpents where you go,
   But harmless as the peaceful dove,
   And let your heav'n-taught conduct show,
   That ye're commissioned from above.

4 Freely from me ye have received,
   Freely, in love to others give;
   Thus shall your doctrines be believ'd,
   And, by your labors, sinners live.

           *J. Logan.*

**289**     *Laborers.*    L. M.
      [ From the German.]

1 High on his everlasting throne,
   The King of saints his work surveys,
   Marks the dear souls he calls his own,
   And smiles on the peculiar race.

2 He rests well pleased their toils to see;
   Beneath his easy yoke they move;
   With all their heart and strength agree
   In the sweet labor of his love.

3 See, where the servants of their God,
   A busy multitude, appear:
   For Jesus day and night employed,
   His heritage they toil to clear.

4 The love of Christ their hearts constrains,
   And strengthens their unwearied hands;
   They spend their sweat and blood, and pains
   To cultivate Immanuel's lands.

5 O multiply thy sowers' seed,
   And fruit we every hour shall bear:
   Throughout the world thy gospel spread,
   Thine everlasting truth declare!

           *J. Wesley.*

     *Doxology.*    L. M.

Praise God, from whom all blessings flow;
Praise him, all creatures here below;
Praise him above, ye heavenly host;
Praise Father, Son, and Holy Ghost.

## MINISTERIAL COMMISSION.

**290  RETREAT. L. M.**

THOS. HASTINGS.

1. "Go preach the gos - pel," saith the Lord, "Bid the whole earth my grace re - ceive;

Ex - plain to them my sa - cred word, Bid them be - lieve, o - bey, and live.

L. M.

*" Go ye into all the world, and preach the gospel to every creature." Mark xvi. 15-20.*

1 " Go preach my gospel," saith th' Lord,
    " Bid the whole earth my grace re-
        ceive;
    Explain to them my sacred word,
    Bid them believe, obey, and live."

2 " I'll make my great commission known,
    And ye shall prove my gospel true,
    By all the works that I have done,
    And all the wonders ye shall do."

3 "Go heal the sick, go raise the dead,
    Go cast out devils in my name;
    Nor let my prophets be afraid,
    Though Greeks reproach, and Jews
        blaspheme."

4 " While thus ye follow my commands,
    I'm with you till the world shall end:
    All power is trusted in my hands,
    I can destroy, and can defend."

5 He spake, and light shone round his
        head;
    On a bright cloud to heav'n he rode;
    They to the farthest nation spread
    The grace of their ascended God.
                                    *Watts.*

**291**      *His universal Effusion.*      L. M.

1 O Spirit of the living God!
    In all the fullness of thy grace,
    Where'er the foot of man hath trod,
    Descend on our apostate race.

2 Give tongues of fire and hearts of love
    To preach the reconciling word:

Give power and unction from above,
    Whene'er the joyful sound is heard.

3 Be darkness, at thy coming, light;
    Confusion, order, in thy path;
    Souls without strength, inspire with might;
    Bid mercy triumph over wrath!

4 Baptize the nations! far and nigh;
    The triumphs of the cross record:
    The name of Jesus glorify,
    Till every kindred call him Lord.

5 God from eternity hath willed
    All flesh shall his salvation see:
    So be the Father's love fulfilled,
    The Saviour's suff'ring crowned through
        thee!
                                *Montgomery.*

**291 b**    *Because thou first loved me.*   L. M.

1 I love, I love thee, Lord most high!
    Because thou first hast loved me;
    I seek no other liberty
    But that of being bound to thee.

2 May memory no thought suggest,
    But shall to thy pure glory tend:
    My understanding find no rest,
    Except in thee, its only end.

3 All mine is thine; say but the word,
    Whate'er thou willest shall be done;
    I know thy love, all-gracious Lord;
    I know it seeks my good alone.

4 Apart from thee all things are naught;
    Then grant, O my supremest Bliss,—
    Grant me to love thee as I ought;
    Thou givest all in giving this.
                                    *Xavier.*

139

# MINISTERIAL COMMISSION.

HANS NAGELI.

1. Hark, how the watch-men cry! At - tend the trum - pet's sound!

Stand to your arms, the foe is nigh; The pow'rs of hell sur - round.

### The Church Militant.                S. M.

1 Hark, how the watchmen cry!
    Attend the trumpet's sound!
  Stand to your arms, the foe is nigh;
    The powers of hell surround.

2 Who bow to Christ's command,
    Your arms and hearts prepare:
  The day of battle is at hand!
    Go forth to glorious war!

3 See, on the mountain top,
    The standard of your God!
  In Jesus' name I lift it up,
    All stained with hallowed blood.

4 His standard-bearer, I
    To all the nations call:
  Let all to Jesus' cross draw nigh:
    He bore the cross for all.

5 All power to him is given:
    He ever reigns the same:
  Salvation, happiness, and heaven,
    Are all in Jesus' name.
                                    C. Wesley.

1 How beauteous are their feet
    Who stand on Zion's hill;

Who bring salvation on their tongues,
    And words of peace reveal!

2 How charming is their voice!
    How sweet the tidings are!
  "Zion, behold thy Saviour King;
    He reigns and triumphs here!"

3 How happy are our ears
    That hear this joyful sound,
  Which kings and prophets waited for,
    And sought, but never found!

4 How blessed are our eyes
    That see this heavenly light!
  Prophets and kings desired it long,
    But died without the sight.

5 The watchmen join their voice,
    And tuneful notes employ :
  Jerusalem breaks forth in songs,
    And deserts learn the joy.

6 The Lord makes bare his arm
    Through all the earth abroad:
  Let every nation now behold
    Their Saviour and their God.
                                    Watts.

## 294 BOYLSTON. S. M.

L. MASON.

1. Ye mes - sen - gers of Christ! His sov - 'reign voice o - bey;

A - rise, and fol - low where he leads, And peace at - tend your way.

S. M.

1 Ye messengers of Christ!
His sovereign voice obey;
Arise, and follow where he leads,
And peace attend your way.

2 The Master whom you serve
Will needful strength bestow;
Depending on his promised aid,
With sacred courage go—

3 Go, spread the Saviour's fame;
And tell his matchless grace
To the most guilty and depraved
Of Adam's numerous race.

4 Mountains shall sink to plains,
And hell in vain oppose;
The cause is God's, and must prevail,
In spite of all his foes.
*Mrs. Voke, from the Presbyterian Coll.*

### 295 *Opening Conference.* S. M.

1 And are we yet alive,
And see each other's face?
Glory and praise to Jesus give
For his redeeming grace!

2 Preserved by power Divine
To full salvation here,
Again in Jesus' praise we join,
And in his sight appear.

3 What troubles have we seen,
What conflicts have we passed,
Fightings without, and fears within,
Since we assembled last;

4 But out of all the Lord
Hath brought us by his love;
And still he doth his help afford,
And hides our life above.

5 Then let us make our boast
Of his redeeming power,
Which saves us to the uttermost,
Till we can sin no more:

6 Let us take up the cross,
Till we the crown obtain;
And gladly reckon all things loss,
So we may Jesus gain.
*C. Wesley.*

### 296 *Closing Conference.* S. M.

1 And let our bodies part,
To diff'rent climes repair;
Inseparably joined in heart
The friends of Jesus are.

2 Jesus the Corner-stone
Did first our hearts unite,
And still he keeps our spirits one,
Who walk with him in white.

3 O let us still proceed
In Jesus' work below,
And, foll'wing our triumphant Head,
To further conquests go.

4 O let our heart and mind
Continually ascend,
That heaven of repose to find,
Where all our labors end!
*C. Wesley.*

# MINISTERIAL COMMISSION.

## 297 CHINA. C. M.

1. Let Zi - on's watch - men all a - wake, And take th' a - larm they give; Now let them from the mouth of God Their aw - ful charge re - ceive.

---

*Zion's Watchmen.*    C. M.

1 Let Zion's watchmen all awake,
   And take th' alarm they give;
Now let them from the mouth of God
   Their awful charge receive.

2 'Tis not a cause of small import
   The pastor's care demands;
But what might fill an angel's heart,
   And filled a Saviour's hands.

3 They watch for souls, for which the Lord
   Did heavenly bliss forego!
For souls which must forever live
   In raptures, or in woe.

4 May they that Jesus whom they preach,
   Their own Redeemer see,
And watch thou daily o'er their souls,
   That they may watch for thee.
                 *C. Wesley.*

## 298    *Christ, the Conqueror.*    C. M.

1 Jesus, immortal King, arise;
   Assert thy rightful sway,
Till earth, subdued, its tribute brings,
   And distant lands obey.

2 Ride forth, victorious Conqueror, ride,
   Till all thy foes submit,
And all the powers of hell resign
   Their trophies at thy feet.

3 Send forth thy word, and let it fly
   The spacious earth around,
Till every soul beneath the sun
   Shall hear the joyful sound.

4 O may the great Redeemer's name
   Through every clime be known,
And heathen gods forsaken, fall,
   And Jesus reign alone.
            *A. C. Hobart Seymour.*

## 299    *The Gospel for all Nations.*    C. M.

1 Great God, the nations of the earth
   Are by creation thine;
And in thy works, by all beheld,
   Thy radiant glories shine.

2 But, Lord, thy greater love has sent
   Thy gospel to mankind,
Unveiling what rich stores of grace
   Are treasured in thy mind.

3 Lord, when shall these glad tidings spread
   The spacious earth around,
Till every tribe and every soul
   Shall hear the joyful sound?

4 Smile, Lord, on each divine attempt
   To spread the gospel's rays,
And build on sin's demolished throne
   The temples of thy praise.
            *Thomas Gibbons.*

MINISTERIAL COMMISSION.

**300 CAMBRIDGE. C. M.** RANDALL.

1. How great the wis-dom, pow'r and grace Which in re - demp-tion shine!

The heav'nly host with joy con - fess The work is all di - vine.

The work is all di - vine, The work is all di - vine.

---

*Let all the angels of God worship him.* C. M.

1 How great the wisdom, power and grace
  Which in redemption shine!
  The heavenly host with joy confess
  The work is all divine.

2 Before his feet they cast their crowns,—
  Those crowns which Jesus gave,—
  And, with ten thousand thousand tongues,
  Proclaim his power to save.

3 They tell the triumphs of his cross,
  The suff'rings which he bore,—
  How low he stooped, how high he rose,
  And rose to stoop no more.

4 O let them still their voices raise,
  And still their songs renew:
  Salvation well deserves the praise
  Of men and angels too.
    *Beddome.*

**301** *Full and Free.* C. M.

1 O what amazing words of grace
  Are in the gospel found!
  Suited to every sinner's case,
  Who knows the joyful sound.

2 Poor, sinful, thirsty, fainting souls
  Are freely welcome here;
  Salvation, like a river, rolls
  Abundant, free and clear.

3 Come then, with all your wants and wounds,
  Your every burden bring:
  Here love, unchanging love, abounds,
  A deep, celestial spring.

4 Whoever will—O gracious word!
  May of this stream partake;
  Come, thirsty souls, and bless the Lord,
  And drink, for Jesus' sake.

5 Millions of sinners, vile as you,
  Have here found life and peace;
  Come, then, and prove its virtues too,
  And drink, adore, and bless.
    *Samuel Medley.*

**301 b** *A blessing from God's presence.* C. M.

1 Great Shepherd of thy people, hear;
  Thy presence now display;
  We kneel within thy house of prayer;
  O give us hearts to pray.

2 The clouds which veil thee from our sight,
  In pity, Lord, remove:
  Dispose our minds to hear aright
  The message of thy love.

3 Help us, with holy fear and joy,
  To kneel before thy face;
  O make us, creatures of thy power,
  The children of thy grace.
    *Newton.*

143

# CHRISTIAN ORDINANCES.

## BAPTISM.

**302 ROCKINGHAM. L. M.**

1. Come, Father, Son and Ho-ly Ghost, Hon - or the means or dained by thee;

Make good our a - pos - tol - ic boast, And own thy glo - rious min - is - try.

L. M.

1 Come, Father, Son, and Holy Ghost,
  Honor the means ordained by thee;
  Make good our apostolic boast,
  And own thy glorious ministry.

2 We now thy promised presence claim:
  Sent to disciple all mankind—
  Sent to baptize into thy name—
  We now thy promised presence find.

3 Father, in these reveal thy Son—
  In these, for whom we seek thy face,
  The hidden mystery make known,
  The inward, pure, baptizing grace.

4 Jesus, with us thou always art:
  Effectuate now the sacred sign,
  The gift unspeakable impart,
  And bless the ordinance divine.

5 Eternal Spirit, come from high,
  Baptizer of our spirits thou!
  The sacramental seal apply,
  And witness with the water now!
  *C. Wesley.*

**303** *The Commission.* L. M.

1 'Twas the commission of our Lord,
  "Go, teach the nations, and baptize;"
  The nations have received the word
  Since he ascended to the skies.

2 "Repent and be baptized," he saith,
  "For the remission of your sins;"
  And thus our sense assists our faith,
  And shows us what his gospel means.

3 Our souls he washes in his blood,
  As water makes the body clean;
  And the good Spirit from our God
  Descends, like purifying rain.

4 Thus we engage ourselves to thee,
  And seal our cov'nant with the Lord:
  O may the great Eternal Three
  In heaven our solemn vows record!
  *Watts.*

**303 b** *Baptism.—Adult.* H. M.
[Tune, Harwich, page 182. H. M]

1 Baptized into thy name,
  Mysterious One in Three,
  Our souls and bodies claim
  A sacrifice to thee:
  We only live our faith to prove,
  The faith which works by humble love.

2 O that our light may shine,
  And all our lives express
  The character Divine,
  The *real* holiness!
  Then, then receive us up t' adore
  The Triune God for evermore.
  *C. Wesley.*

# CHRISTIAN ORDINANCES.

## 304 BROOMSGROVE. C. M.

1. O Lord, while we con-fess the worth Of this the out-ward seal, Do thou the truths here-in set forth To ev - 'ry heart re-veal, To ev - 'ry heart re - veal.

*Significance of Baptism.*   C. M.

1 O Lord, while we confess the worth
Of this the outward seal,
Do thou the truths herein set forth
To every heart reveal.

2 Death to the world we here avow,
Death to each fleshly lust;
Newness of life our calling now,
A risen Lord our trust.

3 And we, O Lord, who now partake
Of resurrection life,
With every sin, for thy dear sake,
Would be at constant strife.

4 Baptised into the Father's name
We'd walk as sons of God;
Baptised in thine, we own thy claim
As ransomed by thy blood.

5 Baptised into the Holy Ghost,
We'd keep his temple pure,
And make thy grace our only boast,
And by thy strength endure.
*Mary P. Bowly.*

**305** *Children in the Arms of Jesus.* C. M.

1 Behold what condescending love
Jesus on earth displays!
To little children he extends
The riches of his grace.

2 He still the ancient promise keeps,
To our forefathers given;

Our infants in his arms he takes,
And calls them heirs of heaven.

3 Forbid them not, whom Jesus calls,
Nor dare the claim resist,
Since his own lips to us declare
Of such will heaven consist.

4 With flowing tears, and thankful hearts,
We give them up to thee;
Receive them, Lord, into thine arms;
Thine may they ever be.
*John Peacock, Augustus M. Toplady.*

**306** *Infant.* C. M.

1 How large the promise, how Divine,
To Abrah'm and his seed!
"I am a God to thee and thine,
Supplying all their need."

2 The words of his extensive love
From age to age endure;
The angel of the cov'nant proves
And seals the blessing sure.

3 Jesus the ancient faith confirms,
To our great father given;
He takes our children to his arms,
And calls them heirs of heaven.

4 O God, how faithful are thy ways!
Thy love endures the same;
Nor from the promise of thy grace
Blots out our children's name.
*Watts.*

145

BAPTISM.

**307 GRIGGS. C. M.**                    J. GRIGG. 1815-1852.

1. See Is - rael's gen - tle Shep - herd stands With all - en - gag - ing charms;

Hark how he calls the ten - der lambs, And folds them in his arms!

*Infant.*                         C. M.

1 See Israel's gentle Shepherd stands
   With all-engaging charms;
   Hark how he calls the tender lambs,
   And folds them in his arms!

2 "Permit them to approach," he cries,
   "Nor scorn their humble name:
   For 'twas to bless such souls as these
   The Lord of angels came."

3 We bring them, Lord, in thankful hands,
   And yield them up to thee:
   Joyful that we ourselves are thine,
   Thine let our offspring be.
                              *Doddridge.*

**308**      *Christ a Fountain.*      S. M.
   [Tune, Kentucky, page 147. S. M.]

1 My Saviour's piercèd side,
   Pour'd out a double flood;
   By water we are purified,
   And pardon'd by the blood.

2 Call'd from above, I rise,
   And wash away my sin;
   The stream to which my spirit flies,
   Can make the foulest clean.

3 It runs divinely clear,
   A fountain deep and wide;
   'Twas opened by the soldier's spear,
   In my Redeemer's side!
                              *Stafford.*

**LORD'S SUPPER.**

**309**                             S. M.

*Communion with Christ and with Saints.*
   [Tune, Kentucky, page 147. S. M.]

1 Jesus invites his saints
   To meet around his board;

Here pardoned rebels sit, and hold
   Communion with their Lord.

2 For food he gives his flesh;
   He bids us drink his blood;
   Amazing favor, matchless grace
   Of our descending God.

3 This holy bread and wine
   Maintain our fainting breath,
   By union with our living Lord,
   And interest in his death.

4 Our heavenly Father calls
   Christ and his members one:
   We the young children of his love,
   And he the first-born Son.
                              *Watts.*

**310**      *The Triumph.*      S. M.
   [Tune, Kentucky, page 147. S. M.]

1 "I the good fight have fought,"
   O when shall I declare!
   The vict'ry by my Saviour got
   I long with Paul to share.

2 O may I triumph so,
   When all my warfare's past;
   And, dying, find my latest foe
   Under my feet at last!

3 This blessed word be mine,
   Just as the port is gained,
   "Kept by the power of grace Divine,
   I have the faith maintained."

4 Th' apostles of my Lord,
   To whom it first was given,—
   They could not speak a greater word,
   Nor all the saints in heaven.
                              *C. Wesley.*

146

CHRISTIAN ORDINANCES.

## 310 KENTUCKY. S. M.

1. "I the good fight have fought," O when shall I de-clare! The

vic-t'ry by my Sav-iour got I long with Paul to share.

**311** *The Invitation.* C. M.

1 The King of heaven his table spreads,
  And blessings crown the board;
  Not paradise. with all its joys,
  Could such delight afford.

2 Pardon and peace to dying men,
  And endless life, are given,
  Through the rich blood that Jesus shed
  To raise our souls to heaven.

3 Millions of souls, in glory now,
  Were fed and feasted here ;
  And millions more, still on the way,
  Around the board appear.

4 All things are ready : come away,
  Nor weak excuses frame ;
  Crowd to your places at the feast,
  And bless the Founder's name.
  *Doddridge.*

## 311 HOWARDS. C. M.

1. The King of heav'n his ta-ble spreads, And bless-ings crown the board ;

Not par-a-dise, with all its joys, Could such de-light af-ford.

117

# THE LORD'S SUPPER.

312 JERUSALEM. C. M.                                          C. F. R.

1 With joy we med - i - tate the grace Of our High Priest a - bove:

His heart is made of ten - der - ness, His bow - els melt with love.

*Heb. iv 14-16.*                    C. M.

1 With joy we meditate the grace
   Of our High Priest above :
   His heart is made of tenderness,
   His bowels melt with love.

2 Touched with a sympathy within,
   He knows our feeble frame ;
   He knows what sore temptations mean,
   For he hath felt the same.

3 He in the days of feeble flesh
   Poured out strong cries and tears ;
   And in his measure feels afresh
   What every member bears.

4 He'll never quench the smoking flax,
   But raise it to a flame :
   The bruised reed he never breaks,
   Nor scorns the meanest name.

5 Then let our humble faith address
   His mercy and his power :
   We shall obtain deliv'ring grace
   In the distressing hour.
                                *Watts.*

313            *The Institution.*        C. M.

1 That doleful night before his death,
   The Lamb for sinners slain,
   Did, almost with his dying breath,
   This solemn feast ordain.

2 To keep the feast, Lord, we have met,
   And to remember thee :
   Help each poor trembler to repeat,
   " For me, he died for me ! "

3 Thy suff'rings, Lord, each sacred sign
   To our remembrance brings :
   We eat the bread, and drink the wine,
   But think on nobler things.

4 O tune our tongues, and set in frame
   Each heart that pants for thee,
   To sing, " Hosanna to the Lamb ! "
   The Lamb that died for me !
                                *Hart.*

314    *Rich gifts of Gospel Grace.*    C. M.

1 O love divine ! O matchless grace !
   Which in this sacred rite
   Shines forth so full, so free, in rays
   Of purest living light.

2 O wondrous death ! O precious blood !
   For us so freely spilt,
   To cleanse our sin-polluted souls
   From every stain of guilt.

3 O covenant of life and peace,
   By blood and suffering sealed !
   All the rich gifts of gospel grace
   Are here to faith revealed.

4 Jesus, we bow our souls to thee,
   Our life, our hope, our all,
   While we, with thankful, contrite hearts,
   Thy dying love recall.

5 O may thy pure and perfect love
   Be written on our minds ;
   Nor earth, nor self, nor sin obscure
   The ever-radiant lines.
                                *Edward Turney.*

148

# CHRISTIAN ORDINANCES.

**315  MOORE. C. M.**                                    SAMUEL WEBBE.

1. Ac - cord - ing  to  thy  gra - cious word,  In  meek  hu - mil - i - ty,

This  will  I  do,  my  dy - ing  Lord,  I  will  re - mem - ber  thee!

*Grateful Remembrance.*    C. M.

1 According to thy gracious word,
　In meek humility,
　This will I do, my dying Lord,
　I will remember thee!

2 Thy body, broken for my sake,
　My bread from heaven shall be;
　Thy testamental cup I take,
　And thus remember thee!

3 Gethsemane can I forget?
　Or there thy conflict see,
　Thine agony and bloody sweat,
　And not remember thee?

4 When to the cross I turn mine eyes,
　And rest on Calvary,
　O Lamb of God, my Sacrifice,
　I must remember thee!

5 Remember thee, and all thy pains,
　And all thy love to me!
　Yea, while a breath, a pulse remains,
　Will I remember thee!
　　　　　　　*James Montgomery.*

**316**    *Approaching the Table.*    C. M.

1 Jesus, at whose supreme command,
　We now approach to God,
　Before us in thy vesture stand,
　Thy vesture dipped in blood.

2 The tokens of thy dying love
　O let us all receive,

And feel the quickening Spirit move,
　And sensibly believe.

3 The cup of blessing, blest by thee,
　Let it thy blood impart;
　The bread thy mystic body be,
　To cheer each languid heart.

4 The living bread sent down from heaven,
　In us vouchsafe to be:
　Thy flesh for all the world is given,
　And all may live by thee.
　　　　　　　*Charles Wesley.*

**316 b**    *Hope Banishing Fear.*    C. M.

1 When I can read my title clear,
　To mansions in the skies,
　I'll bid farewell to every fear,
　And wipe my weeping eyes.

2 Should earth against my soul engage,
　And fiery darts be hurled,
　Then I can smile at Satan's rage,
　And face a frowning world,

3 Let cares, like a wild deluge, come,
　And storms of sorrow fall;
　May I but safely reach my home,
　My God, my heaven, my all.

4 There shall I bathe my weary soul,
　In seas of heavenly rest;
　And not a wave of trouble roll,
　Across my peaceful breast.
　　　　　　　*Watts.*

149

# THE LORD'S SUPPER.

**317 STATE STREET. S. M.**

1. O what de-light is this, Which now in Christ we know,

An earn-est of our glo-rious bliss, Our heav'n be-gun be-low!

*A Foretaste of Glory.*    S. M.

1 O what delight is this,
  Which now in Christ we know,
  An earnest of our glorious bliss,
  Our heaven begun below!

2 When he the table spreads,
  How royal is the cheer!
  With rapture we lift up our heads,
  And own that God is here.

3 The Lamb for sinners slain,
  Who died to die no more,
  Let all the ransomed sons of men,
  With all his hosts, adore.

4 Let earth and heaven be joined,
  His glories to display,
  And hymn the Saviour of mankind
  In one eternal day.

                *Charles Wesley.*

**318**      *Universal Gladness.*      S. M.

1 Glory to God on high.
  Our peace is made with Heaven;
  The Son of God came down to die,
  That we might be forgiven.

2 His precious blood was shed,
  His body bruised, for sin:
  Remember this in eating bread,
  And this in drinking wine.

3 Approach his royal board,
  In his rich garments clad:
  Join every tongue to praise the Lord,
  And every heart be glad.

4 The Father gives the Son:
  The Son, his flesh and blood:
  The Spirit seals; and faith puts on
  The righteousness of God.

                *Joseph Hart.*

**318 DETROIT. S. M.**          E. P. HASTINGS.

1. Glo-ry to God on high, Our peace is made with heav'n;

The Son of God came down to die, That we might be for-giv'n.

**319** EDWARDS. C. M.

*Moderato.*

ANON.

1. If hu-man kind-ness meets re-turn, And owns the grate-ful tie;

If ten-der thoughts within us burn To feel a friend is nigh.

---

*Gratitude and Love.* C. M.

1 If human kindness meets return,
  And owns the grateful tie;
  If tender thoughts within us burn
  To feel a friend is nigh:

2 O shall not warmer accents tell
  The gratitude we owe
  To Him who died our fears to quell,
  And save from endless woe?

3 While yet in anguish he surveyed
  Those pangs he would not flee,
  What love his latest words displayed!
  "Meet, and remember me."

4 Remember thee! thy death, thy shame,
  The griefs which thou didst bear!
  O memory, leave no other name
  So deeply graven there.
  *Gerard T. Noel.*

**320** *The Passion realized.* C. M.

1 Come, Holy Ghost, set to thy seal,
  Thine inward witness give,
  To all our waiting souls reveal
  The death by which we live.

2 Spectators of the pangs Divine
  O that we now may be,
  Discerning in the sacred sign
  His passion on the tree!

3 Give us to hear the dreadful sound
  Which told his mortal pain,
  Tore up the graves, and shook the ground,
  And rent the rocks in twain.

4 Repeat the Saviour's dying cry,
  In every heart so loud,
  That every heart may now reply,
  "This was the Son of God!"
  *C. Wesley.*

**321** *Discerning the Lord's Body.* 7s.

[Tune, Horton, page 152. 7s.]

1 Jesus, all-redeeming Lord,
  Magnify thy dying word;
  In thine ordinance appear;
  Come, and meet thy followers here.

2 In the rite thou hast enjoined,
  Let us now our Saviour find;
  Drink thy blood for sinners shed,
  Taste thee in the broken bread.

3 Thou our faithful hearts prepare;
  Thou thy pardoning grace declare;
  Thou that hast for sinners died,
  Show thyself the Crucified!

4 All the power of sin remove;
  Fill us with thy perfect love;
  Stamp us with the stamp divine;
  Seal our souls forever thine.
  *Charles Wesley.*

# THE LORD'S SUPPER.

## 322  HORTON. 7s.

1. At the Lamb's high feast we sing  Praise to our vic - to - rious King,

Who hath washed us   in   the   tide   Flow - ing   from   his   pierc - ed   side.

---

*Praise to our Victorious King.*  7s.

1 At the Lamb's high feast we sing
Praise to our victorious King,
Who hath washed us in the tide
Flowing from his piercèd side;

2 Praise we him, whose love divine
Gives his sacred blood for wine,
Gives his body for the feast,
Christ the Victim, Christ the Priest.

3 Where the paschal blood is poured,
Death's dark angel sheaths his sword;
Israel's hosts triumphant go
Through the wave that drowns the foe.

4 Praise we Christ, whose blood was shed,
Paschal Victim, paschal Bread;
With sincerity and love
Eat we manna from above.

5 Mighty Victim from the sky!
Hell's fierce powers beneath thee lie;
Thou hast conquered in the fight,
Thou hast brought us life and light:

6 Now no more can death appall,
Now no more the grave enthrall;
Thou hast opened paradise,
And in thee thy saints shall rise.
*Roman Breviary. Tr. by R. Campbell.*

## 323  *Our Paschal Lamb.*  S. M.
[Tune, State Street, page 150. S. M.]

1 Let all who truly bear
The bleeding Saviour's name,
Their faithful hearts with us prepare,
And eat the Paschal Lamb.

---

2 This eucharistic feast
Our every want supplies,
And still we by his death are blest,
And share his sacrifice.

3 Who thus our faith employ,
His sufferings to record,
E'en now we mournfully enjoy
Communion with our Lord.

4 We too with him are dead,
And shall, with him arise;
The cross on which he bows his head
Shall lift us to the skies.
*Charles Wesley.*

## 324  S. M.
*Partaking of the Lord's Supper.*
*Luke* xxi. 19-20.
[Tune, Detroit, page 150. S. M.]

1 Jesus, we thus obey
Thy last and kindest word,
Here in thine own appointed way,
We come to meet thee, Lord.

2 The way thou hast enjoin'd,
Thou wilt therein appear;
We come with confidence to find
Thy special presence here.

3 Whate'er the Almighty can
To pardon'd sinners give,
The fulness of our God made man,
We here with Christ receive.
*C. Wesley.*

# Section 14.
## CHRISTIAN WARFARE AND FAITH UNDER TRIALS.

**325  MANOAH. C. M.**                                    FROM ROSSINI.

1. Sing, O ye ransom'd of the Lord, Your great De - liv - 'rer sing,

Pil - grims, for Zi - on's ci - ty bound, Be joy - ful in your King.

*Isaiah* xxxv. 10.                    C. M.

1 Sing, O ye ransom'd of the Lord,
  Your great Deliv'rer sing;
  Pilgrims, for Zion's city bound,
  Be joyful in your King.

2 A hand Divine shall lead you on,
  Through all the blissful road,
  Till to the sacred mount you rise,
  And see your smiling God.

3 There garlands of immortal joy
  Shall bloom on every head;
  While sorrow, sighing, and distress,
  Like shadows, all are fled.

4 March on in your Redeemer's strength;
  Pursue his footsteps still;
  And let the prospect cheer your eye,
  While lab'ring up the hill.
                              *Doddridge.*

**326**        *Talking with God.*        C. M.

1 Talk with us, Lord, thyself reveal,
  While here o'er earth we rove;
  Speak to our hearts, and let us feel
  The kindling of thy love.

2 With thee conversing, we forget
  All time, and toil, and care;
  Labor is rest, and pain is sweet,
  If thou, my God, art here.

3 Here, then, my God, vouchsafe to stay,
  And bid my heart rejoice;
  My bounding heart shall own thy sway,
  And echo to thy voice.

4 Thou callest me to seek thy face—
  'Tis all I wish to seek;

To attend the whispers of thy grace,
  And hear thee inly speak.

5 Let this my every hour employ,
  Till I thy glory see;
  Enter into my Master's joy,
  And find my heaven in thee.
                              *Charles Wesley.*

**327**        *The Victorious Faith.*        C. M.

1 O for a faith that will not shrink,
  Though pressed by every foe,
  That will not tremble on the brink
  Of any earthly woe!

2 That will not murmur nor complain
  Beneath the chastening rod,
  But, in the hour of grief or pain,
  Will lean upon its God;

3 A faith that shines more bright and clear
  When tempests rage without;
  That when in danger knows no fear,
  In darkness feels no doubt;

4 That bears, unmoved, the world's dread
  Nor heeds its scornful smile;   [frown,
  That seas of trouble cannot drown,
  Nor Satan's art beguile.

5 A faith that keeps the narrow way
  Till life's last hour is fled,
  And with a pure and heavenly ray
  Illumes a dying bed.

6 Lord, give us such a faith as this,
  And then, whate'er may come,
  We'll taste, e'en here, the hallowed bliss
  Of an eternal home.
                              *William H. Bathurst.*

153

# CHRISTIAN WARFARE AND FAITH UNDER TRIALS.

## 328 FRIEND. C. M.

1. Lord, I be-lieve thy ev-'ry word, Thy ev-'ry prom-ise true,

And lo! I wait on thee, my Lord, Till I my strength re-new.

C. M.

*Strength renewed in waiting upon the Lord.*

1 Lord, I believe thy every word,
  Thy every promise true;
  And lo! I wait on thee, my Lord,
  Till I my strength renew.

2 If in this feeble flesh I may
  Awhile show forth thy praise,
  Jesus, support the tottering clay,
  And lengthen out my days.

3 If such a worm as I can spread
  The common Saviour's name,
  Let him who raised thee from the dead,
  Quicken my mortal frame.

4 Still let me live thy blood to show,
  Which purges every stain;
  And gladly linger out below
  A few more years in pain.

*Charles Wesley (when old and worn by sickness.)*

## 329 C. M.

*To live is Christ, and to die is Gain.*
*Phil. 1 : 21.*

1 Lord, it belongs not to my care
  Whether I die or live;
  To love and serve thee is my share,
  And this thy grace must give.

2 If life be long, I will be glad
  That I may long obey;
  If short, yet why should I be sad
  To soar to endless day?

3 Christ leads me through no darker rooms
  Than he went through before;
  He that unto God's kingdom comes
  Must enter by his door.

4 Come, Lord, when grace hath made me meet
  Thy blessed face to see;
  For, if thy work on earth be sweet,
  What will thy glory be?

5 Then I shall end my sad complaints,
  And weary, sinful days,
  And join with the triumphant saints
  Who sing Jehovah's praise.

*Richard Baxter.*

## 329 b *Worth of the soul.* C. M

1 What is the thing of greatest price,
  The whole creation round?
  That which was lost in Paradise,
  That which in Christ is found:

2 The soul of man—Jehovah's breath—
  That keeps two worlds at strife:
  Hell moves beneath to work its death,
  Heaven stoops to give it life.

3 God, to reclaim it, did not spare
  His well-beloved Son:
  Jesus, to save it, deigned to bear
  The sins of all in one.

4 The Holy Spirit sealed the plan,
  And pledged the blood Divine,
  To ransom every soul of man:
  That price was paid for mine.

5 Then let us gather round the cross,
  That knowledge to obtain;
  Not by the soul's eternal loss,
  But everlasting gain.

*Montgomery.*

154

**330  HENRY. C. M.**

1. A - wake, my soul! stretch ev - 'ry nerve, And press with vig - or on:

A heav'n - ly race de - mands thy zeal, And an im - mor - tal crown.

### The Christian Race.  C. M.

1 Awake, my soul! stretch every nerve,
   And press with vigor on :
   A heav'nly race demands thy zeal,
   And an immortal crown.

2 A cloud of witnesses around
   Hold thee in full survey ;
   Forget the steps already trod,
   And onward urge thy way.

3 'Tis God's all-animating voice
   That calls thee from on high ;
   'Tis his own hand presents the prize
   To thine aspiring eye :

4 That prize, with peerless glories bright,
   Which shall new lustre boast,
   When victors' wreaths and monarchs' gems
   Shall blend in common dust.

5 Blest Saviour ! introduced by thee,
   Have I my race begun ;
   And crown'd with vict'ry, at thy feet
   I'll lay my honors down.
                                    *Doddridge.*

**331**      *Taking the Cross.*      C. M.

1 Must Jesus bear the cross alone,
   And all the world go free ?
   No ; there's a cross for every one,
   And there's a cross for me.

2 The consecrated cross I'll bear
   Till death shall set me free,
   And then go home my crown to wear,
   For there's a crown for me.

3 Upon the crystal pavement, down
   At Jesus' piercèd feet,
   Joyful, I'll cast my golden crown
   And his dear name repeat.

4 And palms shall wave and harps shall ring
   Beneath heaven's arches high ;
   The Lord that lives, the ransomed sing,
   That lives no more to die.

5 Oh, precious cross ! oh, glorious crown !
   Oh, resurrection day !
   Ye angels, from the stars come down,
   And bear my soul away.
                                    *G. N. Allen.*

**332**      *Psalm* lxxi. 15.      C. M.

1 My Saviour, my Almighty Friend,
   When I begin thy praise,
   Where will the growing numbers end,
   The numbers of thy grace ?

2 Thou art my everlasting trust ;
   Thy goodness I adore :
   Send down thy grace, O blessed Lord,
   That I may love thee more.

3 My feet shall travel all the length
   Of the celestial road :
   And march with courage in thy strength,
   To see the Lord my God.

4 Awake ! awake ! my tuneful powers :
   With this delightful song
   I'll entertain the darkest hours,
   Nor think the season long.
                                    *Watts.*

155

# CHRISTIAN WARFARE AND FAITH UNDER TRIALS.

333  HE LEADETH ME  L. M. D.                        W. B. BRADBURY. 1816-1868.

1. He lead - eth me! O bless-ed thought! O words with heav'nly comfort fraught!
2. Sometimes 'mid scenes of deep-est gloom, Sometimes where E-den's bow-ers bloom,
3. Lord! I would clasp thy hand in mine, Nor ev - er mur - mur nor re - pine;
4. And when my task on earth is done, When by thy grace the vic-tory's won,

What-e'er I do, wher-e'er I be,   Still 'tis God's hand that lead - eth me.
By wa - ters still, o'er troubled sea,— Still 'tis his hand that lead - eth me.
Con - tent what - ev - er lot I see,  Since 'tis my God that lead - eth me.
E'en death's cold wave I will not flee,  Since God thro' Jor - dan lead - eth me.

REFRAIN.

He lead-eth me! he lead-eth me! By his own hand he lead - eth me;

His faith-ful follower I would be, For by his hand he lead - eth me.

J. H. GILMORE.

156

**334 TALLIS' EVENING HYMN. L. M.**

1. E - ter - nal Beam of light di - vine, Foun-tain of un - ex - haust - ed love,

In whom the Fa-ther's glo-ries shine, Through earth beneath and heav'n a - bove.

*Patient Thankfulness and Trust.* L. M.

1 Eternal Beam of light divine,
  Fountain of unexhausted love,
  In whom the Father's glories shine,
  Through earth beneath, and heaven above;

2 Jesus, the weary wanderer's rest,
  Give me thy easy yoke to bear;
  With steadfast patience arm my breast,
  With spotless love and lowly fear.

3 Thankful I take the cup from thee,
  Prepared and mingled by thy skill;
  Though bitter to the taste it be,
  Powerful the wounded soul to heal.

4 Be thou, O Rock of ages, nigh!
  So shall each murmuring thought be gone,
  And grief, and fear, and care shall fly,
  As clouds before the midday sun.

5 Speak to my warring passions, "Peace;"
  Say to my trembling heart, "Be still;"
  Thy power my strength and fortress is,
  For all things serve thy sovereign will.

6 O Death! where is thy sting? Where now
  Thy boasted victory, O Grave?
  Who shall contend with God? or who
  Can hurt whom God delights to save?
                                *Charles Wesley.*

**335** *In hope, believing against hope.* L. M.

1 Away, my unbelieving fear!
  Fear shall in me no more have place;
  My Saviour doth not yet appear,
  He hides the brightness of his face;

2 But shall I therefore let him go,
  And basely to the tempter yield?
  No, in the strength of Jesus no,
  I never will give up my shield.

3 Although the vine its fruits deny,
  Although the olives yield no oil,
  The withering fig-trees droop and die,
  The fields elude the tiller's toil,

4 The empty stall no herd afford,
  And perish all the bleating race,
  Yet will I triumph in the Lord,—
  The God of my salvation praise.

5 In hope believing against hope.
  Jesus, my Lord, my God, I claim;
  Jesus my strength shall lift me up,
  Salvation is in Jesus' name;

6 To me he soon shall bring it nigh,
  My soul shall then outstrip the wind,
  On wings of love mount up on high,
  And leave the world and sin behind.
                                *Charles Wesley.*

**336 HAMBURG. L. M.** GREGORIAN CHANT.

1. Thy will be done! I will not fear The fate pro-vid-ed by thy love;

Though clouds and darkness shroud me here, I know that all is bright a-bove.

*Resignation.* L. M.

1 Thy will be done! I will not fear
   The fate provided by thy love;
   Though clouds and darkness shroud me here,
   I know that all is bright above.

2 The stars of heaven are shining on,
   Though these frail eyes are dimmed with
      tears;
   The hopes of earth indeed are gone,
   But are not ours the immortal years?

3 Father, forgive the heart that clings,
   Thus trembling, to the things of time;
   And bid my soul on angel wings,
   Ascend into a purer clime.

4 There shall no doubts disturb its trust,
   No sorrows dim celestial love:
   But these afflictions of the dust,
   Like shadows of the night, remove.

5 E'en now, above, there's radiant day,
   While clouds and darkness brood below;
   Then. Father, joyful on my way
   To drink the bitter cup I go.

                              *J. Roscoe.*

**337**  *Sympathetic Love.*  L. M.

1 O love divine, that stooped to share
   Our sharpest pang, our bitterest tear!
   On thee we cast each earthborn care:
   We smile at pain while thou art near.

2 Though long the weary way we tread.
   And sorrow crown each lingering year.
   No path we shun, no darkness dread,
   Our hearts still whispering, "Thou art
      near!"

3 When drooping pleasure turns to grief,
   And trembling faith is changed to fear,
   The murmuring wind. the quivering leaf,
   Shall softly tell us, "Thou art near!"

4 On thee we fling our burdening woe.
   O Love divine. forever dear;
   Content to suffer while we know,
   Living and dying. thou art near!
                          *Oliver W. Holmes.*

**337 b**   *Love the chief joy.*   L. M.

1 Of all the joys we mortals know,
   Jesus, thy love exceeds the rest;
   Love the best blessing here below.
   The nearest image of the blest.

2 While we are held in thine embrace.
   There's not a thought attempts to rove;
   Each smile upon thy beauteous face
   Fixes, and charms, and fires our love.

3 While of thy absence we complain.
   And long, or weep in all we do,
   There's a strange pleasure in the pain,
   And tears have their own sweetness too.

4 When round thy courts by day we rove,
   Or ask the watchman of the night
   For some kind tidings of our love,
   Thy very name creates delight.

5 Jesus, our God, yet rather come,—
   Our eyes would dwell upon thy face:
   'Tis best to see our Lord at home,
   And feel the presence of his grace.
                              *Watts.*

# CHRISTIAN WARFARE AND FAITH UNDER TRIALS.

## 338  HEBRON.  L. M.

1. Thou Lamb of God, thou Prince of peace, For thee my thirst-y soul doth pine; My long-ing heart im - plores thy grace; O make me in thy like-ness shine.

*Meekness and Patience.*  L. M.

1 Thou Lamb of God, thou Prince of peace,
  For thee my thirsty soul doth pine;
  My longing heart implores thy grace;
  O make me in thy likeness shine.

2 When pain o'er my weak flesh prevails,
  With lamb-like patience arm my breast;
  When grief my wounded soul assails
  In lowly meekness may I rest.

3 Close by thy side still may I keep,
  Howe'er life's various currents flow;
  With steadfast eye mark every step,
  And follow thee where'er thou go.

4 Thou, Lord, the dreadful fight hast won;
  Alone thou hast the wine-press trod;
  In me thy strengthening grace be shown:
  O may I conquer through thy blood.

5 So, when on Zion thou shalt stand,
  And all heaven's host adore their King,
  Shall I be found at thy right hand,
  And, free from pain, thy glories sing.
  *C. F. Richter.  Tr. by J. Wesley.*

## 339  The Pilgrim's Song.  7s.
[Tune, Pleyel's Hymn, page 85.  7s.]

1 Children of the heavenly King,
  As we journey let us sing;
  Sing our Saviour's worthy praise,
  Glorious in his works and ways.

2 We are trav'ling home to God
  In the way our fathers trod;
  They are happy now, and we
  Soon their happiness shall see.

3 O ye banished seed, be glad!
  Christ our Advocate is made:

Us to save, our flesh assumes,
  Brother to our souls becomes.

4 Fear not, brethren, joyful stand
  On the borders of our land;
  Jesus Christ, our Father's Son,
  Bids us undismay'd go on.

5 Lord! obediently we'll go,
  Gladly leaving all below:
  Only thou our leader be,
  And we still will follow thee.
  *Cennick.*

## 340  With Christ.  S. M.
[Tune, Franklin Square, page 160.  S. M.]

1 Jesus, one word from thee
  Fills my sad soul with peace:
  My griefs are like a tossing sea;
  They hear thy voice and cease.

2 Soon as thy pitying face
  Shone through my stormy fears,
  The storm swept by, nor left a trace,
  Save the sweet dew of tears.

3 And when thou call'st me, Lord,
  Where thickest dangers be,
  Even the waves a path afford;
  I walk the waves with thee.

4 With thee within my bark
  I'll dare death's threatening tide,
  Nor count the passage strange or dark
  With Jesus by my side.

5 Dear Lord, thy faithful grace
  I know and I adore:
  What shall it be to see thy face
  In heaven, forevermore!
  *Hervey D. Ganse.*

# CHRISTIAN WARFARE AND FAITH UNDER TRIALS.

## 341 FRANKLIN SQUARE. S. M.

*With energy.*

1. My spir - it on thy care, Blest Sav - iour, I re - cline;

Thou wilt not leave me to de - spair, For thou art Love di - vine.

*In the Saviour's Care.* S. M.

1 My spirit on thy care,
  Blest Saviour, I recline ;
  Thou wilt not leave me in despair,
  For thou art Love divine.

2 In thee I place my trust,
  On thee I calmly rest ;
  I know thee good, I know thee just,
  And count thy choice the best.

3 Whate'er events betide,
  Thy will they all perform ;
  Safe in thy breast my head I hide,
  Nor fear the coming storm.

4 Let good or ill befall,
  It must be good for me :
  Secure of having thee in all,
  Of having all in thee.

  *Henry F Lyte.*

## 342 S. M.

*My times are in thy hand. Ps. xxxi. 15.*

1 " My times are in thy hand : "
  My God, I wish them there :
  My life, my friends, my soul, I leave
  Entirely to thy care.

2 "My times are in thy hand,"
  Whatever they may be ;
  Pleasing or painful, dark or bright,
  As best may seem to thee.

3 " My times are in thy hand : "
  Why should I doubt or fear ?
  My Father's hand will never cause
  His child a needless tear.

4 " My times are in thy hand,"
  Jesus, the crucified !
  The hand my cruel sins had pierced
  Is now my guard and guide.

5 " My times are in thy hand ; "
  I'll always trust in thee :
  And, after death, at thy right hand
  I shall forever be.

  *W. F. Lloyd.*

## 343 *Believers Encouraged.* S. M.

1 Your harps, ye trembling saints,
  Down from the willows take :
  Loud to the praise of love divine
  Bid every string awake.

2 Though in a foreign land,
  We are not far from home ;
  And nearer to our house above
  We every moment come.

3 His grace will to the end
  Stronger and brighter shine :
  Nor present things, nor things to come,
  Shall quench the spark divine.

4 When we in darkness walk,
  Nor feel the heavenly flame,
  Then is the time to trust our God,
  And rest upon his name.

5 Soon shall our doubts and fears
  Subside at his control :
  His loving-kindness shall break through
  The midnight of the soul.

  *Toplady, alt. by B. W. Noel.*

160

# CHRISTIAN WARFARE AND FAITH UNDER TRIALS.

## 344 WEBB. 7s & 6s. D.

1. O when shall I see Je - sus, And reign with him above, And from that flowing fountain

D. S.—And with my blessed Je - sus

FINE.

D. S.

Drink ev-er-lasting love? When shall I be de - liv-er'd From this vain world of sin,

Drink endless pleasures in?

*Longing for Heaven.* 7s & 6s.

1 O when shall I see Jesus,
    And reign with him above,
    And from that flowing fountain
    Drink everlasting love?
    When shall I be deliver'd
    From this vain world of sin,
    And with my blessed Jesus
    Drink endless pleasures in?

2 But now I am a soldier;
    My Captain's gone before,
    He's given me my orders,
    And bids me not give o'er;
    And, if I hold out faithful,
    A crown of life he'll give;
    And all his valiant soldiers
    Shall ever with him live.

3 O do not be discouraged,
    For Jesus is your friend;
    And, if you lack for knowledge,
    He'll not refuse to lend :
    Neither will he upbraid you,
    Though often you request :
    He'll give you grace to conquer,
    And take you home to rest.
                        *Unknown.*

## 345 *Peace and Joy.* 7s & 6s.

1 Sometimes a light surprises
    The Christian while he sings;
    It is the Lord who rises
    With healing on his wings;

When comforts are declining,
    He grants the soul again
    A season of clear shining,
    To cheer it after rain.

2 In holy contemplation,
    We sweetly then pursue
    The theme of God's salvation,
    And find it ever new :
    Set free from present sorrow,
    We cheerfully can say,
    Let the unknown to morrow
    Bring with it what it may.

3 It can bring with it nothing
    But he will bear us through;
    Who gives the lilies clothing,
    Will clothe his people too :
    Beneath the spreading heavens
    No creature but is fed;
    And he who feeds the ravens
    Will give his children bread.

4 Though vine nor fig-tree neither
    Their wonted fruit should bear,
    Though all the fields should wither,
    Nor flocks nor herds be there;
    Yet God the same abiding,
    His praise shall tune my voice;
    For while in him confiding,
    I cannot but rejoice.
                        *Wm. Cowper.*

CHRISTIAN WARFARE AND FAITH UNDER TRIALS.

## 346 WELTON. L. M.

1. Je-sus, my Sav-iour, Brother, Friend, On whom I cast my ev-'ry care,

On whom for all things I de-pend,— In-spire, and then ac-cept my prayer.

*A Watchful Spirit.*    L. M.

1 Jesus, my Saviour, Brother, Friend,
On whom I cast my every care,—
On whom for all things I depend,—
Inspire, and then accept my prayer.

2 If I have tasted of thy grace,
The grace that sure salvation brings,
If with me now thy Spirit stays,
And hov'ring, hides me in his wings:

3 Still let him with my weakness stay,
Nor for a moment's space depart;
Evil and danger turn away,
And keep till he renews my heart.

4 When to the right or left I stray,
His voice behind me may I hear,
"Return, and walk in Christ thy way;
Fly back to Christ, for sin is near!"

5 Jesus, I fain would walk in thee.
From nature's every path retreat:
Thou art my way: my leader be,
And set upon the rock my feet.
*C. Wesley.*

**347** *Watchful dependence on Christ.* L. M.

1 Uphold me, Saviour, or I fall:
O reach me out thy gracious hand!
Only on thee for help I call:
Only by thee in faith I stand.

2 Pierce, fill me, with an humble fear;
My utter helplessness reveal!
Satan and sin are always near,
Thee may I always nearer feel.

3 O that to thee my constant mind
Might with an even flame aspire!
Pride in its earliest motions find,
And mark the risings of desire!

4 O that my tender soul might fly
The first abhor'd approach of ill;
Quick, as the apple of an eye,
The slightest touch of sin to feel!

5 Till thou anew my soul create,
Still may I strive, and watch, and pray,—
Humbly and confidently wait,
And long to see the perfect day.
*C. Wesley.*

**347 b**   *Ezekiel* xxxvi. 29, 30.   L. M.

1 Father, supply my every need;
Sustain the life thyself hast given:
O grant the never-failing bread,
The manna that comes down from heaven.

2 The gracious fruits of righteousness,
Thy blessings' unexhausted store,
In me abundantly increase,
Nor ever let me hunger more!

3 Let me no more, in deep complaint,
"My leanness, O my leanness!" cry;
Alone consumed with pining want,
Of all my Father's children, I.

4 The painful thirst, the fond desire,
Thy joyous presence shall remove!
But my full soul shall still require
A whole eternity of love.
*C. Wesley.*

162

**348 INTERCESSION. L. M. 6 Lines.**  J. FAWCETT

1. { Thou hid-den source of calm re - pose, Thou all-suf - fi - cient Love Di-vine, /
   My help and ref-uge from my foes, Se-cure I am if thou art mine: }

And lo! from sin, and grief, and shame, I hide me, Je - sus, in thy name.

---

**" All in All."** L. M. 6 lines.

1 Thou hidden source of calm repose,
 Thou all-sufficient Love Divine,
 My help and refuge from my foes,
 Secure I am if thou art mine!
 And lo! from sin, and grief, and shame.
 I hide me, Jesus, in thy name.

2 Thy mighty name salvation is,
 And keeps my happy soul above :
 Comfort it brings, and power, and peace.
 And joy, and everlasting love :
 To me, with thy great name, are given
 Pardon, and holiness, and heaven.

3 Jesus, my All in all thou art,
 My rest in toil : my ease in pain :
 The med'cine of my broken heart :
 In war, my peace ; in loss, my gain .
 My smile beneath the tyrant's frown ,
 In shame, my glory and my crown,

4 In want, my plentiful supply ,
 In weakness, my almighty power ;
 In bonds, my perfect liberty ;
 My light, in Satan's darkest hour ;
 In grief my joy unspeakable :
 My life in death—my All in all.
 *C. Wesley.*

**349** *General Redemption.* L. M. 6 lines.

1 Would Jesus have the sinner die ?
 Why hangs he then on yonder tree ?
 What means that strange expiring cry ?
 ( Sinners, he prays for you and me : )
 " Forgive them, Father, O forgive,
 They know not that by me they live ! "

2 Jesus, descended from above,
 Our loss of Eden to retrieve,
 Great God of universal love,
 If all the world through thee may live
 In us a quick'ning spirit be,
 And witness thou hast died for me.

3 Thou loving, all-atoning Lamb,
 Thee—by thy painful agony,
 Thy bloody sweat, thy grief and shame,
 Thy cross and passion on the tree,
 Thy precious death and life—I pray,
 Take all, take all my sins away.
 *C. Wesley.*

*Doxology.*

Shout to the great Jehovah's praise !
Ye sons of glory and of grace,
One God in persons three adore,
The same in Majesty and power :
Ye suff'ring and triumphant host
Praise Father, Son, and Holy Ghost.
 *C. Wesley.*

**350** NETTLETON. 8s & 7s. D. JOHN WYETH.

Might-y God, while an-gels bless thee, May a mor-tal lisp thy name?
Lord of men, as well as an-gels, Thou art ev-ery creature's theme.

Lord of ev-ery land and na-tion, An-cient of e-ter-nal days!

Sound-ed through the wide cre-a-tion Be thy just and law-ful praise.

*Praise to the Redeemer.* 8s & 7s. D.

1 Mighty God, while angels bless thee,
    May a mortal lisp thy name?
Lord of men, as well as angels,
    Thou art every creature's theme.
Lord of every land and nation,
    Ancient of eternal days!
Sounded through the wide creation
    By thy just and lawful praise.

2 For the grandeur of thy nature—
    Grand beyond a seraph's thought—
For created works of power.
    Works with skill and kindness wrought:
For thy providence that governs
    Through thine empire's wide domain,
Wings an angel—guides a sparrow—
    Blessed be thy gentle reign.

3 But thy rich, thy free redemption,
    Dark through brightness all along!
Thought is poor, and poor expression;
    Who dare sing that awful song?
Brightness of the Father's glory,
    Shall thy praise unuttered lie?
Fly, my tongue, such guilty silence!
    Sing the Lord who came to die.

*Robinson.*

**351** 8s & 7s. D.

*Praise to Christ for his Divine Grace.*

1 Come, thou fount of every blessing,
    Tune my heart to sing thy grace;
Streams of mercy never ceasing,
    Calls for songs of loudest praise:
Teach me some melodious sonnet,
    Sung by flaming tongues above;
Praise the mount!—I'm fixed upon it,
    Mount of thy redeeming love.

2 Here I'll raise my Ebenezer;
    Hither by thy help I'm come,
And I hope, by thy good pleasure,
    Safely to arrive at home;
Jesus sought me when a stranger,
    Wand'ring from the fold of God:
He, to rescue me from danger,
    Interpos'd his precious blood!

3 O! to grace how great a debtor
    Daily I'm constrain'd to be!
Let thy goodness, like a fetter,
    Bind my wand'ring heart to thee:
Prone to wander, Lord, I feel it;
    Prone to leave the God I love—
Here's my heart, O take and seal it,
    Seal it for thy courts above.

*Huntingdon.*

# CHRISTIAN WARFARE AND FAITH UNDER TRIALS.

**352  MADRID. 8s & 7. D.**  SPANISH AIR.

1. Love Di-vine, all love ex-cell-ing,  Joy of heav'n, to earth come down,
2. Breathe, O breathe thy loving Spir-it  In-to ev-'ry trembling heart!
3. Come, Al-might-y to de-liv-er,  Let us all thy life re-ceive,

Fix in us thy hum-ble dwell-ing,  All thy faith-ful mercies crown!
Let us all in thee in-her-it,  Let us find that second rest.
Sud-den-ly re-turn, and nev-er,  Nev-er more thy temples leave:

Je-sus, thou art all com-pas-sion,  Pure un-bound-ed love thou art;
Take a-way our bent to sin-ning,  Al-pha and O-me-ga be,
Thee we would be al-ways bless-ing;  Serve thee as thy hosts a-bove;

Vis-it us with thy sal-va-tion;  En-ter ev-'ry trembling heart.
End of faith, as its be-gin-ning,  Set our hearts at lib-er-ty.
Pray, and praise thee, with-out ceas-ing,  Glo-ry in thy per-fect love.

C. WESLEY.

165

353 CONTRAST. 8s.

DEFBURY.

1. How tedious and tasteless the hours   When Je-sus no long-er I see!
2. His name yields the richest per-fume,   And sweeter than mu-sic his voice;

Sweet prospects, sweet birds, and sweet flow'rs, Have all lost their sweetness to me:
His presence dis-per-ses my gloom, And makes all with-in me re-joice:

The mid-summer sun shines but dim, The fields strive in vain to look gay;
I should, were he al-ways thus nigh, Have noth-ing to wish or to fear,

But when I am hap-py in him, De-cember's as pleasant as May.
No mor-tal so hap-py as I, My summer would last all the year.

3 Content with beholding his face,
   My all to his pleasure resign'd,
   No changes of season or place
   Would make any change in my mind:
   While bless'd with a sense of his love,
   A palace a toy would appear;
   And prisons would palaces prove,
   If Jesus would dwell with me there.

4 Dear Lord, if indeed I am thine,
   If thou art my sun and my song,
   Say why do I languish and pine?
   And why are my winters so long?
   O drive these dark clouds from my sky,—
   Thy soul-cheering presence restore;
   Or take me to thee up on high,
   Where winters and clouds are no more.

*Newton.*

354 GANGES. C. P. M.
CHANDLER.

1. Come on, my part-ners in dis-tress, My com-rades through the wil-der-ness,

Who still your bod-ies feel: A-while for-get your griefs and fears,

And look be-yond this vale of tears To that ce-les-tial hill.

*Full assurance of hope.*   C. P. M.

1 Come on, my partners in distress,
My comrades through the wilderness,
Who still your bodies feel :
Awhile forget your griefs and fears,
And look beyond this vale of tears
To that celestial hill.

2 Beyond the bounds of time and space
Look forward to that heavenly place,
The saints' secure abode :
On faith's strong eagle-pinions rise,
And force your passage to the skies,
And scale the mount of God.

3 Who suffer with our Master here,
We shall before his face appear.
And by his side sit down :
To patient faith the prize is sure ;
And all that to the end endure
The cross, shall wear the crown.

4 Thrice-blessèd, bliss inspiring hope !
It lifts the fainting spirits up,
It brings to life the dead :
Our conflicts here shall soon be past,
And you and I ascend at last,
Triumphant with our Head.

*C. Wesley.*

355   *Gently lead us.*   8s, 7s & 4s.

[ Tune, Zion, page 136. 8s, 7s & 4s.]

1 Gently, Lord, O gently lead us
Through this gloomy vale of tears ;
And, O Lord, in mercy give us
Thy rich grace in all our fears.
*O refresh us,*
*Travelling through this wilderness.*

2 When temptation's darts assail us,
When in devious paths we stray,
Let thy goodness never fail us,
Lead us in thy perfect way.

3 In the hour of pain and anguish,
In the hour when death draws near,
Suffer not our hearts to languish,
Suffer not our souls to fear.

4 When this mortal life is ended,
Bid us in thine arms to rest.
Till, by angel bands attended,
We awake among the blest.

*Thomas Hastings.*

*Doxology.*   C. P. M.

To Father, Son, and Holy Ghost,
The God whom heaven's triumphant host
And saints on earth adore ;
Be glory as in ages past,
As now it is, and so shall last,
When time shall be no more.

356  RIPLEY.  8s & 7s. D.

DR. L. MASON.

FINE.

{ Full of trem - bling ex - pec - ta - tion,  Feel - ing much, and fear - ing more, }
1. { Might-y God  of  my  sal - va - tion,  I  thy  time - ly  aid  im - plore. }

D.C.—By thy sor - er griefs to cheer me,  By thy more than mor - tal  pain.

D. C.

Suff-'ring Son  of  man, be  near  me,  In my  suff - 'rings to sus - tain;

*In Deep Affliction.*  8s & 7s.

1  Full of trembling expectation,
   Feeling much, and fearing more,
   Mighty God of my salvation,
   I thy timely aid implore.
   Suffering Son of man, be near me,
   In my sufferings to sustain;
   By thy sorer griefs to cheer me,
   By thy more than mortal pain.

2  By thy most severe temptation
   In that dark Satanic hour,
   By thy last mysterious passion,
   Screen me from the adverse power.
   By thy fainting in the garden,
   By thy dreadful death, I pray,
   Write upon my heart the pardon ;
   Take my sins and fears away.
                        *C. Wesley.*

356 b                        8s & 7s.

1  Holy Ghost! dispel our sadness,
   Pierce the clouds of sinful night :
   Come, thou source of joy and gladness,
   Breathe thy life, and spread thy light!
   Come, thou best of all donations
   God doth give when men implore,
   Having thy sweet consolations
   We need wish for nothing more.

2  Author of the new creation!
   Let us now thine influence prove ;
   Make our hearts thy habitation.
   Shed abroad a Saviour's love
   From that height that knows no measure
   As a gracious rain descend,
   Bringing down the richest treasure
   We can ask or God can send.

3  Manifest thy love forever,
   Fence us in on every side ;
   In distress be our Reliever,
   Guard and teach, support and guide.
   Hear, oh hear our supplication,
   Blessed Spirit! God of peace !
   Rest upon this congregation
   With the fullness of thy grace.
                        *Anon.*

**357 PRECIOUS NAME.** 8s & 7s.

W. H. DOANE.

1. Take the name of Je - sus with you, Child of sor - row and of woe,
2. Take the name of Je - sus ev - er, As a shield from ev - 'ry snare;
3. At the name of Je - sus bow - ing, Fall - ing prostrate at his feet,

It will joy and com - fort give you, Take it then where'er you go.
If temp - ta - tions round you gath - er, Breathe that ho - ly name in prayer.
King of kings in heav'n we'll crown him, When our jour - ney is com - plete.

REFRAIN.

Prec - ious name, O how sweet! Hope of earth and joy of heav'n;

Prec-ious name, O how sweet!

Prec-ious name, O how sweet! Hope of earth and joy of heav'n.

Precious name, O how sweet, how sweet!

LYDIA BAXTER. 1873

## 358 FARNHAM. C. M. D.

*Rather Slow.*

Fa - ther, be-hold with gra-cious eyes The souls be-fore thy throne,
Who now pre-sent their sac - ri - fice, And seek thee in thy Son.

Well pleased in him thy - self de-clare, Thy pard-'ning love re - veal,

The peace-ful an - swer of our pray'r To ev - 'ry con-science seal.

*Waiting in the Sanctuary.* C. M.

1 Father, behold with gracious eyes
   The souls before thy throne,
   Who now present their sacrifice,
   And seek thee in thy Son.
   Well pleased in him thyself declare,
   Thy pard'ning love reveal,
   The peaceful answer of our prayer
   To every conscience seal.

2 Meanest of all thy servants, I
   Those happier spirits meet,
   And mix with theirs my feeble cry,
   And worship at thy feet.
   On me, on all, some gift bestow,
   Some blessing now impart:
   The seed of life eternal sow
   In every mournful heart.

3 Thy loving, powerful Spirit shed,
   And speak our sins forgiven,
   Or haste throughout the lump to spread
   The sanctifying leaven.
   Refresh us with a ceaseless shower

Of graces from above
Till all receive the perfect power
Of everlasting love.
                            *C. Wesley.*

## 359 *The Rest of Faith.* C. M.

1 Lord, I believe a rest remains,
   To all thy people known;
   A rest where pure enjoyment reigns,
   And thou art loved alone:
   A rest where all our soul's desire
   Is fixed on things above;
   Where fear, and sin, and grief expire,
   Cast out by perfect love.

2 O that I now the rest might know,
   Believe, and enter in!
   Now, Saviour, now the power bestow,
   And let me cease from sin!
   Remove this hardness from my heart,
   This unbelief remove:
   To me the rest of faith impart,
   The Sabbath of thy love.
                            *C. Wesley.*

# CHRISTIAN WARFARE AND FAITH UNDER TRIALS.

**360 MORROW. C. M.**

*God, my Sufficient Portion.* C. M.

1 My God, my Portion, and my Love,
My everlasting All,
I've none but thee in heaven above,
Or on this earthly ball.

2 What empty things are all the skies,
And this inferior clod!
There's nothing here deserves my joys,
There's nothing like my God.

3 To thee I owe my wealth, and friends,
And health, and safe abode:
Thanks to thy name for meaner things;
But they are not my God.

4 How vain a toy is glittering wealth,
If once compared to thee!
Or what's my safety, or my health,
Or all my friends to me?

5 Were I possessor of the earth,
And called the stars my own,
Without thy graces and thyself,
I were a wretch undone.

6 Let others stretch their arms like seas,
And grasp in all the shore;
Grant me the visits of thy grace,
And I desire no more.

*Isaac Watts.*

**DEEMS. C. M. (Second Tune.)**

171

361 ROLLAND. L. M.

1. Lord, how secure and blest are they Who feel the joys of pardon'd sin! Should storms of wrath shake earth and sea, Their minds have heav'n and peace within, Their minds have heav'n and peace within.

*"Our Rejoicing is This"* — L. M.

1 Lord, how secure and blest are they
   Who feel the joys of pardoned sin !
Should storms of wrath shake earth and sea,
   Their minds have heaven and peace
      within.

2 The day glides sweetly o'er their heads,
   Made up of innocence and love :
And soft and silent as the shades
   Their nightly minutes gently move.

3 Quick as their thoughts their joys come on,
   But fly not half so fast away ;
Their souls are ever bright as noon,
   And calm as summer evenings be.

4 They scorn to seek our golden toys,
   But spend the day and share the night
In numbering o'er the richer joys
   That heaven prepares for their delight.
                              *Watts.*

362      *Friend of the friendless.*      L. M.

1 God of my life, to thee I call,
   Afflicted at thy feet I fall ;
When the great water-floods prevail,
   Leave not my trembling heart to fail.

2 Friend of the friendless and the faint,
   Where should I lodge my deep complaint ?
Where, but with thee, whose open door
   Invites the helpless and the poor ?

3 Did ever mourner plead with thee,
   And thou refuse that mourner's plea ?
Does not the promise still remain,
   That none shall seek thy face in vain ?

4 Poor I may be, despised, forgot,
   Yet God, my God, forgets me not ;
And he is safe, and must succeed,
   For whom the Saviour deigns to plead.
                              *William Cowper.*

363      *Psalm* lxviii. 17–18.      L. M.

1 Lord, when thou didst ascend on high,
   Ten thousand angels filled the sky ;
Those heavenly guards around thee wait,
   Like chariots that attend thy state.

2 Not Sinai's mountain could appear
   More glorious, when the Lord was there :
While he pronounced his dreadful law,
   And struck the chosen tribes with awe.

3 How bright the triumph none can tell,
   When the rebellious powers of hell,
That thousand souls had captives made,
   Were all in chains, like captives, led.

4 Raised by his Father to the throne,
   He sent the promised Spirit down,
With gifts and grace for rebel men,
   That God might dwell on earth again.
                              *Watts.*

**364  SWEET HOUR OF PRAYER. L. M.**  WM. B. BRADBURY.

1. Sweet hour of prayer, sweet hour of prayer! That calls me from a world of care,

*D.C.*—And oft es-caped the temp-ter's snare By thy re-turn, sweet hour of prayer;

FINE.

And bids me at my Fa-ther's throne Make all my wants and wish-es known,

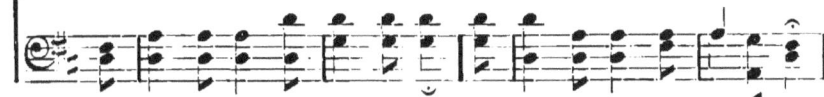

And oft es-caped the temp-ter's snare By thy re-turn, sweet hour of prayer.

*D.C.*

In sea-sons of dis-tress and grief, My soul has oft-en found re-lief,

2 Sweet hour of prayer! sweet hour of prayer!
Thy wings shall my petition bear,
To him whose truth and faithfulness,
Engage the waiting soul to bless:
And since he bids me seek his face,
Believe his word, and trust his grace,
I'll cast on him my every care,
And wait for thee, sweet hour of prayer!

3 Sweet hour of prayer! sweet hour of prayer!
May I thy consolation share;
Till from Mount Pisgah's lofty height,
I view my home, and take my flight;
This robe of flesh I'll drop, and rise
To seize the everlasting prize:
And shout, while passing through the air,
Farewell, farewell, sweet hour of prayer.

CHRISTIAN WARFARE AND FAITH UNDER TRIALS.

**365 CREATION. L. M.**

HAYDN.

1. Je - sus, thou Joy of lov - ing hearts! Thou Fount of life! thou Light of men!

From the best bliss that earth im - parts, We turn un - filled to thee a - gain.

*The joy of loving hearts.* L. M.

1 Jesus, thou Joy of loving hearts!
  Thou Fount of life! thou Light of men!
  From the best bliss that earth imparts,
  We turn unfilled to thee again.

2 Thy truth unchanged hath ever stood ;
  Thou savest those that on thee call !
  To them that seek thee, thou art good,
  To them that find thee, all in all.

3 We taste thee, O thou Living Bread,
  And long to feast upon thee still ;
  We drink of thee, the Fountain Head,
  And thirst our souls from thee to fill !

4 Our restless spirits yearn for thee,
  Where'er our changeful lot is cast ;
  Glad, when thy gracious smile we see.
  Blest, when our faith can hold thee fast.

5 O Jesus, ever with us stay ;
  Make all our moments calm and bright ;
  Chase the dark night of sin away,
  Shed o'er the world thy holy light !
    *Bernard of Clairvaux. Tr. by R. Palmer.*

**366** L. M.

*His loving-kindness better than life.*

1 O God, thou art my God alone ;
  Early to thee my soul shall cry :
  A pilgrim in a land unknown,
  A thirsty land, whose springs are dry.

2 Thee in the watches of the night,
  When I remember on my bed,

Thy presence makes the darkness light ;
Thy guardian wings are round my head.

3 Better than life itself, thy love ;
  Dearer than all beside to me ;
  For whom have I in heaven above,
  Or what on earth, compared with thee ?

4 Praise with my heart, my mind, my voice,
  For all thy mercy I will give ;
  My soul shall still in God rejoice,
  My tongue shall bless thee while I live.
    *James Montgomery.*

**367** *At home with God anywhere.* L. M.

1 My Lord, how full of sweet content
  I pass my years of banishment !
  Where'er I dwell, I dwell with thee,
  In heaven, in earth or on the sea.

2 To me remains nor place nor time ;
  My country is in every clime :
  I can be calm and free from care
  On any shore, since God is there.

3 While place we seek, or place we shun
  The soul finds happiness in none ;
  But with a God to guide our way,
  'Tis equal joy to go or stay.

4 Could I be cast where thou art not,
  That were indeed a dreadful lot ;
  But regions none remote I call,
  Secure of finding God in all.
    *Mad. J. M. B. De La Motte Guyon.*
    *[ Tr. by Wm. Cowper ]*

171

# CHRISTIAN WARFARE AND FAITH UNDER TRIALS.

**368** SHIRLAND. S. M.

H. STANLEY.

1. Gra - cious Re - deem - er, shake This slum - ber from my soul!

Say to me now, "A - wake, a - wake! And Christ shall make thee whole."

*Watchfulness.* S. M.

1 Gracious Redeemer, shake
This slumber from my soul!
Say to me now, "Awake, awake!
And Christ shall make thee whole."

2 Lay to thy mighty hand;
Alarm me in this hour;
And make me fully understand
The thunder of thy power!

3 Give me on thee to call.
Always to watch and pray,
Lest I into temptation fall,
And cast my shield away.

4 For each assault prepar'd
And ready may I be;
For ever standing on my guard,
And looking up to thee.

5 O do thou always warn
My soul of evil near!
When to the right or left I turn,
Thy voice still let me hear:

6 "Come back! this is the way!
Come back! and walk herein!"
O may I hearken and obey,
And shun the paths of sin! *C. Wesley.*

**369** *The mind that was in Christ.* S. M.

1 Equip me for the war,
And teach my hands to fight;
My simple, upright heart prepare
And guide my words aright.

2 Control my every thought,
My whole of sin remove;
Let all my works in thee be wrought,
Let all be wrought in love.

3 O arm me with the mind,
Meek Lamb, that was in thee:
And let my knowing zeal be joined
With perfect charity.

4 With calm and tempered zeal
Let me enforce thy call;
And vindicate thy gracious will,
Which offers life to all. *C. Wesley.*

**370** *Watch and pray. Matt.* xxiv. 41. S. M.

1 My soul, be on thy guard,
Ten thousand foes arise;
And hosts of sins are pressing hard,
To draw thee from the skies.

2 O watch, and fight, and pray,
The battle ne'er give o'er;
Renew it boldly every day,
And help divine implore.

3 Ne'er think the victory won,
Nor once at ease sit down;
Thy arduous work will not be done
Till thou hast got the crown.

4 Fight on, my soul, till death
Shall bring thee to thy God:
He'll take thee, at thy parting breath,
Up to his blest abode. *Heath.*

**371** *Make haste to live.* S. M.

1 Make haste, O man, to live,
For thou so soon must die;
Time hurries past thee like the breeze:
How swift its moments fly!

2 Make haste, O man, to do
Whatever must be done;
Thou hast no time to lose in sloth,
Thy day will soon be gone.

3 Up, then, with speed, and work;
Fling ease and self away;
This is no time for thee to sleep,
Up, watch, and work, and pray!

4 Make haste, O man, to live,
Thy time is almost o'er;
O sleep not, dream not, but arise,
The Judge is at the door. *Horatius Bonar.*

175

# CHURCH ACTIVITIES.

## PRAYER.

372 HURSLEY., L. M.                                     GERMAN.

1. Pray'r is ap - point - ed to con - vey The bless - ings

God de - signs to give: Long as they live should

Chris - tians pray, They learn to pray when first they live.

*Prevailing Prayer.*   L. M.

1 Prayer is appointed to convey
The blessings God designs to give:
Long as they live should Christians pray,
They learn to pray when first they live.

2 If pain afflict, or wrongs oppress;
If cares distract, or fears dismay;
If guilt deject; if sin distress;—
In every case, still watch and pray.

3 'Tis prayer supports the soul that's weak:
Though thought be broken, language lame,
Pray if thou canst, or canst not speak:
But pray with faith in Jesus' name.

4 Depend on him; thou canst not fail;
Make all thy wants and wishes known:
Fear not; his merits must prevail;
Ask but in faith, it shall be done.

*Hart.*

373   *A Morning Prayer.*   L. M.

1 Awake, my soul, and with the sun
Thy daily stage of duty run:
Shake off dull sloth, and early rise
To pay thy morning sacrifice.

2 Wake, and lift up thyself, my heart,
And with the angels bear thy part;
Who all night long unwearied sing
High praises to th' eternal King.

3 Glory to thee, who safe hast kept,
And hast refreshed me while I slept:
Grant, Lord, when I from death shall wake,
I may of endless life partake.

4 Direct, control, suggest this day,
All I design, or do, or say,
That all my powers, with all their might,
In thy sole glory may unite.

*T. Ken.*

## 374 HARMONY GROVE. L. M.

H. K. OLIVER.

*Slowly.*

1. My God, ac-cept my ear-ly vows, Like morning in-cense in thy house,

And let my night-ly wor-ship rise Sweet as the even-ing sac - ri - fice.

---

### Early Vows. L. M.

1 My God, accept my early vows,
Like morning incense in thy house,
And let my nightly worship rise
Sweet as the evening sacrifice.

2 Watch o'er my lips, and guard them, Lord,
From every rash and heedless word;
Nor let my feet incline to tread
The guilty path where sinners lead.

3 O, may the righteous, when I stray,
Smite, and reprove my wand'ring way!
Their gentle words, like ointment shed,
Shall never bruise, but cheer my head.

4 When I behold them pressed with grief,
I'll cry to heaven for their relief;
And by my warm petitions prove
How much I prize their faithful love.
*Watts.*

### 375 Evening Song. L. M.

1 How do thy mercies close me round!
Forever be thy name ador'd;
I blush in all things to abound;
The servant is above his Lord!

2 Inur'd to poverty and pain,
A suff'ring life my Master led;
The Son of God, the Son of man,
He had not where to lay his head.

3 But, lo! a place he hath prepar'd
For me, whom watchful angels keep;
Yea, he himself becomes my guard;
He smoothes my bed, and gives me sleep.

4 Jesus protects; my fears, begone!
What can the rock of ages move!
Safe in thy arms I lay me down,
Thy everlasting arms of love.
*C. Wesley.*

### 376 C. M.

*How frail I am. Psalm* xxxix.
[ Tune, Maitland, page 178. C. M.]

1 Teach me the measure of my days,
Thou Maker of my frame:
I would survey life's narrow space,
And learn how frail I am.

2 A span is all that we can boast,
An inch or two of time:
Man is but vanity and dust,
In all his flower and prime.

3 What should I wish, or wait for, then,
From creatures, earth, and dust?
They make our expectations vain
And disappoint our trust.

4 Now I forbid my carnal hope,
My fond desires recall;
I give my mortal interest up,
And make my God my all.
*Watts.*

177

# CHURCH ACTIVITIES.

**377 MAITLAND. C. M.**

1. O God, our help in a - ges past, Our hope for years to come,

Our shel-ter from the storm-y blast, And our e-ter-nal home:

*The Lord our Help.*    *Psalm* xc.   C. M.

1 O God, our help in ages past,
  Our hope for years to come,
Our shelter from the stormy blast,
  And our eternal home:

2 Under the shadow of thy throne,
  Still may we dwell secure;
Sufficient is thine arm alone,
  And our defense is sure.

3 Before the hills in order stood,
  Or earth received her frame,
From everlasting thou art God,
  To endless years the same.

4 A thousand ages, in thy sight,
  Are like an evening gone:
Short as the watch that ends the night
  Before the rising sun.

5 Time, like an ever-rolling stream,
  Bears all its sons away;
They fly, forgotten, as a dream
  Dies at the op'ning day.

6 O God, our help in ages past,
  Our hope for years to come,
Be thou our guard while life shall last,
  And our perpetual home!
              *Watts*

**378**    *A Morning meditation.*    C. M.

1 Once more, my soul, the rising day,
  Salutes thy waking eyes;
Once more, my voice, thy tribute pay
  To him that rules the skies.

2 Night unto night his name repeats,
  The day renews the sound,—
Wide as the heavens on which he sits,
  To turn the seasons round.

3 'Tis he supports my mortal frame;
  My tongue shall speak his praise:
My sins might rouse his wrath to flame,
  But yet his wrath delays.

4 O God, let all my hours be thine,
  While I enjoy the light!
Then shall my sun in smiles decline,
  And bring a pleasant night.
              *Watts.*

**379**    *Awake, my soul.*    C. M.

1 Awake, my soul, to meet the day,
  Unfold thy drowsy eyes,
And burst the pond'rous chain that loads
  Thine active faculties.

2 God's guardian shield was round me spread
  In my defenseless sleep:
Let him have all my waking hours
  Who doth my slumbers keep.

3 Pardon, O God, my former sloth,
  And arm my soul with grace;
As rising now, I seal my vows
  To prosecute thy ways.

4 Bright Sun of righteousness, arise;
  Thy radiant beams display,
And guide my dark, bewilder'd soul
  To everlasting day.
              *Doddridge.*

**380 HATTIE. C. M.**

MUSIC BY J. B. STANSBERRY, D. D.

1. Giv - er and guard - ian of my sleep, To praise thy name I
wake: Still, Lord, thy help - less ser - vant keep, For thine own mer - cy's sake.

*Meditation.* C. M.

1 Giver and guardian of my sleep.
   To praise thy name I wake:
   Still, Lord, thy helpless servant keep,
   For thine own mercy's sake.

2 The blessing of another day
   I thankfully receive:
   O may I only thee obey,
   And to thy glory live!

3 Upon me lay thy mighty hand,
   My words and thoughts restrain:
   Bow my whole soul to thy command,
   Nor let my faith be vain.

4 Pris'ner of hope, I wait the hour
   Which shall salvation bring;
   When all I am shall own thy power,
   And call my Jesus King.
                                    *C. Wesley.*

**381** C. M.

*Sabbath Morning. Psalm v. 1-8.*

1 Lord, in the morning thou shalt hear
   My voice ascending high;
   To thee will I direct my prayer,
   To thee lift up mine eye:

2 Up the hills where Christ is gone,
   To plead for all his saints,
   Presenting at his Father's throne
   Our songs and our complaints.

3 Thou art a God before whose sight
   The wicked shall not stand:
   Sinners shall ne'er be thy delight,
   Nor dwell at thy right hand.

4 But to thy house will I resort,
   To taste thy mercies there;
   I will frequent thy holy court,
   And worship in thy fear.

5 O may thy Spirit guide my feet
   In ways of righteousness,
   Make ev'ry path of duty straight
   And plain before my face.
                                    *Watts.*

**381 b** *Life, light and love.* C. M.

1 Enthroned on high, almighty Lord,
   The Holy Ghost send down;
   Fulfil in us thy faithful word,
   And all thy mercies crown.

2 Though on our heads no tongues of fire
   Their wondrous powers impart,
   Grant, Saviour, what we more desire,—
   Thy Spirit in our heart.

3 Spirit of life, and light, and love,
   Thy heavenly influence give;
   Quicken our souls, our guilt remove,
   That we in Christ may live.

4 To our benighted minds reveal
   The glories of his grace,
   And bring us where no clouds conceal
   The brightness of his face.

5 His love within us shed abroad,
   Life's ever-spreading well;
   Till God in us, and we in God,
   In love eternal dwell.
                                    *Thomas Haweis.*

## 382 WILMOT. 7s.

VON WEBER.

1. Now the shades of night are gone; Now the morn-ing light is come;

Lord, may we be thine to - day, Drive the shades of sin a - way.

*Morning Hymn.* 7s.

1 Now the shades of night are gone;
Now the morning light is come;
Lord, may we be thine to-day,
Drive the shades of sin away.

2 Fill our souls with heavenly light,
Banish doubt and clear our sight;
In thy service, Lord, to-day,
May we labor, watch, and pray.

3 Keep our haughty passions bound;
Save us from our foes around;
Going out and coming in
Keep us safe from every sin.

4 When our work of life is past,
O receive us then at last;
Night and sin will be no more,
When we reach the heav'nly shore.
*Unknown.*

**383** *Evening.* 7s.

1 Omnipresent God! whose aid
No one ever asked in vain,
Be this night about my bed,
Every evil thought restrain:

2 Lay thy hand upon my soul,
God of my unguarded hours!
All my enemies control,
Hell, and earth and nature's powers.

3 O thou jealous God! come down,
God of spotless purity;
Claim and seize me for thine own,
Consecrate my heart to thee:

4 Under thy protection take;
Songs in the night season give;
Let me sleep to thee, and wake;
Let me die to thee, and live.

5 Let me of thy life partake,
Thy own holiness impart;
O that I may sweetly wake,
With my Saviour in my heart!

6 O that I may know thee mine!
O that I may thee receive!
Only live the life Divine!
Only to thy glory live!
*C. Wesley.*

**384** *For reviving grace.* 7s.

1 Light of life, seraphic fire,
Love Divine, thyself impart;
Every fainting soul inspire;
Shine in every drooping heart;

2 Every mournful sinner cheer;
Scatter all our guilty gloom;
Son of God, appear! appear!
To thy human temples come.

3 Come in this accepted hour;
Bring thy heavenly kingdom in;
Fill us with thy glorious power,
Rooting out the seeds of sin.

4 Nothing more can we require,
We will covet nothing less;
Be thou all our hearts' desire,
All our joy, and all our peace.
*C. Wesley.*

PRAYER.

JAMES LUCAS.

1. Come, let us a-new our jour-ney pur-sue, Roll round with the year,

And nev-er stand still till the Mas-ter ap-pear. His a-dor-a-ble

will let us glad-ly ful-fil, And our tal-ents im-prove, By the pa-tience of

hope and the la-bor of love, By the pa-tience of hope, and the la-bor of love.

*Renewed devotedness.*        10. 5, 11.

1 Come, let us anew our journey pursue,
    Roll round with the year,
  And never stand still till the Master appear.
  His adorable will let us gladly fulfil,
    And our talents improve,
  By the patience of hope, and the labor of
      love.

2 Our life is a dream; our time, as a stream,
    Glides swiftly away,
  And the fugitive moment refuses to stay,

The arrow is flown,— the moment is gone;
    The millennial year
  Rushes on to our view, and eternity's here.

3 O that each in the day of his coming may say,
    "I have fought my way through;
  I have finished the work thou didst give me
      to do!"
  O that each from his Lord may receive the
      glad word,
    "Well and faithfully done!
  Enter into my joy, and sit down on my
      throne!"        *Charles Wesley.*

181

**386 HARWICH. H. M.**  DR. L. MASON

*Allegro moderato.*

1. The Lord of earth and sky, The God of a - ges praise! Who
reigns enthroned on high, An - cient of end - less days! Who
lengthens out our tri - als here, And spares us yet an - oth - er year.

*The opening year.*  H. M.

1 The Lord of earth and sky,
    The God of ages praise!
Who reigns enthroned on high,
    Ancient of endless days!
Who lengthens out our trials here,
And spares us yet another year.

2 Barren and wither'd trees,
    We cumber'd long the ground!
No fruit of holiness
    On our dead souls was found;
Yet doth he us in mercy spare
Another and another year.

3 When justice gave the word,
    To cut the fig-tree down,
The pity of the Lord
    Cried, "Let it still alone!"
The Father mild inclines his ear,
And spares us yet another year.

4 Jesus, thy speaking blood,
    From God obtain'd the grace;
Who therefore hath bestow'd
    On us a longer space:
Thou didst in our behalf appear,
And lo! we see another year!

5 Then dig about the root,
    Break up our fallow ground,
And let our gracious fruit
    To thy great praise abound!
O let us all thy praise declare,
And fruit unto perfection bear!
                                C. Wesley.

**387**  *Lo, I am with you alway.*  8, 7.
[ Tune, Ripley, page 168.  8s, 7s.]

1 Always with us, always with us;—
    Words of cheer and words of love;
Thus the risen Saviour whispers,
    From his dwelling-place above.
With us when we toil in sadness,
    Sowing much, and reaping none;
Telling us that in the future
    Golden harvests shall be won.

2 With us when the storm is sweeping
    O'er our pathway dark and drear;
Waking hope within our bosoms,
    Stilling every anxious fear.
With us in the lonely valley,
    When we cross the chilling stream;
Lighting up the steps to glory
    With salvation's radiant beam.
                                Edwin H. Nevin.

182

# PRAYER.

**388  FERGUSON. S. M.**                     GEO. KINGSLEY.

1. God of al - might - y love,— By whose suf - fic - ient grace I

lift my heart to things a - bove, And hum - bly seek thy face.

---

*A holy life.*                     S. M.

1 God of almighty love,—
  By whose sufficient grace
  I lift my heart to things above,
  And humbly seek thy face,—

2 Through Jesus Christ, the just,
  My faint desires receive,
  And let me in thy goodness trust,
  And to thy glory live.

3 Whate'er I say or do,
  Thy glory be my aim;
  My off'rings all be offer'd through
  The ever-blessed name.

4 Jesus, my single eye
  Be fix'd on thee alone:
  Thy name be prais'd on earth, on high,
  Thy will by all be done!

5 Spirit of faith, inspire
  My consecrated heart:
  Fill me with pure, celestial fire,
  With all thou hast and art.

6 My feeble mind transform,
  And, perfectly renew'd,
  Into a saint exalt a worm—
  A worm exalt to God!
                     *C. Wesley.*

**389**          *Trust in old age.*     S. M.

1 Thou seest my feebleness;
  Jesus, be thou my power,
  My help and refuge in distress,
  My fortress and my tower.

2 Give me to trust in thee;
  Be thou my sure abode:
  My horn, and rock; and buckler be,
  My Saviour and my God.

3 Myself I cannot save,
  Myself I cannot keep;
  But strength in thee I surely have,
  Whose eyelids never sleep.

4 My soul to thee alone,
  Now, therefore, I commend:
  Thou, Jesus, love me as thine own,
  And love me to the end!
                     *C. Wesley.*

**389 b**     *The victory and song.*     S. M.

1 The people of the Lord
  Are on their way to heaven;
  There they obtain their great reward;
  The prize will there be given.

2 'Tis conflict here below;
  'Tis triumph there, and peace:
  On earth we wrestle with the foe;
  In heaven our conflicts cease.

3 'Tis gloom and darkness here;
  'Tis light and joy above;
  There all is pure, and all is clear;
  There all is peace and love.

4 Then let us joyful sing;
  The conflict is not long:
  We hope in heaven to praise our King
  In one eternal song.

183

**390 LUTHER. S. M.**    T. HASTINGS.

1. To God your ev - - ry want In in - stant prayer dis - play:

Pray al - - ways; pray, and nev er faint: Pray

with - out ceas - ing, pray, Pray with - - out ceas - ing, pray.

*" Praying always, with all prayer."* S. M.

1 To God your every want
In instant prayer display:
Pray always; pray, and never faint:
Pray without ceasing, pray.

2 In fellowship,—alone—
To God with faith draw near:
Approach his courts, besiege his throne,
With all the power of prayer:

3 Go to his temple, go,
Nor from his altar move:
Let every house his worship know,
And every heart his love.

4 To God your spirits dart;
Your souls in words declare;
Or groan, to him who reads the heart,
Th' unutterable prayer:

5 His mercy now implore;
And now show forth his praise;
In shouts, or silent awe, adore
His miracles of grace.

6 Pour out your souls to God,
And bow them with your knees;
And spread your hearts and hands abroad,
And pray for Zion's peace.
                        *C. Wesley.*

**391**    *Thyself the way.*    S. M.

1 O thou that wouldst not have
One wretched sinner die:
Who diedst thyself, my soul to save
From endless misery!

2 Show me the way to shun
Thy dreadful wrath severe;
That when thou comest on thy throne,
I may with joy appear!

3 Thou art thyself the way,
Thyself in me reveal;
So shall I spend my life's short day
Obedient to thy will.

4 So shall I love my God,
Because he first lov'd me;
And praise thee in thy bright abode
To all eternity.
                        *C. Wesley.*

**391 b**    *The Harvest.*    S. M.

1 The harvest dawn is near,
The year delays not long;
And he who sows with many a tear,
Shall reap with many a song.

2 Sad to his toil he goes,
His seed with weeping leaves:
But he shall come, at twilight's close,
And bring his golden sheaves.
                        *Burgess.*

184

# PRAYER.

**392**     *Intercession.*     S. M.

[ Tune, Schumann, page 189.   S. M. ]

1 We lift our hearts to thee,
    O Day-Star from on high !
  The sun itself is but thy shade,
    Yet cheers both earth and sky.

2 O let thy orient beams
    The night of sin disperse,
  The mists of error and of vice
    Which shade the universe !

3 May we this life improve,
    To mourn for errors past,—
  And live this short revolving day
    As if it were our last.

4 To God, the Father, Son,
    And Spirit,—One in Three,—
  Be glory, as it was, is now,
    And shall forever be.

                         *John Wesley.*

**393  DUANE STREET.  L. M.**                   REV. J. COLES.

1. Je - sus! and shall it ev - er be, A mor - tal man a-shamed of thee!

A - shamed of thee, whom an-gels praise, Whose glo-ries shine through end-less days.

FINE.

*D.S.*—He sheds the beams of light di - vine O'er this be-night - ed soul of mine.

*D.S.*

A-shamed of Je - sus! soon - er far Let ev'n-ing blush to own a star;

*Not ashamed of Christ.*     L. M.

1 Jesus! and shall it ever be,
  A mortal man ashamed of thee!
  Ashamed of thee, whom angels praise,
  Whose glories shine through endless days.
  Ashamed of Jesus! sooner far
  Let evening blush to own a star;
  He sheds the beams of light divine
  O'er this benighted soul of mine.

2 Ashamed of Jesus! just as soon
  Let midnight be ashamed of noon;
  'Tis midnight with my soul, till he,
  Bright morning star, bid darkness flee.

Ashamed of Jesus! that dear friend
On whom my hopes of heaven depend.
No, when I blush, be this my shame,
That I no more revere his name.

3 Ashamed of Jesus! yes, I may
  When I've no guilt to wash away,
  No tear to wipe, no good to crave,
  No fears to quell, no soul to save.
  Till then—nor is my boasting vain—
  Till then I boast a Saviour slain !
  And O, may this my glory be,
  That Christ is not ashamed of me !

                              *Gregg.*

185

# CHURCH ACTIVITIES.

## 394 ALBERT. L. M.

*Moderato.*

1. Thus far the Lord hath led me on,— Thus far his pow'r pro-longs my days;

And ev-'ry ev'n-ing shall make known Some fresh mem-or-ial of his grace.

---

*Evening: Memorials of his Grace.* L. M.

1 Thus far the Lord hath led me on,—
  Thus far his pow'r prolongs my days;
  And every evening shall make known
  Some fresh memorial of his grace.

2 Much of my time has run to waste,
  And I, perhaps, am near my home:
  But he forgives my follies past,
  And gives me strength for days to come.

3 I lay my body down to sleep;
  Peace is the pillow for my head:
  While well-appointed angels keep
  Their watchful stations round my bed.

4 Thus, when the night of death shall come
  My flesh shall rest beneath the ground,
  And wait thy voice to rouse my tomb,
  With sweet salvation in the sound.

*Watts.*

## 395 L. M.

" *Thou crownest the Year with thy Goodness.*"

1 Eternal Source of every joy,
  Well may thy praise our lips employ,
  While in thy temple we appear,
  Whose goodness crowns the circling year.

2 The flow'ry spring, at thy command,
  Embalms the air, and paints the land;
  The summer rays with vigor shine,
  To raise the corn and cheer the vine.

3 Thy hand in autumn richly pours,
  Through all our coasts, redundant stores;
  And winters, soften'd by thy care,
  No more a face of horror wear.

4 Seasons, and months, and weeks, and days
  Demand successive songs of praise:
  Still be the cheerful homage paid
  With op'ning light and ev'ning shade.

5 Here in thy house shall incense rise,
  As circling Sabbaths bless our eyes;
  Still we will make thy mercies known
  Around thy board, and round our own.

6 O may our more harmonious tongue
  In worlds unknown pursue the song;
  And in those brighter courts adore,
  Where days and years revolve no more!

*Doddridge.*

## 395 b L. M.

1 My spirit sinks within me, Lord!
  But I will call thy name to mind,
  And times of past distress record
  When I have found my God was kind.

2 Yet will the Lord command his love
  When I address his throne by day;
  Nor in the night his grace remove:
  The night shall hear me sing and pray.

3 I'll cast myself before his feet,
  And say, " My God, my heavenly Rock!
  Why doth thy love so long forget
  The soul that groans beneath thy stroke?

4 Thy light and truth shall guide me still:
  Thy word shall my best thoughts employ
  And lead me to thy heavenly hill,
  My God! my most exceeding joy!

PRAYER.

**396 BECKER. L. M.**

FROM THE GERMAN.

1. Great God, we sing that mighty hand, By which sup-port-ed still we stand: The opening year thy mer-cy shows; Let mer-cy crown it till it close.

*A Song for the opening year.*    L. M.

1 Great God, we sing that mighty hand,
By which supported still we stand:
The opening year thy mercy shows;
Let mercy crown it till it close.

2 By day, by night, at home, abroad,
Still we are guarded by our God;
By his incessant bounty fed,
By his unerring counsel led.

3 With grateful hearts the past we own.
The future—all to us unknown—
We to thy guardian care commit,
And peaceful leave before thy feet.

4 In scenes exalted or depress'd,
Be thou our joy, and thou our rest;
Thy goodness all our hope shall raise,
Ador'd through all our changing days.

5 When death shall close our earthly songs
And seal in silence mortal tongues,
Our Helper, God, in whom we trust,
In brighter worlds our souls shall boast.
*Doddridge*

**397**    *Worth of prayer.*    L. M.

1 What various hind'rances we meet
In coming to a mercy-seat!
Yet who that knows the worth of prayer
But wishes to be often there?

2 Prayer makes the darkened cloud withdraw;
Prayer climbs the ladder Jacob saw;
Gives exercise to faith and love;
Brings every blessing from above.

3 Restraining prayer, we cease to fight:
Prayer makes the Christian's armor bright;
And Satan trembles when he sees
The weakest saint upon his knees.

4 Have you no words? Ah! think again,
Words flow apace when you complain,
And fill your fellow creature's ear
With the sad tale of all your care.

5 Were half the breath thus vainly spent,
To heaven in supplication sent,
Your cheerful song would oft'ner be,
"Hear what the Lord has done for me."
*Cowper.*

**397 b**    *The doubter's plea.*    L. M.

1 My God! permit me not to be
A stranger to myself and thee;
Amidst a thousand thoughts I rove,
Forgetful of my highest love.

2 Why should my passions mix with earth,
And thus debase my heav'nly birth?
Why should I cleave to things below,
And let my God, my Saviour, go?

3 Call me away from flesh and sense,
One sov'reign word can draw me thence;
I would obey the voice divine,
And all inferior joys resign.

4 Be earth, with all her scenes, withdrawn,
Let noise and vanity be gone;
In secret silence of the mind,
My heav'n, and there my God, I find.
*Watts.*

187

**398 SILVER STREET. S. M.** I. SMITH.

1. Our Heav'nly Fa - ther, hear   The prayer we   of - fer   now:   Thy

name be   hal - lowed far   and   near;   To   thee   all   na - tions   bow.

### The Lord's Prayer. S. M.

1 Our Heavenly Father, hear
  The prayer we offer now:
  Thy name be hallowed far and near;
  To thee all nations bow,

2 Thy kingdom come; thy will
  On earth be done in love.
  As saints and seraphim fulfil
  Thy perfect law above.

3 Our daily bread supply
  While by the word we live;
  The guilt of our iniquity
  Forgive, as we forgive.

4 From dark temptation's power,
  From Satan's wiles defend;
  . Deliver in the evil hour,
  And guide us to the end.

5 Thine shall forever be
  Glory and power Divine;
  The sceptre, throne, and majesty,
  Of heaven and earth, are thine.
  *Montgomery.*

### 398 Evening. S. M.

1 The day is past and gone,
  The evening shades appear:
  O may we all remember well,
  The night of death draws near!

2 We lay our garments by,
  Upon our beds to rest;
  So death will soon disrobe us all
  Of what is here possess'd.

3 Lord, keep us safe this night,
  Secure from all our fears;
  May angels guard us while we sleep,
  Till morning light appears.

4 And when we early rise,
  And view th' unwearied sun,
  May we set out to win the prize,
  And after glory run.

5 And when our days are past,
  And we from time remove,
  O may we in thy bosom rest,
  The bosom of thy love.
  *J. Leland.*

### 399 b "Give Me Thine Heart." L. M.

[Tune, Blake, page 191. L. M.]

1 Jesus demands this heart of mine,
  Demands my love, my joy, my care;
  But ah! how dead to things divine,
  How cold my best affections are!

2 'Tis sin, alas! with dreadful power,
  Divides my Saviour from my sight;
  Oh, for one happy, cloudless hour
  Of sacred freedom, sweet delight!

3 Come, gracious Lord! thy love can raise
  My captive powers from sin and death,
  And fill my heart and life with praise,
  And tune my last expiring breath.
  *A. Steele.*

# PRAYER.

**400 SCHUMANN. S. M.**  ROBERT SCHUMANN.

1. Se - rene I laid me down Be - neath his guard-ian care;

I slept, and I a - woke, and found My kind pre - serv - er near!

---

*Dedication to God, our Preserver.*  S. M.
*Psalm iii. 5.*

1 Serene I laid me down
  Beneath his guardian care :
I slept, and I awoke, and found
  My kind preserver near!

2 Thus does thine arm support
  This weak, defenseless frame :
But whence these favors, Lord, to me,
  All worthless as I am ?

3 O, how shall I repay
  The bounties of my God ?
This feeble spirit pants beneath
  The pleasing, painful load.

4 Dear Saviour, to thy cross
  I bring my sacrifice ;
Ting'd with thy blood, it shall ascend
  With fragrance to the skies.

5 My life I would anew
  Devote, O Lord, to thee ;
And in thy service I would spend
  A long eternity.
    *Dwight.*

**401**  S. M.

*Whoso putteth his trust in the Lord shall be
  safe.*

1 Commit thou all thy griefs
  And ways into his hands,
To his sure trust and tender care
  Who earth and heaven commands.

2 Who points the clouds their course,
  Whom winds and seas obey,
He shall direct thy wandering feet,
  He shall prepare thy way.

3 Thou on the Lord rely,
  So, safe, shalt thou go on :
Fix on his work thy steadfast eye,
  So shall thy work be done.

4 No profit canst thou gain
  By self-consuming care ;
To him commend thy cause; **his ear**
  Attends the softest prayer.

5 Thy everlasting truth,
  Father, thy ceaseless love,
Sees all thy childrens' wants, and knows
  What best for each will prove.
    *Tr. by J. Wesley.*

**402**  C. M.
*An Evening Prayer. Psalm iv.*
  [ Tune, Avon, page 190. C. M.]

1 Lord, thou wilt hear me when I pray ;
  I am forever thine :
I fear before thee all the day,
  Nor would I dare to sin.

2 And while I rest my weary head,
  From cares and business free,
'Tis sweet conversing on my bed,
  With my own heart and thee.

3 I pay this ev'ning sacrifice :
  And when my work is done,
Great God, my faith, my hope, relies
  Upon thy grace alone.

4 Thus, with my tho'ts compos'd to peace,
  I'll give mine eyes to sleep ;
Thy hand in safety keeps my days,
  And will my slumbers keep.
    *Watts.*

**403 AVON. C. M.**

1. All praise to him who dwells in bliss, Who made both day and night:

Whose throne is dark-ness in th' a-byss Of un - cre - a - ted light.

C. M.

*" And is a discerner of the thoughts and intents of the heart." Heb. iv. 12, 13.*

1 All praise to him who dwells in bliss,
   Who made both day and night:
   Whose throne is darkness in th' abyss
   Of uncreated light.

2 Each thought and deed his piercing eyes,
   With strictest search survey;
   The deepest shades no more disguise.
   Than the full blaze of day.

3 Whom thou dost guard, O King of kings,
   No evil shall molest:
   Under the shadow of thy wings
   Shall they securely rest.

4 Thy angels shall around their beds
   Their constant stations keep;
   Thy faith and truth shall shield their heads,
   For thou dost never sleep.

5 May we, with calm and sweet repose
   And heavenly thoughts refresh'd,
   Our eyelids with the morn unclose,
   And bless thee, ever bless'd.
                                        *C. Wesley.*

**404**      *Twilight Meditation.*      C. M.

1 I love to steal awhile away
   From every cumbering care;
   And spend the hours of setting day
   In humble, grateful pray'r.

2 I love in solitude to shed
   The penitential tear,
   And all his promises to plead,
   Where none but God can hear.

3 I love to think on mercies past,
   And future good implore,
   And all my cares and sorrows cast
   On him whom I adore.

4 I love by faith to take a view
   Of brighter scenes in heav'n;
   The prospect does my strength renew,
   While here by tempest driv'n.

5 Thus, when life's toilsome day is o'er,
   May its departing ray
   Be calm as this impressive hour,
   And lead to endless day.
                                        *Mrs. Browne.*

**405** *Evening Hymn. Psalm cxli. 2.* C. M.

1 Dread Sovereign, let my ev'ning song
   Like holy incense rise;
   Assist the off'ring of my tongue
   To reach the lofty skies.

2 Through all the dangers of the day
   Thy hand was still my guard;
   And still to drive my wants away
   Thy mercy stood prepared.

3 Perpetual blessings from above
   Encompass me around;
   But, O, how few returns of love
   Hath my Creator found!

4 Lord, with this guilty heart of mine,
   To thy dear cross I flee,
   And to thy grace my soul resign,
   To be renew'd by thee.
                                        *Watts.*

PRAYER.

**406 WARD. L. M.**

1. Great God, in-dulge my hum-ble claim, Be thou my hope, my joy, my rest;

The glo-ries that com-pose thy name Stand all en-gaged to make me blest.

*The greatness and goodness of God.*
*Psalm lxiii. 1–4.*

1 Great God, indulge my humble claim,
Be thou my hope, my joy, my rest;
The glories that compose thy name
Stand all engaged to make me blest.

2 Thou great and good, thou just and wise,
Thou art my Father and my God!
And I am thine by sacred ties,
Thy son, thy servant bought with blood.

3 With heart, and eyes, and lifted hands,
For thee I long, to thee I look,
As travellers in thirsty lands
Pant for the cooling water-brook.

4 E'en life itself, without thy love,
No lasting pleasure can afford;
Yea, 'twould a tiresome burden prove,
If I were banished from thee, Lord!

5 I'll lift my hands, I'll raise my voice,
While I have breath to pray or praise:
This work shall make my heart rejoice,
And spend the remnant of my days.
*Watts.*

**406 b** L. M.

1 Soon may the last glad song arise,
Through all the millions of the skies;
That song of triumph which records
That all the earth is now the Lords.

2 Let thrones, and powers, and kingdoms be
Obedient, mighty God, to thee;
And over land, and stream, and main,
Now wave the scepter of thy reign.

3 O let that glorious anthem swell,
Let host to host the triumph tell,
Till not one rebel heart remains,
But over all the Saviour reigns.
*Mrs. Voke.*

**406 b BLAKE. L. M.**

1. Soon may the last glad song a-rise, Thro' all the mill-ions of the skies;

That song of tri-umph which re-cords That all the earth is now the Lords.

191

# CHURCH ACTIVITIES.

**407 MENDON. L. M.**

GERMAN.

1. Au-thor of faith, we seek thy face, For all who feel thy work be-gun:

Con-firm, and strengthen them in grace, And bring thy feeb-lest chil - dren on.

---

*For the lambs of the flock.* L. M.

1 Author of faith, we seek thy face,
  For all who feel thy work begun:
  Confirm, and strengthen them in grace,
  And bring thy feeblest children on.

2 Thou seest their wants, thou knowest
    their names.
  Be mindful of thy youngest care;
  Be tender of the new-born lambs,
  And gently in thy bosom bear.

3 The lion roaring for his prey,
  With rav'ning wolves on every side,
  Watch over them to tear and slay,
  If found one moment from their Guide.

4 In safety lead thy little flock!
  From hell, the world, and sin, secure:
  And set their feet upon the rock,
  And make in thee their goings sure.
                              *C. Wesley.*

**408** L. M.

*Praise on Earth, in Heaven.* Rev. i. 5, 6.

1 Now to the Lord, who makes us know
  The wonders of his dying love,
  Be humble honors paid below,
  And strains of nobler praise above.

2 'Twas he who cleansed our foulest sins,
  And washed us in his richest blood:
  'Tis he who makes us priests and kings,
  And brings us rebels near to God.

3 To Jesus, our atoning Priest,
  To Jesus, our superior King,
  Be everlasting power confessed—
  Let every tongue his glory sing.
                              *Watts.*

**409** L. M.

*The Mercy-seat.* Exod. xxv. 22.

1 From every stormy wind that blows,
  From every swelling tide of woes,
  There is a calm, a sure retreat;
  'Tis found beneath the mercy-seat.

2 There is a place where Jesus sheds
  The oil of gladness on our heads—
  A place of all on earth most sweet;
  It is the blood-bought mercy-seat.

3 There is a scene where spirits blend,
  Where friend holds fellowship with friend;
  Though sunder'd far, by faith they meet
  Around one common mercy-seat.

4 There, there, on eagle wings we soar,
  And sin and sense molest no more;
  And heaven comes down our souls to greet,
  And glory crowns the mercy-seat.

5 Oh, let my hand forget her skill,
  My tongue be silent, cold and still,
  This bounding heart forget to beat,
  If I forget thy mercy-seat!
                              *Stowell.*

PRAYER.

## 410 COVENTRY. C. M.

1. Blest be the dear u - nit - ing love, That will not let us part:

Our bod - ies may far off re - move, We still are one in heart.

---

### United—though separate. C. M.

1 Blest be the dear uniting love,
   That will not let us part:
   Our bodies may far off remove,
   We still are one in heart.

2 Joined in one spirit to our Head,
   Where he appoints we go;
   And still in Jesus' footsteps tread,
   And show his praise below.

3 O may we ever walk in him,
   And nothing know beside;
   Nothing desire, nothing esteem,
   But Jesus crucified.

4 Closer and closer let us cleave
   To his beloved embrace;
   Expect his fulness to receive,
   And grace to answer grace.

5 Partakers of the Saviour's grace,
   The same in mind and heart,
   Nor joy, nor grief, nor time, nor place,
   Nor life, nor death can part.
                        *C. Wesley.*

### 411 "Thy Will be done." C. M.
#### Matt. vi. 10.

1 Thy presence, Lord, the place shall fill,
   My heart shall be thy throne;
   Thy holy, just, and perfect will,
   Shall in my flesh be done.

2 I thank thee for the present grace,
   And now in hope rejoice,
   In confidence to see thy face,
   And always hear thy voice.

3 I have the things I ask of thee,
   What shall I more require?
   That still my soul may restless be,
   And only thee desire.

4 Thy only will be done, not mine,
   But make me, Lord, thy home;
   Come as thou wilt, I that resign,
   But O, my Jesus, come!
                        *C. Wesley.*

### 412 Lord, teach us to pray. C. M.
#### Luke xi. 1.

1 Lord, teach thy servants how to pray
   With reverence and with fear:
   Though dust and ashes, yet we may,
   We must to thee draw near.

2 We come, then, God of grace to thee;
   Give broken, contrite hearts:
   Give—what thine eyes delight to see—
   Truth in the inward parts.

3 Give deep humility; the sense
   Of godly sorrow give;
   A strong, desiring confidence
   To see thy face and live.

4 Give faith in that one sacrifice
   Which can for sin atone;
   To cast our hopes, to fix our eyes,
   On Christ, and Christ alone.
                        *Montgomery.*

193

CHURCH ACTIVITIES.

**413  MEAR. C. M.**  WELSH AIR. AARON WILLIAMS.

1. Sing to the great Je - ho - vah's praise! All praise to him be - longs,

Who kind - ly length - ens out our days, De-mands our choic - est songs:

*New Year's Day.* C. M.

1 Sing to the great Jehovah's praise!
   All praise to him belongs,
   Who kindly lengthens out our days,
   Demands our choicest songs:

2 His providence hath brought us through
   Another various year;
   We all with vows and anthems new
   Before our God appear.

3 Father, thy mercies past we own,
   Thy still continued care:
   To thee presenting, through thy Son,
   Whate'er we have or are:

4 Our lips and lives shall gladly show
   The wonders of thy love,
   While on in Jesus' steps we go
   To seek thy face above.

5 Our residue of days or hours,
   Thine, wholly thine, shall be;
   And all our consecrated powers
   A sacrifice to thee:

6 Till Jesus in the clouds appear
   To saints on earth forgiv'n,
   And bring the grand sabbatic year,
   The jubilee of heav'n.
                    *C. Wesley.*

**414**  *Winter.  Psalm* cxlvii.  C. M.

1 With songs and honors sounding loud,
   Address the Lord on high:
   Over the heavens he spreads his cloud,
   And waters veil the sky.

2 His steady counsels change the face
   Of the declining year:

He bids the sun cut short his race,
   And wintry days appear.

3 His hoary frost, his fleecy snow,
   Descend and clothe the ground:
   The liquid streams forbear to flow,
   In icy fetters bound.

4 When, from his dreadful stores on high,
   He pours the sounding hail,
   The wretch that dares his God defy
   Shall find his courage fail.

5 The changing wind, the flying cloud,
   Obey his mighty word;
   With songs and honors sounding loud,
   Praise ye the sov'reign Lord.
                    *Watts.*

**415**  *End of the year.*  C. M.

1 And now, my soul, another year
   Of thy short life is past;
   I cannot long continue here,
   And this may be my last.

2 Awake, my soul! with utmost care
   Thy true condition learn:
   What are thy hopes? how sure? how fair?
   What is thy great concern?

3 Behold, another year begins!
   Set out afresh for heaven;
   Seek pardon for thy former sins,
   In Christ so freely given.

4 Devoutly yield thyself to God,
   And on his grace depend;
   With zeal pursue the heav'nly road,
   Nor doubt a happy end.
                    *Browne.*

194

**416** ANTIOCH. C. M.         HANDEL.

1. A-wake, ye saints, and raise your eyes, And raise your voic - es high:

A - wake, and praise that sov - 'reign love That shows sal - va - tion

nigh, That shows sal-va-tion nigh, That shows, that shows sal - va -tion nigh.

*Close of the year.*      C. M.

1 Awake, ye saints, and raise your eyes,
  And raise your voices high :
Awake, and praise that sov'reign love
  That shows salvation nigh.

2 On all the wings of time it flies,
  Each moment brings it near,
Then welcome, each declining day!
  Welcome, each closing year!

3 Ye wheels of nature, speed your course;
  Ye mortal powers, decay ;
Fast as ye bring the night of death,
  Ye bring eternal day.
            *Doddridge.*

**417** *Morning: Confident Security.* C. M.

1 On thee, each morning, O my God,
  My waking thoughts attend ;
In thee are founded all my hopes,—
  In thee my wishes end.

2 My soul, in pleasing wonder lost,
  Thy boundless love surveys ;
And, fired with grateful zeal, prepares
  A sacrifice of praise.

3 God leads me through the maze of sleep,
  And brings me safe to light ;
And, with the same paternal care,
  Conducts my steps till night.

4 When eve'ning slumbers press mine eyes,
  With his protection blest,
In peace and safety I commit
  My wearied limbs to rest.

5 My spirit, in his hand secure,
  Fears no approaching ill ;
For, whether waking or asleep,
  The Lord is with me still.
            *Knapp.*

**417 b**    *Deeds of Charity.*    C. M.

1 High on a throne of light, O Lord,
  Dost thou exalted shine :
What can our poverty bestow,
  Since all the world is thine ?

2 But thou hast brethren here below,
  Partakers of thy grace,
Whose humble names thou wilt confess
  Before thy Father's face.

3 In them may'st thou be clothed and fed,
  And visited and cheered ;
And, in their accents of distress,
  The Saviour's voice be heard.

4 Whate'er our willing hands can give,
  Lord, at thy feet we lay ;
Grace will the humble gift receive,
  And grace at length repay.
            *Pratt's Coll.*

# CHRISTIAN ACTIVITIES.

## ERECTION AND CONSECRATION OF CHURCHES.

**418  PARK STREET. L. M.**

1. And will the great, e - ter - nal God, On earth es - tab - lish his a - bode? And will he, from his ra - diant throne, A - vow our tem - ple for his own, A - vow our tem - ple for his own?

*Dedication.*   L. M.

1 And will the great, eternal God,
On earth establish his abode?
And will he, from his radiant throne,
Avow our temple for his own?

2 We bring the tribute of our praise ;
And sing that condescending grace,
Which to our notes will lend an ear,
And call us sinful mortals near.

3 These walls we to thy honor raise,
Long may they echo to thy praise,
And thou, descending, fill the place
With choicest tokens of thy grace.

4 And in the great, decisive day,
When God the nations shall survey,
May it before the world appear
That crowds were born to glory here!
*Doddridge.*

**419**   *A House for God.*   L. M.

1 Where shall I go to seek and find
A habitation for our God ?
A dwelling for th' Eternal Mind
Among the sons of flesh and blood?

2 The God of Jacob chose the hill
Of Zion for his ancient rest ;
And Zion is his dwelling still ;
His church is with his presence blest.

3 Here will he meet the hungry poor,
And fill their souls with living bread ;
Here sinners, waiting at his door,
With sweet provision shall be fed.

4 " Here will I fix my gracious throne,
And reign forever," saith the Lord ;
" Here shall my powers and love be
known,
And blessings shall attend my word."
*Watts.*

*Doxology.*   L. M.

1 Dismiss us with thy blessing Lord,
Help us to feed upon thy word,
All that has been amiss, forgive
And let thy truth within us, live.

2 Though we are guilty thou art good,
Wash all our souls in Jesus blood,
Give every fettered soul release,
And let us all depart in peace.

**420 HAMBURG. L. M.**  ARR. BY DR. L. MASON.

1. Be-hold thy tem-ple, God of grace, The house that we have rear'd for thee,
Re-gard it as thy rest-ing place, And fill it with thy maj-es-ty.

---

*Dedication.* L. M.

1 Behold thy temple, God of grace,
The house that we have rear'd for thee,
Regard it as thy resting-place,
And fill it with thy majesty.

2 When from its altars shall arise
Joint supplications to thy name,
Deign to accept the sacrifice,
Thyself our answ'ring God proclaim.

3 And when from hence the voice of praise
Shall lift its triumphs to thy throne,
Show thy acceptance of our lays,
By making all thy glory known.

4 When here thy ministers shall stand,
To speak what thou shalt bid them say,
Maintain thy cause with thine own hand,
And give thy truth a winning way.

5 Now, therefore, O our God, arise!
In this thy resting-place appear;
And let thy people's longing eyes
Behold thee fix thy dwelling here.
*Palmer.*

**421** L. M.
*God's Earthly House.* I *Kings* viii. 13.

1 Here, in thy name, eternal God,
We build this earthly house for thee;
O, choose it for thy fixed abode,
And guard it long from error free.

2 Here, when thy people seek thy face,
And dying sinners pray to live,
Hear thou, in heav'n, thy dwelling-place,
And when thou hearest, Lord, forgive.

3 Here, when thy messengers proclaim
The blessed gospel of thy Son,
Still by the power of his great name
Be mighty signs and wonders done.

4 But will, indeed, Jehovah deign
Here to abide, no transient guest?
Here will our great Redeemer reign,
And here the Holy Spirit rest?

5 Thy glory never hence depart:
Yet choose not, Lord, this house alone;
Thy kingdom come to every heart;
In every bosom fix thy throne.
*Montgomery.*

**421 b** *Art thou my Father.* L. M.

1 Great God, and wilt thou condescend
To be my Father and my Friend?
I, a poor child, and thou, so high,
The Lord of earth, and air, and sky?

2 Art thou my Father? Let me be
A meek, obedient child to thee;
And try in word and deed and thought,
To serve and please thee as I ought.

3 Art thou my Father? I'll depend
Upon the care of such a Friend;
And only wish to do and be
Whatever seemeth good to thee.

4 Art thou my Father? Then, at last,
When all my days on earth are past,
Send down and take me in thy love,
To be thy better child above.
*Ann Taylor Gilbert,* 1809.

**422** CLAUDE. 8s & 7s. 8 Lines.   ALTERED FROM CLAUDE GOUDIMEL, CIR. 1562, OR GUILLAUME FRANC, 1543.

God of thun - der and the light-ning Cloth'd in ma - jes - ty di - vine,
To thy feet we bring this trib - ute Lord ac-cept this house as thine.

To thy name, O Lord Je - ho - vah, We this tem - ple ded - i - cate,

Lord re - ceive this hum - ble trib - ute, Sanc - ti - fy it, ear - ly, late.

8s & 7s.

1 God of thunder and the lightning
  Cloth'd in majesty divine.
To thy feet we bring this tribute
Lord accept this house as thine.
To thy name, O Lord Jehovah,
  We this temple dedicate;
Lord receive this humble tribute,
  Sanctify it, early, late.

2 Send thy Spirit, Lord from heav'n,
  Consecrate its sacred halls:
Let thy ever biding presence
  Dwell within these humble walls.
Here may sinners be converted,
  While we sing our Saviour's praise;
May the deaf, the halt, the blinded,
  Now their Ebenezer raise.
                        *H. M. Turner.*

**422 b**   *A Funeral Hymn.*   8s & 7s.

1 In this world of sin and sorrow,
  Compassed round with many a care,
From eternity we borrow
  Hope that can exclude despair.
Thee, triumphant God and Saviour!
  In the glass of faith we see,
Oh! assist each faint endeavor,
  Raise our earth-born souls to thee.

2 Place that awful scene before us,
  Of the last tremendous day,
When to life thou shalt restore us, —
  Lingering ages! haste away.
Then this vile and sinful nature
  Incorruption shall put on:
Life-renewing, glorious Saviour!
  Let thy gracious will be done.
          *Mrs. Judith [ Cowper ] Madan, 1763.*

**422 c**   *Onward and Upward.*   8s & 7s.

1 Take, my soul! thy full salvation,
  Rise o'er sin, and fear, and care;
Joy to find, in every station,
  Something still to do or bear:
Think what Spirit dwells within thee;
  What a Father's smile is thine:
What a Saviour died to win thee!
  Child of heaven, shouldst thou repine?

2 Haste, then, on from grace to glory,
  Armed by faith, and winged by prayer!
Heaven's eternal days before thee,
  God's own hand shall guide thee there:
Soon shall close thy earthly mission,
  Swift shall pass thy pilgrim days,
Hope soon change to glad fruition,
  Faith to sight, and prayer to praise.
          *Henry Francis Lyte, 1829.*

**423 LISCHER. H. M.**　　　　　　　DR. L. MASON.

God of thine Is - rael true, Their pil - lar, shield, and rock,
Who, all the des - ert through, Didst lead them like a flock;

In this our sanc - tu - a - ry dwell, Thou glo - rious, felt, in -

vis - i - ble, Thou glo - rious, felt, in - vis - i - ble!

*Dedication.*　　　H. M.

1 God of thine Israel true,
　Their pillar, shield, and rock,
Who, all the desert through,
　Didst lead them like a flock;
In this our sanctuary dwell,
Thou glorious, felt, invisible !

2 That holy peace shed down,
　The world can never give ;
Thy truth with triumph crown,
　Command the dead to live ;
And fill this consecrated place
With living trophies of thy grace.

3 Great Shepherd of thy flock,
　Our glorious Leader be ;
Our pillar, shield, and rock,
　Till the fair land we see :
Ruler of heaven's eternal sphere,
Be thou the guardian glory here !
　　　　　　　　*Robinson.*

**424**　*Invoking God's Presence.*　H. M.

1 Great King of glory, come,
　And with thy favor crown

This temple as thy home,
　This people as thine own
Beneath this roof, O deign to show
How God can dwell with men below.

2 Here may thine ears attend
　Our interceding cries,
And grateful praise ascend,
　Like incense to the skies :
Here may thy word melodious sound,
And spread celestial joys around.

3 Here may our unborn sons
　And daughters sound thy praise,
And shine, like polished stones,
　Through long-succeeding days :
Here, Lord, display thy saving power,
While temples stand and men adore.

4 Here may the listening throng
　Receive thy truth in love :
Here Christians join the song
　Of seraphim above ;
Till all, who humbly seek thy face,
Rejoice in thy abounding grace.
　　　　　　· *Benjamin Francis.*

**425  ELTHAM. 7s. Double.**  L. MASON.
FINE.

Lord of hosts, to thee we raise Here a house of prayer and praise;
Thou thy peo-ple's hearts pre-pare Here to meet for praise and prayer.

D.C.—Here, in hope of glo-ry blest, May the dead be laid to rest.

D.C.

Let the liv - ing here be fed With thy word, the heav'nly bread;

---

*I have put my name there forever.* 7s.
1 *Kings* ix. 3.

1 Lord of hosts, to thee we raise
Here a house of prayer and praise;
Thou thy people's hearts prepare
Here to meet for praise and prayer.
Let the living here be fed
With thy word, the heavenly bread;
Here, in hope of glory blest,
May the dead be laid to rest.

2 Here to thee a temple stand,
While the sea shall gird the land;
Here reveal thy mercy sure,
While the sun and moon endure.
Hallelujah!—earth and sky
To the joyful sound reply;
Hallelujah!—hence ascend
Prayer and praise till time shall end.
*Montgomery.*

**426  Sinai, Tabor, Calvary.**  7s.

1 When on Sinai's top I see
God descend, in majesty,
To proclaim his holy law,
All my spirit sinks with awe.
When, in ecstasy sublime,
Tabor's glorious steep I climb,
At the too transporting light,
Darkness rushes o'er my sight.

2 When on Calvary I rest,
God, in flesh made manifest,
Shines in my Redeemer's face,
Full of beauty, truth, and grace.
Here I would forever stay,
Weep and gaze my soul away:
Thou art heaven on earth to me,
Lovely, mournful Calvary.
*Montgomery.*

**426 b  Filial Submission.**  C. M.

[Tune, Downs, page 201. C. M.]

1 And can my heart aspire so high,
To say,—"My Father, God!"
Lord! at thy feet I fain would lie,
And learn to kiss the rod.

2 I would submit to all thy will,
For thou art good and wise;
Let every anxious thought be still,
Nor one faint murmur rise.

3 Thy love can cheer the darksome gloom,
And bid me wait serene,
Till hopes and joys immortal bloom,
And heighten all the scene.

4 "My Father!" Oh! permit my heart
To plead her humble claim.
And ask the bliss those words impart,
In my Redeemer's name.
*Anne Steele.* 1760.

200

# ERECTION AND CONSECRATION.

## 427 DOWNS. C. M.

1. A - rise, O King of grace, a - rise, And en - ter to thy rest!

Lo! thy church waits, with long-ing eyes, Thus to be own'd and bless'd.

---

*Psalm* cxxxii. 8, 15.     C. M.

1 Arise, O King of grace, arise,
  And enter to thy rest!
Lo! thy church waits, with longing eyes,
  Thus to be own'd and bless'd.

2 Enter, with all thy glorious train,
  Thy Spirit and thy word:
All that the ark did once contain
  ·Could no such grace afford.

3 Here, mighty God, accept our vows;
  Here let thy praise be spread :
Bless the provisions of thy house,
  And fill thy poor with bread.
                      *Watts.*

## 428    *God dwelling among men.*    C. M.
### 2 *Chron.* vi. 18.

1 Will God in every deed descend,
  And dwell with men below ?
An ear to mortal worship lend ?
  To us his glory show?

2 While heaven's exalted spheres resound
  With hymns which angels sing,
Will God in mercy so abound,
  T' accept the praise we bring?

3 Allow'd within thy courts to meet,
  Thy presence we implore;
Smile on us from thy mercy-seat,
  And we desire no more.

4 Here let thy gospel be declar'd ;
  Here make thy power be known;
May every heart, by grace prepar'd,
  Be the Redeemer's throne.

5 Here make thyself a glorious name,
  And form us for thy praise ;
Thy promis'd presence, Lord, we claim,
  And supplicate thy grace.
                  *Shepherd's Col.*

## 429    *Divine blessing solicited.*    C. M.

1 To thee this temple we devote,
  Our Father and our God;
Accept it thine, and seal it now
  Thy Spirit's blest abode.

2 Here may the prayer of faith ascend,
  The voice of praise arise ;
O, may each lowly service prove
  Accepted sacrifice.

3 Here may the sinner learn his guilt,
  And weep before his Lord ;
Here, pardoned, sing a Saviour's love
  And here his vows record.

4 Here may affliction dry the tear,
  And learn to trust in God,
Convinced it is a Father smites,
  And love that guides the rod.

5 Peace be within these sacred walls;
  Prosperity be here ;
Long smile upon thy people, Lord,
  And evermore be near.
                  *J. R. Scott.*

CHRISTIAN ACTIVITIES.

**430 CAMPBELL. S. M.**     W. H. GIBSON, SR.

1. Fa-ther of life de-scend! With-in this sa-cred fane, Before thy throne our spir-its bend, O here come down and reign!
Thou Son of God, de-scend! And con-se-crate this place, O
make it Lord, till time shall end, The tem-ple of thy grace!

S. M.

*Hymn for the Consecration of Churches.*

1 Father of life, descend!
Within this sacred fane,
Before thy throne our spirits bend,
O here come down and reign!
Thou Son of God, descend!
And consecrate this place,
O make it Lord, till time shall end,
The temple of thy grace!

2 Spirit of light, descend!
And shed thy glory here,
Thine unction with our worship blend,
And waft to heav'n our prayer.
There let the gospel sound
Its tones of peace and love;
Spread holiness and life around,
And lift our hopes above.

3 Give to the blind their sight,
Bind up the broken heart,
The erring spirit guide aright,
And strength to all impart.

Bid the lame leap for joy,
The dead, awake and rise,
Let righteousness our lives employ,
Then lift us to the skies.
*Bishop D. A. Fayne.*

**431**    *Psalm xlviii.*    S. M.

1 Great is the Lord our God,
And let his praise be great:
He makes his churches his abode,
His most delightful seat.

2 These temples of his grace,
How beautiful they stand!
The honors of our native place
And bulwarks of our land.

3 In Sion God is known
A refuge in distress:
How bright has his salvation shone
Through all her palaces.

4 In every new distress
We'll to his house repair;
We'll think upon his wondrous grace,
And seek deliv'rance there. *Watts.*

202

**432 MISSIONARY HYMN. 7, 6, 7, 6.**  DR. L. MASON.

1. From Greenland's icy mountains, From India's cor-al strand; Where Afric's sunny fountains Roll down their golden sand; From many an ancient riv - er, From many a palm-y plain, They call us to de - liv - er Their land from error's chain.

## MISSIONS.

*"Come over—and help us."*   7, 6, 7, 6.

1 From Greenland's icy mountains,
  From India's coral strand;
Where Afric's sunny fountains
  Roll down their golden sand;
From many an ancient river,
  From many a palmy plain,
They call us to deliver
  Their land from error's chain.

2 What though the spicy breezes
  Blow soft o'er Ceylon's isle,
Though every prospect pleases,
  And only man is vile:
In vain with lavish kindness
  The gifts of God are strown;
The heathen in his blindness
  Bows down to wood and stone.

3 Shall we, whose souls are lighted
  With wisdom from on high,
Shall we to men benighted
  The lamp of life deny?
Salvation! O salvation!
  The joyful sound proclaim,
Till earth's remotest nation
  Has learned Messiah's name.

4 Waft, waft, ye winds, his story,
  And you, ye waters, roll,
Till, like a sea of glory,
  It spreads from pole to pole:
Till o'er our ransom'd nature,
  The Lamb for sinners slain,
Redeemer, King, Creator,
  In bliss returns to reign.
             *Bishop Heber.*

**432 b**   7, 6, 7, 6.

1 Hail to the Lord's Anointed,
  Great David's greater Son;
Hail, in the time appointed,
  His reign on earth begun;
He comes to break oppression,
  To set the captive free,
To take away transgression,
  And rule in equity.

2 He comes with succor speedy
  To those who suffer wrong;
To help the poor and needy,
  And bid the weak be strong;
To give them songs for sighing,
  Their darkness turn to light,
Whose souls, condemned and dying,
  Were precious in his sight.
             *Montgomery.*

**433 HENDON. 7s.**

C. MALAN.

1. See how great a flame as - pires, Kin - dled by a spark of grace! Je - sus' love the na - tions fires, Sets the king-doms on a blaze, Sets the king - doms on a blaze.

*Success.* 7s.

1 See how great a flame aspires,
    Kindled by a spark of grace!
  Jesus' love the nations fires,
    Sets the kingdoms on a blaze.

2 To bring fire on earth he came;
    Kindled in some hearts it is:
  O that all might catch the flame,
    All partake the glorious bliss!

3 When he first the work begun,
    Small and feeble was his day:
  Now the word doth swiftly run,
    Now it wins its wid'ning way:

4 More and more it spreads and grows
    Ever mighty to prevail;
  Sin's strongholds it now o'erthrows,
    Shakes the trembling gates of hell.

5 Saw ye not the cloud arise,
    Little as a human hand?
  Now it spreads along the skies,
    Hangs o'er all the thirsty land:

6 Lo! the promise of a shower
    Drops already from above:
  But the Lord will shortly pour
    All the Spirit of his love.
      *C. Wesley.*

**434** *The Song of Jubilee.* 7s.

1 Hark! the song of Jubilee,
    Loud—as mighty thunders roar!
  Or the fullness of the sea,
    When it breaks upon the shore.—

2 Hallelujah! for the Lord,
    God Omnipotent, shall reign!
  Hallelujah! let the word
    Echo round the earth and main.

3 Hallelujah! hark! the sound,
    From the centre to the skies,
  Wakes, above, beneath, around,
    All creation's harmonies!

4 See Jehovah's banners furl'd,
    Sheath'd his sword! he speaks—'tis done,
  And the kingdoms of this world
    Are the kingdoms of his Son.

5 He shall reign from pole to pole
    With illimitable sway:
  He shall reign, when, like a scroll,
    Yonder heav'ns have pass'd away!

6 Then the end—beneath his rod,
    Man's last enemy shall fall:
  Hallelujah! Christ in God,
    God in Christ, is All in All.
      *Montgomery.*

201

# MISSIONS.

[ Tune, Fulton, page 61. 7s.]

**435**     *Missions.*     7s.

1 Hasten, Lord, the glorious time,
    When, beneath Messiah's sway,
Every nation, every clime,
    Shall the gospel call obey.

2 Mightiest kings his power shall own,
    Heathen tribes his name adore;
Satan and his host, o'erthrown,
    Bound in chains, shall hurt no more.

3 Then shall wars and tumults cease,
    Then be banish'd grief and pain;
Righteousness, and joy, and peace,
    Undisturbed shall ever reign.

4 Bless we, then, our gracious Lord,
    Ever praise his glorious name;
All his mighty acts record,
    All his wondrous love proclaim.

*Lincoln.*

**436 OCEAN WAVE. 6s & 4s, or 10s.**     WM. B. BRADBURY, BY PER.

1. O - ver the o - cean wave, far, far a - way, There the poor
2. Here in this hap - py land we have the light Shin - ing from
3. Then, while the mis - sion ships glad ti - dings bring, List! as that

CHO.—Pit - y them, pit - y them, Chris-tians at home, Haste with the

*FINE.*

hea - then live, wait - ing for day; Grop-ing in ig - no - rance,
God's own word, free, pure, and bright; Shall we not send to them
hea - then band joy - ful - ly sing, "O - ver the o - cean wave,

bread of life, has - ten and come.

*D. C. CHORUS.*

dark as the night, No bless-ed Bi - ble to give them the light.
Bi - bles to read, Teachers, and preach-ers, and all that they need?
oh, see them come, Bring-ing the bread of life, guid-ing us home."

205

**437 KENLEY. 8s & 7s. D.**

FINE.

1. { Hark! the voice of Je - sus cry - ing—"Who will go and work to - day?
   { Fields are white, and har - vest wait - ing; Who will bear the sheaves a - way?"

*D.C.*—Who will an - swer, glad-ly say - ing, "Here am I; send me, send me!"

Loud and strong the Mas - ter call - eth, Rich re - ward he of - fers thee;

*D.C.*

*Who will go To-day.* 8s & 7s. D.

1 Hark! the voice of Jesus crying—
   "Who will go and work to-day?
   Fields are white, and harvest waiting;
   Who will bear the sheaves away?"
   Loud and strong the Master calleth,
   Rich reward he offers thee;
   Who will answer, gladly saying,
   "Here am I; send me, send me!"

2 If you cannot cross the ocean,
   And the heathen lands explore,
   You can find the heathen nearer,
   You can help them at your door.
   If you cannot give your thousands,
   You can give the widow's mite;
   And the least you do for Jesus,
   Will be precious in his sight.

3 If you cannot be the watchman
   Standing high on Zion's wall,
   Pointing out the path to heaven.
   Offering life and peace to all;—
   With your prayers and with your bounties
   You can do what heaven demands;
   You can be like faithful Aaron,
   Holding up the prophet's hands.

4 Let none hear you idly saying,
   "There is nothing I can do,"
   While the souls of men are dying,
   And the Master calls for you.
   Take the task he gives you gladly,

Let his work your pleasure be;
Answer quickly when he calleth,
   "Here am I; send me, send me!"
                        *Dan'l March.*

**437 b** *The Light of the world.* 8s & 7s. D.

1 Light of those whose dreary dwelling
   Borders on the shades of death,
   Come, and, by thyself revealing.
   Dissipate the clouds beneath.
   Thou, new heaven and earth's Creator,
   In our deepest darkness rise;
   Scattering all the night of nature,
   Pouring day upon our eyes.

2 Still we wait for thine appearing;
   Life and joy thy beams impart,
   Chasing all our fears, and cheering
   Every poor, benighted heart.
   Come, and manifest thy favor
   To our ruined, guilty race;
   Come, thou universal Saviour;
   Come, and bring the gospel grace.

3 Save us in thy great compassion,
   O thou mild, pacific Prince;
   Give the knowledge of salvation,
   Give the pardon of our sins:
   By thine all-atoning merit,
   Every burdened soul release;
   Every weary, wandering spirit,
   Guide me into perfect peace.
                        *Charles Wesley.*

**438** HAIL TO THE BRIGHTNESS. 11s & 10s.                    L. MASON.

1. Hail to the bright-ness of Zi - on's glad morn-ing! Joy to the
lands that in dark-ness have lain; Hushed be the ac - cents of
sor - row and mourning, Zi - on in tri - umph be - gins her mild reign.

*Dawn of the Millennium.*                    11s & 10s.

1 Hail to the brightness of Zion's glad morning!
   Joy to the lands that in darkness have lain;
   Hushed be the accents of sorrow and mourning,
   Zion in triumph begins her mild reign.

2 Hail to the brightness of Zion's glad morning,
   Long by the prophets of Israel foretold;
   Hail to the millions from bondage returning;
   Gentiles and Jews the blest vision behold.

3 Lo! in the desert rich flowers are springing,
   Streams ever copious are gliding along;
   Loud from the mountain-tops echoes are ringing,
   Wastes rise in verdure, and mingle in song.

4 See, from all lands—from the isles of the ocean,
   Praise to Jehovah ascending on high;
   Fallen are the engines of war and commotion,
   Shouts of salvation are rending the sky.

**439 NORTHFIELD. C. M.** JER. INGALLS.

1. The na-tions call! from sea to sea Ex-tends the thrill-ing cry,

"Come o-ver, Christians, if there be, And

"Come o-ver Chris-tians
"Come

"Come o-ver, Chris-tians, if there be, Come o-ver, Chris-tians,

help us, ere we die."

if there be, And help us, ere we die."

o-ver, Chris-tians, if there be,

if there be,

*Responding to the Appeal.* C. M.

1 The nations call! from sea to sea
Extends the thrilling cry,
"Come over, Christians, if there be,
And help us, ere we die."

2 Our hearts, O Lord, the summons feel;
Let hand with heart combine,
And answer to the world's appeal
By giving "that is thine."

3 Say to thy gifted servants, "Speed!
Behold the world your field;"
Say to the gold, "The Lord hath need,"
Till hoarded treasures yield.

4 Say to the slumb'ring soul, "Awake!
Ere wanes thy noon away;
Lo! soon I come th' account to take,
Ye stewards of a day."

5 Saviour, forgive; asham'd we lie,
Thy gracious will we know:
Behold, while we delay, they die!
Bid, bid us send, or go:
*Gilbert.*

**440** C. M.

*Glory of the latter days.* Isa. ii. 1-5

1 Behold, the mountain of the Lord
In latter days shall rise
Above the mountains and the hills,
And draw the wond'ring eyes.

2 To this the joyful nations round,
All tribes and tongues, shall flow:
"Up to the hill of God," they say,
"And to his house, we'll go."

3 The beam that shines on Zion's hill
Shall lighten every land:
The King who reigns in Zion's towers
Shall all the world command.

4 Among the nations he shall judge:
His judgments truth shall guide;
His sceptre shall protect the just,
And quell the sinner's pride.

5 Come, then, O house of Jacob! come
To worship at his shrine;
And, walking in the light of God,
With holy beauties shine.
*Logan.*

**441** STERLING. L. M.                                                        HARRISON.

1. Be - hold, the heathen waits to know    The joy the gos-pel will be - stow;

The ex - iled cap - tive to re - ceive    The free-dom Je - sus has to give

*Missions to the Heathen.*        L. M.

1 Behold, the heathen waits to know
The joy the gospel will bestow;
The exiled captive to receive
The freedom Jesus has to give.

2 "Come, let us, with a grateful heart,
In this blest labor share a part;
Our prayers and offerings gladly bring
To aid the triumphs of our King."

3 Our hearts exult in songs of praise,
That we have seen these latter days,
When our Redeemer shall be known
Where Satan long hath held his throne.

4 Where'er his hand hath spread the skies,
Sweet incense to his name shall rise,
And slave and freeman, Greek and Jew,
By sovereign grace be formed anew.
                                        *Voke,*

**442**    *Missionaries Encouraged.*    L. M.

1 Ye Christian heralds, go, proclaim
Salvation in Immanuel's name ;
To distant climes the tidings bear,
And plant the rose of Sharon there.

2 He'll shield you with a wall of fire,
With holy zeal your hearts inspire,
Bid raging winds their fury cease,
And calm the savage breast to peace.

3 And when our labors all are o'er,
Then we shall meet to part no more—
Meet, with the blood-bought throng to fall,
And crown the Saviour, Lord of all.
                            *Winchell's Sel.*

**443**    *Hebrew Missionaries.*    S. M.
[ Tune, Golden Hill, page 222. S. M.]

1 Almighty God of love,
Set up th' attracting sign,

And summon whom thou dost approve
For messengers Divine.

2 From favor'd Abrah'm's seed
The new apostles choose,
In isles and continents to spread
The dead-reviving news.

3 O send thy servants forth,
To call the Hebrews home !
From East, and West, and South and
North,
Let all the wand'rers come.

4 With Israel's myriad's seal'd,
Let all the nations meet,
And show the mystery fulfill'd,
The family complete !
                            *C. Wesley.*

**444**    *God giveth the Increase.*    S. M.
[ Tune, Golden Hill, page 222. S. M.]

1 Lord, if at thy command
The word of life we sow,
Watered by thy almighty hand,
The seed shall surely grow.

2 The virtue of thy grace
A large increase shall give,
And multiply the faithful race,
Who to thy glory live.

3 Now, then, the ceaseless shower
Of gospel-blessings send,
And let the soul-converting power
Thy ministers attend.

4 On multitudes confer
The heart-renewing love,
And by the joy of grace prepare
For fuller joys above.
                            *C. Wesley.*

# CHRISTIAN ACTIVITIES.

**445 PROCTOR. 8s, 7s & 4s.**

J. P. HOLBROOK.

1. O'er the gloom-y hills of dark-ness, Look, my soul, be still and gaze;

See the prom-is-es ad-vanc-ing To a glo-rious day of grace;

Bless-ed jub-'lee, Bless-ed jub-'lee, Let thy glo-rious morn-ing dawn.

*The Acceptable Year.* 8s, 7s & 4s.

1 O'er the gloomy hills of darkness,
Look, my soul, be still and gaze;
See the promises advancing
To a glorious day of grace;
‖: Blessed jub lee,:‖
Let thy glorious morning dawn.

2 Let the dark, benighted pagan,
Let the rude barbarian, see
That divine and glorious conquest,
Once obtain'd on Calvary:
‖: Let the gospel, :‖
Loud resound, from pole to pole.

3 Kingdoms wide, that sit in darkness,
Grant them, Lord, the glorious light;
Now, from eastern coast to western,
May the morning chase the night:
‖: Let redemption, :‖
Freely purchased, win the day.

4 Fly abroad, thou mighty gospel,
Win and conquer—never cease:
May thy lasting, wide dominions,
Multiply and still increase:

‖: Sway thy sceptre, :‖
Saviour, all the world around.
*P. Williams.*

**446** 8s & 7s.
*Collection for the spread of the Gospel.*
[Tune, Stockwell, page 211. 8s & 7s.]

1 With my substance I will honor
My Redeemer and my Lord;
Were ten thousand worlds my manor,
All were nothing to his word.

2 While the heralds of salvation
His abounding grace proclaim;
Let his friends of every station,
Gladly join to spread his fame.

3 May his kingdom be promoted;
May the world the Saviour know:
Be my all to him devoted;
To my Lord my all I owe.

4 Praise the Saviour, all ye nations;
Praise him, all ye hosts above;
Shout, with joyful acclamations,
His divine—victorious love.
*Francis*

# CHRISTIAN ACTIVITIES.

**447  STOCKWELL.  8s & 7s.**

D. E. JONES.

1. Saviour, sprin-kle ma- ny na - tions, Fruit-ful let thy sor-rows be;

By thy pain and con-so-la-tions, Draw the Gen-tiles un - to thee.

*So shall He sprinkle many Nations.* 8s & 7s.

*Isaiah* lii. 15.

1 Saviour, sprinkle many nations,
   Fruitful let thy sorrows be;
By thy pains and consolations,
   Draw the Gentiles unto thee:

2 Of thy cross the wondrous story,
   Be it to the nations told;
Let them see thee in thy glory,
   And thy mercy manifold.

3 Far and wide, though all unknowing,
   Pants for thee each mortal breast;
Human tears for thee are flowing;
   Human hearts in thee would rest;

4 Thirsting, as for dews of even,
   As the new-mown grass for rain,
Thee they seek, as God of heaven,
   Thee, as Man for sinners slain.

5 Saviour, lo! the isles are waiting,
   Stretched the hand, and strained the sight,
For thy Spirit, new creating
   Love's pure flame and wisdom's light;

6 Give the word, and of the preacher
   Speed the foot, and touch the tongue,
Till on earth by every creature
   Glory to the Lamb be sung.

*A. Cleveland Coxe.*

**448**

*Fields white to the harvest.*  8, 7, 4.

[ Tune, Proctor, page 210.  8, 7, 4.]

1 Who but thou, almighty Spirit,
   Can the heathen world reclaim?
Men may preach, but till thou favor,
   Heathens will be still the same:
      Mighty Spirit!
   Witness to the Saviour's name.

2 Thou hast promised by thy prophets
   Glorious light in latter days:
Come, and bless bewildered nations,
   Change our prayers and tears to praise:
      Promised Spirit!
   Round the world diffuse thy rays.

3 All our hopes, and prayers, and labors
   Must be vain without thine aid:
But thou wilt not disappoint us,
   All is true that thou hast said:
      Faithful Spirit!
   O'er the world thine influence shed.

*Unknown*

211

# CHRISTIAN ACTIVITIES.

**449  WOODWORTH. L. M.**                                        WM. B. BRADBURY.

1. Go, mes-sen-ger of peace and love, To peo-ple plunged in shades of night,

Like an-gels sent from fields a-bove, Be thine to shed ce-les-tial light.

L. M.

*The missionary charged and encouraged.*

1 Go, messenger of peace and love,
    To people plunged in shades of night,
  Like angels sent from fields above,
    Be thine to shed celestial light.

2 On barren rock and desert isle,
    Go, bid the rose of Sharon bloom;
  Till arid wastes around thee smile,
    And bear to heaven a sweet perfume.

3 Go to the hungry—food impart;
    To paths of peace the wanderer guide;
  And lead the thirsty, panting heart
    Where streams of living water glide.

4 Go, bid the bright and morning star
    From Bethlehem's plain resplendent shine,
  And, piercing through the gloom afar,
    Shed heav'nly light and love divine.

5 O, faint not in the day of toil,
    When harvest waits the reaper's hand;
  Go, gather in the glorious spoil,
    And joyous in his presence stand.

6 Thy love a rich reward shall find
    From Him who sits enthron'd on high;
  For they who turn the erring mind
    Shall shine like stars above the sky.
                                    *A. Balfour.*

**450  *Approaching Millenium.*  L. M.**

1 Behold the expected time draw near,
  The shades disperse, the dawn appear;
  Behold the wilderness assume
  The beauteous tints of Eden's bloom.

2 The untaught heathen waits to know
  The joy the gospel will bestow;
  The exiled captive, to receive
  The freedom Jesus has to give.

3 Come, let us with a grateful heart,
  In the blest labor share a part;
  Our pray'rs and off'rings gladly bring
  To aid the triumphs of our King.

4 Invite the world to come and prove
  A Saviour's condescending love;
  And humbly fall before his feet,
  Assured they shall acceptance meet.
                                    *Coxe.*

**450 b  *For Jews and Gentiles.*  L. M.**

1 Head of the Church, whose Spirit fills
    And flows through every faithful soul,
  Unites in mystic love, and seals
    Them one, and sanctifies the whole;

2 "Come, Lord," thy glorious Spirit cries,
    And souls beneath the altar groan;
  "Come, Lord," the bride on earth replies,
    "And perfect all our souls in one."

3 Pour out the promised gift on all;
    Answer the universal "Come!"
  The fullness of the Gentiles call,
    And take thine ancient people home.

4 To thee let all the nations flow;
    Let all obey the gospel word;
  Let all their bleeding Saviour know,
    Filled with the glory of the Lord.

5 O for thy truth and mercy's sake
    The purchase of thy passion claim;
  Thine heritage, the Gentiles, take,
    And cause the world to know thy name.
                                    *Charles Wesley.*

212

**451 BEULAH. 7s. D.** JOIS.

1. Watch-man, tell us of the night, What its signs of prom - ise are:

Trav'l - ler, o'er yon moun - tain height, See that glo - ry - beam - ing star.

*D.S.*—Trav'l - ler, yes; it brings the day, Prom-is'd day of Is - ra - el.

Watch-man, does its beau - teous ray Aught of hope or joy fore - tell?

*Watchman, what of the night?* 7s. D.

1 Watchman, tell us of the night,
  What its signs of promise are:
  Trav'ller, o'er yon mountain height,
  See that glory-beaming star.
  Watchman, does its beauteous ray
  Aught of hope or joy foretell?
  Trav'ller, yes; it brings the day,
  Promis'd day of Israel.

2 Watchman, tell us of the night:
  Higher yet that star ascends,
  Trav'ller, blessedness and light,
  Peace and truth, its course portends.
  Watchman, will its beams alone
  Gild the spot that gave them birth?
  Trav'ller, ages are its own,
  See! it bursts o'er all the earth.

3 Watchman, tell us of the night,
  For the morning seems to dawn,
  Trav'ller, darkness takes its flight,
  Doubt and terror are withdrawn,
  Watchman, let thy wand'rings cease;

Hie thee to thy quiet home.
Trav'ller, lo! the Prince of peace,
Lo! the Son of God is come.

*Bowring.*

**451 b** *The Banner of the Cross.* 7s. D.

1 Go, ye messengers of God;
  Like the beams of morning, fly.
  Take the wonder-working rod;
  Wave the banner cross on high.
  Go to many a tropic isle
  In the bosom of the deep,
  Where the skies forever smile,
  And th' oppress'd forever weep.

2 O'er the pagan's night of care
  Pour the living light of heaven;
  Chase away his wild despair;
  Bid him hope to be forgiven.
  Where the golden gates of day
  Open on the palmy East,
  High the bleeding cross display;
  Spread the Gospel's richest feast.

*Marsden.*

213

CHRISTIAN ACTIVITIES.

452 LUTHER. S. M.  DR. HASTINGS.

1. O Thou whom we a-dore! To bless our earth a-gain, As-sume thine own al-might-y power, And o'er the na-tions reign. And o'er the na-tions reign.

*Phil.* ii. 10, 11.    S. M.

1 O thou whom we adore!
  To bless our earth again,
Assume thine own almighty power,
  And o'er the nations reign.

2 The world's Desire and Hope,
  All power to thee is given;
Now set the last great empire up,
  Eternal Lord of heaven!

3 A gracious Saviour, thou
  Wilt all thy creatures bless;
And every knee to thee shall bow;
  And every tongue confess.

4 According to thy word,
  Now be thy grace revealed;
And with the knowledge of the Lord,
  Let all the earth be filled.
                          *C. Wesley.*

453    *Rev.* xxii. 20.    S. M.

1 Come, Lord, and tarry not!
  Bring the long-looked for day;
Oh, why these years of waiting here,
  These ages of delay?

2 Come for thy saints still wait;
  Daily ascends their sigh;
The Spirit and the Bride say, Come!
  Dost thou not hear the cry?

3 Come, for creation groans,
  Impatient of thy stay,
Worn out with these long years of ill,
  These ages of delay.

4 Come, and make all things new,
  Build up this ruined earth,
Restore our faded paradise,—
  Creation's second birth.

5 Come and begin thy reign
  Of everlasting peace;
Come, take the kingdom to thyself,
  Great King of Righteousness.
                          *Bonar.*

454    *Hab.* iii. 3.    S. M.

1 O Lord, thy work revive,
  In Zion's gloomy hour,
And make her dying graces live
  By thy restoring power.

2 Awake thy chosen few
  To fervent, earnest prayer;
Again may they their vows renew,
  Thy blessed presence share.

3 Thy Spirit then will speak
  Through lips of feeble clay,
And hearts of adamant will break,
  And rebels will obey.

4 Lord, lend thy gracious ear;
  Oh, listen to our cry;
Oh, come and bring salvation here!
  Our hopes on thee rely.
                          *Mrs. Brown.*

455    *Lam.* i. 4.    S. M.

1 Oh, for the happy hour
  When God will hear our cry,
And send, with a reviving power,
  His Spirit from on high.

2 We meet, we sing, we pray,
  We listen to the word,
In vain;—we see no cheering ray,
  No cheering voice is heard.

3 While many crowd thy house,
  How few, around thy board,
Meet to recount their solemn vows,
  And bless thee as their Lord!

214

4 Thou, thou alone, canst give
Thy gospel sure success;
Canst bid the dying sinner live
Anew in holiness,

5 Come, then, with power divine,
Spirit of life and love!
Then shall this people all be thine,
This church like that above.

*Bethune.*

## LOVE FEASTS.

**456 MARTYN. 7s. D.**            S. B. MARSH.

1. { Come, and let us sweet-ly join, Christ to praise in hymns di - vine!
{ Give we all, with one ac- cord, Glo - ry to our com - mon Lord;

*D.C.*—An - te - date the joys a - bove; Cel - e - brate the feast of love.

Hands, and hearts, and voi-ces raise; Sing as in the an - cient days;

*With One Accord.*     7s. D.

1 Come, and let us sweetly join,
Christ to praise in hymns divine!
Give we all, with one accord,
Glory to our common lord;
Hands, and hearts, and voices, raise;
Sing as in the ancient days;
Antedate the joys above;
Celebrate the feast of love.

2 Strive we, in affection strive:
Let the purer flame revive,
Such as in the martyrs glow'd,
Dying champions for their God.
We for Christ, our Master, stand,
Lights in a benighted land:
We our dying Lord confess,
We are Jesus' witnesses.

3 Witnesses that Christ hath died:
We with him are crucified:
Christ hath burst the bands of death,
We his quick'ning Spirit breathe:
Christ is now gone up on high;
Thither all our wishes fly;
Sits at God's right hand above;
There with him we reign in love.

*C. Wesley.*

**457**     *Unity.*     7s. D.

1 Come, thou high and lofty Lord!
Lowly, meek, incarnate Word:
Humbly stoop to earth again:
Come and visit abject man!
Jesus, dear expected guest,
Thou art bidden to the feast:
For thyself our hearts prepare:
Come, and sit, and banquet there!

2 Jesus, we thy promise claim:
We are met in thy great name:
In the midst do thou appear,
Manifest thy presence here!
Sanctify us, Lord, and bless!
Breathe thy Spirit, give thy peace!
Thou thyself within us move:
Make our feast a feast of love.

3 Make us all in thee complete;
Make us all for glory meet—
Meet t' appear before thy sight,
Partners with the saints in light.
Call, O call us each by name,
To the marriage of the Lamb:
Let us lean upon thy breast;
Love be there our endless feast.

*C. Wesley.*

# CHRISTIAN ACTIVITIES.

**458  HENDON. 7s.**

DR. MALAN.

1. Let us join, ('tis God com - mands,) Let us join our hearts and hands; Help to gain our call - ing's hope, Build we each the oth - er up, Build we each the oth - er up:

*Fitly joined together.* 7s.

1 Let us join, ( 'tis God commands,)
Let us join our hearts and hands ;
Help to gain our calling's hope,
Build we each the other up:

2 Still forget the things behind,
Follow Christ in heart and mind ;
Toward the mark unwearied press,
Seize the crown of righteousness.

3 Plead we thus for faith alone,
Faith which by our works is shown:
God it is who justifies,
Only faith the grace applies ;

4 Active faith that lives within ;
Conquers earth, and hell, and sin ;
Sanctifies and makes us whole ;
Forms the Saviour in the soul.

5 Let us for this faith contend ;
Sure salvation is its end :
Heav'n already is begun,
Everlasting life is won :

6 Only let us persevere,
Till we see our Lord appear ;
Never from the Rock remove,
Saved by faith, which works by love.

*C. Wesley.*

**459**  *Of one heart and mind.* 7s.

1 Jesus, Lord, we look to thee ;
Let us in thy name agree ;
Show thyself the Prince of peace ;
Bid our jars forever cease.

2 By thy reconciling love,
Every stumbling block remove ;
Each to each unite, endear,
Come, and spread thy banner here.

3 Make us of one heart and mind,
Courteous, pitiful, and kind,
Lowly, meek, in thought and word,
Altogether like our Lord.

4 Let us for each other care.
Each the other's burden bear ;
To thy Church the pattern give,
Show how true believers live.

5 Free from anger and from pride,
Let us thus in God abide ;
All the depths of love express,
All the heights of holiness.

6 Let us then with joy remove
To the family above ;
On the wings of angels fly ;
Show how true believers die.

*Charles Wesley.*

216

# LOVE FEASTS.

**460  METROPOLITAN. C. M.**    J. T. LAYTON.

*Andante.*    *mf*

1. How sweet and heav'n-ly is the sight, When those who love the Lord

In one an-oth-er's peace de-light, And so ful-til his word!

---

*Brotherly Love.*    C. M.

1 How sweet and heav'nly is the sight,
  When those who love the Lord
  In one another's peace delight,
  And so fulfil his word!

2 Oh! may we feel each brother's sigh,
  And with him bear a part;
  May sorrows flow from eye to eye,
  And joy from heart to heart.

3 Let love, in one delightful stream,
  Through every bosom flow;
  Let union sweet, and dear esteem,
  In every action, glow.

4 Love is the golden chain that binds
  The happy souls above;
  And he's an heir of heaven, who finds
  His bosom glow with love.
                                    *Swain.*

**461**    *Love to Christ's Disciples.*    C. M.

1 Lord, thou on earth didst love thine own;
  Didst love them to the end;
  Oh! still from thy celestial throne,
  Let gifts of love descend.

2 As thou for us didst stoop so low,
  Warm'd by love's holy name,
  So let our deeds of kindness flow
  To all who bear thy name.

3 One blessed fellowship in love
  Thy living church should stand,
  Till, faultless, she at last above
  Shall shine at thy right hand.

4 Oh! glorious day when she the bride,
  With her dear Lord appears;
  When robed in beauty at his side,
  She shall forget her tears.
                                    *Ray Palmer.*

**462**    *Mutual Aid.*    C. M.

1 Try us, O God, and search the ground
  Of every sinful heart:
  Whate'er of sin in us is found,
  O bid it all depart!

2 When to the right or left we stray,
  Leave us not comfortless;
  But guide our feet into the way
  Of everlasting peace.

3 Help us to help each other, Lord,
  Each other's cross to bear:
  Let each his friendly aid afford,
  And feel his brother's care.

4 Help us to build each other up,
  Our little stock improve:
  Increase our faith, confirm our hope,
  And perfect us in love.

5 Up into thee, our living Head,
  Let us in all things grow:
  Till thou hast made us free indeed,
  And spotless here below.

6 Then, when the mighty work is wrought,
  Receive thy ready bride:
  Give us in heaven a happy lot
  With all the sanctified.
                                    *C. Wesley.*

217

# CHRISTIAN ACTIVITIES.

463 OLWELL. C. M. ANON.

1. My God, what gen-tle cords are thine, How soft, and yet how strong!

While pow'r, and truth, and love com-bine To draw our souls a-long.

*Christians drawn with cords of Love.* C. M.

1 My God, what gentle cords are thine,
How soft, and yet how strong!
While pow'r, and truth, and love combine
To draw our souls along.

2 Thou saw'st us crush'd beneath the yoke
Of Satan and of sin;
Thy hand the iron bondage broke,
Our sinful hearts to win.

3 The guilt of twice ten thousand sins
One offering takes away;
And grace, when first the war begins,
Secures the crowning day.
*Doddridge.*

464 *Christian Love.* C. M.

1 Happy the heart where graces reign,
Where love inspires the breast;
Love is the brightest of the train,
And strengthens all the rest.

2 Knowledge, alas! 'tis all in vain,
And all in vain our fear;
Our stubborn sins will fight and reign,
If love be absent there.

3 'Tis love that makes our cheerful feet
In swift obedience move;
The devils know and tremble too,
But devils cannot love.

4 This is the grace that lives and sings,
When faith and hope shall cease;
'Tis this shall strike our joyful strings,
In the sweet realms of bliss.
*Watts.*

465 *Safety in Union.* C. M.

1 Jesus, great Shepherd of the sheep,
To thee for help we fly;
Thy little flock in safety keep,
For O, the wolf is nigh!

2 He comes, of hellish malice full,
To scatter, tear, and slay;
He seizes every straggling soul
As his own lawful prey.

3 Us into thy protection take,
And gather with thine arm;
Unless the fold we first forsake,
The wolf can never harm.

4 We laugh to scorn his cruel power
While by our Shepherd's side;
The sheep he never can devour,
Unless he first divide.

5 O do not suffer him to part
The souls that here agree;
But make us of one mind and heart,
And keep us one in thee.

6 Together let us sweetly live,
Together let us die;
And each a starry crown receive,
And reign above the sky.
*Charles Wesley.*

# FUNERALS AND OTHER OCCASIONS.

## DEATH—THE JUDGMENT—HEAVEN.

466 BALERMA. C. M.　　　　　　　　　　　R. SIMPSON.

1. Thee we a - dore, e - ter - nal Name! And humb-ly own to thee

How feeb - le is our mor - tal frame, What dy - ing worms we be!

---

**Brevity of life.**　　　C. M.

1 Thee we adore, eternal Name!
　And humbly own to thee
　How feeble is our mortal frame,
　What dying worms we be!

2 The years roll round, and steals away
　The breath that first it gave:
　Whate'er we do, where'er we be,
　We're trav'ling to the grave.

3 Dangers stand thick through all the
　　　ground
　To push us to the tomb;
　And fierce diseases wait around
　To hurry mortals home.

4 Great God! on what a slender thread,
　Hang everlasting things!
　Th' eternal states of all the dead
　Upon life's feeble strings.

5 Infinite joy, or endless woe,
　Attends on every breath;
　And yet how unconcern'd we go
　Upon the brink of death!

6 Waken, O Lord, our drowsy sense,
　To walk this dang'rous road;
　And if our souls be hurried hence
　May they be found with God!
　　　　　　　　　　　　　*Watts.*

---

467　*A voice from the Tombs.*　C. M.

1 Hark! from the tombs a doleful sound,
　My ears attend the cry;
　" Ye living men, come view the ground
　Where you must shortly lie.

2 " Princes, this clay must be your bed,
　In spite of all your towers:
　The tall, the wise, the rev'rend head,
　Must lie as low as ours."

3 Great God! is this our certain doom!
　And are we still secure!
　Still walking downward to the tomb,
　And yet prepared no more!

4 Grant us the power of quick'ning grace,
　To fit our souls to fly;
　Then, when we drop this dying flesh,
　We'll raise above the sky.
　　　　　　　　　　　　　*Watts.*

*Doxology.*

To Father, Son, and Holy Ghost,
　Who sweetly all agree,
To save a world of sinners lost,
　Eternal glory be.

**468** MEAR. C. M.

1. And must I be to judg-ment brought, And an-swer in that day

For ev-'ry vain and i-dle thought, And ev-'ry word I say?

---

*The Day of Judgment.* C. M.

1 And must I be to judgment brought,
And answer in that day
For every vain and idle thought,
And every word I say?

2 Yes, every secret of my heart
Shall shortly be made known,
And I receive my just desert
For all that I have done.

3 How careful, then, ought I to live!
With what religious fear!
Who such a strict account must give
For my behaviour here!

4 Thou awful Judge of quick and dead,
The watchful power bestow;
So shall I to my ways take heed,
To all I speak or do.

5 If now thou standest at the door,
O let me feel thee near!
And make my peace with God, before
I at thy bar appear.
*C. Wesley.*

**469** *The vain man warned.* C. M.

1 Vain man thy vain pursuits forbear;
Repent, thy end is nigh:
Death, at the farthest, can't be far:
O! think before thou die.

2 Reflect: thou hast a soul to save;
Thy sins, how high they mount!
What are thy hopes beyond the grave?
How stands that dark account?

3 Death enters, and there's no defense,
His time there's none can tell;
He'll in a moment call thee hence,
To heaven, or down to hell.

4 Thy flesh, perhaps thy greatest care,
Shall crawling worms consume:
But ah! destruction stops not there;
Sin kills beyond the tomb.
*Joseph Hart.*

**470** *Eternal Death.* C. M.

1 That awful day will surely come,
Th' appointed hour makes haste,
When I must stand before my Judge
And pass the solemn test.

2 Jesus, thou Source of all my joys,
Thou Ruler of my heart,
How could I bear to hear thy voice
Pronounce the sound, "Depart!"

3 The thunder of that awful word,
Would so torment my ear,
'Twould tear my soul asunder, Lord,
With most tormenting fear.

4 What, to be banished from my Lord,
And yet forbid to die!
To linger in eternal pain,
And death forever fly!

5 O wretched state of deep despair,
To see my God remove,
And fix my doleful station where
I must not taste his love!
*Watts.*

**471 PHUVAH. C. M.** MELCHIOR VULPIUS.

1 Come, let us join our friends a - bove, That have ob - tain'd the prize;

And on the eag - le wings of love To joys ce - les - tial rise.

2 Let all the saints terrestial sing,
With those to glory gone;
For all the servants of our King,
In earth and heaven, are one.

3 One family we dwell in him,
One Church above, beneath.
Though now divided by the stream,
The narrow stream of death.

4 One army of the living God,
To his command we bow;
Part of his host have cross'd the flood,
And part are crossing now.

5 Our spirits too shall quickly join,
Like theirs with glory crown'd,
And shout to see our Captain's sign,
To hear his trumpet sound.

6 O that we now might grasp our Guide!
O that the word were given!
Come, Lord of hosts, the waves divide,
And land us all in heaven!

*C. Wesley.*

**471 b** *The New Jerusalem.* C. M.

1 Lo, what a glorious sight appears
To our believing eyes!
The earth and seas are passed away,
And the old rolling skies.

2 From the third heaven, where God resides,
That holy, happy place,
The New Jerusalem comes down,
Adorned with shining grace.

3 Attending angels shout for joy,
And the bright armies sing,
"Mortals, behold the sacred seat
Of your descending King!"

4 "The God of glory down to men
Removes his blest abode;
Men, the dear objects of his grace,
And he the loving God."

5 "His own soft hand shall wipe the tears
From every weeping eye;
And pains, and groans, and griefs, and fears,
And death itself, shall die."

*Isaac Watts.*

**471 b ST. ANN'S C. M.** WM. CROFT.

1. Lo, what a glo - rious sight ap - pears To our be - liev - ing eyes!

The earth and seas are passed a - way, And the old roll - ing skies.

221

472 GOLDEN HILL. S. M.               CHAPIN.

*Slow.*

1. Thou judge of quick and dead, Be - fore whose bar se - vere,

With ho - ly joy, or guilt - y dread, We all shall soon ap - pear.

*The seat of Judgment.*      S. M.

1 Thou Judge of quick and dead,
   Before whose bar severe,
With holy joy, or guilty dread,
   We all shall soon appear.

2 Our caution'd souls prepare
   For that tremendous day,
And fill us now with watchful care,
   And stir us up to pray.

3 To pray, and wait the hour,
   That awful hour unknown,
When, robed in majesty and power,
   Thou shalt from heaven come down.

4 Th' immortal Son of man,
   To judge the human race,
With all thy Father's dazzling train,
   With all thy glorious grace.

5 O may we thus be found,
   Obedient to his word ;
Attentive to the trumpet's sound,
   And looking for our Lord !

6 O may we thus insure
   A lot among the blest ;
And watch a moment to secure
   An everlasting rest !

                    *C. Wesley.*

473 *A house not made with hands.*    S. M.
          *2 Cor.* v. 1–9.

1 We know, by faith we know,
   If this vile house of clay,
This tabernacle, sink below,
   In ruinous decay.

2 We have a house above,
   Not made with mortal hands ;
And firm as our Redeemer's love
   That heavenly fabric stands.

3 It stands securely high,
   Indissolubly sure :
Our glorious mansion in the sky
   Shall evermore endure:

4 O were we enter'd there !
   To perfect heav'n restored !
O were we all caught up to share
   The triumph of our Lord !

5 For this in faith we call ;
   For this we weep and pray :
O might the tabernacle fall !
   O might we 'scape away.

6 Full of immortal hope,
   We urge the restless strife,
And hasten to be swallowed up
   Of everlasting life,

                    *C. Wesley.*

**474 OLNEY. S. M.**                                    DR. L. MASON.

1. And must this bod - y die, This well-wrought frame de - cay?

And must these ac - tive limbs of mine Lie mould -'ring in the clay!

---

*The momentous question.*     S. M.

1 And must this body die.
   This well-wrought frame decay?
   And must these active limbs of mine
   Lie mould'ring in the clay!

2 Corruption, earth, and worms,
   Shall but refine this flesh,
   Till my triumphant spirit comes
   To put it on afresh.

3 God my Redeemer lives,
   And ever from the skies
   Looks down, and watches all my dust,
   Till he shall bid it rise.

4 Array'd in glorious grace
   Shall these vile bodies shine,
   And every shape, and every face,
   Be heavenly and divine.

5 These lively hopes we owe,
   Lord, to thy dying love:
   O may we bless thy grace below,
   And sing thy grace above!
                                    *Watts.*

**475**     *The end of Life.*     S. M.

1 And am I born to die?
   To lay this body down?
   And must my trembling spirit fly
   Into a world unknown?

2 A land of deepest shade,
   Unpierced by human thought;
   The dreary regions of the dead,
   Where all things are forgot!

3 Soon as from earth I go,
   What will become of me?
   Eternal happiness or woe
   Must then my portion be!

4 Waked by the trumpet's sound,
   I from my grave shall rise;
   And see the Judge with glory crown'd,
   And see the flaming skies.

5 How shall I leave my tomb—
   With triumph or regret?
   A fearful or a joyful doom,
   A curse or blessing meet?

6 Will angel bands convey
   Their brother to the bar?
   Or devils drag my soul away
   To meet its sentence there?
                                    *C. Wesley.*

**475 b**     *Eccles.* xi. 6.     S. M.

1 Sow in the morn thy seed,
   At eve hold not thy hand;
   To doubt and fear give thou no heed—
   Broad-cast it o'er the land.

2 Beside all waters sow,
   The highway furrows stock,
   Drop it where thorns and thistles grow,
   Scatter it on the rock.

3 The good, the fruitful ground,
   Expect not here nor there;
   O'er hill, o'er dale, by plots, 'tis found;
   Go forth, then, everywhere.
                                    *Montgomery.*

476 MERIBAH. C. P. M.  DR. L. MASON.

1. How hap - py, gracious Lord, are we, Di - vine - ly drawn to fol - low thee! Whose hours di - vid - ed are Be - twixt the mount and mul - ti - tude; Our day is spent in do - ing good, Our night in praise and prayer.

*Always rejoicing.* C. P. M.

1 How happy, gracious Lord, are we,
Divinely drawn to follow thee!
Whose hours divided are
Betwixt the mount and multitude;
Our day is spent in doing good,
Our night in praise and prayer.

2 With us no melancholy void,
No moment lingers unemployed,
Or unimproved, below:
Our weariness of life is gone,
Who live to serve our God alone,
And only thee to know.

3 The winter's night, the summer's day,
Glide imperceptibly away,
Too short to sing thy praise;
Too few we find the happy hours,
And haste to join those heavenly powers
In everlasting lays.

4 With all who chant thy name on high,
And, "Holy, holy, holy," cry,—
A bright, harmonious throng!
We long thy praises to repeat,
And ceaseless sing around thy seat
The new, eternal song.

*Charles Wesley.*

221

# DEATH—THE JUDGMENT—HEAVEN.

**477 BEATUS-MINOR. 8s.**  OLD MELODY.

1. O when shall we sweet-ly re - move, O when shall we en - ter our rest,

Re - turn to the Zi - on a - bove, The moth - er of spir - its dis-tressed!

---

*To be with Christ is far better.* 8s.

1 O when shall we sweetly remove,
  O when shall we enter our rest,
Return to the Zion above,
  The mother of spirits distressed!

2 That city of God the great King,
  Where sorrow and death are no more,
But saints our Immanuel sing,
  And cherub and seraph adore.

3 Not all the archangels can tell
  The joys of that holiest place,
Where Jesus is pleased to reveal
  The light of his heavenly face:

4 When, caught in the rapturous flame,
  The sight beatific they prove,
And walk in the light of the Lamb,
  Enjoying the beams of his love.

5 Thou know'st in the spirit of prayer
  We long thy appearing to see,
Resigned to the burden we bear,
  But longing to triumph with thee:

6 'Tis good at thy word to be here;
  'Tis better in thee to be gone.
And see thee in glory appear,
  And rise to a share in thy throne.

*Charles Wesley.*

---

**478**  *Desiring to depart.*  8s.

1 I long to behold him arrayed
  With glory and light from above;
The King in his beauty displayed,
  His beauty of holiest love;

2 I languish and sigh to be there,
  Where Jesus hath fixed his abode;
O when shall we meet in the air,
  And fly to the mountain of God!

3 With him I on Zion shall stand,
  For Jesus hath spoken the word;
The breadth of Immanuel's land
  Survey by the light of my Lord:

4 But when, on thy bosom reclined,
  Thy face I am strengthened to see,
My fullness of rapture I find,
  My heaven of heavens in thee.

5 How happy the people that dwell
  Secure in the city above!
No pain the inhabitants feel,
  No sickness or sorrow shall prove.

6 Physician of souls, unto me
  Forgiveness and holiness give;
And then from the body set free,
  And then to the city receive.

*Charles Wesley.*

479 HORTON. 7s.  VON WARTENSEE.

1. Lift your eyes of faith and see Saints and an - gels joined in one:

What a count-less com - pa - ny Stand be - fore yon dazz - ling throne!

*Saints and angels round the throne.* 7s.

1 Lift your eyes of faith, and see
  Saints and angels joined in one:
  What a countless company
  Stand before yon dazzling throne!

2 Each before his Saviour stands,
  All in whitest robes arrayed;
  Palms they carry in their hands,
  Crowns of glory on their head.

3 Saints begin the endless song,
  Cry aloud in heavenly lays,
  Glory doth to God belong,
  God, the glorious Saviour, praise.

4 All salvation from him came,
  Him, who reigns enthroned on high:
  Glory to the bleeding Lamb,
  Let the morning stars reply.

5 Angel powers the throne surround,
  Next the saints in glory they;
  Lulled with the transporting sound,
  They their silent homage pay:

6 Prostrate on their face, before
  God and his Messiah fall:
  Then in hymns of praise adore,
  Shout the Lamb that died for all.
  *Charles Wesley.*

480 *Make his praise glorious.* C. P. M.

[Tune, Ganges, page 167. C. P. M.]

1 O could I speak the matchless worth,
  O could I sound the glories forth,
    Which in my Saviour shine,
  I'd soar and touch the heavenly strings,
  And vie with Gabriel while he sings
    In notes almost divine.

2 I'd sing the precious blood he spilt,
  My ransom from the dreadful guilt
    Of sin, and wrath divine:
  I'd sing his glorious righteousness,
  In which all-perfect heavenly dress
    My soul shall ever shine.

3 I'd sing the characters he bears,
  And all the forms of love he wears,
    Exalted on his throne;
  In loftiest songs of sweetest praise,
  I would to everlasting days
    Make all his glories known.

4 Well, the delightful day will come
  When my dear Lord will bring me home,
    And I shall see his face:
  Then with my Saviour, Brother, Friend,
  A blest eternity I'll spend,
    Triumphant in his grace
    *Samuel Medley.*

**481  VARINA. C. M. D.**

ARR. BY GEO. F. ROOT.

1. { There is a land of pure de-light, Where saints im-mor-tal reign; }
{ In - fi - nite day ex - cludes the night, And pleas-ures ban - ish pain: }

There ev - er - last - ing spring a - bides, And nev - er - with-'ring flowers:

Death, like a nar - row sea, di - vides This heav'n-ly land from ours.

*The Heavenly Canaan.* C. M. D.

1 There is a land of pure delight,
 Where saints immortal reign;
Infinite day excludes the night,
 And pleasures banish pain:
There everlasting spring abides
 And never-with'ring flowers:
Death, like a narrow sea, divides
 This heavenly land from ours.

2 Sweet fields beyond the swelling flood
 Stand dress'd in living green;
So to the Jews old Canaan stood,
 While Jordan rolled between.
Could we but climb where Moses stood,
 And view the landscape o'er,
Not Jordan's stream, nor death's cold flood,
 Should fright us from the shore.

*Watts.*

**482**    *Visions of Heaven.*    C. M. D.

1 And let this feeble body fail,
 And let it droop or die :
My soul shall quit the mournful vale,

And soar to worlds on high,—
Shall join the disembodied saints,
 And find its long-sought rest,
That only bliss for which it pants,
 In my Redeemer's breast.

2 In hope of that immortal crown,
 I now the cross sustain ;
And gladly wander up and down,
 And smile at toil and pain:
I suffer out my threescore years,
 Till my Deliv'rer come,
And wipe away his servant's tears,
 And take his exile home.

3 O what are all my suff'rings here,
 If, Lord, thou count me meet
With that enraptured host to appear,
 And worship at thy feet!
Give joy or grief, give ease or pain : —
 Take life or friends away,
I come to find them all again
 In that eternal day.

*Charles Wesley.*

**483 GENEVA. C. M.** COLE.

1. My thoughts sur-mount these low - er skies, And look with - in the veil;
2. There I be - hold with sweet de - light The bless-ed Three in One,
3. His prom - ise stands for - ev - er firm, His grace shall ne'er de-part;
4. I would not be a stran - ger still To that ce - les - tial place,

There springs of end - less pleas - ure rise, The wa - ters nev - er fail.
And strong af - fec - tions fix my sight On God's in - car - nate Son.
He binds my name up - on his arm, And seals it on his heart.
Where I for - ev - er hope to dwell Near my Re - deem-er's face.

WATTS.

**484** *Vision of Heaven.* C. M.

1 Give me the wings of faith to rise
Within the veil, and see
The saints above, how great their joys,
How bright their glories be.

2 Once they were mourning here below,
And wet their couch with tears;
They wrestled hard, as we do now,
With sins and doubts and fears.

3 I asked from whence their vict'ry came;
They, with united breath,

Ascribe their conquest to the Lamb,
Their triumph to his death.

4 They marked the footsteps that he trod,
His zeal inspired their breast,
And following their incarnate God,
Possess the promised rest.

5 Our glorious Leader claims our praise
For his own pattern given,
While the long cloud of witnesses
Show the same path to heaven.

*Watts.*

**484 b SWANWICK. C. M.** LUCAS.

1. There is a fold whence none can stray; And pastures ev - er green, Where sul-try
2. Far up the ev - er - last - ing hills In God's own light it lies; His smile its
3. One nar-row vale, one dark-some wave, Di - vides that land from this: I have a
4. Soon at his feet my soul will lie In life's last strug-gling breath; But I shall
5. Far from this guilt-y world to be Ex - empt from toil and strife—To spend e -

sun, or stormy day, Or night is nev - er seen, Or night is nev - er seen.
vast di - men-sion fills With joy that nev - er dies, With joy that nev - er dies.
Shepherd pledged to save And bear me home to bliss, And bear me home to bliss.
on - ly seem to die. I shall not taste of death, I shall not taste of death.
ter - ni - ty with thee—My Saviour, this is life, My Sa-viour, this is life!

UNKNOWN.

228

**485** *Resting in hope.* S. M.

1 Rest for the toiling hand,
Rest for the anxious brow,
Rest for the weary, way-sore feet,
Rest from all labor now.

2 Rest for the fevered brain,
Rest for the throbbing eye;
Through these parched lips of thine no
Shall pass the moan or sigh. [more

3 Soon shall the trump of God
Give out the welcome sound,
That shakes thy silent chamber-walls,
And breaks the turf-sealed ground.

4 Ye dwellers in the dust,
Awake, come forth and sing!
Sharp has your frost of winter been,
But bright shall be your spring.
*H. Bonar.*

**486** DOVER. S. M.                              AARON WILLIAMS.

1. "Ser - vant of God, well done! Rest from thy loved em - ploy;
The bat - tle fought, the vic - t'ry won, En - ter thy Mas - ter's joy."

*Funeral of an aged Minister.* S. M.

1 "Servant of God, well done!
Rest from thy loved employ;
The battle fought, the vict'ry won,
Enter thy Master's joy."

2 The voice at midnight came:
He started up to hear;
A mortal arrow pierced his frame;
He fell,—but felt no fear.

3 His sword was in his hand,
Still warm with recent fight,
Ready that moment, at command,
Through rock and steel to smite.

4 Bent on such glorious toils,
The world to him was loss,
Yet all his trophies, all his spoils,
He hung upon the cross.

5 At midnight came the cry,
"To meet thy God prepare!"
He woke,—and caught his Captain's eye,
Then, strong in faith and prayer,

6 His spirit, with a bound,
Left its encumb'ring clay;
His tent, at sunrise, on the ground
A darken'd ruin lay.

7 The pains of death are past,
Labor and sorrow cease;
And, life's long warfare closed at last,
His soul is found in peace.

8 Soldier of Christ, well done!
Praise be thy new employ;
And while eternal ages run,
Rest in thy Saviour's joy.
*Montgomery.*

**487  ELTON. L. M.**                                DR. L. MASON.

*Energetic.*

1. Life is' the time to serve the Lord, The time t'in - sure the great re - ward;

And while the lamp holds out to burn, The vil - est sin - ner may re - turn.

---

*Life, the day of grace.*  L. M.

1 Life is the time to serve the Lord,
  The time t' insure the great reward;
  And while the lamp holds out to burn,
  The vilest sinner may return.

2 Life is the hour that God has given
  To escape from hell, and fly to heaven;
  The day of grace, and mortals may
  Secure the blessings of the day.

3 The living know that they must die,
  But all the dead forgotten lie;
  Their mem'ry and their sense is gone,
  Alike unknowing and unknown.

4 Their hatred and their love is lost,
  Their envy buried in the dust;
  They have no share in all that's done
  Beneath the circuit of the sun.

5 Then what my thoughts design to do,
  My hands, with all your might pursue;
  Since no device nor work is found,
  Nor faith, nor hope, beneath the ground.

6 There are no acts of pardon pass'd
  In the cold grave, to which we haste;
  But darkness, death, and long despair,
  Reign in eternal silence there.
                                    *Watts.*

**488**   *Funeral of a Youth.*   L. M.

1 The morning flowers display their sweets,
  And gay their silken leaves unfold,
  As careless of the noontide heats,
  As fearless of the evening cold.

2 Nipp'd by the wind's untimely blast,
  Parch'd by the sun's directer ray,
  The momentary glories waste,
  The short-liv'd beauties die away.

3 So blooms the human face divine,
  When youth its pride of beauty shows;
  Fairer than spring the colors shine,
  And sweeter than the virgin rose.

4 Or worn by slowly-rolling years,
  Or broke by sickness in a day,
  The fading glories disappears,
  The short-lived beauties die away.

5 Yet these, new-rising from the tomb,
  With lustre brighter far shall shine,
  Revive with ever-during bloom,
  Safe from diseases and decline.

6 Let sickness blast, let death devour,
  If heaven must recompense our pains:
  Perish the grass, and fade the flower,
  If firm the word of God remains.
                                    *S. Wesley, Jr.*

DEATH—THE JUDGMENT—HEAVEN.

**489 ROLLAND. L. M.**    W. B. BRADBURY. 1816-1868.

1. The saints who die of Christ possess'd Enter in - to immediate rest; For them no far-ther

test remains Of purging fires and torturing pains, Of purg-ing fires and torturing pains.

---

*Disembodied saints.*    L. M.

1 The saints who die of Christ possessed
Enter into immediate rest ;
For them no further test remains
Of purging fires and torturing pains.

2 Who trusting in their Lord depart,
Cleans'd from all sin and pure in heart,
The bliss unmix'd, the glorious prize,
They find with Christ in paradise.

3 Close followed by their works they go,
Their Master's purchas'd joy to know ;
Their works enhance the bliss prepar'd,
And each hath its distinct reward.

4 Yet glorified by grace alone,
They cast their crowns before the throne :
And fill the echoing courts above
With praises of redeeming love.
                                    *C. Wesley.*

**490**    *Dies iræ.*    L. M.

1 The day of wrath, that dreadful day,
When heaven and earth shall pass away!
What power shall be the sinner's stay ?
How shall he meet that dreadful day—

2 When, shriv'lling like a parchèd scroll,
The flaming heavens together roll ;
And louder yet, and yet more dread,
Swells the high trump that wakes the dead ?

3 O, on that day, that wrathful day,
When man to judgment wakes from clay,

Be thou, O Christ, the sinner's stay,
Though heaven and earth shall pass away.
                                    *W. Scott.*

**490 b**    *Watch Night.*    H. M.
[Tune, Harwich, page 182. H. M.]

1 Ye virgin souls, arise,
   With all the dead awake !
Unto salvation wise,
   Oil in your vessels take :
Upstarting at the midnight cry,
"Behold the heavenly Bridegroom nigh."

2 He comes, he comes, to call
   The nations to his bar,
And raise to glory all
   Who fit for glory are :
Made ready for your full reward,
Go forth with joy to meet your Lord.

3 Go meet him in the sky,
   Your everlasting Friend
Your dead to glorify,
   With all his saints ascend :
Ye pure in heart, obtain the grace
To see, without a veil, his face !

4 The everlasting doors
   Shall soon the saints receive,
Above yon angel powers
   In glorious joy to live ;
Far from a world of grief and sin,
With God eternally shut in.
                                    *C. Wesley.*

231

**491 ZEPHYR. L. M.** W. B. BRADBURY.

1. Shrinking from the cold hand of death, I soon shall gath-er up my feet;

Shall soon re-sign this fleet-ing breath, And die,—my fa-ther's God to meet.

*Death welcome to the Christian.* L. M.

1 Shrinking from the cold hand of death,
I soon shall gather up my feet;
Shall soon resign this fleeting breath,
And die,—my father's God to meet.

2 Number'd among thy people, I
Expect with joy thy face to see:
Because thou didst for sinners die,
Jesus, in death remember me!

3 O that without a lingering groan
I may the welcome word receive!
My body with my charge lay down,
And cease at once to work and live!

4 Walk with me through the dreadful shade,
And, certified that thou art mine,
My spirit, calm and undismayed,
I shall into thy hands resign.

5 No anxious doubt, no guilty gloom,
Shall damp whom Jesus' presence cheers:
My light, my life, my God is come,
And glory in his face appears!
                                    *C. Wesley.*

**492** *The Peaceful Death.* L. M.

1 Why should we start and fear to die?
What tim'rous worms we mortals are!
Death is the gate to endless joy,
And yet we dread to enter there.

2 The pains, the groans, the dying strife,
Fright our approaching souls away;
And we shrink back again to life,
Fond of our prison and our clay.

3 O if my Lord would come and meet,
My soul would stretch her wings in haste,
Fly fearless through death's iron gate,
Nor feel the terrors as she passed,

4 Jesus can make a dying-bed
Feel soft as downy pillows are,
While on his breast I lean my head,
And breathe my life out sweetly there.
                                    *Watts.*

**493** *God eternal, and man mortal.* L. M.
                *Psalm xc.*

1 Through every age, eternal God,
Thou art our rest, our safe abode:
High was thy throne ere heaven was made,
Or earth, thy humble footstool, laid.

2 Long hadst thou reign'd ere time begun
Or dust was fashion'd into man:
And long thy kingdom shall endure,
When earth and time shall be no more.

3 But man, weak man, is born to die,
Made up of guilt and vanity:
Thy dreadful sentence, Lord, is just—
"Return ye sinners, to your dust."

4 Death, like an ever-flowing stream,
Sweeps us away: our life's a dream—
An empty tale—a morning flower
Cut down and withered in an hour.

5 Teach us, O Lord, how frail is man,
And kindly lengthen out our span,
Till, cleans'd by grace, we all may be
Prepar'd to die, and dwell with thee.
                                    *Watts.*

232

# DEATH—THE JUDGMENT—HEAVEN.

**494 FREDERICK. 11s.**

GEO. KINGSLEY.

1. I would not live al-way; I ask not to stay Where storm af - ter

storm ris - es dark o'er the way; The few lur-id morn-ings that

dawn on us here, Are e-nough for life's woes, full e - nough for its cheer.

---

*"I would not live alway."* 11s.

1 I would not live alway : I ask not to stay
Where storm after storm rises dark o'er the
way ;
The few lurid mornings that dawn on us
here,
Are enough for life's woes, full enough for
its cheer.

2 I would not live alway : no—welcome the
tomb ;
Since Jesus hath lain there, I dread not its
gloom ;
There, sweet be my rest, till he bid me arise,
To hail him in triumph descending the skies.

3 Who, who would live alway, away from his
God,—
Away from yon heaven, that blissful abode,
Where rivers of pleasure flow o'er the bright
plains,
And the noontide of glory eternally reigns :

4 Where the saints of all ages in harmony
meet,
Their Saviour and brethren transported to
greet ;
While the anthems of rapture unceasingly
roll,
And the smile of the Lord is the feast of
the soul !
*Muhlenberg.*

233

**495  LUCAS.  10, 5, 11.**                                    ENGLISH.

1. Ho - san - na to God, in his high-est a-bode: All heav - en be join'd

T' ex - tol the Re-deem-er and Friend of man-kind! He claims all our

*Tenor or Alto ad lib.*

praise, who in in - fin-ite grace A - gain hath stoop'd down And caught up a

worm to in - her - it a crown, And caught up a worm to in - her - it a crown.

2 Our friend is restor'd to the joy of his Lord,
　With triumph departs,
But speaks by his death to our echoing
　hearts:
Follow after, he cries, as he mounts to the
　skies,
　Follow after your friend
To the blissful enjoyment that never shall
　end.

3 Through Jesus's name our comrade o'er-
　came,
　And Jesus is ours,
And arms us with all his invincible powers:

He looks from the skies, he shows us the
　prize,
　And gives us a sign
That we shall o'ercome by the mercy Di-
　vine.

4 For us is prepar'd the angelical guard;
　The convoy attends—
A minist'ring host of invisible friends—
Ready-wing'd for their flight to the regions
　of light,
　The horses are come,
The chariots of Israel, to carry us home.

C. Wesley.

234

DEATH—THE JUDGMENT—HEAVEN.

**496** MERCY. 7s.                                    GOTTSCHALK.

1. Hark! a voice di-vides the sky, Hap-py are the faith-ful dead!

In the Lord who sweet-ly die, They from all their toils are freed.

---

*Funeral of a Christian.*    7s.
*Rev.* xiv. 13.

1 Hark! a voice divides the sky,
  Happy are the faithful dead!
  In the Lord who sweetly die,
  They from all their toils are freed.

2 Them the Spirit hath declar'd
  Blest, unutterably blest;
  Jesus is their great reward,
  Jesus is their endless rest.

3 Follow'd by their works, they go
  Where their Head has gone before;
  Reconcil'd by grace below,
  Grace hath open'd Mercy's door.

4 Justified through faith alone,
  Here they know their sins forgiven;
  Here they laid their burden down,
  Hallow'd, and made meet for heaven.
                              C. Wesley.

**497**    *Death of a Relative.*    C. P. M.
[ Tune, Meribah, page 224.  C. P. M.]

1 If death my friend and me divide,
  Thou dost not, Lord, my sorrow chide,
  Or from, my tears to see;
  Restrain'd from passionate excess,
  Thou bidd'st me mourn in calm distress
  For them that rest in thee.

2 I feel a strong, immortal hope,
  Which bears my mournful spirit up,
  Beneath its mountain-load;

Redeem'd from death, and grief, and pain,
  I soon shall find my friend again
  Within the arms of God.

3 Pass a few fleeting moments more,
  And death the blessing shall restore
  Which death has snatch'd away;
  For me thou wilt the summons send,
  And give me back my parted friend
  In that eternal day.
                              C. Wesley.

**498**    *Rev.* xxii. 17.    8s.
[ Tune, Beatus-Minor, page 225.  8s.]

1 The Church in her militant state
  Is weary, and cannot forbear!
  The saints in an agony wait,
  To see him again in the air!

2 The Spirit invites in the bride
  Her heavenly Lord to descend,
  And place her enthron'd at his side,
  In glory that never shall end.

3 The news of his coming I hear,
  And join in the catholic cry:
  O Jesus, in triumph appear!
  Appear in the clouds of the sky!

4 Whom only I languish to love,
  In fulness of majesty come;
  And give me a mansion above,
  And take to my heavenly home!
                              C. Wesley.

235

**499 SHINING SHORE. 8s & 7s.**  G. F. ROOT.

1. My days are gliding swiftly by, And I, a pilgrim stranger, Would not detain them

**Chorus.**

as they fly, Those hours of toil and dan-ger.  For O, we stand on Jordan's strand, Our

friends are passing o-ver, And just before, the shining shore We may almost dis-cov-er.

*The Shining Shore.*  8, 7.

1 My days are gliding swiftly by,
  And I, a pilgrim stranger,
  Would not detain them as they fly,
  Those hours of toil and danger.

  CHORUS:—

  For O, we stand on Jordan's strand,
  Our friends are passing over,
  And just before, the shining shore
  We may almost discover.

2 We'll gird our loins, my brethren dear,
  Our heavenly home discerning;
  Our absent Lord has left us word,
  Let every lamp be burning.

3 Should coming days be cold and dark,
  We need not cease our singing:
  That perfect rest naught can molest
  Where golden harps are ringing.

4 Let sorrow's rudest tempest blow,
  Each chord on earth to sever;
  Our King says come, and there's our home,
  Forever, O forever.

**500**  *The heavenly Jerusalem.*  C. M.
  [Tune, Valentia, page 237.  C. M.]

1 Jerusalem, my happy home!
  Name ever dear to me!

When will my sorrows have an end?
  Thy joys, when shall I see?

2 Thy walls are all of precious stone,
  Most glorious to behold;
  Thy gates are richly set with pearl,
  Thy streets are pav'd with gold.

3 Thy garden and thy pleasant walks,
  My study long have been;
  Such dazzling views by human sight
  Have never yet been seen.

4 If heaven be thus so glorious, Lord,
  Why should I stay from thence?
  What folly's this that I should dread
  To die and go from hence?

5 Reach down, O Lord, thine arm of grace,
  And cause me to ascend,
  Where congregations ne'er break up,
  And Sabbaths never end.

6 Jesus, my Lord, to glory's gone,
  Him will I go and see;
  And all my brethren here below,
  Will soon come after me.

7 My friends, I bid you all adieu,
  I leave you in God's care,
  And if I never more see you,
  Go on, I'll meet you there.

*Dickson.*

DEATH—THE JUDGMENT—HEAVEN.

## 500  VALENTIA. C. M.

ARR. BY KINGSLEY.

1. Je - ru - sa - lem, my hap - py home! Name ev - er dear to me!

When will my sor - rows have an end? Thy joys, when shall I see?

**501**  *Death the gate to Heaven.*  C. M.

1 Why do we mourn departing friends,
  Or shake at death's alarms?
  'Tis but the voice that Jesus sends,
  To call them to his arms.

2 Are we not tending upward too,
  As fast as time can move?
  Nor should we wish the hours more slow
  To keep us from our love.

3 Why should we tremble to convey
  Their bodies to the tomb?
  There once the flesh of Jesus lay,
  And left a long perfume.

4 The graves of all his saints he blest,
  And softened every bed:
  Where should the dying members rest,
  But with their dying Head?

5 Thence he arose, ascending high,
  And showed our feet the way;
  Up to the Lord our flesh shall fly,
  At the great rising-day.

6 Then let the last loud trumpet sound,
  And bid our kindred rise:
  Awake, ye nations under ground;
  Ye saints, ascend the skies!

*Isaac Watts.*

## 501  CHINA. C. M.

SWAN.

1. Why do we mourn de - part - ing friends, Or shake at death's a - larms?

'Tis but the voice that Je - sus sends, To call them to his arms.

237

FUNERALS AND OTHER OCCASIONS.

**502** ST. MARTINS. C. M.

1. There is a house not made with hands, E - ter - nal and on high;

And here my spir - it, wait - ing, stands, Till God shall bid it fly.

*Faith contemplating Heaven.* C. M.

1 There is a house not made with hands,
  Eternal and on high;
  And here my spirit, waiting, stands,
  Till God shall bid it fly.

2 Shortly this prison of my clay
  Must be dissolved and fall;
  Then, O my soul, with joy obey
  Thy heavenly Father's call.

3 'Tis he, by his almighty grace,
  That forms thee fit for heaven;
  And, as an earnest of the place,
  Has his own Spirit giv'n.

4 We walk by faith of joys to come;
  Faith lives upon his word;
  But while the body is our home,
  We're absent from the Lord.
                                 *Watts.*

**503** *Looking from earth to Heaven.* C. M.

1 Death may dissolve my body now,
  And bear my spirit home:
  Why do my days so sluggish move,
  Nor my salvation come?

2 God has laid up in heaven for me
  A crown which cannot fade;
  The righteous Judge, at that great day,
  Shall place it on my head.

3 Jesus, the Lord, will guard me safe
  From every ill design,
  And to his heavenly kingdom take
  This feeble soul of mine.

4 God is my everlasting aid,
  My portion and my friend,
  To him be highest glory paid,
  Through ages without end.
                                 *Watts.*

**504** *What are these?* Rev. vii. 13-17. 7s.
          [ Tune, Mercy, page 235. 7s.]

1 What are these arrayed in white,
  Brighter than the noonday sun?
  Foremost of the sons of light,
  Nearest the eternal throne?

2 These are they that bore the cross,
  Nobly for their Master stood,
  Suff'rers in his righteous cause,
  Foll'wers of the dying God.

3 Out of great distress they came,
  Wash'd their robes by faith below,
  In the blood of yonder Lamb,
  Blood that washes white as snow.

4 Therefore are they next the throne,
  Serve their Maker day and night,
  God resides among his own,
  God doth in his saints delight.

6 More than conquerors at last,
  Here they find their trials o'er;
  They have all their suff'rings past,
  Hunger now and thirst no more.

6 No excessive heat they feel
  From the sun's directer ray;
  In a milder clime they dwell,
  Region of eternal day.
                                 *C. Wesley.*

238

## DEATH—THE JUDGMENT—HEAVEN.

**505**  *The city that hath foundations.*  8s.

[ Tune, Beatus-Minor, page 225.  8s.]

1  Away with our sorrow and fear !
    We soon shall recover our home ;
    The city of saints shall appear;
    The day of eternity come.

2  From earth we shall quickly remove,
    And mount to our native abode ;

The house of our Father above,
    The palace of angels and God.

3  Our morning is all at an end,
    When rais'd by the life-giving word,
    We see the new city descend,
    Adorned as a bride for her Lord.

4  The city so holy and clean,
    No sorrow can breathe in the air :
    No gloom of affliction or sin,
    No shadow of evil is there.

**506  TALLIS' EVENING HYMN. L. M.**  TH. TALLIS. 1650.

1. Lo ! round the throne, a glo - rious band, The saints in count-less myr-iads stand;

Of ev - 'ry tongue re-deem'd of God, Ar - rayed in gar - ments washed in blood.

*The redeemed in heaven.*  L. M.

1  Lo ! round the throne, a glorious band,
    The saints in countless myriads stand ;
    Of every tongue redeemed of God,
    Arrayed in garments washed in blood.

2  Through tribulation great they came ;
    They bore the cross, despised the shame ;
    But now from all their labors rest,
    In God's eternal glory blest.

3  They see the Saviour face to face ;
    They sing the triumph of his grace ;
    And day and night, with ceaseless praise,
    To him their loud hosannas raise.

4  O may we tread the sacred road
    That holy saints and martyrs trod ;
    Wage to the end the glorious strife,
    And win, like them, a crown of life !

*Mary L. Duncan.*

**507**  L. M.

*They shall behold the land that is very far off.*
*Isa.* xxxiii. 17.

1  There is a land mine eye hath seen
    In visions of enraptured thought,
    So bright, that all which spreads between
    Is with its radiant glories fraught.

2  A land upon whose blissful shore
    There rests no shadow, falls no stain ;
    There those who meet shall part no more,
    And those long parted meet again.

3  Its skies are not like earthly skies,
    With varying hues of shade and light;
    It hath no need of suns to rise
    To dissipate the gloom of night.

4  There sweeps no desolating wind
    Across that calm serene abode ;
    The wanderer there a home may find
    Within the paradise of God.

*Gurdon Robins.*

# FUNERALS AND OTHER OCCASIONS.

## 508 EFFINGHAM. L. M.

*Allegretto.*

1. Me-thinks the last great day is come, Me-thinks I hear the trump-et sound, That shakes the earth, rends ev-'ry tomb, And wakes the pris - 'ners un - der ground.

---

*The last great day.* L. M.

1 Methinks the last great day is come,
Methinks I hear the trumpet sound,
That shakes the earth, rends every tomb,
And wakes the prisoners under ground.

2 The mighty deep gives up her trust,
Aw'd by the Judge's high command ;
Both small and great now quit their dust
And round the great tribunal stand.

3 Behold the awful books displayed,
Big with th' important fates of men ;
Each deed a word more public made,
As wrote by heaven's unerring pen.

4 To every soul the books assign
The joyous or the dread reward ;
Sinners in vain lament and pine—
No plea the Judge will here regard,

5 Lord, when these awful leaves unfold,
May life's fair book my soul approve,
There may I read my name enroll'd,
And triumph in redeeming love !

## 509 *The Heavenly Zion.* L. M.

1 Arm of the Lord, awake, awake !
Thine own immortal strength put on !
With terror cloth'd, hell's kingdom shake,
And cast thy foes with fury down.

2 By death and hell pursued in vain,
To thee the ransomed seed shall come ;
Shouting, their heavenly Zion gain,
And pass through death triumphant home.

3 The pain of life shall then be o'er,
The anguish and distracting care ;
There sighing grief shall weep no more,
And sin shall never enter there.

4 Where pure, essential joy is found,
The Lord's redeem'd their heads shall
With everlasting gladness crowned, [raise,
And filled with love, and lost in praise.
*Charles Wesley.*

## 510 *The Land of Peace.* S. M.
[ Tune, St. Thomas, page 241. S. M.]

1 Come to the land of peace;
From shadows come away ;
Where all the sounds of weeping cease,
And storms no more have sway.

2 Fear hath no dwelling here;
But pure repose and love
Breathe through the bright, celestial air
The spirit of the dove.

3 Come to the bright and blest,
Gathered from every land ;
For there thy soul shall find its rest
Amid the shining band.

4 In this divine abode
Change leaves no saddening trace;
Come, trusting spirit, to thy God,
Thy holy resting-place.

5 " Come to our peaceful home,"
The saints and angels say.
" Forsake the world, no longer roam ;
O wanderer, come away ! "
*Unknown,*

# DEATH—THE JUDGMENT—HEAVEN

**511 ST. THOMAS. S. M.** GEORGE FREDERICK HANDEL.

1. "For - ev - er with the Lord!" A - men, so let it be!

Life from the dead is in that word, 'Tis im - mor - tal - i - ty.

*At home in Heaven.* S. M.

1 " Forever with the Lord!
Amen, so let it be!
Life from the dead is in that word,
'Tis immortality.

2 Here in the body pent,
Absent from him I roam,
Yet nightly pitch my moving tent
A day's march nearer home.

3 " Forever with the Lord!"
Father, if 'tis thy will,
The promise of that faithful word,
E'en here to me fulfil.

4 So when my latest breath
Shall rend the vail in twain,
By death I shall escape from death,
And life eternal gain.

5 Knowing as I am known,
How shall I love that word,
And oft repeat before the throne,
" Forever with the Lord!"
*James Montgomery.*

**512** *The goodly land.* S. M.

1 Far from these scenes of night,
Unbounded glories rise,
And realms of joy and pure delight,
Unknown to mortal eyes.

2 Fair land! could mortal eyes
But half its charms explore,
How would our spirits long to rise,
And dwell on earth no more!

3 No cloud those regions know,
Realms ever bright and fair:
For sin, the source of mortal woe,
Can never enter there.

4 O, may the prospect fire
Our hearts with ardent love,
Till wings of faith and strong desire,
Bear every thought above.

5 Prepared, by grace divine,
For thy bright courts on high,
Lord, bid our spirits rise and join
The chorus of the sky.
*Anne Steele.*

**513** *No night in Heaven.* S. M.

1 There is no night in heaven;
In that blest world above
Work never can bring weariness,
For work itself is love.

2 There is no grief in heaven;
For life is one glad day,
And tears are of those former things
Which all have passed away.

3 There is no sin in heaven;
Behold that blessed throng,
All holy in their spotless robes,
All holy in their song.

4 There is no death in heaven;
For they who gain that shore
Have won their immortality,
And they can die no more.
*Frederick D. Huntington.*

241

Section 17.

# DEVOTIONAL MISCELLANY.

**514 METROPOLITAN. C. M.**  J. T. LAYTON,

*Andante.*  *mf*

1. How vain are all things here be-low! How false, and yet how fair!

*ff*  *p*

Each pleas-ure hath its poi-son, too, And ev-'ry sweet a snare.

*Surrendering all for Christ.*  C. M.

1 How vain are all things here below!
  How false, and yet how fair!
  Each pleasure hath its poison, too,
  And every sweet a snare.

2 The brightest things below the sky
  Give but a flatt'ring light:
  We should suspect some danger nigh
  Where we possess delight.

3 Our dearest joys and nearest friends,
  The partners of our blood,

How they divide our wav'ring minds,
  And leave but half for God!

4 The fondness of a creature's love,
  How strong it strikes the sense!
  Thither the warm affections move,
  Nor can we call them thence.

5 Dear Saviour, let thy beauties be
  My soul's eternal food:
  And grace command my soul away
  From all created good.

*Watts.*

**514 AMANDA. C. M. (Second tune.)**  M. T. STERLING.

1. How vain are all things here be-low! How false, and yet how fair!

Each pleas-ure hath its poi-son, too, And ev-'ry sweet a snare.

242

**515  WARING.  8s & 6s.**                    FROM LOUIS SPOHR.

I. Ye wea - ry, heav-y lad - en souls, Who are op - pres - sed sore,

Ye trav'llers through the wil - der - ness, To Ca - naan's peace-ful shore:

Ye trav'llers through the wil-der - ness, To Ca - naan's peaceful shore:

*The Pilgrim's Song.*     8s & 6s.

1 Ye weary, heavy laden souls,
  Who are oppressèd sore,
  ‖: Ye trav'llers through the wilderness,
  To Canaan's peaceful shore. :‖

2 Through chilling winds and beating rain,
  The waters deep and cold,
  ‖: And enemies surrounding you,
  Take courage and be bold. :‖

3 Though storms and hurricanes arise,
  The desert all around,
  ‖: And fiery serpents oft appear
  Through the enchanted ground. :‖

4 Dark nights, and clouds, and gloomy fear,
  And dragons often roar;
  ‖: But while the gospel trump we hear,
  We'll press for Canaan's shore. :‖

5 Methinks I now begin to see
  The borders of that land;
  ‖: The trees of life, with heavenly fruit,
  In beauteous order stand. :‖

6 The wintry time is past and gone,
  Sweet flowers now appear.
  ‖: The fiftieth year hath now rolled round,
  The great Sabbatic year. :‖

*Unknown.*

**516**     *Remember Me.*     C. M.

[Tune, Dundee, page 244.  C. M.]

1 Jesus! thou art the sinner's friend,
  As such I look to thee;
  Now in the bowels of thy love,
  O Lord! remember me.

2 Remember thy pure word of grace,
  Remember Calvary;
  Remember all thy dying groans,
  And then remember me.

3 Thou wondrous Advocate with God!
  I yield myself to thee;
  While thou art sitting on thy throne,
  O Lord! remember me.

4 I own I'm guilty, own I'm vile,
  Yet thy salvation's free;
  Then, in thy all-abounding grace,
  O Lord! remember me.

5 Howe'er forsaken, or distress'd,
  Howe'er oppress'd I be,
  Howe'er afflicted here on earth,
  Do thou remember me.

*Unknown.*

**517 DUNDEE. C. M.**

*Moderato.*

1 In - quire, ye pil - grims, for the way That leads to Si - on's hill,

And thith - er set your stead - y face, With a de - ter - min'd will.

---

*Admission into the Church.* C. M.

1 Inquire, ye pilgrims, for the way
That leads to Sion's hill,
And thither set your steady face,
With a determin'd will.

2 Invite the strangers all around
Your pious march to join,
And spread the sentiments you feel
Of faith and love divine.

3 O come, and join your souls to God
In everlasting bands :
Accept the blessings he bestows,
With thankful hearts and hands.
*Doddridge.*

**518** *Scenes of the Resurrection.* C. M.

1 How long shall Death, the tyrant, reign,
And triumph o'er the just ?
How long the blood of martyrs slain
Lie mingled with the dust ?

2 Lo! I behold the scatter'd shades :
The dawn of heaven appears :
The bright, immortal morning spreads
Its blushes round the spheres.

3 I see the Lord of glory come,
And flaming guards around :
The skies divide to make him room :
The trumpet shakes the ground.

4 I hear the voice, "Ye dead, arise!"
And, lo! the graves obey;

And waking saints, with joyful eyes,
Salute th' expected day.

5 O may our humble spirits stand
Among them, cloth'd in white :
The meanest place at his right hand
Is infinite delight.
*Watts.*

**519** C. M.

"*Thy kingdom come.*" *Matt.* vi. 10.

1 Father of me, and all mankind
And all the hosts above
Let every understanding mind
Unite to praise thy love.

2 To know thy nature and thy name,
One God in persons three ;
And glorify the great I AM
Through all eternity.

3 Thy kingdom come, with power and grace,
To every heart of man :
Thy peace, and joy, and righteousness,
In all our bosoms reign.
*C. Wesley.*

*Doxology.*

To Father, Son, and Holy Ghost,
One God whom we adore,
Be glory as it was, is now,
And shall be evermore.

244

# DEVOTIONAL MISCELLANY.

*1. O Sun of right - eous - ness, a - rise With heal - ing in thy wing! To*

*my dis - eas'd, my faint-ing soul, Life and sal - va - tion bring, Life*

*and sal - va - tion bring, Life and sal - va - tion, sal - va - tion bring.*

*Lighten mine eyes. Ps. xiii. 3.*    C. M.

1 O sun of righteousness, arise
  With healing in thy wing!
To my diseas'd, my fainting soul,
  Life and salvation bring.

2 These clouds of pride and sin dispel,
  By thine all-piercing beam :
Lighten mine eyes with faith, my heart
  With holy hope inflame.

3 My mind, by thy all-quickening power,
  From low desires set free :
Unite my scattered thoughts, and fix
  My love entire on thee.

4 Father, thy long-lost son receive ;
  Saviour, thy purchase own ;
Blest Comforter, with peace and joy
  Thy new-made creature crown.

5 Eternal, undivided Lord,
  Coëqual One and Three,
On thee all faith, all hope be placed,
  All love be paid to thee.
              *C. Wesley.*

**521**     *Evening.*     C. M.

1 The work of one more day is done—
  Is done, as best we could.
And yet, O Lord, we must confess
  'Tis not done as we would.

2 We would have lived throughout the hours
  As though we saw thee near ;
That thou shouldst know each thought and
  Should bring to us no fear.   [word,

3 But as we retrospect the day,
  Our heart is made to grieve,
In pity, Lord, we pray look down,
  Our burdened souls relieve.

4 O make us not to close our eyes,
  Till we shall feel thy love,
Hear thou our song, hear thou our pray'r
  "Come quickly from above."
            *B. T. Tanner.*

**521 b**   *"Saints' Inventory."*   C. M.

1 If God is mine, then present things
  And things to come are mine ;
Yea, Christ, his word, and Spirit, too,
  And glory all divine.

2 If he is mine, then from his love
  He every trouble sends ;
All things are working for my good,
  And bliss his rod attends.

3 If he is mine, let friends forsake,
  Let wealth and honor flee ;
Sure he who giveth me himself
  Is more than these to me.
            *B. Beddome.*

522 FALLS CITY. C. M. Double.

W. H. GIBSON, 8R.

1. Giv - er of con-cord, Prince of peace, Meek, lamb-like Son of God,
2. Sub - due in us the car - nal mind, Its en - mi - ty de - stroy,

Bid our un - ru - ly pas-sions cease, By thy a - ton - ing blood.
With cords of love our spir - its bind, And melt us in - to joy.

Re - buke our rage, our pas - sions chide, Our stub-born wills con - trol,
Us in - to clos - est un - ion draw, And in our in - ward parts

Beat down our wrath, root out our pride, And calm our trou-bled soul.
Let kind-ness sweet - ly write her law, And love com-mand our hearts.

523　　*The Farewell.*　　C. M. D.

1 Ye golden lamps of heaven, farewell,
　With all your feeble light;
Farewell, thou ever-changing moon,
　Pale empress of the night.
And thou, refulgent orb of day,
　In brighter flames arrayed,
My soul, that springs beyond thy sphere
　No more demands thy aid.

2 Ye stars are but the shining dust
　Of my divine abode,
The pavement of those heavenly courts,
　Where I shall see my God.
There all the millions of his saints
　Shall in one song unite:
And each the bliss of all shall view,
　With infinite delight.
　　　　　　*Doddridge.*

246

**524  MARLOW. C. M.**

*Moderato.*

1. Dear friends, farewell, I  do you tell,  Since you and I  must  part;
I  go a - way  but  here you stay;  But  still we're joined in  heart.

C. M.

*A minister or brethren parting on earth.*
Acts. xx. 36–38.

1 Dear friends, farewell, I do you tell,
Since you and I must part;
I go away but here you stay;
But still we're joined in heart.

2 Your love to me has been so free,
Your conversation sweet;
How can I bear to journey, where
With you I cannot meet!

3 Yet I do find my heart inclined
To do my work below;
When Christ doth call, I trust I shall
Be ready then to go.

4 I leave you all, both great and small,
To Christ's encircling arms,
Which can you save from hell's dark grave,
And shield you from all harms.

5 I long to go where pleasures flow,
My soul shall be at rest,
No more complain or sigh again,
But be forever blest.

6 There we shall meet in bliss complete,
And long together dwell,
To love the Lord with one accord;
So, brethren, all farewell.
*Unknown.*

**525**      *Patriot's Song.*      C. M.

1 Lord, while for all mankind we pray,
Of every clime and coast,

O hear us for our native land,—
The land we love the most.

2 O guard our shores from every foe,
With peace our borders bless,
With prosp'rous times our cities crown,
Our fields with plenteousness.

3 Here may religion shed her light
On days of rest and toil;
And piety and virtue reign,
And bless our native soil.

4 Lord of the nations, thus to thee
Our country we commend;
Be thou her refuge and her trust,
Her everlasting friend.
*Wreford.*

**525 b**      C. M.

1 Keep silence, all created things,
And wait your Maker's nod;
My soul stands trembling while she sings
The honors of her God.

2 Life, death and hell, and worlds unknown,
Hang on his firm decree;
He sits on no precarious throne,
Nor borrows leave to be.

3 Chained to his throne a volume lies,
With all the fates of men,
With every angel's form and size,
Drawn by th' eternal pen.

4 In thy fair book of life and grace
May I but find my name
Recorded in some humble place,
Beneath my Lord, the Lamb.

247

# DEVOTIONAL MISCELLANY.

**526 BETHANY. 6s & 4s.**   L. MASON.

1. Near-er, my God, to thee, Near-er to thee! E'en tho' it be a cross

*D. S.—*Near-er, my God, to thee,

That rais-eth me, Still all my song shall be, Near-er, my God, to thee,

Near-er to thee!

### Nearer to thee.   6s & 4s.

1 Nearer, my God, to thee,
　Nearer to thee!
　E'en though it be a cross
　That raiseth me,
　Still all my song shall be,
　Nearer, my God, to thee,
　Nearer to thee!

2 Though like the wanderer,
　The sun gone down,
　Darkness be over me,
　My rest a stone;
　Yet in my dreams I'd be
　Nearer, my God, to thee,
　Nearer to thee!

3 There let the way appear
　Steps unto heaven;
　All that thou sendest me,
　In mercy given;
　Angels to beckon me
　Nearer, my God, to thee,
　Nearer, to thee.

4 Then with my waking thoughts
　Bright with thy praise,
　Out of my stony griefs
　Bethel I'll raise;
　So by my woes to be
　Nearer, my God, to thee,
　Nearer to thee!

5 Or if on joyful wing,
　Cleaving the sky,
　Sun, moon, and stars forgot,
　Upward I fly,
　Still all my song shall be,
　Nearer, my God, to thee,
　Nearer to thee,
　　　　*Sarah F. Adams.*

### 527   6s & 4s.

1 Saviour! thy gentle voice
　Gladly we hear;
　Author of all our joys,
　Ever be near;
　Our souls would cling to thee,
　Let us thy fulness see,
　Our life to cheer.

2 Fountain of life divine!
　Thee we adore;
　We would be wholly thine
　Forevermore;
　Freely forgive our sin,
　Grant heavenly peace within,
　Thy light restore.

3 Though to our faith unseen,
　While darkness reigns,
　On thee alone we lean
　While life remains;
　By thy free grace restored,
　Our souls shall bless the Lord
　In joyful strains!
　　　　*Hastings.*

248

**528  ROWLEY.  12 & 9.**

1. Come a-way to the skies, my be-lov-ed a-rise, And re-joice in the day thou was born: On this fes-ti-val day, come ex-ult-ing a-way, And with sing-ing to Si-on re-turn, And with sing-ing to Si-on re-turn.

*Birthday of a consort.*    12 & 9.

1  Come away to the skies, my beloved arise,
    And rejoice in the day thou was born:
On this festival day, come exulting away,
    And with singing to Sion return.

2  We have laid up our love and our treasure
        above,
    Though our bodies continue below:
The redeem'd of our Lord, we remember
        his word,
    And with singing to paradise go.

3  With singing we praise the original grace
    By our Heavenly Father bestow'd;
Our being receive from his bounty, and live
    To the honor and glory of God.

4  For thy glory we are created to share
        Both the nature and kingdom Divine;
    Created again, that our souls may remain
        In time and eternity thine.

5  With thanks we approve the design of thy
        love,
    Which hath joined us in Jesus' name;
So united in heart that we never can part,
    Till we meet at the feast of the Lamb.

6  There, there at his feet we shall suddenly
        meet,
    And be parted in body no more!
We shall sing to our lyres, with the heav-
        enly choirs,
    And our Saviour in glory adore.
                                    *C. Wesley.*

249

**529 BOYLSTON. S. M.**

LOWELL MASON.

1. Did Christ o'er sin - ners weep, And shall our cheeks be dry? Let

floods of pen - i - ten - tial grief Burst forth from ev - 'ry eye.

*"He beheld the city, and wept over it."* S. M.

1 Did Christ o'er sinners weep,
   And shall our cheeks be dry?
   Let floods of penitential grief
   Burst forth from every eye.

2 The Son of God in tears
   The wond'ring angels see:
   Be thou astonished, O my soul;
   He shed those tears for thee.

3 He wept that we might weep:
   Each sin demands a tear:
   In heaven alone no sin is found
   And there's no weeping there.
                                    *Beddome.*

**530** *Household consecrated to God.* S. M.

1 The power to bless my house
   Belongs to God alone;
   Yet rend'ring him my constant vows,
   He sends his blessings down.

2 Shall I not then engage
   My house to serve the Lord,
   To search the soul-converting page,
   And feed upon his word,—

3 To ask with faith and hope
   The grace which he supplies,
   In prayer and praise to offer up
   Their daily sacrifice?

4 Let each his sin eschew,
   Through thy restraining grace,
   Our father Abrah'm's steps pursue,
   And walk in all thy ways.

5 Saviour of men, incline
   The hearts which thou hast made,
   Which thou hast bought with blood Divine,
   To ask thy promis'd aid.

6 Me and my house receive,
   Thy family t' increase,
   And let us in thy favor live,
   And let us die in peace.
                                    *C. Wesley.*

**530 b**                        L. M.

*Light for those who sit in darkness.*

[Tune, Hamburg, page 252. L. M.]

1 Though now the nations sit beneath
   The darkness of o'erspreading death,
   God will arise with light divine,
   On Zion's holy towers to shine.

2 That light shall shine on distant lands,
   And wandering tribes, in joyful bands,
   Shall come, thy glory, Lord, to see,
   And in thy courts to worship thee.

3 O light of Zion, now arise!
   Let the glad morning bless our eyes;
   Ye nations, catch the kindling ray,
   And hail the splendors of the day.
                                    *Leonard Bacon*

## 531  STATE STREET. S. M.

JONATHAN CALL WOODMAN.

1. Through all the loft - y sky, Through all th' in - fer - ior ground,

Th' Al-might-y Mak - er shines con-fess'd, And pours his bless - ings round.

---

*General Thanksgiving.*    S. M.

1 Through all the lofty sky,
   Through all the inferior ground,
  Th' Almighty Maker shines confess'd,
   And pours his blessings round.

2 Each year the teeming earth
   With flowers and fruits is crown'd;
  And grass, and herbs, and harvests, grow
   And send their joys around.

3 The world of waters yields
   A rich supply of food,
  And distant lands their treasures send
   Upon the rolling flood.

4 To serve and bless our land
   The elements conspire;
  And mercies mix themselves with earth,—
   With ocean, air and fire.

5 O that the sons of men
   To God their songs would raise,
  And celebrate his power and love
   In never-ceasing praise!
               *Thomas Gibbons.*

## 532    *Glorious in holiness.*    S. M.

1 God is in Judah known,
   Israel extols his name,
  In Salem he has placed his throne,
   In Zion lives his fame.

2 There did he break the shield,
   The battle and the bow;
  There to his glorious might shall yield
   The desolating foe.

3 There is the spoiler spoil'd,
   The proud have slept their sleep;
  There are the men of battle foil'd,
   In one promiscuous heap.

4 When thy rebuke is heard,
   Both horse and car expire;
  Thou God of Jacob shalt be fear'd;
   O who shall meet thine ire?

6 Heaven utter'd thy decree,
   Earth, trembling, paused to hear:
  Soon shall the world thy judgments see,
   Thy saints no more shall fear.
               *Marsh.*

# DEVOTIONAL MISCELLANY.

**533** *On changing place of abode.* L. M.

1 Sole Sov'reign of the earth and skies,
Supremely good, supremely wise,
Fix thou the place of our abode,
But let it still be near our God.

2 On earth we weary pilgrims roam,
Nor find, nor hope, a lasting home;

We seek a house not made with hands,
A heavenly house which ever stands.

3 Yet while we sojourn here below,
Let streams of mercy round us flow;
And when our destin'd race is run,
Assign us mansions near thy throne.

**534** HAMBURG. L. M. ARR. BY LOWELL MASON.

1. Come, ye that love the Lord in - deed, Who are from sin and bond - age freed,

Sub - mit to all the ways of God, And walk that nar-row hap - py road.

*The Prosperous Saint.* *Rev.* vii. 13–17. L. M.

1 Come, ye that love the Lord indeed,
Who are from sin and bondage freed,
Submit to all the ways of God,
And walk that narrow happy road.

2 Great tribulation you shall meet,
But soon shall walk the golden street;
Though hell may rage and vent her spite
Yet Christ will save his heart's delight.

3 That happy day will soon appear,
When Gabriel's trumpet you shall hear
Sound through the earth, yea, down to hell,
To call the nations, great and small.

4 Behold the earth in burning flames,
The trumpet louder still proclaims;
The earth must hear and know her doom,
The separation day is come.

5 Behold the righteous marching home,
And all the angels bid them come;
When Christ himself these words proclaims.
Here come my saints, I know their names.
*Unknown.*

252

**535 MIGDOL. L. M.**

1. Lord, I am thine, en - tire - ly thine, Pur - chased and saved by blood Di - vine; With full con - sent thine would I be, And own thy sov - 'reign right in me.

---

*Self-dedication.* L. M.

1 Lord, I am thine, entirely thine,
Purchased and saved by blood Divine;
With full consent thine would I be,
And own thy sovereign right in me.

2 Grant one poor sinner more a place
Among the children of thy grace;
A wretched sinner, lost to God,
But ransom'd by Immanuel's blood.

3 Thine would I live, thine would I die,
Be thine through all eternity;
The vow is past beyond repeal,
Now will I set the solemn seal.

4 Here at that cross where flows the blood
That bought my guilty soul for God,
Thee, my new Master, now I call,
And consecrate to thee my all.

5 Do thou assist a feeble worm
The great engagement to perform:
Thy grace can full assistance lend,
And on that grace I dare depend.

*Davies.*

**536** *National Praise.* L. M.

1 We bless thy name, Almighty God,
For all the kindness thou hast shown,
To this fair land our fathers trod,
This land we fondly call our own.

2 Here freedom spreads her banner wide,
And casts her soft and hallow'd ray;
For thou our country's arms didst guide,
And led them on their conqu'ring way.

3 We praise thee, that the gospel light
Through all our land its radiance sheds;
Scatters the shades of error's night,
And heavenly blessings round us spreads.

4 When foes without and foes within,
With threatening ills our land have press'd,
Thou hast our nation's bulwark been,
And, smiling, sent us peaceful rest.

5 O God, preserve us in thy fear,
In troublous times our helper be;
Diffuse thy truth's bright precepts here,
And may we worship only thee.

*Presb. Hymns.*

**537 CHRISTIAN VICTOR. 10s.**

1. { Joy - ful - ly, joy - ful - ly    on-ward I move, Bound to the land of bright
   { An - gel - ic chor - is - ters    sing as I come, Joy - ful - ly, joy - ful - ly

spir - its   a - bove; } Soon with my pil - grim - age end - ed be - low,
haste to thy home! }

Home to the land of bright spir-its I go;   Pil - grim and stran - ger no

more shall I roam,    Joy - ful - ly,   joy - ful - ly rest - ing at home.

2 Friends, fondly cherished, have passed on
    before;
Waiting, they watch me approaching the
    shore;
Singing to cheer me thro' death's chilling
    gloom:
Joyfully, joyfully haste to thy home.
Sounds of sweet melody fall on my ear;
Harps of the blessed, your voices I hear!
Rings with the harmony heaven's high
    dome—
Joyfully, joyfully haste to thy home.

3 Death, with thy weapons of war lay me
    low,
Strike, king of terrors! I fear not the blow;
Jesus hath broken the bars of the tomb!
Joyfully, joyfully will I go home.
Bright will the morn of eternity dawn,
Death shall be banished, his scepter be
    gone;
Joyfully, then, shall I witness his doom,
Joyfully, joyfully, safely at home.
*W. Hunter.*

538  AMSTERDAM. 7s & 6s.

NARES.

1. Rise, my soul, and stretch thy wings, Thy bet - ter por- tion trace;
2. Riv - ers to the o - cean run, Nor stay in all their course;
3. Fly me, rich - es, fly me, cares, Whilst I that coast ex - plore;
4. Cease, ye pil - grims, cease to mourn, Press on - ward to the prize;

Rise from tran - si - to - ry things T'wards heav'n, thy na - tive place:
Fire, as - cend- ing, seeks the sun; Both speed them to their source:
Flat-t'ring world, with all thy snares, So - lic - it me no more!
Soon our Sa - viour will re - turn Tri - um - phant in the skies:

Sun, and moon, and stars de - cay; Time shall soon this earth re-move;
So a soul that's born of God, Pants to view his glo - rious face,
Pil - grims fix not here their home; Stran - gers tar - ry but a night;
Yet a sea - son, and you know Hap - py en - trance will be giv'n,

Rise, my soul and haste a - way To seats pre-pared a - bove.
Up- ward tends to his a - bode, To rest in his em - brace.
When the last dear morn is come, They'll rise to joy - ful light.
All our sor - rows left be - low, And earth ex-changed for heav'n.

SEAGRAVE.

**539 LYONS. 10s & 11s.** FRANCIS JOSEPH HAYDN.

1. O tell me no more of this world's vain store, The time for such
tri - fles with me now is o'er; A coun-try I've found where
true joys a - bound, To dwell I'm de - ter-mined on that hap-py ground.

2 The souls that believe, in paradise live,
And me in that number will Jesus receive;
My soul, don't delay—he calls thee away,
Rise, follow thy Saviour, and bless the glad day.

3 No mortal doth know what he can bestow,
What light, strength, and comfort—go after him, go;
Lo, onward I move to a city above,
None guesses how wondrous my journey will prove.

4 Great spoils I shall win from death, hell, and sin,
Midst outward afflictions shall feel Christ within;
And when I'm to die, receive me, I'll cry,
For Jesus hath loved me, I cannot tell why.

5 But this I do find, we two are so join'd,
He'll not live in glory and leave me behind:
So this is the race I'm running through grace,
Henceforth—till admitted to see my Lord's face.

6 And now I'm in care, my neighbors may share
These blessings: to seek them will none of you dare?
In bondage, O why, and death will you lie,
When one here assures you free grace is so nigh.

*Gambold,*

**540 DULCIANA. 11s & 6s.**

J. C. EMRRY.
HAR. BY J. T. LAYTON, 1897.

By faith I view my Sa-viour dy-ing, On the tree; on the tree;
To ev-'ry na-tion he is cry-ing, Look to me! look to me!

He bids the guilt-y now draw near, Re-pent, be-lieve, dis-miss their fear;—

Hark! hark! what precious words I hear! Mer-cy's free! mer-cy's free!

---

**First Part.** 11s & 6s.

1 By faith I view my Saviour dying
On the tree; on the tree;
To every nation he is crying,
Look to me! look to me!
He bids the guilty now draw near,
Repent, believe, dismiss their fear;—
Hark! hark! what precious words I hear!
Mercy's free! mercy's free!

2 Did Christ, when I was sin pursuing,
Pity me? pity me?
And did he snatch my soul from ruin?
Can it be? can it be?
O yes! he did salvation bring:
He is my Prophet, Priest, and King;
And now my happy soul can sing,—
Mercy's free! mercy's free!

3 Jesus my weary soul refreshes;—
Mercy's free! mercy's free!
And every moment, Christ is precious
Unto me! unto me!
None can describe the bliss I prove,
While through this wilderness I rove:
All may enjoy the Saviour's love,
Mercy's free! mercy's free!

**541 Second Part.** 11s & 6s.

1 Jesus, the mighty God, hath spoken
Peace to me, peace to me:
Now all my chains of sin are broken—
I am free, I am free:
Soon as I in his name believed,
The Holy Spirit I received,
And Christ from death my soul retrieved:
Mercy's free! mercy's free!

2 This precious truth, ye sinners, hear it—
Mercy's free! mercy's free!
Ye ministers of God, declare it—
Mercy's free! mercy's free!
Visit the heathen's dark abode,
Proclaim to all the love of God,
And spread the glorious news abroad—
Mercy's free! Mercy's free!

3 Long as I live I'll still be crying,
Mercy's free! mercy's free!
And this shall be my theme when dying,
Mercy's free! mercy's free!
And when the vale of death I've pass'd,
When lodg'd above the stormy blast,
I'll sing, while endless ages last,
Mercy's free! mercy's free!

*Unknown.*

257

# DEVOTIONAL MISCELLANY.

**542  WILL YOU GO?  8s & 3s.**  J. C. EMBRY.

FINE.

1. We're travelling home to heav'n a-bove, Will you go? Will you go?

D.C.—And mill-ions more are on the road, Will you go, Will you go?

To sing the Sav-iour's dy - ing love, Will you go? Will you go?

D. C.

Mill-ions have reached that blest a-bode, A - noint - ed kings and priests to God,

**8s & 3s.**

1 We're travelling home to heaven above,
　Will you go?
To sing the Saviour's dying love,
　Will you go?
Millions have reached that blest abode,
Anointed kings and priests to God,
And millions more are on the road,
　Will you go?

2 We're going to see the bleeding Lamb,
　Will you go?
In rapturous strains to praise his name,
　Will you go?
The crown of life we there shall wear,
The conqueror's palm our hands shall bear
And all the joys of heaven we'll share,
　Will you go?

3 We're going to join the heavenly choir,
　Will you go?
To raise our voice and tune the lyre,
　Will you go?
There saints and angels gladly sing
Hosanna to their God and King.
And make the heavenly arches ring,
　Will you go?

4 We're going to walk the plains of light,
　Will you go?
Where perfect day excludes the night:
　Will you go?
Our sun will there no more go down,
In that blest world of great renown,
Our days of mourning past and gone,
　Will you go?

5 The way to heaven is free for all,
　Will you go?
For Jew and Gentile, great and small,
　Will you go?
Make up your mind, give God your heart,
With every sin and idol part,
And now for glory make a start.
　Will you go?

6 The way to heaven is straight and plain:
　Will you go?
Repent, believe, be born again:
　Will you go?
The Saviour cries aloud to thee :
Take up thy cross and follow me,
And thou shalt my salvation see.
　Will you go?

*Unknown.*

258

**543 GREENVILLE.** 8s & 7s. D.                    J. J. ROUSSEAU, 1775.

Breth-ren, we have met to wor-ship And a-dore our God the Lord:
Will you pray with all your pow-er, While we try to preach the word?

All is vain, un-less the Spir-it Of the Ho-ly One come down:

Breth-ren, pray, and ho-ly man-na Will be show-er'd all a-round.

*Opening Worship.*    8s, 7s. D.

1 Brethren, we have met to worship
    And adore our God the Lord:
  Will you pray with all your power,
    While we try to preach the word!
  All is vain unless the Spirit
    Of the Holy One come down:
  Brethren, pray, and holy manna
    Will be shower'd all around.

2 Brethren, see poor sinners round you
    Slumbering on the brink of woe:
  Death is coming, hell is moving,
    Can you bear to let them go?
  See our fathers, and our mothers,
    And our children sinking down:
  Brethren, pray, and holy manna
    Will be shower'd all around.

3 Sister, will you join and help us?
    Moses' sister join'd with him:
  While you see the trembling sinners,
    Have you no concern for them?
  Tell them all about the Saviour,
    Tell them that he will be found:
  Pray on, sisters, and the manna
    Will be shower'd all around.

4 Let us love our God supremely,
    Let us love each other, too:
  Let us love and pray for sinners,
    Till our God makes all things new.
  Then he'll call us home to heaven,
    At his table we'll sit down:
  Christ will gird himself, and serve us
    With sweet manna all around.
                            *Unknown.*

**544 HENDON. 7s.**  REV. HENRI ABRAHAM CÆSAR MALAN.

1. Christ, from whom all bless - ings flow, Per - fect - ing the saints be - low, Hear us who thy na - ture share, Who thy mys - tic bod - y are, Who thy mys - tic bod - y are.

*"The unity of the Spirit."*  7s.
*Eph.* iv. 3.

1 Christ, from whom all blessings flow,
  Perfecting the saints below,
  Hear us who thy nature share,
  Who thy mystic body are.

2 Join us in one spirit join,
  Let us still receive of thine:
  Still for more on thee we call,
  Thou who fillest all in all.

3 Move, and actuate, and guide:
  Divers gifts to each divide:
  Placed according to thy will,
  Let us all our work fulfil:

4 Never from our office move,
  Needful to each other prove:
  Use the grace on each bestow'd,
  Temp'red by the art of God!

5 Sweetly may we all agree,
  Touch'd with softest sympathy;
  Kindly for each other care;
  Every member feel its share.

6 Many are we now and one,
  We who Jesus have put on:
  Names, and sects, and parties, fall:
  Thou, O Christ, art all in all.
                                    *C. Wesley.*

**545**  *Cleaving to God.*  7s.

1 God of love, that hear'st pray'r,
  Kindly for thy people care,
  Who on thee alone depend:
  Love us, save us to the end.

2 Save us in the prosp'rous hour,
  From the flatt'ring tempter's power;
  From his unsuspected wiles,
  From the world's pernicious smiles.

3 Men of worldly, low design,
  Let not these thy people join,
  Poison our simplicity,
  Drag us from our trust in thee.

4 Save us from the great and wise,
  Till they sink in their own eyes,
  Tamely to thy yoke submit,
  Lay their honors at thy feet.

5 Never let the world break in,
  Fix a mighty gulf between:
  Keep us little and unknown,
  Priz'd and lov'd by God alone.
                                    *C. Wesley.*

# DEVOTIONAL MISCELLANY.

1. God of mer - cy, hear our pray'r  For the child-ren thou hast giv'n;

Let them all  thy  bless-ings share—  Grace on earth and  bliss in heav'n.

*Prayer for the Salvation of Children.*  7s,

1 God of mercy, hear our prayer
  For the children thou hast giv'n;
  Let them all thy blessings share—
  Grace on earth and bliss in heaven.

2 In the morning of their days
  May their hearts be drawn to thee;
  Let them learn to lisp thy praise
  In their earliest infancy.

3 When we see their passions rise,
  Sinful habits unsubdued,
  Then to thee we lift our eyes,
  That their hearts may be renew'd.

4 Cleanse their souls from every stain,
  Through the Saviour's precious blood;
  Let them all be born again,
  And be reconciled to God.

5 For this mercy, Lord, we cry;
  Bend thine ever-gracious ear:
  While on thee our souls rely,
  Hear our prayer—in mercy hear.
                          *Campbell's Coll.*

**546 b**  *The Lord our Righteousness.*  7s.

1 In thy presence we appear;
  Lord! we love to worship here,

  When, within the veil, we meet
  Thee upon thy mercy-seat.

2 While thy glorious Name is sung,
  Touch our lips, and loose our tongue;
  Then our joyful souls shall bless
  Thee, the Lord our righteousness.

3 While to thee our prayers ascend,
  Let thine ear in love attend;
  Hear, for Jesus intercedes;
  Hear us, for thy Spirit pleads.

4 While thy word is heard with awe,
  And we tremble at thy law,
  Let thy Gospel's wondrous love
  Every doubt and fear remove.

5 While thy ministers proclaim
  Peace and pardon through thy name,
  In their voices let us own
  Jesus, speaking from the throne.

6 From thy house when we return,
  Let our hearts within us burn;
  That at evening we may say,—
  We have walk'd with God to-day.
                          *Montgomery.*

**547 PASS ME NOT.**

W. H. DOANE, BY PER.

1. Pass me not, O gen - tle Sav - iour, Hear my hum - ble cry;
2. Let me at a throne of mer - cy, Find a sweet re - lief,
3. Trust - ing on - ly in thy mer - it, Would I seek thy face;
4. Thou the Spring of all my com - fort, More than life to me,

While on oth - ers thou art smil - ing, Do not pass me by.
Kneel - ing there in deep con - tri - tion, Help my un - be - lief.
Heal my wound - ed, brok - en spir - it, Save me by Thy grace.
Whom have I on earth be - side thee? Whom in Heav'n but thee?

CHORUS.

Sav - iour, Sav - iour, hear my hum - ble cry,

While on oth - ers thou art call - ing, Do not pass me by.

FANNIE J. CROSBY, 1868.

262

**548  REGENT SQUARE.  8s & 7s.**    SIR H. SMART.

1. Dark and thorn-y is the des-ert Through which pil-grims make their

way; Yet be-yond this vale of sor-row Lie the

fields of end-less day, Lie the fields of end-less day.

*Scenes of Glory.*     8s & 7s.

1 Dark and thorny is the desert
   Through which pilgrims make their way;
   Yet beyond this vale of sorrow
   Lie the fields of endless day.

2 Fiends, loud howling through the desert,
   Make them tremble as they go;
   And the fiery darts of Satan
   Often bring their courage low.

3 O young pilgrims, are you weary
   Of the roughness of the way?
   Does your strength begin to fail you,
   And your vigor to decay?

4 Jesus, Jesus, will go with you:
   He will lead you to his throne:—
   He who dyed his garments for you,
   And the wine-press trod alone.

5 There, on flowery hills of pleasure,
   Lie the fields of endless rest;
   There shall love and joy forever
   Reign and triumph in your breast:

6 Hail, ye happy, happy spirits!
   Death no more shall make you fear,
   Grief or sorrow, pain or anguish,
   Never shall distress you there.
                         *Unknown*

**548 b**     8s & 7s.
*Pressing onward to the prize.*

1 Pilgrims in this vale of sorrow,
   Pressing onward to the prize,
   Strength and comfort here we borrow
   From the Hand that rules the skies,

2 'Mid these scenes of self-denial,
   We are called the race to run;
   We must meet full many a trial
   Ere the victor's crown is won.

3 Love shall every conflict lighten,
   Hope shall urge us swifter on,
   Faith shall every prospect brighten,
   Till the morn of heaven shall dawn.
                         *Hastings.*

**548 c**     *Jesus calls us.*     8 & 7s.

1 Jesus calls us, o'er the tumult
   Of our life's wild restless sea,
   Day by day his sweet voice soundeth,
   Saying, "Christian, follow me."

2 Jesus calls us—from the worship
   Of the vain world's golden store,
   From each idol that would keep us—
   Saying, "Christian, love me more."

3 In our joys and in our sorrows,
   Days of toil, and hours of ease,
   Still he calls, in cares and pleasures,
   "Christian, love me more than these."
                         *Anon.*

263

**549 THE GATE AJAR FOR ME.**

8. J. VAIL.

1. There is a gate that stands a - jar, And through its por - tals gleam - ing,
2. That gate a - jar stands free for all Who seek through it sal - va - tion;
3. Press on - ward then, though foes may frown, While mer-cy's gate is o - pen:
4. Be - yond the riv - er's brink we'll lay The cross that here is giv - en,

A ra-diance from the Cross a - far, The Sav-iour's love re - veal - ing.
The rich and poor, the great and small, Of ev - 'ry tribe and na - tion.
Ac - cept the cross, and win the crown, Love's ev - er - last - ing tok - en.
And bear the crown of life a - way, And love him more in heav - en.

**REFRAIN.**

Oh, depth of mer - cy! can it be That gate was left a - jar for me?

For me, for me? Was left a - jar for me?
for me, for me?

MRS. LYDIA BAXTER.

**550 ALMOST PERSUADED.**

P. P. BLISS. BY PER.

1. "Al - most per - suad - ed" now to be - lieve;
2. "Al - most per - suad - ed" come, come to - day;
3. "Al - most per - suad - ed," har - vest is past!

"Al - most per - suad - ed" Christ to re - ceive;
"Al - most per - suad - ed," turn not a - way;
"Al - most per - suad - ed," doom comes at last!

Seems now some soul to say, "Go, Spir - it, go Thy way,
Je - sus in - vites you here, An - gels are ling - 'ring near,
"Al - most" can not a - vail; "Al - most" is but to fail!

Some more con - ven - ient day On thee I'll call."
Prayers rise from hearts so dear: O wan - d'rer, come.
Sad, sad, that bit - ter wail— "Al - most *but lost!*"

**551 MEDITATION. 11s & 8s.**   FREEMAN LEWIS, ARR. BY H. P. MAIN.

1. O thou, in whose pres - ence my soul takes de - light, On whom in af - flic - tion I call, My com - fort by day, and my song in the night, My hope, my sal - va - tion, my all!

*My Beloved.*     11s & 8s.

1 O thou, in whose presence my soul takes
    delight,
  On whom in affliction I call,
  My comfort by day and my song in the night,
  My hope, my salvation, my all!

2 Where dost thou, dear Shepherd, resort with
    thy sheep,
  To feed them in pastures of love?
  Say, why in the valley of death should I
    weep,
  Or alone in this wilderness rove?

3 O why should I wander an alien from thee,
  Or cry in the desert for bread?
  Thy foes will rejoice when my sorrows they
    see,
  And smile at the tears I have shed.

4 Ye daughters of Zion, declare have you seen
    The star that on Israel shone?
  Say, if in your tents my Beloved has been,
    And where with his flocks he is gone.

5 He looks! and ten thousands of angels re-
    joice,
  And myriads wait for his word:
  He speaks! and eternity, filled with his
    voice,
  Re-echoes the praise of the Lord.

6 Dear Shepherd, I hear, and will follow thy
    call;
  I know the sweet sound of thy voice:
  Restore and defend me, for thou art my all,
    And in thee I will ever rejoice.

                                    *Unknown.*

**552  THE ROCK THAT IS HIGHER. P. M.**   W. G. FISCHER.

1. Oh, sometimes the shadows are deep, And rough seems the path to the goal;
2. Oh, sometimes how long seems the day, And sometimes how wea-ry my feet,
3. Oh, near to the Rock let me keep, If bless-ings, or sor-rows pre-vail;

And sor-rows sometimes how they sweep Like tempests down o-ver the soul.
But toil-ing in life's dust-y way, The Rock's bless-ed shadow how sweet.
Or climb-ing the mountain way steep, Or walk-ing the shad-ow-y vale.

REFRAIN.

Oh, then to the Rock let me fly,......... To the Rock that is higher than I :.........
let me fly, is higher than I :

Oh, then to the Rock let me fly,......... To the Rock that is high-er than I.
let me fly,   E. JOHNSON.

## 553 IS MY NAME WRITTEN THERE?

FRANK M. DAVIS, BY PER.

1. Lord, I care not for rich-es, Neither sil-ver nor gold; I would make sure of heav-en, I would en-ter the fold. In the book of thy king-dom, With its pa-ges so fair, Tell me, Je-sus, my Sav-iour, Is my name writ-ten there?

2. Lord, my sins they are man-y, Like the sands of the sea, But thy blood, oh, my Sav-iour! Is suf-fi-cient for me; For thy prom-ise is writ-ten, In bright let-ters that glow, "Tho' your sins be as scar-let, I will make them like snow."

3. Oh! that beau-ti-ful cit-y, With its man-sions of light, With its glo-ri-fied be-ings, In pure garments of white; Where no e-vil thing com-eth, To de-spoil what is fair; Where the an-gels are watch-ing, Yes, my name's written there.

CHORUS.

Is my name writ-ten there, On the page white and fair? In the book of thy king-dom, Is my name writ-ten there?

MRS. MARY A. KIDDER.

**554 AMO TE. 11s.**

ENGLISH MELODY, ARR. BY J. T. LAYTON.

1. My Je - sus, I love thee, I know thou art mine, For
2. I love thee be - cause thou hast first lov - ed me, And
3. I'll love thee in life, I will love thee in death, And
4. In man - sions of glo - ry and end - less de - light, I'll

thee all the fol - lies of sin I re - sign; My grac - ious Re -
pur - chased my par - don on Cal - va - ry's tree; I love thee for
praise thee as long as thou lend - est me breath: And say when the
ev - er a - dore thee in heav - en so bright: I'll sing with the

CHORUS.

deem - er, my Sav - iour art thou,
wear - ing the thorns on thy brow,
death - dew lies cold on my brow,
glit - ter - ing crown on my brow,

If ev - er I loved thee, my

Je - sus, 'tis now, If ev - er I loved thee, my Je - sus, 'tis now.

ENGLISH BAPTIST COL.

**555 ORTONVILLE. C. M.**  THOMAS HASTINGS.

1. Je - sus, the ver - y thought of thee With sweet-ness fills the breast; But sweeter far thy face to see, And in thy presence rest, And in thy presence rest.

*The thought of thee.*  C. M.

1 Jesus, the very thought of thee
   With sweetness fills the breast;
   But sweeter far thy face to see,
   And in thy presence rest.

2 No voice can sing, no heart can frame,
   Nor can the memory find
   A sweeter sound than Jesus' name,
   The Saviour of mankind.

3 O Hope of every contrite heart,
   O Joy of all the meek,
   To those who ask, how kind thou art!
   How good, to those who seek!

4 But what to those who find? Ah, this
   Nor tongue nor pen can show:
   The love of Jesus, what it is,
   None but his loved ones know.

5 Jesus, our only joy be thou,
   As thou our prize wilt be;
   In thee be all our glory now,
   And through eternity.
                           *Bernard.*

**556**  *"All things are of God."*  C. M.
       1 *Sam.* iii. 18.

1 It is the Lord—enthroned in light,
   Whose claims are all divine,

Who has an undisputed right
   To govern me and mine.

2 It is the Lord—who gives me all—
   My wealth, my friends, my ease;
   And of his bounties may recall
   Whatever part he please.

3 It is the Lord—my Covenant God,
   Thrice blessèd be his name;
   Whose gracious promise, sealed with blood,
   Must ever be the same.

4 Can I, with hopes so firmly built,
   Be sullen, or repine?
   No, gracious God, take what thou wilt,
   To thee I all resign.
                           *Green.*

*Doxology.*

*The Apostolic Benediction.*

1 May the grace of Christ the Saviour,
   And the Father's boundless love,
   With the Holy Spirit's favor,
   Rest upon us from above.

2 Thus may we abide in union
   With each other and the Lord;
   And possess, in sweet communion,
   Joys which earth cannot afford.

557 WOODSTOCK. C. M. DEODATUS DUTTON, JR.

1. Grant me with-in thy courts a place, A-mong thy saints a seat,

For ev-er to be-hold thy face, And wor-ship at thy feet.

*Lord, grant my Prayer.* C. M.

1 Grant me within thy courts a place,
    Among thy saints a seat,
  For ever to behold thy face,
    And worship at thy feet ;

2 In thy pavilion to abide
    When storms of trouble blow,
  And in thy tabernacle hide,
    Secure from every foe.

3 Then leave me not when griefs assail
    And earthly comforts flee ;
  When father, mother, kindred fail,
    My God! remember me.
                    *Montgomery.*

558    *The Saviour Welcomed.*    C. M.
       *Prov.* xxiii. 26.

1 Welcome. O Saviour! to my heart;
    Possess thine humble throne ;
  Bid every rival hence depart,
    And claim me for thine own.

2 The world and Satan I forsake—
    To thee I all resign :
  My longing heart, O Jesus! take,
    And fill with love divine.

3 O! may I never turn aside,
    Nor from thy bosom flee ;
  Let nothing here my heart divide—
    I give it all to thee.
                    *Bourne.*

559    *Desiring Salvation.*    *Psa.* li.    C. M.

1 O God of mercy! hear my call,
    My load of guilt remove ;
  Break down this separating wall,
    That bars me from thy love.

2 Give me the presence of thy grace ;
    Then my rejoicing tongue
  Shall speak aloud thy righteousness,
    And make thy praise my song.

3 No blood of goats, nor heifer slain,
    For sin could e'er atone ;
  The death of Christ shall still remain
    Sufficient and alone.

4 A soul, oppressed with sin's desert,
    My God will ne'er despise ;
  An humble groan, a broken heart,
    Is our best sacrifice.
                    *Watts.*

271

# DEVOTIONAL MISCELLANY.

560 WARD. L. M.                    SCOTCH TUNE, ARR. BY LOWELL MASON.

1. Go, la-bor on; spend and be spent,—Thy joy to do the Fa-ther's will;

It is the way the Mas-ter went; Should not the ser-vant tread it still?

Zeal. *John* xii. 43.          L. M.

1 Go, labor on; spend and be spent,—
    Thy joy to do the Father's will;
    It is the way the Master went;
    Should not the servant tread it still?

2 Go, labor on; 'tis not for naught;
    Thine earthly loss is heavenly gain;
    Men heed thee, love thee, praise thee not;
    The Master praises,—what are men?

3 Go, labor on; enough, while here,
    If he shall praise thee, if he deign
    Thy willing heart to mark and cheer:
    No toil for him shall be in vain.

4 Toil on, and in thy toil rejoice;
    For toil comes rest, for exile home;
    Soon shalt thou hear the Bridegroom's voice.
    The midnight peal: "Behold, I come!"
                        *Bonar.*

561          Zeal. *John* ix. 4.          L. M.

1 Go, labor on, while it is day;
    The world's dark night is hastening on:
    Speed, speed thy work,—cast sloth away!
    It is not thus that souls are won.

2 Men die in darkness at your side,
    Without a hope to cheer the tomb;
    Take up the torch and wave it wide—
    The torch that lights time's thickest gloom.

3 Toil on,—faint not; keep watch and pray!
    Be wise the erring soul to win;
    Go forth into the world's highway;
    Compel the wanderer to come in.

4 Go, labor on; your hands are weak;
    Your knees are faint, your soul cast down;
    Yet falter not; the prize you seek
    Is near,—a kingdom and a crown!
                        *Bonar.*

562                              L. M.
" *Though thou slay me, yet will I trust thee.*"
            *Heb.* vii. 11.

1 I bless thee, Lord, for sorrows sent
    To break the dream of human power,
    For now my shallow cistern's spent,
    I find thy fount and thirst no more.

2 I take thy hand, and fears grow still;
    Behold thy face, and doubts remove;
    Who would not yield his wavering will
    To perfect truth and boundless love!

3 That truth gives promise of a dawn,
    Beneath whose light I am to see,
    When all these blinding veils are drawn,
    This was the wisest path for me.

4 That love this restless soul doth teach
    The strength of thy eternal calm;
    And tunes its sad and broken speech,
    To sing ev'n now the angels' psalm.
                        *Anon.*

272

**563 WELTON. L. M.**

C.ÆSAR MALAN, 1830.

1. I can-not al - ways trace the way Where thou, Al-might-y One, dost move,

But I can al - ways, al - ways say, That God is love, that God is love.

*God is love. Heb. xii. 6.* L. M.

1 I cannot always trace the way
  Where thou, Almighty One, dost move;
But I can always, always say,
  That God is love, that God is love.

2 When fear her chilling mantle flings
  O'er earth, my soul to heaven above,
As to her native home, upsprings,
  For God is love, for God is love.

3 When mystery clouds my darkened path,
  I'll check my dread, my doubts reprove;
In this my soul sweet comfort hath,
  That God is love, that God is love.

4 Yes, God is love;—a thought like this
  Can every gloomy thought remove,
And turn all tears, all woes, to bliss,
  For God is love, for God is love.
    *Anon.*

**563 b** *The better Choice.* L. M.

1 What sinners value I resign;
  Lord! 'tis enough that thou art mine;
I shall behold thy blissful face,
  And stand complete in righteousness.

2 This life's a dream, an empty show,
  But the bright world to which I go
Hath joys substantial and sincere;
  When shall I wake and find me there?

3 Oh, glorious hour! oh, blest abode!
  I shall be near and like my God,
And flesh and sin no more control
  The sacred pleasures of the soul.

4 My flesh shall slumber in the ground
  Till the last trumpet's joyful sound;
Then burst the chains with sweet surprise,
  And in my Saviour's image rise.
    *Watts.*

**563 b ANTIGUA. L. M.**

ENGLISH MELODY.

1. What sin-ners val-ue I re - sign; Lord! 'tis e - nough that thou art mine;

I shall be-hold thy blis - ful face, And stand com-plete in rightousness.

273

**564 LAYTON. 8s & 7s.**   J. T. LAYTON.

*Moderato.*

1. Sav - iour, hear us, through thy mer - it; Low - ly bend - ing at thy feet;

Oh, draw near us by thy Spir - it; Pros - trate at thy mer - cy seat.

---

*O draw near us. John viii. 36.*   8s & 7s.

1 Saviour, hear us, through thy merit;
Lowly bending at thy feet;
Oh, draw near us by thy Spirit;
Prostrate at thy mercy-seat.

For the joys of thy salvation,
Still we raise our cries to thee:
Hear the voice of supplication,
Set our souls at liberty.
*Anon.*

**565** *The Sower. Ps. cxxvi. 6.*   8s & 7s.

1 He that goeth forth with weeping,
Bearing precious seed in love,
Never tiring, never sleeping,
Findeth mercy from above.

2 Soft descend the dews of heaven,
Bright the rays celestial shine;
Precious fruits will thus be given,
Through an influence all divine.

3 Sow thy seed, be never weary,
Let no fears thy soul annoy;
Be the prospect ne'er so dreary,
Thou shalt reap the fruits of joy.

4 Lo, the scene of verdure brightening!
See the rising grain appear;
Look again! the fields are whitening,
For the harvest time is near.
*Hastings.*

**566** *Glorying in the Cross.*   8s & 7s.

1 In the cross of Christ I glory,
Towering o'er the wrecks of time;
All the light of sacred story,
Gathers round its head sublime.

2 When the woes of life o'ertake me,
Hopes deceive, and fears annoy,
Never shall the cross forsake me;
Lo! it glows with peace and joy.

3 When the sun of bliss is beaming
Light and love upon my way,
From the cross the radiance streaming
Adds more lustre to the day.

4 Bane and blessing, pain and pleasure,
By the cross are sanctified;
Peace is there, that knows no measure,
Joys that through all time abide.
*Sir John Bowring.*

*Doxology.*

*Dismission.*

1 Lord, dismiss us with thy blessing;
Bid us now depart in peace;
Still on heavenly manna feeding,
Let our faith and love increase:

2 Fill each breast with consolation:
Up to thee our hearts we raise:
When we reach our blissful station,
Then we'll give thee nobler praise.

# DEVOTIONAL MISCELLANY.

1. Je - sus on - ly, when the morn - ing Beams up - on the path I tread;

Je - sus on - ly, when the dark - ness Gath - ers round my wea - ry head.

---

*Only Jesus.  Matt.* xvii. 8.  8s & 7s.

1 Jesus only, when the morning
 Beams upon the path I tread;
 Jesus only, when the darkness
 Gathers round my weary head.

2 Jesus only, when the billows
 Cold and sullen o'er me roll;
 Jesus only, when the trumpet
 Rends the tomb and wakes the soul.

3 Jesus only, when in judgment
 Boding fears my heart appal;
 Jesus only, when the wretched
 On the rocks and mountains call.

4 Jesus only, when, adoring,
 Saints their crowns before him bring;
 Jesus only, I will, joyous,
 Through eternal ages sing.
  *Nason.*

**568**  *Lover of Sinners.*  8s & 7s.
  *Prov.* xviii. 24.

1 One there is, above all others,
 Well deserves the name of Friend;
 His is love beyond a brother's,
 Costly, free, and knows no end.

2 Which of all our friends, to save us,
 Could or would have shed his blood?
 But our Jesus died to save us
 Reconciled in him to God.

3 When he lived on earth abaséd,
 Friend of sinners was his name;
 Now above all glory raiséd,
 He rejoices in the same.

4 Oh! for grace our hearts to soften,
 Teach us, Lord, at length, to love;
 We, alas! forget too often
 What a friend we have above.
  *Newton.*

**568 b**  *Penitent Prayer.*  10s.

[ Words Ed.  Tune, Eventide, page 317.  10s.]

1 Not worthy, Lord! to gather up the crumbs
 With trembling hand, that from thy table
  fall,
 A weary, heavy laden sinner comes
 To plead thy promise and obey thy call.

2 I am not worthy to be thought thy child;
 Nor sit the last and lowest at thy board;
 Too long a wanderer, and too oft beguiled,
 I only ask one reconciling word.

3 One word from thee, my Lord! one smile,
  one look,
 And I could face the cold, rough world
  again,
 And with that treasure in my heart could
  brook
 The wrath of devils and the scorn of men.

4 And is not mercy thy prerogative—
 Free mercy, boundless, fathomless, divine?
 Me, Lord! the chief of sinners, me forgive,
 And thine the greater glory, only thine.

5 I hear thy voice; thou bid'st me come and
  rest;
 I come, I kneel, I clasp thy piercéd feet;
 Thou bid'st me take my place, a welcome
  guest,
 Among thy saints, and of thy banquet eat.

6 My praise can only breathe itself in prayer,
 My prayer can only lose itself in thee;
 Dwell thou for ever in my heart, and there,
 Lord! let me sup with thee; sup thou
  with me.
  *E. H. Bickersteth.*

# DEVOTIONAL MISCELLANY.

**569 HOME. L. M.**

ARR. REV. WILLIAM MCDONALD.

1. My heav'nly home is bright and fair; Nor pain nor death can en - ter there;

Its glitt'ring tow'rs the sun out-shine; That heav'nly man - sion shall be mine.

**Chorus.**

{ I'm go - ing home, I'm go - ing home, I'm go - ing home to die no more; }
{ To die no more, to die no more, I'm go - ing home to die no more. }

*My Heavenly Home.* L. M.

1 My heavenly home is bright and fair;
Nor pain nor death can enter there;
Its glittering towers the sun outshine;
That heavenly mansion shall be mine.

CHORUS:—

I'm going home, I'm going home,
I'm going home to die no more;
To die no more, to die no more,
I'm going home to die no more.

2 My Father's house is built on high,
Far, far above the starry sky.
When from this earthly prison free,
That heavenly mansion mine shall be.

3 While here, a stranger far from home,
Affliction's waves may round me foam;
Although, like Lazarus, sick and poor,
My heavenly mansion is secure.

4 Let others seek a home below,
Which flames devour, or waves o'erflow,
Be mine the happier lot to own
A heavenly mansion near the throne.

5 Then fail the earth, let stars decline,
And sun and moon refuse to shine,
All nature sink and cease to be,
That heavenly mansion stands for me.

*William Hunter.*

**570 MISSIONARY. 6, 6 & 9s.** FROM "INDIAN MELODIES." THS. COMMUCK.

1. Come, let us as-cend, My com-pan-ion and friend, To a taste of the ban-quet a-bove: If thy heart be as mine, If for Je-sus it pine, Come up in-to the char-iot of love.

*Rapturous Anticipation.* 6, 6 & 9s.

1 Come, let us ascend,
My companion and friend,
To a taste of the banquet above:
If thy heart be as mine,
If for Jesus it pine,
Come up into the chariot of love.

2 Who in Jesus confide,
We are bold to outride
The storms of affliction beneath;
With the prophet we soar
To the heavenly shore,
And outfly all the arrows of death.

3 By faith we are come
To our permanent home;
By hope we the rapture improve;
By love we still rise,
And look down on the skies,
For the heaven of heavens is love.

4 Who on earth can conceive
How happy we live
In the palace of God the great King?
What a concert of praise,
When our Jesus's grace
The whole heavenly company sing!

5 What a rapturous song,
When the glorified throng
In the spirit of harmony join;
Join all the glad choirs,
Hearts, voices and lyres,
And the burden is, "Mercy divine!"

6 "Hallelujah," they cry,
To the King of the sky,
To the great everlasting I Am;
To the Lamb that was slain,
And that liveth again,—
"Hallelujah to God and the Lamb!"
*Charles Wesley.*

277

# ΘHE SABBAΘH.

**571  CHRISTMAS.  C. M.**    GEORGE FREDERICK HANDEL.

1. This   is the day the Lord hath made, He   calls the hours his   own;   Let

heav'n rejoice, let earth be glad, And praise surround the throne, And praise surround the throne.

C. M.

*Christ's Resurrection.    Psalm* cxviii. 24.

1 This is the day the Lord hath made,
    He calls the hours his own ;
  Let heaven rejoice, let earth be glad,
    And praise surround the throne.

2 To-day he rose and left the dead,
    And Satan's empire fell ;
  To-day the saints his triumphs spread,
    And all his wonders tell.

3 Hosanna to the annointed King,
    To David's holy Son !
  Help us, O Lord! descend and bring
    Salvation from thy throne.

4 Blest be the Lord who comes to men
    With messages of grace ;
  Who comes in God his Father's name,
    To save our sinful race.

5 Hosanna in the highest strains
    The church on earth can raise ;
  The highest heavens, in which he reigns,
    Shall give him nobler praise.
                                *Watts.*

**572**                              C. M.

*O come, let us worship and bow down.*

1 Come, let us join with one accord
    In hymns around the throne !

  This is the day our rising Lord
  Hath made and called his own.

2 This is the day which God hath blessed,
    The brightest of the seven,
  Type of that everlasting rest
    The saints enjoy in heaven.

3 Then let us in his name sing on,
    And hasten to that day
  When our Redeemer shall come down,
    And shadows pass away.

4 Not one, but all our days below,
    Let us in hymns employ;
  And in our Lord rejoicing, go
    To his eternal joy.
                                *C. Wesley.*

**573**    *In the Spirit.  Rev.* i. 10.    C. M.

1 May I throughout this day of thine
    Be in thy Spirit, Lord :
  Spirit of humble fear divine,
    That trembles at thy word;—

2 Spirit of faith, my heart to raise,
    And fix on things above ;
  Spirit of sacrifice and praise,
    Of holiness and love.
                                *C. Wesley.*

278

# THE SABBATH.

**HEBRON. L. M.**
*Slow and soft.*

1. Far from my thoughts, vain world, begone! Let my re-lig-ious hours a-lone:

Fain would my eyes my Sav-iour see; I wait a vis-it, Lord, from thee.

---

*In the Sanctuary.* L. M.

1 Far from my thoughts, vain world, begone!
Let my religious hours alone :
Fain would my eyes my Saviour see ;
I wait a visit, Lord, from thee.

2 My heart grows warm with holy fire,
And kindles with a pure desire :
Come, my dear Jesus, from above,
And feed my soul with heavenly love.

3 Blest Jesus, what delicious fare !
How sweet thine entertainments are !
Never did angels taste above
Redeeming grace and dying love.
*Watts.*

**575** *The day of rest.* L. M.

1 Another six days' work is done ;
Another Sabbath is begun ;
Return, my soul, enjoy thy rest ;
Improve the day thy God hath blessed.

2 O that our thoughts and thanks may rise,
As grateful incense, to the skies ;
And draw from Christ that sweet repose
Which none but he that feels it knows !

3 This heavenly calm within the breast
Is the dear pledge of glorious rest,
Which for the Church of God remains,
The end of cares, the end of pains.

4 In holy duties let the day,
In holy comforts, pass away :
How sweet, a Sabbath thus to spend,
In hope of one that ne'er shall end !
*J. Stennett.*

**576** *Sweet is the work.* Psalm xcii. L. M.

1 Sweet is the work, my God, my King,
To praise thy name, give thanks, and sing,
To show thy love by morning light,
And talk of all thy truth by night.

2 Sweet is the day of sacred rest :
No mortal cares shall seize my breast :
O may my heart in tune be found,
Like David's harp of solemn sound !

3 My heart shall triumph in my Lord,
And bless his works, and bless his word :
Thy works of grace, how bright they shine !
How deep thy counsels ! how divine !

4 Then I shall share a glorious part
When grace hath well refined my heart,
And fresh supplies of joy are shed,
Like holy oil, to cheer my head.

5 Then shall I see, and hear, and know,
All I desired or wished below ;
And every hour find sweet employ
In that eternal world of joy.
*Watts.*

# THE SABBATH.

**577 HAMBURG. L. M.**                    ARR. FROM A GREGORIAN CHANT BY LOWELL MASON.

1. Thine earthly Sab-baths, Lord, we love; But there's a no - bler rest a - bove;

To that our lab - 'ring souls as - pire, With ar-dent pangs of strong de - sire.

*The Eternal Sabbath.*      L. M.

1 Thine earthly Sabbaths, Lord, we love;
But there's a nobler rest above;
To that our lab'ring souls aspire,
With ardent pangs of strong desire.

2 No more fatigue, no more distress;
Nor sin nor hell shall reach the place;
No sighs shall mingle with the songs
Which warble from immortal tongues.

3 No rude alarms of raging foes;
No cares to break the long repose;
No midnight shade, no clouded sun,
But sacred, high, eternal noon.

4 O long expected day, begin;
Dawn on these realms of woe and sin:
Fain would we leave this weary road,
And sleep in death, to rest with God.

*Doddridge.*

**577 ST. CROSS. L. M. Second Tune.**                    DYKES.

1. Thine earthly Sab - baths, Lord, we love; But there's a no - bler rest a - bove;

To that our la-b'ring souls as - pire, With ar - dent pangs of strong de - sire.

280

# THE SABBATH.

DANIEL READ.

1. Wel - come, sweet day of rest, That saw the Lord a - rise:

Wel - come to this re - viv-ing breast, And these re - joic - ing eyes!

*Welcome Sabbath.*     S. M.

1 Welcome, sweet day of rest,
   That saw the Lord arise:
Welcome to this reviving breast,
   And these rejoicing eyes!

2 The King himself comes near,
   And feasts his saints to-day;
Here we may sit, and see him here,
   And love, and praise, and pray.

3 One day within the place
   Which thou dost, Lord, frequent,
Is sweeter than ten thousand days
   In sinful pleasure spent.

4 My willing soul would stay
   In such a frame as this,
And sit and sing herself away
   To everlasting bliss.
                *Watts.*

**579**     *The Eternal Sabbath.*     S. M.

1 Hail to the Sabbath day!
   The day divinely given,
When men to God their homage pay,
   And earth draws near to heaven.

2 Lord, in this sacred hour,
   Within thy courts we bend,
And bless thy love, and own thy power,
   Our Father and our Friend.

3 But thou art not alone
   In courts by mortal trod;
Nor only is the day thine own
   When man draws near to God:

4 Thy temple is the arch
   Of yon unmeasured sky;
Thy Sabbath, the stupendous march
   Of vast eternity.

5 Lord, may that holier day
   Dawn on thy servants' sight;
And purer worship may we pay
   In heaven's unclouded light.
          *Stephen G. Bulfinch.*

**579 b**     *The opened Fountain.*     S. M.

1 Call'd from above, I rise,
   And wash away my sin;
The stream to which my spirit flies,
   Can make the foulest clean.

2 It runs divinely clear,
   A fountain deep and wide:
'Twas open'd by the soldier's spear,
   In my Redeemer's side.

# THE SABBATH.

REV. JOHN CHETHAM.

1. This is the day, the sa - cred day When Je - sus left the grave:

Of him we sing, and well we may, His arm is strong to save.

*Now is Christ risen from the dead.* C. M.
1 *Cor.* xv. 20.

1 This is the day, the sacred day
When Jesus left the grave:
Of him we sing, and well we may,
His arm is strong to save.

2 'Tis sweet to know that by his death
We live—this grace is sweet:
The Saviour, with his dying breath,
Proclaim'd his work complete.

3 He lives, he reigns the God of love,
He reigns for evermore:
His throne, all other thrones above;
His name, all names before.

4 To him who died and rose again,
The Lord of earth and heav'n:
To him, by angels and by men,
Be endless glory giv'n:

5 The glory due to him alone,
Who reigns in heav'n above;
Who fills the everlasting throne;
The God of grace and love.
*Kelley's Hymns.*

*Doxology.* C. M.

To Father, Son, and Holy Ghost,
Who sweetly all agree
To save the world of sinners lost,
Eternal glory be.

**581** C. M.
*Hitherto hath the Lord helped us.*
1 *Sam.* vii. 12.

1 Another week is past and gone,
Rejoice, we're nearer home,
Our gracious Lord has led us on;
And thus far have we come.

2 Our Ebenezer here we'll raise:
The Lord our help has been:
We'll publish, to our Saviour's praise,
The things our eyes have seen.

3 We've seen our foes before us flee,
They turned and fled apace:
To God alone the glory be;
We'll sing his pow'r and grace.

4 We've seen the timid lose their fears,
And valiant wax in fight.
We've seen the mourners dry their tears,
And put their griefs to flight.

5 We've seen the pris'ners burst their chains,
And walk at liberty;
We've seen the guilty lose his stains,
And without blemish be.

6 His word, on which we rest, is true,
Himself a faithful friend:
And He, who kept us hitherto,
Will keep us to the end.
*Kelley's Hymns.*

282

# THE SABBATH.

582 AUSTRIA. 8s & 7s. D.                                FRANCIS JOSEPH HAYDN.

1. Neith-er "voice" we have nor "vis - ion," Yet we walk as if we had;
2. One "un-seen" we own as mas - ter, And with him we look to be;
3. Then we shall be what we should be, Which, till then, can nev - er be;

Ob - jects of the world's de - ris - ion; Sor - row - ful, yet al - ways "glad."
Fly, ye sea - sons, fly still fast - er, Till our "Lord from heav'n" we see.
Then we shall be where we would be, Dwell-ing, Lord, in heav'n with thee.

On the word of truth re - ly - ing, Word of him who can - not lie,
Nev - er can we rest, no nev - er, Till the day when he ap - pears,
What a hope! to be for - ev - er In thy pres - ence, Lord, a - bove;

We go on, the foe de - fy - ing, Know-ing that the Lord is nigh.
Then we cease from sin for - ev - er, And he wipes a - way our tears.
To be - hold thee there, and nev - er Cease to sing thy grace and love.

KELLY'S HYMNS.

# SELECTIONS FROM THE PSALMS.

**583** ST. AGNES. C. M. 

REV. JOHN BACCHUS DYKES.

1. A - mong as - semb - led men of might, The might-y God doth stand:

He stands to or - der judg - ment right To judg - es of the land.

*Psalm* lxxxii. C. M.

1 Among assembled men of might,
The mighty God doth stand:
He stands to order judgment right
To judges of the land.

2 How long will ye, with wrongful aid,
The oppressor's cause protect?
How long, by gift and favor swayed,
The wicked man respect?

3 Protect the fatherless and weak,
Defend the poor distressed;
And give deliv'rance to the meek
By lawless power oppressed.

4 They will not know nor understand,
In darkness on they go:
Quake all ye pillars of the land;
They totter to and fro.

5 "True, ye are gods, ye kings," I said;
"And sons of God Most High;
Yet as the sons of men ye fade,
And as the princes die."

6 Arise, O God, assert thy right,
Pronounce thy just decree:
The heritage of earth by right
Belongs, O Lord, to thee.

**584** *Psalm* xci. C. M.

1 The man that doth in secret place
Of God Most High reside,
Beneath the shade of him that is
Th' Almighty shall abide.

2 I of the Lord, my God, will say,
He is my refuge still,
He is my fortress, and my God;
And trust in him I will.

3 Assuredly he shall thee save,
And give deliverance
From cunning fowler's snare, and from
The deadly pestilence.

4 His feathers shall thee hide; thy trust
Beneath his wings shall be:
His faithfulness shall be a shield
And buckler unto thee.

5 Thou shalt not need to be afraid
For terrors of the night;
Nor for the arrow that doth fly
By day, while it is light;

6 Nor for the pestilence, that walks
In darkness secretly;
Nor for destruction, that doth waste
At noon-day openly.

SELECTIONS FROM THE PSALMS.

**585 NAOMI. C. M.**  HANS GEORGE NAGELI, ARR. BY LOWELL MASON.

1. O Lord of hosts, how love - ly  is  The place where thou dost dwell!

The tab - er - na - cles  of  thy grace  In pleas - ant - ness ex - cel.

*Psalm* lxxxiv.    **C. M.**
*First Part.*

1 O Lord of hosts, how lovely is
The place where thou dost dwell!
The tabernacles of thy grace
In pleasantness excel.

2 My soul doth long, yea even faint,
Jehovah's courts to see ;
My heart and flesh are crying out,
O living God, for thee.

3 Behold, the sparrow findeth out
A house wherein to rest ;
The swallow also for herself
Hath found a peaceful nest.

**586**    *Second Part.*    **C. M.**

1 So they from strength unwearied go
Still forward unto strength ;
And they in Zion shall appear
Before the Lord at length.

2 Lord God of hosts, my prayer now hear ;
O Jacob's God, give ear,
See, God, our shield, look on the face
Of thy anointed dear.

3 For in thy courts one day excels
A thousand ; rather in
My God's house will I keep a door,
Than dwell in tents of sin.

4 For God the Lord's a sun and shield,
He'll grace and glory give ;

And no good thing will he withhold
From them that justly live.

5 O thou that art the Lord of hosts,
That man is truly blest,
Who with unshaken confidence,
On thee alone doth rest.

**587**    *Psalm* cxi.    **C. M.**

1 Praise ye the Lord : with all my heart
I will God's praise declare,
Ev'n where assemblies of the just
And congregations are.

2 Jehovah's works are very great,
The wonders of his might ;
Sought out they are of every one
Who in them takes delight.

3 His work most honorable is,
Most glorious and pure,
And his untainted righteousness
Forever doth endure.

4 His works of wonder he hath made
To be remembered well :
In grace and in compassion great
Jehovah doth excel.

5 The Lord provideth food for all
Who truly do him fear ;
And evermore his covenant
He in his mind will bear.

6 He did the power of his works
To his own people show,
That he the heathen's heritage
Upon them might bestow.

285

**588  SICILY.  8s & 7s.**

*Moderato.*

1. O my soul, bless thou Je - ho - vah, All with - in me bless his name,

Bless Je - ho - vah, and for - get not All his mer - cies to pro-claim.

---

*Psalm* ciii.  8s & 7s.

1 O my soul, bless thou Jehovah,
  All within me bless his name,
  Bless Jehovah, and forget not
  All his mercies to proclaim.

2 Who forgives all thy transgressions,
  Thy diseases all who heals;
  Who redeems thee from destruction,
  Who with thee so kindly deals.

3 Who with tender mercies crowns thee,
  Who with good things fills thy mouth,
  So that even like the eagle
  Thou hast been restored to youth.

4 In his righteousness, Jehovah
  Will deliver those distressed;
  He will execute just judgment
  In the cause of all oppressed.

5 He made known his ways to Moses,
  And his acts to Israel's race;
  God is plentiful in mercy,
  Slow to anger, rich in grace.

6 He will not forever chide us,
  Nor keep anger in his mind,

Hath not dealt as we offended,
Nor rewarded as we sinned.

**589**  *Psalm* vi.  8s & 7s.

1 Lord in anger do not chasten;
  Thy fierce wrath from me restrain;
  I am weak; in mercy hasten,
  O relieve my flesh from pain.

2 Sorrows deep my soul are grieving;
  Lord, how long!—O pity take;
  Lord, return, my soul relieving;
  Save me for thy mercy's sake.

3 Thee the grave no more remembers:
  Who gives thanks among the dead?
  Weary groans distract my slumbers,
  Tears have overflowed my bed.

4 Sorely vexed by my oppressors,
  Grief like age has dimmed my eye,
  Hence, and leave me, all transgressors,
  For the Lord hath heard my cry.

5 God hath heard my supplication;
  My petition will not spurn,
  Let my foes, with sore vexation,
  Back in sudden shame return.

**590 MEDITATION. 11s & 8s.** FREEMAN LEWIS, ARR. BY H. P. MAIN.

1. Make haste, O my God, to de - liv - er, I pray, O

Lord, to my suc - cor make haste: Let them be con - found - ed who

seek me to slay, And in their own fol - ly dis - graced.

*Psalm lxx.* 11s & 8s.

1 Make haste, O my God, to deliver I pray,
  O Lord, to my succor make haste:
  Let them be confounded who seek me to slay,
  And in their own folly disgraced.

2 Let them be turned back in confusion, O Lord,
  Who wish my destruction to see;
  Let shame and defeat be their only reward,
  Who laugh in derision at me.

3 Let all them that seek thee be glad and re-
    joice,
  And who thy salvation would see;
  In anthems of praise let them lift up their
    voice,
  And constantly magnify thee.

4 But I, poor and needy, still trust in thy word;
  Make haste to the rescue, I pray;
  My helper thou art, and my Saviour, O Lord
  No longer thy coming delay.

**591** *Psalm ii.* L. M.

*First Part.*

[Tune, Hamburg, page 280. L. M.]

1 Why do the heathen storm with ire?
  The people vanity devise?
  The rulers craftily conspire,
  The kings of earth rebellious rise.

2 Against the Lord they lift their hands,
  Against him and his Christ they say,

"Asunder let us break their bands,
  And from us cast their cords away."

3 He that in heaven sits shall laugh,
  Jehovah shall deride them all;
  Then as he speaks in burning wrath,
  Dismay and dread shall on them fall.

4 "Yet notwithstanding I ordain,"
  Thus shall he speak his sov'reign will,
  "He my anointed King shall reign
  On Zion, my own holy hill."

**592** *Second Part.* L. M.

[Tune, St. Cross, page 280. L. M.]

5 Thus spake to me the Holy One,
  I utter now the Lord's decree,
  "Thou art proclaimed my only Son,
  This day have I begotten thee.

6 "Ask for inheritance of me,
  And I will make the heathen thine,
  And for possession, give to thee
  The earth to its remotest line.

7 "An iron sceptre thou shalt sway,
  And with it break and crush them all;
  E'en like the potter's brittle clay,
  Thou shalt them dash in pieces small."

8 And now, ye kings, be wise and hear;
  Be warned, ye judges of the earth;
  See that ye serve the Lord with fear,
  And mingle trembling with your mirth.

**593 WELLS. L. M.**

HOLDRAYD.

1. Je - ho-vah reigns, let earth be glad    And all her is - lands clap their hands;

With clouds and darkness he is clad,    His throne in right and judgment stands.

*Psalm* xcvii.    L. M.

1 Jehovah reigns, let earth be glad,
  And all her islands clap their hands;
  With clouds and darkness he is clad,
  His throne in right and judgment stands.

2 A fiery stream before him goes,
  And burns around him all his foes;
  His lightning shafts, in vengeance hurled,
  Blaze lurid o'er the trembling world.

3 Like wax the mountains melt away,
  Before his majesty divine;
  The heavens his righteousness display,
  All nations see his glory shine.

4 Be shamed who idols serve and boast,
  Fear him, ye gods, with all your host;
  When Zion glad, thy judgments heard,
  Then Judah's daughters praised the Lord.

5 Exalted is thy throne, O Lord,
  Above all gods, above all lands;
  Hate evil, ye who love his word,
  His saints he frees from wicked hands.

6 For all the righteous sown is light,
  And joy for men in heart upright,
  Ye saints rejoice in God; him bless,
  When musing on his holiness.

**594**    *Psalm* xcviii.    L. M.

1 Come, let us sing unto the Lord,
  New songs of praise with sweet accord;
  For wonders great by him are done;
  His hand and arm have vict'ry won.

2 The great salvation of our God
  Is seen through all the earth abroad;
  Before the heathen's wondering sight,
  He hath revealed his truth and right.

3 He called to mind his truth and grace
  In promise made to Israel's race;
  And unto earth's remotest bound,
  Glad tidings of salvation sound.

4 All lands to God lift up your voice;
  Sing praise to him, with shouts rejoice;
  With voice of joy and loud acclaim,
  Let all unite and praise his name.

**595**    *Psalm* c.    L. M.

1 All people that on earth do dwell,
  Sing to the Lord with cheerful voice.
  Him serve with mirth, his praise forth tell,
  Come ye before him and rejoice.

2 Know that the Lord is God indeed;
  Without our aid he did us make:
  We are his flock, he doth us feed,
  And for his sheep he doth us take.

3 O enter then his gates with joy,
  Within his courts his praise proclaim;
  Let thankful songs your tongues employ,
  O bless and magnify his name.

4 Because the Lord our God is good,
  His mercy is forever sure;
  His truth at all times firmly stood,
  And shall from age to age endure.

**596  HARWICH. H. M.**

1. The glo-ry of the Lord The heav'ns de-clare a-broad;

The fir-ma-ment dis-plays The hand-i-work of God;

Day un-to day de-clar-eth speech, And night to night doth knowledge teach.

| Psalm xix. | H. M. | **597** | Psalm xix. | H. M. |
| First Part. | | | Second Part. | |

1 The glory of the Lord
  The heavens declare abroad;
  The firmament displays
  The handiwork of God;
  Day unto day declareth speech,
  And night to night doth knowledge teach.

2 Aloud they do not speak,
  They utter forth no word,
  Nor into language break;
  Their voice is never heard.
  Their line through all the earth extends,
  Their words to earth's remotest ends.

3 In them he for the sun
  Hath set a dwelling place;
  Rejoicing as a man
  Of strength to run a race;
  He, bridegroom-like in his array,
  Comes from his chamber, bringing day.

4 His daily going forth
  Is from the end of heaven;
  The firmament to him
  Is for his circuit given—
  His circuit reaches to its ends,
  And everywhere his heat extends.

1 God's perfect law converts
  The soul in sin that lies;
  His testimony sure
  Doth make the simple wise;
  His statutes just delight the heart;
  His holy precepts light impart.

2 The fear of God is clean,
  And ever doth endure;
  His judgments all are truth,
  And righteousness most pure.
  To be desired are they far more
  Than finest gold in richest store.

3 God's judgments to the taste
  More sweet than honey are,
  Than honey from the comb
  That droppeth, sweeter far,
  With counsel they thy servant guard;
  In keeping them is great reward.

4 Who can his errors know?
  From secret faults me cleanse;
  Thy servant keep thou back
  From all presumptuous sins,
  O let them not my way control,
  Nor gain dominion o'er my soul.

# SELECTIONS FROM THE PSALMS.

**598  HEBRON. L. M.**                                          LOWELL MASON.

1. My Shepherd is the Lord Most High, And all my wants shall be sup-plied;

In pas-tures green he makes me lie, And leads by streams which gently glide.

*Psalm* xxiii.                    L. M.

1  My Shepherd is the Lord Most High,
   And all my wants shall be supplied ;
   In pastures green he makes me lie,
   And leads by streams which gently glide.

2  He in his mercy doth restore
   My soul when sinking in distress ;
   For his name's sake he evermore
   Leads me in paths of righteousness.

3  Yea, though I walk through death's dark
                                   vale,

Ev'n there no evil will I fear.
Because thy presence shall not fail,
Thy rod and staff my soul shall cheer.

4  For me a table thou hast spread,
   Prepared before the face of foes ;
   With oil thou dost annoint my head ;
   My cup is filled and overflows.

5  Goodness and mercy shall not cease
   Through all my days to follow me ;
   And in God's house my dwelling place
   With him forevermore shall be.

**598  MENDON. L. M. (Second Tune.)**

*Spirited.*

1. My Shepherd is the Lord Most High, And all my wants shall be sup-plied;

In pas-tures green he makes me lie, And leads by streams which gent-ly glide.

290

**599 PORTUGUESE HYMN. 11s.**

UNKNOWN.

1. The earth and the ful - ness with which it is stored The world and its

dwell - ers be - long to the Lord; For he on the seas its foun -

da - tion hath laid, And firm on the wa - ters its pil - lars hath

stayed, And firm on the wa - ters its pil - lars hath stayed.

*Psalm* xxiv.                    11s.

1 The earth and the fulness with which it is
    stored,
  The world and its dwellers belong to the
    Lord;
  For he on the seas its foundation hath
    laid,
  And firm on the waters its pillars hath
    stayed.

2 What man shall the hill of Jehovah ascend?
  And who in the place of his holiness stand?
  The man of pure heart, and of hands with-
    out stain,
  Who swears not to falsehood, nor loves what
    is vain.

3 He shall from Jehovah the blessing receive.
  The God of salvation shall righteousness
    give;
  For this is the people, yea, this is the race,
  The Israel true who are seeking thy face.

4 Ye gates, lift your heads, and an entrance
    display,
  Ye doors everlasting, wide open the way;
  The King of all glory high honors await,
  The King of all glory shall enter in state.

5 What King of all glory is this that ye sing?
  The Lord, strong and mighty, the conquer-
    ing King.
  Ye gates, lift your heads, and an entrance
    display,
  Ye doors everlasting, wide open the way.

# SELECTIONS FROM THE PSALMS.

## 600 WALNUT GROVE. C. M.

H. K. OLIVER.

1. To thee I lift my soul, O Lord My God, I trust in thee;

O let me nev er be a-shamed, Nor foes ex-ult o'er me.

*Psalm xxv.* C. M.

1 To thee I lift my soul, O Lord
My God, I trust in thee;
O let me never be ashamed,
Nor foes exult o'er me.

2 O Lord, let none be put to shame
Upon thee who attend;
But make all those to be ashamed
Who causelessly offend.

3 Thy ways, Lord, show: teach me thy paths;
Lead me in truth, teach me;
For of my safety thou art God;
All day I wait on thee.

4 Thy mercies that most tender are,
To mind, O Lord, recall,
And loving kindnesses, for they
Have been through ages all.

## DEVOTIONAL MISCELLANY.

### 601 C. M.

*A Prayer for deliverance from Oppression.*

1 Regard in tenderness, O Lord,
The ills thy children bear:
Do thou thy gracious help afford,
And answer this our prayer.

2 We trust not in the arms of flesh,
We lean upon thy word;
For thine own arm omnipotent,
Is mightier than the sword.

3 What care we for the midnight foe?
Or arrows winged with light?
Or pestilence's fatal touch,
Since thou, Lord, art our might?

4 We need not fear the cruel hate
Of those we've done no wrong;
We look to thee, our Advocate,
For weapons sure and strong.

5 In common Fatherhood above,
Thou reignest o'er the world;
The poor thou liftest from the dust,
The proud are downward hurled.
*Rev. H. T. Johnson.*

### 602 *Cold Gethsemane.* C. M.

*Luke xxii. 44.*

1 Cold Gethsemane! the sweat and tears,
Witnessed by thee, from him
Who came to save and calm our fears,
And bring us back to heav'n.

2 *The thought of that sad hour*—the day,
So chill, the night so cold,
The amazing grief that on him lay,
Might well amaze my soul.

3 They all forsake him now, weak men!
Alas! men always do,
Forsake their God, always—ah then,
Can sinful man be true?

4 How shall I thee requite, my Lord,
For all thy grief and pain,
How magnify thy gracious word,
Or how, extend thy fame?

5 I'll take the cup of blessing now,
And drink before thy face,
And sound throughout the world below,
The wonders of thy grace.
*J. C. Embry.*

292

**603 PILGRIMS. 9s & 8s.**　　　　　　　　　HENRY SMART.

1. In deep e - ter - ni - ty, out - ly - ing, The a - ges

mark'd by cir - cling bands, Our God, in cy - cles still out -

vie - ing, Cre - a - tion wrought by his own hands.

9s & 8s.

*The mystery of Power—wisdom—love.*
*Gen.* i. 1–5 & *2 Cor.* viii. 9.

1 In deep eternity, out-lying,
　The ages mark'd by circling bands,
　Our God in cycles still out-vieing,
　Creation wrought by his own hands.

2 He spake, and said, let light go flying,
　Beneath, from the eternal throne,
　Creation heard his voice with crying,
　Behold, the mighty work is done.

3 His plans in wisdom now arranging,
　For darkness he hath given light,
　His perfect law shall know no changing,
　And brings the morning after night.

4 The morning stars began with singing,
　An anthem to his wondrous name,
　And flaming clusters join in ringing,
　The chorus, through the shining frame.

5 Let men unite their humbler voices,
　With those that hymn his praise above,
　And sing—the universe rejoices—
　The mystery of life is love!

6 O love of God in Jesus bringing,
　Bright image of the Father's face,
　Let earth and heaven continue ringing,
　O love and grace to answer grace.
　　　　　　　　　　　*J. C. Embry.*

**603 b**　　　　　　　　　　9s & 8s.

1 Bread of the world in mercy broken,
　Wine of the soul in mercy shed,
　By whom the words of life were spoken,
　And in whose death our sins are dead!

2 Look on the heart by sorrow broken,
　Look on the tears by sinners shed,
　And be thy feast to us the token
　That by thy grace our souls are fed.
　　　　　　　　　　　*Heber.*

**603 c EMBRY. 11s & 10s.**   J. C. EMBRY, 1897.

1. Hith - er, ye faith - ful, haste with songs of tri - umph,
2. O, Je - sus! for such won - drous con - de - scen - sion,
3. Shout his al - might - y name, ye choirs of an - gels,

To Bethlehem go, the Lord of Life to meet; To you, this day, is
Our praise and rev - 'rence are an offering meet, Now is the Word made
Let the ce - les - tial courts His praise re-peat; Un - to our God be

born a Prince and Sav - iour, O, come, and let us wor - ship at his feet.
flesh, and dwells a - momg us, O, come, and let us wor - ship at his feet.
glo - ry in the high - est; O, come, and let us wor - ship at his feet.

**603 d**   *"We would see Jesus."*   11s & 10s.

1 We would see Jesus—for the shadows lengthen,
   Across this little landscape of our life:
   We would see Jesus our weak faith to strengthen,
   For the last weariness—the final strife.

2 We would see Jesus—the great Rock Foundation,
   Whereon our feet were set by sovereign grace;
   Not life, nor death, with all their agitation,
   Can thence remove us, if we see his face.

3 We would see Jesus—other lights are fading,
   Which for long years we have rejoiced to see;
   The blessings of our pilgrimage are failing,
   We would not mourn them, for we go to thee.

4 We would see Jesus—this is all we're needing
   Strength, joy and willingness come with the sight;
   We would see Jesus, dying, risen, pleading,
   Then welcome day, and farewell mortal night!

                                        *Anon.*

# SUPPLEMENT.
## FOR SOCIAL AND PUBLIC WORSHIP.

**604  JENIFER. C. M.**                    BRAXTON,

1. Am I a sol - dier of the cross,— A follower of the Lamb,—

And shall I fear to own his cause, Or blush to speak his name?

*Courage.*                    C. M.

1 Am I a soldier of the cross,—
A follower of the Lamb,—
And shall I fear to own his cause,
Or blush to speak his name?

2 Must I be carried to the skies
On flowery beds of ease,
While others fought to win the prize,
And sailed through bloody seas?

3 Are there no foes for me to face?
Must I not stem the flood?
Is this vile world a friend to grace,
To help me on to God?

4 Sure I must fight if I would reign:
Increase my courage, Lord;
I'll bear the toil, endure the pain,
Supported by thy word.

5 Thy saints, in all this glorious war,
Shall conquer, though they die:
They see the triumph from afar,
By faith they bring it nigh.

6 When that illustrious day shall rise,
And all thy armies shine,
In robes of vict'ry, through the skies,
The glory shall be thine.
*Watts.*

**605**    *The Pilgrimage.*    8, 7, 8, 7, 4, 7.

[ Tune, Proctor, page 210.   8, 7, 4.]

1 Guide me, O thou great Jehovah,
Pilgrim through this barren land:
I am weak, but Thou art mighty;
Hold me with thy powerful hand:
Bread of heaven,
Feed me till I want no more.

2 Open, Lord, the crystal fountain
Whence the healing waters flow:
Let the fiery, cloudy pillar,
Lead me all my journey through:
Strong Deliv'rer!
Be thou still my strength and shield.

3 When I tread the verge of Jordan,
Bid my anxious fears subside:
Death of death, and hell's destruction,
Lead me safe on Canaan's side;
Songs of praises
I will ever give to thee.
*Williams.*

**606**                    S. M.

*"For ye are members one of another."*

[ Tune, Dennis, page 296.   S. M.]

1 Blest be the tie that binds
Our hearts in Jesus' love;
The fellowship of Christian minds
Is like to that above.

2 Before our Father's throne
We pour united prayers;
Our fears, our hopes, our aims are one;
Our comforts and our cares.

3 We share our mutual woes,
Our mutual burdens bear;
And often for each other flows
The sympathizing tear.

4 When we at death must part,
Not like the world's, our pain:
But one in Christ, and one in heart,
We part to meet again.

5 From sorrow, toil, and pain,
And sin we shall be free;
And perfect love and friendship reign
Throughout eternity.
*Fawcett.*

295

**606 b DENNIS. S. M.**　　　　　　　　　　　HANS GEORGE NAEGELI.

1. Thou ve - ry pres - ent Aid In suff - 'ring and dis - tress,

The mind which still on thee is stayed Is kept in per - fect peace.

*Peace.*　　　　　　　　S. M.

1 Thou very present Aid
　In suffering and distress,
　The mind which still on thee is stayed
　Is kept in perfect peace.

2 The soul by faith reclined
　On the Redeemer's breast,
　'Mid raging storms, exults to find
　An everlasting rest.

3 Sorrow and fear are gone,
　Whene'er thy face appears;
　It stills the sighing orphan's moan,
　And dries the widow's tears.

4 Jesus, to whom I fly,
　Doth all my wishes fill;
　What though created streams are dry?
　I have the fountain still.

5 Stripped of each earthly friend,
　I find them all in One,
　And peace and joy which never end,
　And heaven, in Christ, alone.
　　　　　　　　　　　*C. Wesley.*

**606 c**　　　　　　　　S. M.

*Thy gentleness hath made me great.*

*Psalm 18: 35.*

1 How gentle God's commands!
　How kind his precepts are!
　Come, cast your burdens on the Lord,
　And trust his constant care.

2 Beneath his watchful eye
　His saints securely dwell;
　That hand which bears all nature up
　Shall guard his children well.

3 Why should this anxious load
　Press down your weary mind?
　Haste to your heavenly Father's throne,
　And sweet refreshment find.

4 His goodness stands approved,
　Unchanged from day to day:
　I'll drop my burden at his feet,
　And bear a song away.
　　　　　　　　　　　*Philip Doddridge.*

**607**　　　　　*Before His cross.*　　　　Ss & 7s.

[Tune, Greenville, page 259. 8s & 7s.]

1 Sweet the moments, rich in blessing,
　Which before the cross I spend;
　Life, and health, and peace possessing,
　From the sinner's dying Friend.

2 Truly blessed is this station,
　Low before his cross to lie,
　While I see divine compassion
　Beaming in his gracious eye.

3 Here it is I find my heaven
　While upon the cross I gaze;
　Love I much? I've much forgiven;
　I'm a miracle of grace.

4 Love and grief my heart dividing,
　With my tears his feet I'll bathe:
　Constant still, in faith abiding,
　Life deriving from his death.

5 Here in tender, grateful sorrow
　With my Saviour I will stay:
　Here new hope and strength will borrow;
　Here will love my fears away.
　　　　　　　　　　　*James Allen.*

**608** **WHAT A FRIEND WE HAVE IN JESUS.** CHARLES CONVERSE, BY PER.

1. What a friend we have in    Je - sus,    All our sins and griefs to bear;
2. Have we tri - als and temp - ta - tions?    Is there trou-ble an - y - where?
3. Are we weak and heav - y    la - den,    Cum-bered with a load of    care?

What a priv - i - lege to    car - ry    Ev - 'ry thing to God in    prayer.
We should nev-er be    dis - cour - aged,    Take it    to the Lord in    prayer.
Pre - cious Sav-iour, still our    ref - uge,—    Take it    to the Lord in    prayer.

Oh, what peace we oft - en    for - feit,    Oh, what need-less pain we    bear—
Can we find a Friend so faith - ful,    Who will all our sor - rows share?
Do thy friends despise, for - sake thee?    Take it    to the Lord in    prayer;

All    be-cause we do not    car - ry    Ev - 'ry thing to God in    prayer.
Je - sus knows our ev - 'ry    weak - ness,    Take it    to the Lord in    prayer.
In    his arms he'll take and shield thee,    Thou wilt find a    sol - ace there.

"JUBILEE HARP."

**609  HIDE THOU ME.**

REV. ROBERT LOWRY.

1. In thy cleft, O Rock of A - ges, Hide thou me; When the
2. From the snare of sin - ful pleas - ure, Hide thou me; Thou, my
3. In the lone - ly night of sor - row, Hide thou me; Till in

fit - ful tem - pest ra - ges, Hide thou me; Where no
soul's e - ter - nal treas - ure, Hide thou me; When the
glo - ry dawns the mor - row, Hide thou me; In the

mor - tal arm can sev - er From my heart thy love for -
world its power is wield - ing, And my heart is al - most
sight of Jor - dan's bil - low, Let thy bo - som be my

ev - er, Hide me, O Thou Rock of A - ges, Safe in thee.
yield - ing, Hide me, O Thou Rock of A - ges, Safe in thee.
pil - low; Hide me, O Thou Rock of A - ges, Safe in thee.

FANNY J. CROSBY.

**610 SHALL WE MEET?**

ELIHU S. RICE, 1866, BY PER.

*Moderato.*

1. Shall we meet be - yond the riv - er, Where the sur - ges cease to roll?
2. Shall we meet in that blest har - bor, When our storm - y voyage is o'er?
3. Shall we meet in yon - der cit - y, Where the tow'rs of crys - tal shine?
4. Shall we meet with Christ our Sav-iour, When he comes to claim his own?

Where in all the bright for - ev - er, Sor - row ne'er shall press the soul?
Shall we meet and cast the an - chor, By the fair, ce - les - tial shore?
Where the walls are all of jas - per, Built by work - man-ship di - vine?—
Shall we know his bless - ed fa - vor, And sit down up - on His throne?

CHORUS.

Shall we meet, shall we meet, Shall we meet be - yond the riv - er?

Shall we meet be - yond the riv - er, Where the sur - ges cease to roll?

HORACE L. HASTINGS.

# SUPPLEMENT.

**611  REST. L. M.**

*Tenderly.*

1. A - sleep in Je - sus! Bless-ed sleep, From which none ev - er wakes to weep—

A calm and un - dis - turbed re - pose, Un - brok-en by the last of foes.

*Rest.*      L. M.

1 Asleep in Jesus! Blessed sleep,
From which none ever wakes to weep—
A calm and undisturbed repose,
Unbroken by the last of foes.

2 Asleep in Jesus! Oh how sweet
To be for such a slumber meet,
With holy confidence to sing
That death has lost his venomed sting!

3 Asleep in Jesus! Peaceful rest,
Whose waking is supremely blest;
No fear, no woe, shall dim that hour
That manifests the Saviour's power.

4 Asleep in Jesus! Far from thee
Thy kindred and their graves may be,
But thine is still a blessed sleep,
From which none ever wakes to weep.

**612** *Before Receiving Appointments.* L. M.

1 Jesus, the truth and power Divine,
Send forth these messengers of thine,
Their hands confirm, their hearts inspire,
And touch their lips with hallowed fire.

2 Be thou their mouth and wisdom, Lord;
Thou, by the hammer of thy word,
The rocky hearts in pieces break,
And bid the sons of thunder speak.

3 To those who would their Lord embrace,
Give them to preach the word of grace,—
Sweetly their yielding bosoms move,
And melt them with the fire of love.

4 Let all with thankful hearts confess
Thy welcome messengers of peace,
Thy power in their report be found,
And let thy feet behind them sound.

**613** *The living and the dead.* L. M.

1 Where are the dead? In heaven or hell
Their disembodied spirits dwell!
Their perished forms in bonds of clay,
Reserv'd until the judgment day.

2 Who are the dead? The sons of time
In every age and state and clime—
Renown'd, dishonour'd, or forgot—
The place that knew them knows them not.

3 Where are the living? On the ground
Where prayer is heard and mercy found,
Where, in the compass of a span,
The mortal makes th' immortal man.

4 Who are the living? They whose breath
Draws every moment nigh to death:
Of endless bliss or woe the heirs,
O what a solemn state is theirs!

5 Then, timely warn'd, let us begin
To follow Christ, and flee from sin,
Daily grow up in him our head;
Lord of the living and the dead.

*Montgomery.*

*Doxology.*      L. M.

Praise God, from whom all blessings flow;
Praise him, all creatures here below;
Praise him above, ye heavenly host;
Praise Father, Son, and Holy Ghost.

*T. Ken.*

300

# SUPPLEMENT.

## 614  WINDHAM. L. M.

READ.

1. Un - veil thy bos - om, faith-ful tomb! Take this new treas-ure    to    thy trust,

And  give these sa-cred   rel - ics room   To  slum-ber in   the   si-lent dust.

---

*A Burial Hymn.*     L. M.

1 Unveil thy bosom, faithful tomb!
  Take this new treasure to thy trust,
  And give these sacred relics room
  To slumber in the silent dust.

2 Nor pain, nor grief, nor anxious fear
  Invade thy bounds; no mortal woes
  Can reach the peaceful sleeper here,
  While angels watch the soft repose.

3 So Jesus slept;—God's dying Son
  Passed through the grave, and blessed
      the bed!
  Rest here, blest saint, till from his throne,
  The morning break, and pierce the shade.

## 615     *Camp-meeting.*     L. M.

1 A twelve month more has rolled around,
  Since we were on this tented ground:
  Ten thousand scenes have mar'd the year,
  Since we last met to worship here.

2 Relentless death has hurl'd his darts,
  And lodged them deep in noblest hearts:
  O'er old and young, in every sphere,
  He's triumph'd since we worshipp'd here.

3 Yet we are spared, to Heaven be praise,
  Our God has lengthen'd out our days:
  We've left our homes with hearts sincere,
  And met, once more, to worship here.

4 My Father's children—heirs of heaven,
  Let all your hearts to prayer be given,

That God may lend a listening ear
And answer, while we worship here.

5 Come sinners, come, your pardoning God
  Now waits t' impart his cleansing blood:
  O! loathe your sins, to Christ draw near,
  And seek him while we worship here.

6 Ye mourners, raise your languid eyes:
  Your home's beyond the starry skies!
  Your Saviour smiles, renounce your fear,
  And praise him while we worship here.
                        *A. Means.*

## 616       *Will you meet us?*     P. M.

1 Say, brothers, will you meet us,
  Say, brothers, will you meet us,
  Say, brothers, will you meet us,
  On Canaan's happy shore?

2 By the grace of God we'll meet you,
  By the grace of God we'll meet you,
  By the grace of God we'll meet you,
  Where parting is no more.

3 Jesus lives and reigns for ever,
  Jesus lives and reigns for ever,
  Jesus lives and reigns for ever,
  On Canaan's happy shore.

4 Glory, glory, hallelujah,
  Glory, glory, hallelujah,
  Glory, glory, hallelujah,
  For ever, evermore.

301

617 OLIVET. 6s & 4s.

L. MASON.

1. My faith looks up to thee, Thou Lamb of Cal - va - ry, Sav - iour di - vine,

{ Now hear me while I pray, }
{ Take all my guilt a - way, } Oh, let me from this day Be whol - ly thine.

6s & 4s.

1 My faith looks up to thee,
Thou Lamb of Calvary,
Saviour divine!
Now hear me while I pray,
Take all my guilt away,
Oh, let me from this day
Be wholly thine.

2 May thy rich grace impart
Strength to my fainting heart;
My zeal inspire;
As thou hast died for me,
Oh, may my love to thee
Pure, warm, and changeless be,
A living fire.

3 While life's dark maze I tread,
And griefs around me spread,
Be thou my guide;
Bid darkness turn to day,
Wipe sorrow's tears away,
Nor let me ever stray
From thee aside.

4 When ends life's transient dream,
When death's cold, sullen stream
Shall o'er me roll,
Blest Saviour! then, in love,

Fear and distrust remove;
Oh, bear me safe above,
A ransomed soul!

*Ray Palmer.*

618                    6s & 4s.

1 Saviour, I look to thee,
Be not thou far from me,
'Mid storms that lower:
On me thy care bestow,
Thy loving-kindness show,
Thine arms around me throw,
This trying hour.

2 Saviour, I look to thee,
Feeble as infancy,
Gird up my heart.
Author of life and light,
Thou hast an arm of might,
Thine is the sovereign right,
Thy strength impart.

3 Saviour, I look to thee,
Thine shall the glory be,
Hearer of prayer:
Thou art my only aid,
On thee my soul is stayed,
Naught can my heart invade,
While thou art near.

*Hastings.*

**619 INGLESIDE. C. M. D.** WIESENTHAL.

1. On Jordan's stormy banks I stand, And cast a wishful eye To Canaan's fair and

hap - py land, Where my posses - sions lie. O the transporting, rapt'rous scene That

ris - es to my sight Sweet fields array'd in liv-ing green, And riv - ers of delight!

### The Heavenly Canaan. C. M. D.

1 On Jordan's stormy banks I stand,
  And cast a wishful eye
To Canaan's fair and happy land
  Where my possessions lie.
O the transporting, rapt'rous scene
  That rises to my sight
Sweet fields array'd in living green,
  And rivers of delight!

2 There gen'rous fruits that never fail
  On trees immortal grow:
There rocks, and hills, and brooks, and vales,
  With milk and honey flow.
All o'er those wide-extended plains
  Shines one eternal day;
There God the Son forever reigns,
  And scatters night away.

3 When shall I reach that happy place,
  And be for ever blest?
When shall I see my Father's face,
  And in his bosom rest?
Filled with delight, my raptur'd soul
  Would here no longer stay!
Though Jordan's waves around me roll
  Fearless I'd launch away.

### 620 Heaven. C. M. D.

1 Arise and shine, on Zion fair,
  Behold thy light is come!
Thy glorious conq'ring King is near
  To take his exiles home:

The trumpet sounding through the sky,
  To set poor captives free;
The day of wonder now is nigh:
  The year of Jubilee.

2 Ye heralds, blow your trumpets loud,
  The earth must know her doom;
Go spread the news from pole to pole,
  Behold the Judge is come:
Blow out the sun! burn up the earth!
  Consume the rolling flood!
While every star shall disappear,
  Go turn the moon to blood!

3 Arise ye nations under ground,
  Before the Judge appear:
All tongues and languages shall come,
  Their final doom to hear!
King Jesus on his dazzling throne,
  Ten thousand angels round;
And Gabriel with a silver trump,
  Echoes the awful sound!

4 The glorious news of gospel grace
  To sinners now is o'er;
The trump in Zion now is still,
  And to be heard no more!
The watchmen all have left their walls,
  And with their flocks above,
On Canaan's peaceful shore they sing,
  And shout redeeming love!

SUPPLEMENT.

**621 MEAR. C. M.**  WELSH AIR. AARON WILLIAMS' COLL., CIR. 1760.

1. Be - neath our feet and o'er our head Is e - qual warn - ing given;

Be - neath us lie the count-less dead, And far a - bove is heaven.

*A Warning from the Grave.* C. M.

1 Beneath our feet and o'er our head
  Is equal warning given;
  Beneath us lie the countless dead,
  And far above is heaven.

2 Death rides on every passing breeze,
  And lurks in every flower;
  Each season has its own disease,
  Its peril every hour.

3 Turn, sinner, turn: thy danger know:
  Where'er thy foot can tread,
  The earth rings hollow from below,
  And warns thee of her dead.

4 Turn, Christian, turn: thy soul apply
  To truths which hourly tell
  That they who underneath thee lie
  Shall live in heaven—or hell.
  *Heber.*

**622** *We shall know Him as he is.* C. M.

1 The heavenly treasure now we have
  In a vile house of clay;
  But Christ will to the utmost save,
  And keep us to that day.

2 Our souls are in his mighty hand,
  And he shall keep them still;
  And you and I shall surely stand
  With him on Zion's hill.

3 Him eye to eye we there shall see,
  Our face like his shall shine;
  O what a glorious company,
  When saints and angels join!

4 O what a joyful meeting there!
  In robes of white arrayed,
  Palms in our hands we all shall bear,
  And crowns upon our head.

5 Then let us lawfully contend,
  And fight our passage through:
  Bear in our faithful minds the end,
  And keep the prize in view.
  *Charles Wesley.*

**623** *Prepare us for that day.* S. M.
[Tune, State Street, page 150. S. M.]

1 Behold! with awful pomp
  The Judge prepares to come;
  Th' archangel sounds the dreadful trump
  And wakes the gen'ral doom.

2 Nature, in wild amaze,
  Her dissolution mourns;
  Blushes of blood the moon deface,
  The sun to darkness turns.

3 The living look with dread;
  The frighted dead arise,
  Start from the monumental bed,
  And lift their ghastly eyes.

4 Horrors all hearts appal:
  They quake, they shriek, they cry;
  Bid rocks and mountains on them fall;
  But rocks and mountains fly.

5 Great God, in whom we live,
  Prepare us for that day:
  Help us in Jesus to believe,—
  To watch, and wait, and pray.
  *Anon.*

304

**624  DIRGE. 7s. 6 Lines.**                   W. H. GIBSON, SR.

1. Sleep, thou dust and ash - es, sleep, When the trump shall wake the dead;

Pure im - mor - tal, thou shalt leap From thy nar - row, earth - y bed,

Like an an - gel thou shalt fly Far a - bove the star - ry sky.

---

7s. 6 lines.

*On the death and burial of a friend.*

1 Sleep, thou dust and ashes, sleep,
    When the trump shall wake the dead;
Pure-immortal, thou shalt leap
    From thy narrow, earthy bed,
Like an angel thou shalt fly
Far above the starry sky.

2 Grant, Thou Triune Deity,
    We, with him, may then arise,
Hear Thee in benignity
Bid us reign above the skies,
Strike our golden harps above,
In the bright abode of love.
                                *Bishop Payne.*

**625    *Christ enthroned.*    7s. 6 lines.**

1 Glory, glory to our King!
    Crowns unfading wreathe his head;
Jesus is the name we sing.—
    Jesus, risen from the dead;

Jesus, Conqueror o'er the grave;
Jesus, mighty now to save.

2 Jesus is gone up on high:
    Angels come to meet their King;
Shouts triumphant rend the sky,
    While the Victor's praise they sing:
"Open now, ye heavenly gates!
'Tis the King of glory waits."

3 Now behold him high enthroned,
    Glory beaming in his face,
By adoring angels owned,
    God of holiness and grace!
Oh! for hearts and tongues to sing—
    "Glory, glory to our King!"

4 Jesus! on thy people shine:
    Warm our hearts and tune our tongues,
That with angels we may join,
    Share their bliss, and swell their songs:
Glory, honor, praise, and power,
Lord! be thine for evermore!
                          *Thomas Kelly, 1804.*

**626 RHINE. L. M. D.**

GERMAN AIR.

1. Je - sus shall reign where-e'er the sun Does his suc - cess - ive jour-neys run; His
2. Peo - ple and realms, of ev - 'ry tongue, Dwell on his love with sweet-est song, And
3. Where he dis-plays his heal-ing pow'r, Death and the curse are known no more : In

king-dom stretch from shore to shore, Till moons shall wax and wane no more. For
in - fant voi - ces shall pro - claim Their ear - ly bless-ings on his name. Bless-
him the tribes of A-dam boast More bless-ings than their fa - ther lost. Let

him shall end-less pray'r be made, And end-less prais-es crown his head ; His name, like
ings a-bound where'er he reigns, The pris-'ner leaps to loose his chains, The wea-ry
ev - 'ry crea- ture rise and bring Pe- cul- iar hon-ors to our King; An - gels de -

sweet per-fume shall rise With ev-'ry morn - ing sac - ri - fice.
find e - ter - nal rest, And all the sons of want are blessed.
scend with songs a - gain, And earth re - peat the long A - men!

**627 RUSSIAN HYMN. 10s.** ALEXIS LWOF.

1. Rise, crown'd with light, im - pe - rial Sa - lem, rise; Ex - alt thy

tower - ing head and lift thine eyes: See heav'n its spark - ling por - tals

wide dis - play, And break up - on thee in a flood of day.

1 Rise, crown'd with light, imperial Salem, rise;
Exalt thy towering head and lift thine eyes:
See heaven its sparkling portals wide display,
And break upon thee in a flood of day.

2 See a long race thy spacious courts adorn,
See future sons and daughters yet unborn,
In crowding ranks on every side arise,
Demanding life, impatient for the skies.

3 See barbarous nations at thy gates attend,
Walk in thy light, and in thy temple bend:
See thy bright altars throng'd with prostrate kings,
While every land its joyous tribute brings.

4 The seas shall waste, the skies to smoke decay,
Rocks fall to dust, and mountains melt away;
But fix'd his word, his saving power remains;
Thy realm shall last, thy own Messiah reigns.

*Alexander Pope.*

307

## 628 BEAR THE CROSS.

1. Bear the cross ye sons of men, With love's best am - bi - tion,
2. "It is fin - ished," hear him say, Prec - ious prom - ise giv - en,
3. Bear the cross then un - til death, Shall re - lieve the bur - den,

Je - sus bore it all a - lone, For the world's re - mis - sion.
Will you at the cross to - day, Fix your hearts for Heav - en?
And you'll find sweet rest and peace, Just be - yond the Jor - dan.

REFRAIN.

Bear the cross, bear the cross, He bore all for thee,

With a Sav - iour's lov - ing heart, 'Twas on Cal - va - ry.

JAMES T. WALKER.

**629 ELLERS. 10s.**

E. J. HOPKINS.

1. Sav-iour, a-gain to thy dear name we raise, With one ac-cord our part-ing hymn of praise; We stand to bless thee ere our wor-ship cease, Then, low-ly kneel-ing, wait thy word of peace.

1 Saviour, again to thy dear Name we raise,
With one accord our parting hymn of praise;
We stand to bless thee ere our worship cease,
Then, lowly kneeling, wait thy word of peace.

2 Grant us thy peace upon our homeward way;
With thee began, with thee shall end the day;
Guard thou the lips from sin, the hearts from shame,
That in this house have called upon thy Name.

3 Grant us thy peace, Lord, thro' the coming night,
Turn thou for us its darkness into light;
From harm and danger keep thy children free,
For dark and light are both alike to thee.

4 Grant us thy peace throughout our earthly life,
Our balm in sorrow, and our stay in strife;
Then, when thy voice shall bid our conflict cease,
Call us, O Lord, to thine eternal peace.

*J. Ellerton,* 1868.

**630 LEAD, KINDLY LIGHT.**                                J. B. DYKES.

1. Lead, kindly Light, a - mid th' encircling gloom,    Lead thou me    on;
2. I was not ev - er thus, nor pray'd that thou    Shouldst lead me    on;
3. So long thy power has blest me, sure it    still    Will lead me    on

The night is dark, and I am far from home,    Lead thou me    on.
I loved to choose and see my path: but    now    Lead thou me    on.
O'er moor and fen, o'er crag and torrent,    till    The night is    gone.

Keep thou my    feet:    I    do not ask    to    see...........
I loved the    gar - ish    day; and, spite    of    fears,.........
And with the    morn    those    an - gel fa - ces    smile,.........

The    dis - tant    scene:    one step e - nough    for    me.
Pride ruled    my    will:    re - mem - ber    not    past    years.
Which    I    have loved    long since, and    lost    a - while.

BISHOP NEWMAN.

310

# SUPPLEMENT.

**631 BROWNELL. L. M. 6 Lines.** FROM J. HAYDN.

1. Come, O thou Trav-el-er un-known, Whom still I hold, but can-not see;

My com-pa-ny be-fore is gone, And I am left a-lone with thee:

With thee all night I mean to stay, And wres-tle till the break of day.

*First Part.*

L. M. 6 lines.

*Wrestling Jacob—the struggle.*

1 Come, O thou Traveler unknown,
   Whom still I hold, but cannot see;
My company before is gone,
   And I am left alone with thee:
With thee all night I mean to stay,
And wrestle till the break of day.

2 I need not tell thee who I am,
   My sin and misery declare;
Thyself has called me by my name,
   Look on thy hands, and read it there:
But who, I ask thee, who art thou?
Tell me thy name, and tell me now.

3 In vain thou strugglest to get free,
   I never will unloose my hold:
Art thou the Man that died for me?
   The secret of thy love unfold:
Wrestling, I will not let thee go,
Till I thy name, thy nature know.

4 Wilt thou not yet to me reveal
   Thy new, unutterable name?
Tell me, I still beseech thee, tell;
   To know it now resolved I am:
Wrestling, I will not let thee go,
Till I thy name, thy nature know.

5 What though my shrinking flesh complain,
   And murmur to contend so long?
I rise superior to my pain;

When I am weak, then I am strong;
And when my all of strength shall fail,
I shall with the God-man prevail.

*Second Part.*

**632** L. M. 6 lines.

*The name revealed.*

1 Yield to me now, for I am weak,
   But confident in self-despair;
Speak to my heart, in blessing speak,
   Be conquered by my instant prayer:
Speak, or thou never hence shalt move,
And tell me if thy name be Love.

2 'Tis Love! 'tis Love! thou diedst for me!
   I hear thy whisper in my heart;
The morning breaks, the shadows flee;
   Pure, universal love thou art;
To me, to all, thy bowels move;
Thy nature and thy name is Love.

3 My prayer hath power with God; the grace
   Unspeakable I now receive;
Through faith I see thee face to face,
   I see thee face to face, and live!
In vain I have not wept and strove;
Thy nature and thy name is Love.

4 I know thee, Saviour, who thou art,
   Jesus, the feeble sinner's Friend;
Nor wilt thou with the night depart,
   But stay and love me to the end:
Thy mercies never shall remove;
Thy nature and thy name is Love.

*Charles Wesley.*

# SUPPLEMENT.

**633 ST. THOMAS. S. M.**  WILLIAM TANSUR. 1768.

1. Stand up, and bless the Lord, Ye peo - ple of his choice:

Stand up, and bless the Lord your God, With heart, and soul, and voice.

"*Fearful in Praises.*"  S. M.

1 Stand up, and bless the Lord,
  Ye people of his choice :
  Stand up, and bless the Lord your God,
  With heart, and soul, and voice.

2 Though high above all praise,
  Above all blessing high,
  Who would not fear his holy name,
  And laud, and magnify ?

3 O for the living flame
  From his own altar brought,
  To touch our lips—our minds inspire,
  And wing to heaven our thought!

4 There, with benign regard,
  Our hymns he deigns to hear :
  Though unrevealed to mortal sense,
  The spirit feels him near.

5 God is our strength and song,
  And his salvation ours :
  Then be his love in Christ proclaimed
  With all our ransomed powers.

6 Stand up, and bless the Lord,
  The Lord, your God adore ;

Stand up, and bless his glorious name,
Henceforth, for evermore.
*Montgomery.*

**634**  S. M.

1 By faith, I see uplaid,
  A land, with beauty crowned ;
  Where trees, and flowers, that never fade,
  And richest fruits abound.

2 A land of endless day,
  Of bright, unclouded sky,
  Ungirt, by wave and billowy sea,
  Or sand of golden dye.

3 The home of angels bright,
  And saints, from earth set free,
  Who walk with Christ, in spotless white
  'Midst shouts of victory.

4 Thither, my wayworn feet,
  Their constant steps shall tend ;
  Till to its shining, golden street,
  They finally ascend.

5 To this delightful end,
  O Lord, thy grace bestow,
  And teach me humbly to depend
  On thee, my journey through.
*James G. Sampson.*

312

# SUPPLEMENT.

**635 DULCIMER. 11s & 8s.** ANON. "MISSOURI HARMONY." 1827.

1. All hail to the day when the Sav - iour a - rose! His work of re - demp - tion com - plete, He rest - ed in tri - umph, de - spite all his foes, With glo - ry of King - ship re - plete.

*Joy of the Sabbath Rest.* 11s & 8s.

1 All hail to the day when the Saviour arose!
  His work of redemption complete,
  He rested in triumph, despite all his foes,
  With glory of Kingship replete.

2 Cease, pilgrims, your toiling and banish all care,
  The Sabbath has dawned—it is rest,
  That all its communion and gladness may share,
  The day God has hallowed and blest.

3 Let reading and converse be cheerful and pure,
  Reflection and worship be sweet :
  Let naught from a holy observance allure
  In by-ways your scrupulous feet.

4 Responsive and joyous, exultingly sing,
  Earth smiles in her garments of peace :
  In glad convocation, devout homage bring,
  To him who has brought such release.

5 Our fathers, the pilgrims, heroic and true,
  Devoutly remembered this day,
  They hallowed the sod, the first Lord's day they trod
  The bleak shores of New Plymouth bay.

6 All hail to the day of devotion and rest,
  The brightest and best of the week !
  Assembled for worship in name of our Guest,
  The aid of the Spirit we seek.

C. B. Botsford.

313

**636 GUIDANCE. 6s & 5s.**  J. BARNBY.

1. Je - sus, meek and gen - tle, Son of God Most High,

Pity - ing, lov - ing Sav - iour, Hear thy chil - dren's cry.

Pity - ing, lov - ing Sav-iour, Hear thy chil - - dren's cry.

**6s & 5s.**

1 Jesus, meek and gentle,
  Son of God Most High,
  Pitying, loving Saviour,
  Hear thy children's cry.

2 Pardon our offences,
  Loose our captive chains,
  Break down every idol
  Which our soul detains.

3 Give us holy freedom,
  Fill our hearts with love;
  Draw us, holy Jesus,
  To the realms above.

4 Lead us on our journey,
  Be thyself the way
  Through terrestrial darkness
  To celestial day.

5 Jesus, meek and gentle,
  Son of God Most High,
  Pitying, loving Saviour,
  Hear thy children's cry.
      *George R. Prynne.* 1856.

**637** *The pilgrim's Song.*  L. M. 6 lines.
  [Tune, Home, page 276. L. M.]
1 Leader of faithful souls, and Guide
  Of all that travel to the sky,
  Come, and with us, e'en us, abide
  Who would on thee alone rely.
  On thee alone our spirits stay,
  While held in life's uneven way.

2 Strangers and pilgrims here below,
    This earth we know is not our place;
  But hasten through the vale of woe
    And, restless to behold thy face,
  Swift to our heavenly country move,
  Our everlasting home above.

3 We have no 'biding city here,
    But seek a city out of sight;
  Thither our steady course we steer,
    Aspiring to the plains of light,
  Jerusalem, the saint's abode,
  Whose founder is the living God.

4 Patient th' appointed race to run,
    This weary world we cast behind;
  From strength to strength we travel on
    The New Jerusalem to find;
  Our labor this, our only aim,
  To find the New Jerusalem.

5 Through thee, who all our sins hast borne,
    Freely and graciously forgiven,
  With songs to Zion we return,
    Contending for our native heaven,
  That palace of our glorious King:
  We find it nearer while we sing.

6 E'en now we taste the pleasures there!
    A cloud of spicy odors comes,
  Soft wafted by the balmy air,
    Sweeter than Araby's perfumes;
  From Zion's top the breezes blow,
  And cheer us in the vale below!
      *C. Wesley.*

314

# SUPPLEMENT.

**638  REST. L. M.**  WILLIAM B. BRADBURY.

1. By faith in Christ I walk with God, With heav'n, my journey's end, in view:

Sup-port-ed by his staff and rod, My road is safe and pleas-ant too.

---

### By Faith.  L. M.

1 By faith in Christ I walk with God,
  With heaven, my journey's end, in view;
  Supported by his staff and rod,
  My road is safe and pleasant too.

2 Though snares and dangers throng my path,
  And earth and hell my course withstand,
  I triumph over all by faith,
  Guarded by his almighty hand.

3 The wilderness affords no food,
  But God for my support prepares,
  Provides me every needful good,
  And frees my soul from wants and cares.

4 With him sweet converse I maintain;
  Great as he is, I dare be free;
  I tell him all my grief and pain,
  And he reveals his love to me.

5 Some cordial from his word he brings,
  Whene'er my feeble spirit faints;
  At once my soul revives and sings,
  And yields no more to sad complaints.

**639**  *The Christian's parting hour.*  L. M.

1 How sweet the hour of closing day,
  When all is peaceful and serene,
  And when the sun, with cloudless ray,
  Sheds mellow luster o'er the scene!

2 Such is the Christian's parting hour;
  So peacefully he sinks to rest,
  When faith, endued from heaven with power,
  Sustains and cheers his languid breast.

3 Mark but that radiance of his eye,
  That smile upon his wasted cheek;
  They tell us of his glory nigh,
  In language that no tongue can speak.

4 A beam from heaven is sent to cheer
  The pilgrim on his gloomy road;
  And angels are attending near,
  To bear him to their bright abode.

5 Who would not wish to die like those
  Whom God's own Spirit deigns to bless?
  To sink into that soft repose,
  Then wake to perfect happiness?
          *William H. Bathurst.*

**640**  *The vision of faith.*  L. M.

1 Shall man, O God of light and life,
  Forever molder in the grave?
  Canst thou forget thy glorious work,
  Thy promise, and thy power to save?

2 In those dark, silent, realms of night,
  Shall peace and hope no more arise?
  No future morning light the tomb,
  Nor day-star gild the darksome skies?

3 Cease, cease, ye vain, desponding fears:
  When Christ, our Lord, from darkness sprang,
  Death, the last foe, was captive led,
  And heaven with praise and wonder rang.

4 Faith sees the bright, eternal doors
  Unfold, to make his children way;
  They shall be clothed with endless life,
  And shine in everlasting day.
          *Timothy Dwight.*

315

**641 NAZREY.**

J. T. LAYTON.

*With Spirit.*

1. We'll praise the Lord for he is great, And in his pres-ence an-gels wait;
2. We'll praise the Lord for he is wise; His wisdom shines thro' all the skies
3. We'll praise the Lord for he is just; And in him we may ev-er trust;
4. We'll praise the Lord for he is true; His word the same all a-ges through;—
5. Oh, praise him for his name is Love, And from his glo-rious throne a-bove,

All heav'n is swell-ing with his praise—Shall we not, too, our an-thems raise?
The earth he measures with a span, And crowns us with his im-age—man.
Prin-ces and kings may turn a-side, But God by RIGHT will e'er a-bide.
Earth, sea and sky may pass a-way, But firm, God's truth will ev-er stay.
He bends to wel-come our weak praise, Shall we not then our an-them raise?

CHORUS.

*Organ.*

Oh, we will praise him, Oh, we will praise him, Oh, we will praise his ho-ly name,

Oh, we will praise him, Oh, we will praise him, Oh, we will praise his ho-ly name.

REV. T. G. STEWART.

**642 EVENTIDE. 10s.** MONK.

1. A - bide with me: fast falls the e - ven - tide; The dark-ness

deep - ens; Lord, with me a - bide: When oth - er help - ers

fail, and com-fort flee, Help of the help-less, O a - bide with me.

10s.

1 Abide with me: fast falls the eventide;
    The darkness deepens; Lord, with me
        abide:
When other helpers fail, and comfort flee,
    Help of the helpless, O abide with me.

2 Swift to its close ebbs out life's little day;
    Earth's joys grow dim, its glories pass
        away,
Change and decay in all around I see;
    O thou who changest not, abide with me.

3 I need thy presence every passing hour;
    What but thy grace can foil the tempter's
        power?
Who, like thyself, my guide and stay can be?
    Through cloud and sunshine, Lord, a-
        bide with me.

4 I fear no foe, with thee at hand to bless:
    Ills have no weight, and tears no bitter-
        ness,
Where is death's sting? where, grave, thy
        victory?
    I triumph still, if thou abide with me.

5 Hold thou thy cross before my closing eyes;
    Shine through the gloom, and point me
        to the skies;
Heaven's morning breaks, and earth's vain
        shadows flee;
    In life, in death, O Lord, abide with me.

*H. F. Lyte.*

**643** *Sweet Foretastes.* 10s.

1 Here, O my Lord, I see thee face to face;
    Here would I touch and handle things
        unseen;
Here grasp with firmer hand the eternal
        grace,
    And all my weariness upon thee lean.

2 Here would I feed upon the bread of God;
    Here drink with thee the royal wine of
        heaven;
Here would I lay aside each earthly load,
    Here taste afresh the calm of sin
        forgiven.

3 Too soon we rise; the symbols disappear;
    The feast, though not the love, is passed
        and gone;
The bread and wine remove, but thou art
        here—
    Nearer than ever—still my Shield and
        Sun.

4 Feast after feast thus comes and passes by;
    Yet, passing, points to the glad feast
        above,
Giving sweet foretastes of the festal joy,
    The Lamb's great bridal feast of bliss
        and love.

*H. Bonar.*

317

**644** STEWARD. L. M.

*Moderato.*

J. T. LAYTON.

1. Go, mes - sen - ger of Christ, pro - claim The glo - ries

of Em - manu - el's name; The na - tions wait to

hear thee tell Of him who saves from death and hell.

L. M.

1 Go, messenger of Christ, proclaim
The glories of Emmanuel's name;
The nations wait to hear thee tell
Of him who saves from death and hell.

2 Go, armed with truth and filled with love,
Go, harmless as the gentle dove,
In wisdom and with burning zeal,
Go, and the way of life reveal.

3 Go, clothed in majesty divine.
Go, and thy face with glory shine;
Go, while the Spirit's quickening power
Doth fit thee for each trying hour.

4 And when against thee foes shall rise,
And former friends shall thee despise;
Remember that the Lord will be
A comfort and defense for thee.

5 And when thy work on earth is o'er,
And thou shalt preach to men no more,
Unceasing joys shall thee await
In thine eternal blest estate.

*W. H. Brooks.*

**645**　　　　　　　　L. M.

*The Presence of Christ in Heaven.*

1 Oh! for a sweet inspiring ray,
To animate our feeble strains,

From the bright realms of endless day,—
The blissful realms, where Jesus reigns!

2 There, low before his glorious throne,
Adoring saints and angels fall!
And, with delightful worship, own　[all.
His smile their bliss, their heaven, their

3 Immortal glories crown his head,
While tuneful hallelujahs rise,
And love, and joy, and triumph spread
Through all the assemblies of the skies.

4 He smiles,—and seraphs tune their songs
To boundless rapture, while they gaze;
Ten thousand, thousand joyful tongues
Resound his everlasting praise.

5 There, all the favorites of the Lamb
Shall join at last the heavenly choir;
Oh! may the joy-inspiring theme,
Awake our faith and warm desire.

6 Dear Saviour! let thy Spirit seal
Our interest in that blissful place;
Till death remove this mortal veil,
And we behold thy lovely face.

*Anne Steele, 1760.*

**646 PORTUGAL. L. M.**  THOMAS THORLEY. 17—.

1. Lord, how mys-te-rious are thy ways! How blind are we, how mean our praise!

Thy steps no mor-tal eyes ex-plore; 'Tis ours to won-der and a-dore.

---

*Providence.*  L. M.

1 Lord, how mysterious are thy ways!
How blind are we, how mean our praise!
Thy steps no mortal eyes explore;
'Tis ours to wonder and adore.

2 Great God! I do not ask to see
What in futurity shall be;
Let light and bliss attend my days,
And then my future hours be praise.

3 Are darkness and distress my share?
Give me to trust thy guardian care;
Enough for me, if love divine
At length through every cloud shall shine.

4 Yet this my soul desires to know,
Be this my only wish below:
That Christ is mine!—this great request,
Grant, bounteous God, and I am blest.

*A. Steele.*

**647**  *The glory of God.*  L. M.

1 God is a name my soul adores,
Th' almighty Three, th' eternal One:
Nature and grace, with all their powers,
Confess the Infinite unknown.

2 Thy voice produced the sea and spheres,
Bade the waves roar, the planets shine;
But nothing like thyself appears
Through all these spacious works of thine.

3 Still restless nature dies and grows,
From change to change the creatures run:

Thy being no succession knows,
And all thy vast designs are one.

4 A glance of thine runs through the globe,
Rules the bright worlds and moves their
frame:
Of light thou form'st thy dazzling robe,
Thy ministers are living flame.

5 How shall polluted mortals dare
To sing thy glory or thy grace?
Beneath thy feet we lie afar,
And see but shadows of thy face.

6 Who can behold the blazing light?
Who can approach consuming flame?
None but thy Wisdom knows thy might,
None but thy Word can speak thy name.

*Watts.*

*Doxology.*  8s & 7s.

*Dismission.*

Lord, dismiss us with thy blessing,
Bid us now depart in peace;
Still on heavenly manna feeding,
Let our faith and love increase;
Fill each breast with consolation;
Up to thee our hearts we raise:
When we reach our blissful station,
Then we'll give thee nobler praise.

*Tr. by J. Wesley.*

**648** NICÆA. P. M.                                          J. B. DYKES.

1. Ho - ly, ho - ly, ho - ly! Lord God Al - might - y!

. Ear - ly in the morn - ing our song shall rise to thee;

Ho - ly, ho - ly, ho - ly! mer - ci - ful and might - y!

God in three Per - sons, bless - ed Trin - i - ty!

2 Holy, holy, holy! all the saints adore thee,
    Casting down their golden crowns around the glassy sea,
    Cherubim and seraphim falling down before thee,
    Which wert, and art, and evermore shalt be.

3 Holy, holy, holy! though the darkness hide thee,
    Though the eye of sinful man thy glory may not see,
    Only thou art holy: there is none beside thee
    Perfect in power, in love, and purity.

4 Holy, holy, holy! Lord God Almighty!
    All thy works shall praise thy name, in earth and sky and sea,
    Holy, holy, holy! merciful and mighty!
    God in Three Persons, blessed Trinity.

*Bishop Reginald Heber, 1827.*

\* The small notes are intended for the second and third verses.

# SUPPLEMENT.

**649 ST. GEORGE'S. 7s. D.** G. J. ELVEY.

1. Pleas - ant are thy courts a - bove, In the land of light and love;

Pleas - ant are thy courts be - low, In this land of sin and woe.

O, my spir - it longs and faints For the con - verse of thy saints,

For the brightness of thy face, King of Glo - ry, God of grace!

2 Happy birds that sing and fly
Round thy altars, O Most High!
Happier souls, that find a rest,
In a Heavenly Father's breast!
Like the wandering dove, that found
No repose on earth around,
They can to their ark repair,
And enjoy it ever there.

3 Happy souls! their praises flow,
Ever in this vale of woe;
Waters in the desert rise,
Manna feeds them from the skies;

On they go from strength to strength,
Till they reach thy throne at length;
At thy feet adoring fall,
Who hast led them safe through all.

4 Lord, be mine this prize to win;
Guide me through a world of sin,
Keep me by thy saving grace,
Give me at thy side a place;
Sun and shield alike thou art,
Guide and guard my erring heart;
Grace and glory flow from thee,
Shower, O shower them, Lord, on me.

*Henry F. Lyte,* 1834.

321

**650 AMERICA. 6s & 4s.** ADAPTED BY HENRY CAREY, OBIT., 1743.

1. My country! 'tis of thee, Sweet land of lib - er - ty, Of thee I sing; Land, where my

fathers died! Land of the pilgrims' pride! From ev-'ry mountain side, Let freedom ring!

*Native Country.* 6s & 4s.

1 My country! 'tis of thee,
Sweet land of liberty,
  Of thee I sing;
Land, where my fathers died!
Land of the pilgrims' pride!
From every mountain side,
  Let freedom ring!

2 My native country! thee,—
Land of the noble, free,—
  Thy name—I love;
I love thy rocks and rills,
Thy woods and templed hills:
My heart with rapture thrills
  Like that above.

3 Let music swell the breeze,
And ring, from all the trees,
  Sweet freedom's song:
Let mortal tongues awake;
Let all that breathe partake;
Let rocks their silence break,—
  The sound prolong.

4 Our fathers' God! to thee,
Author of liberty,
  To thee we sing:
Long may our land be bright,
With freedom's holy light;
Protect us, by thy might,
  Great God, our King!
    *Samuel F. Smith*, 1832.

**651** *The national Anniversary.* 6s & 4s.

1 Auspicious morning! hail!
Voices, from hill and vale,
  Thy welcome sing:

Joy on thy dawning breaks;
Each heart that joy partakes,
While cheerful music wakes,
  Its praise to bring.

2 When, on the tyrant's rod,
Our patriot fathers trod,
  And dared be free,
'T was not in burning zeal,
Firm nerves, and hearts of steel,
Our country's joy to seal,
  But, Lord! in thee.

3 Thou, as a shield of power,
In battle's awful hour,
  Didst round us stand;
Our hopes were in thy throne;
Strong in thy might alone,
By thee our banners shone,
  God of our land!

4 Long, o'er our native hills,
Long, by our shaded rills,
  May freedom rest;
Long may our shores have peace,
Our flag grace every breeze,
Our ships the distant seas,
  From east to west.

5 Peace on this day abide,
From morn till eventide;
  Wake tuneful song;
Melodious accents raise;
Let every heart, with praise,
Bring high and grateful lays,
  Rich, full, and strong.
    *Samuel F. Smith*, 1841.

**652 BROWN. C. M.** H. F. GRANT.

1. My God! I know, I feel thee mine, And will not quit my claim,

Till all I have is lost in thine, And all renewed I am.

2 I hold thee with a trembling hand,
But will not let thee go,
Till steadfastly by faith I stand,
And all thy goodness know.

3 Jesus, thine all-victorious love
Shed in my heart abroad;
Then shall my feet no longer rove,
Rooted and fixed in God.

4 O that in me the sacred fire
Might now begin to glow!

Burn up the dross of base desire,
And make the mountains flow!

5 O that it now from heaven might fall,
And all my sins consume!
Come, Holy Ghost, for thee I call,
Spirit of burning, come.

6 Refining fire, go through my heart,
Illuminate my soul;
Scatter thy life through every part,
And sanctify the whole.

*C. Wesley.*

**653 DALSTON. S. P. M.** A. WILLIAMS.

1. How pleased and blest was I To hear the people cry, "Come, let us seek our God to-day!"

Yes, with a cheerful zeal, We haste to Zi-on's hill, And there our vows and honors pay.

2 Zion, thrice happy place,
Adorned with wondrous grace,
And walls of strength embrace thee round;
In thee our tribes appear,
To pray, and praise, and hear
The sacred gospel's joyful sound.

3 May peace attend thy gate,
And joy within thee wait,
To bless the soul of every guest;

The man who seeks thy peace,
And wishes thine increase,
A thousand blessings on him rest.

4 My tongue repeats her vows,
"Peace to this sacred house!"
For here my friends and kindred dwell;
And, since my glorious God
Makes thee his blest abode,
My soul shall ever love thee well.

*Watts*

**654 SHIRLAND. S. M.**

SAMUEL STANLEY.

1. O come, and dwell in me, Spir - it of power with - in! And

bring the glo - rious lib - er - ty From sor - row, fear, and sin.

2 This inward, dire disease,
   Spirit of health, remove,
Spirit of finished holiness,
Spirit of perfect love.

3 Hasten the joyful day
   Which shall my sins consume,
When old things shall be done away,
And all things new become.

4 I want the witness, Lord,
   That all I do is right,
According to thy will and word,
Well pleasing in thy sight.

5 I ask no higher state;
   Indulge me but in this;
And soon or later then translate
To my eternal bliss.

C. Wesley.

**655 WRIGHT. S. M.**

M. T. STERLING.

1. "The Lord is risen in - deed:" He lives to die no more: He lives the

sinner's cause to plead, Whose curse and shame he bore, Whose curse and shame he bore.

2 "The Lord is risen indeed:"
   Then hell has lost his prey,
With him has risen the ransomed seed,
To reign in endless day.

3 "The Lord is risen indeed:"
   Attending angels hear,—

Up to the courts of heaven, with speed,
   The joyful tidings bear.

4 Then wake your golden lyres,
   And strike each cheerful chord;
Join, all ye bright, celestial choirs,
To sing our risen Lord.

Kelly.

324

## 656 INVITATION.

1. Art thou wea - ry, art thou lan - guid,

Art thou sore dis - tressed? "Come to me," saith

One, "and com - ing, Be.................. at rest."

1 Art thou weary, art thou languid,
Art thou sore distress'd?
"Come to me," saith One, "and coming,
Be at rest."

2 Hath he marks to lead me to him,
If he be my Guide?
"In his feet and hands are wound-prints,
And his side."

3 Is there diadem as Monarch
That his brow adorns?
"Yea, a crown, in very surety,
But of thorns."

4 If I find him, if I follow,
What his guerdon here?

"Many a sorrow, many a labor,
Many a tear."

5 If I still hold closely to him,
What hath he at last?
"Sorrow vanquished, labor ended,
Jordan pass'd."

6 If I ask him to receive me,
Will he say me nay?
"Not till earth, and not till heaven
Pass away."

7 Finding, following keeping, struggling,
Is he sure to bless!
"Saints, apostles, prophets, martyrs,
Answer, "Yes."

*S. Stephen the Sabaite; Tr. J. M. Neale, 1862.*

657  GRIMKE. L. M.                                   H. F. GRANT.

1. 'Twas on that night when doomed to know The ea - ger rage of  ev - 'ry foe—

That night in which he  was be - trayed,  The  Sav - iour  of  the world took bread:

*Lord's Supper established.*   L. M.

1 *Cor.* 11: 25.

1 'Twas on that night when doomed to know
   The eager rage of every foe—
   That night in which he was betrayed,
   The Saviour of the world took bread:

2 And, after thanks and glory given
   To him that rules in earth and heaven,
   That symbol of his flesh he broke,
   And thus to all his followers spoke:

3 "My broken body thus I give
   For you, for all; take, eat, and live;
   And oft the sacred rite renew,
   That brings my wondrous love to view."

4 Then in his hands the cup he raised,
   And God anew he thanked and praised;
   While kindness in his bosom glowed,
   And from his lips salvation flowed.

5 "My blood I thus pour forth," he cries,
   "To cleanse the soul in sin that lies;
   In this the covenant is sealed,
   And Heaven's eternal grace revealed.

6 "With love to man this cup is fraught,
   Let all partake the sacred draught;

Through latest ages let it pour,
In memory of my dying hour."
                                *Unknown.*

658      *The Dawn of Heaven.*   L. M.

1 Now let our souls, on wings sublime,
   Rise from the vanities of time,
   Draw back the parting veil, and see
   The glories of eternity.

2 Born by a new celestial birth,
   Why should we grovel here on earth?
   Why grasp at transitory toys,
   So near to heaven's eternal joys?

3 Shall ought beguile us on the road,
   While we are traveling back to God?
   For strangers into life we come,
   And dying is but going home.

4 Welcome, sweet hour of full discharge!
   That sets my longing soul at large,
   Unbinds my chains, breaks up my cell,
   And gives me with my God to dwell.

5 To dwell with God, to feel his love,
   Is the full heaven enjoyed above;
   And the sweet expectation now
   Is the young dawn of heaven below.
                       *Thomas Gibbons, 1762.*

326

**659 · ADVENT HYMN. 8s, 7s & 4.**                    V. NOVELLO.

1. Lo! he comes, with clouds de-scend-ing, Once for fa - vor'd sin - ners slain;

Thous-and thous-and saints at - tend-ing Swell the tri - umph of his train:

Al - le - lu - ia! Al - le - lu - ia! Christ, the Lord, re - turns to reign.

8s, 7s & 4s.

1 Lo! he comes, with clouds descending,
Once for favored sinners slain ;
Thousand thousand saints attending
Swell the triumph of his train :
Alleluia!
Christ, the Lord, returns to reign.

2 Ev'ry eye shall now behold him,
Robed in dreadful majesty ;
Those who set at nought and sold him,
Pierced, and nail'd him to the tree,
Deeply wailing,
Shall the true Messiah see.

3 Every island, sea, and mountain,
Heaven and earth, shall flee away ;
All who hate him must, confounded,

Hear the trump proclaim the day ;
Come to judgment,
Come to judgment, come away.

4 Now redemption, long expected,
See in solemn pomp appear :
All his saints, by men rejected,
Now shall meet him in the air.
Alleluia!
See the day of God appear.

5 Yea, Amen ; let all adore Thee,
High on thine eternal throne :
Saviour, take the power and glory;
Claim the kingdom for thine own.
O come quickly,
Alleluia! Come, Lord, come.

*M. Madan, 1760; C. Wesley, 1758; J. Connick, 1752.*

327

**660 WHITE. C. M.** HENRY WHITE.

1. Je - sus, I love thy charm - ing name, 'Tis mu - sic to my ear;

Fain would I sound it out so loud, That earth and heaven should hear.

*" He is precious."* C. M.

1 Jesus, I love thy charming name,
'Tis music to my ear;
Fain would I sound it out so loud,
That earth and heaven should hear.

2 Yes, thou art precious to my soul,
My transport and my trust;
Jewels, to thee, are gaudy toys,
And gold is sordid dust.

3 All my capacious powers can wish
In thee doth richly meet;
Nor to mine eyes is light so dear,
Nor friendship half so sweet.

4 Thy grace still dwells upon my heart,
And sheds its fragrance there;
The noblest balm of all its wounds,
The cordial of its care.

5 I'll speak the honors of thy name
With my last lab'ring breath!

Then speechless clasp thee in mine arms,
The antidote of death.
*Doddridge.*

**661** *A Morning Offering.* C. M.

1 Awake, my soul, to sound his praise;
Awake, my harp, to sing;
Join, all my powers, the song to raise,
And morning incense bring.

2 Among the people of his care,
And through the nations round,
Glad songs of praise will I prepare,
And there his name resound.

3 Be thou exalted, O my God,
Above the starry frame;
Diffuse thy heavenly grace abroad,
And teach the world thy name.

4 So shall thy chosen sons rejoice,
And throng thy courts above,
While sinners hear thy pardoning voice,
And taste redeeming love.
*Barlow.*

328

SUPPLEMENT.

**662** AVON. C. M.
HUGH WILSON, 1768,

1. Cre - a - tive week, O wond-rous thought! When God the tru - ly wise,
2. Be - fore the time when sun and moon, And stars their cour-ses ran,
3. From age to age in cease-less rounds, His power he'll still dis - play,

By his al - might - y power be - gan, To form the earth and skies.
In un-known a - ges of the past, The first day's work be - gan.
Till all the crea - tures of his hand, Shall hail the crown-ing day.

C. MAX MANNING.

**663** *Latter-day Glory.* C. M.

1 Rejoice, ye nations of the world,
   And hail the happy day,
When Satan's kingdom, downward hurl'd,
   Shall perish with dismay.

2 Rejoice, ye heathen, wood and stone
   Shall form your gods no more;
Jehovah ye shall trust alone
   And him alone adore.

3 Christians, rejoice—each party name,
   Each diff'rent sect shall cease;
Your error, grief, and wrath, and shame,
   Shall yield to truth and peace.

4 Ye sons of peace, the triumph share,
   Trumpets no more shall sound;
The murd'rous sword, the bloody spear
   Shall cultivate the ground.

5 Bright o'er the mountains, may we see
   This blessed morning ray;
And glorious may its splendour be,
   E'en to the perfect day.

329

**664 AURELIA. 7s & 6s. D.**

DR. S. S. WESLEY.

1. The Church's one foun - da - tion Is Je - sus Christ the Lord;

She is his new cre - a - tion The spir - it and the word:

From heav'n he came and sought her To be his ho - ly bride;

With his own blood he bought her, And for her life he died.

2 Elect from every nation,
　Yet one o'er all the earth,
　Her charter of salvation
　One Lord, one faith, one birth
　One Holy Name she blesses,
　Partakes one holy food,
　And to one hope she presses,
　With every grace endued.

3 Though with a scornful wonder
　Men see her sore opprest,
　By schisms rent asunder,
　By heresies distrest;
　Yet Saints their watch are keeping,
　Their cry goes up, " How long?"
　And soon the night of weeping
　Shall be the morn of song.

4 'Mid toil and tribulation,
　And tumult of her war,
　She waits the consummation
　Of peace for evermore;
　Till with the vision glorious
　Her longing eyes are blest,
　And the great Church victorious
　Shall be the Church at rest.

5 Yet she on earth hath union
　With God the Three in One,
　And mystic sweet communion
　With those whose rest is won.
　O happy ones and holy!
　Lord, give us grace that we
　Like them, the meek and lowly,
　On high may dwell with thee.

*S. J. Stone.* 1860.

SUPPLEMENT.

**665  LAUDES DOMINI.  6s.**  FROM AN OLD GERMAN AIR, BY JOSEPH BARNBY.

1. When morn-ing gilds the skies, My heart a-wak-ing cries,
May Je-sus Christ be praised. A-like at work and prayer.
To Je-sus I re-pair; May Je-sus Christ be praised.

2 Whene'er the sweet church bell
Peals over hill and dell,
May Jesus Christ be praised.
Oh, hark to what it sings,
As joyously it rings,
May Jesus Christ be praised.

3 My tongue shall never tire
Of chanting with the choir,
May Jesus Christ be praised:
This song of sacred joy,
It never seems to cloy;
May Jesus Christ be praised.

4 When sleep her balm denies,
My silent spirit sighs
May Jesus Christ be praised.
When evil thoughts molest
With this I shield my breast,
May Jesus Christ be praised.

5 Does sadness fill my mind?
A solace here I find,
May Jesus Christ be praised:

Or fades my earthly bliss?
My comfort still is this,
May Jesus Christ be praised.

6 The night becomes as day,
When from the heart we say
May Jesus Christ be praised:
The powers of darkness fear,
When this sweet chant they hear,
May Jesus Christ be praised.

7 In heaven's eternal bliss
The lovliest strain is this,
May Jesus Christ be praised:
Let earth, and sea, and sky
From depth to height reply,
May Jesus Christ be praised.

8 Be this, while life is mine,
My canticle divine,
May Jesus Christ be praised:
Be this th' eternal song,
Through all the ages on,
May Jesus Christ be praised.

331

**666 THATCHER. S. M.**  FROM GEORGE FREDERICK HANDEL, 1732.

1. Sol - diers of Christ, a - rise, And gird your ar - mor on, Strong in the strength which God sup - plies Through his e - ter - nal Son.

*Fight the good fight of faith.* 1 *Tim.* vi. 12.

1 Soldiers of Christ, arise,
  And gird your armor on,
Strong in the strength which God supplies
  Through his eternal Son.

2 Strong in the Lord of hosts,
  And in his mighty power,
The man who in the Saviour trusts
  Is more than conqueror.

3 Stand, then, in his great might,
  With all his strength endued,
And take, to arm you for the fight,
  The panoply of God;—

4 That, having all things done,
  And all your conflicts past,
You may o'ercome through Christ alone,
  And stand complete at last.

5 From strength to strength go on;
  Wrestle, and fight, and pray:
Tread all the powers of darkness down,
  And win the well-fought day.

6 Still let the Spirit cry,
  In all his soldiers, "Come,"
Till Christ the Lord descends from high,
  And takes the conquerors home.
                                    *C. Wesley.*

**GLORIA PATRI. Irr.**  GREATOREX COLL.

Glo - ry be to the Fa - ther, and to the Son, and to the Ho - ly Ghost; As it was in the be - gin-ning, is now, and ev-er shall be, world without end. A-men, A-men.

**667 CREATION. L. M.** FRANCIS JOSEPH HAYDN, 1798.

1. The spa-cious firm-a-ment on high, With all the blue e-the-real sky, And span-gled heav'ns, (a shin-ing frame,) Their great O-rig-i-nal pro-claim.

**Psalm xix.** L. M.

1 The spacious firmament on high,
With all the blue ethereal sky,
And spangled heavens, (a shining frame,)
Their great Original proclaim:

2 Th' unwearied sun from day to day
Doth his Creator's power display,
And publishes to every land
The work of an almighty hand.

3 Soon as the evening shades prevail,
The moon takes up the wondrous tale,
And nightly to the list'ning earth
Repeats the story of her birth:

4 While all the stars that round her burn,
And all the planets, in their turn
Confirm the tidings as they roll,
And spread the truth from pole to pole.

5 What though in solemn silence all
Move round the dark terrestrial ball:
What though no real voice nor sound
Amid the radiant orbs be found;

6 In reason's ear they all rejoice,
And utter forth a glorious voice,
For ever singing as they shine,
"The hand that made us is Divine."
*Addison.*

**668** *The minister's welcome.* L. M

1 We bid thee welcome in the name
Of Jesus, our exalted Head;—
Come as a servant,—so *He* came,
And we receive thee in his stead.

2 Come as a shepherd;—guard and keep
This fold from hell, and earth, and sin;
Nourish the lambs, and feed the sheep,
The wounded heal, the lost bring in.

3 Come as a watchman;—take thy stand
Upon the tower amidst the sky,
And when the sword comes on the land,
Call us to fight, or warn to fly.

4 Come as an angel:—hence to guide
A band of pilgrims on their way,
That, safely walking at thy side,
We fail not, faint not, turn nor stray.

5 Come as a teacher—sent from God,
Charged his whole counsel to declare;
Lift o'er our ranks the prophet rod,
While we uphold thy hands with prayer.
*Montgomery.*

333

**669 DE FLEURY. 8s, 8 lines.** MARIA DE FLEURY, 1806.

I. { Ho - san - na to Je - sus on high! An - oth - er has en - ter'd his rest; }
{ An - oth - er has 'scap'd to the sky, And lodg'd in Im - man - u - el's breast: }

The soul of our *sis - ter* is gone, To heighten the tri - umph a - bove:

Ex - alt - ed to Je - sus's throne, And clasp'd in the arms of his love.

8s, 8 lines.

*The Triumphs of a Believer over Death.*

*Rev. xiv. 13.*

1 Hosanna to Jesus on high!
  Another has enter'd his rest:
Another has 'scap'd to the sky,
  And lodg'd in Immanuel's breast:
The soul of our *sister* is gone,
  To heighten the triumph above:
Exalted to Jesus's throne,
  And clasp'd in the arms of his love.

2 What fulness of rapture is there,
  While Jesus his glory displays;
And purples the heavenly air,
  And scatters the odors of grace!
He looks—and his servants in light,
  The blessing ineffable meet:
He smiles—and they faint at his sight,
  And fall overwhelm'd at his feet.

3 How happy the angels that fall
  Transported to Jesus's name:
The saints whom he soonest shall call
  To share in the feast of the Lamb!
No longer imprison'd in clay,
  Who next from his dungeon shall fly?
Who first shall be summon'd away—
  My merciful God—Is it I?

4 O Jesus if this be thy will
  That suddenly I should depart;
Thy counsel of mercy reveal,
  And whisper thy call to my heart:
O give me a signal to know,
  If soon thou wouldst have me remove,
And leave the dull body below,
  And fly to the regions above.
*Unknown.*

**670** 8s, 8 lines.
*Longing for still closer communion.*

1 Thou Shepherd of Israel, and mine,
  The joy and desire of my heart,
For closer communion I pine;
  I long to reside where thou art:
The pasture I languish to find,
  Where all, who their Shepherd obey,
Are fed, on thy bosom reclined,
  And screen'd from the heat of the day

2 'Tis there, with the lambs of thy flock,
  There only, I covet to rest;
To lie at the foot of the rock,
  Or rise to be hid in thy breast:
'Tis there I would always abide,
  And never a moment depart,—
Conceal'd in the cleft of thy side,
  Eternally held in thy heart.
*Wesley.*

**671  NASHVILLE. L. M. 6 lines.**  FROM A GREGORIAN CHANT.

1. Fa - ther of lights, from whom proceeds  What-e'er thy  ev -'ry creature needs,—

Whose goodness, prov - i - dent-ly nigh,  Feeds the young ra - vens when they cry,—

To thee I look, my heart pre-pare;  Sug-gest, and heark-en  to my pray'r.

*Praying for repentance.* L. M. 6 lines.

1 Father of lights, from whom proceeds
Whate'er thy every creature needs,—
Whose goodness, providently nigh,
Feeds the young ravens when they cry,—
To thee I look, my heart prepare;
Suggest, and hearken to my prayer.

2 Since, by thy light, myself I see
Naked, and poor, and void of thee,
Thine eyes must all my thoughts survey
Preventing what my lips would say :
Thou seest my wants, for help they call,
And ere I speak thou know'st them all.

3 Thou know'st the baseness of my mind,
Wayward, and impotent, and blind ;
Thou know'st how unsubdued my will,
Averse to good, and prone to ill ;
Thou know'st how wide my passions rove,
Nor checked by fear, nor charmed by love.

4 Fain would I know, as known by thee,
And feel the indigence I see :
Fain would I all my vileness own,
And deep beneath the burden groan !
Abhor the pride that lurks within,
Detest and loathe myself and sin.

5 Ah! give me, Lord, myself to feel,
My total misery reveal :

Ah ! give me, Lord, (I still would say,)
A heart to mourn, a heart to pray ;
My business this, my only care,
My life, my every breath, be prayer.

*C. Wesley.*

**672**  L. M. 6 lines.
*Priesthood of Christ.*

1 O thou eternal Victim, slain,
A sacrifice for guilty man,
By the eternal Spirit made
An off'ring in the sinner's stead :
Our everlasting Priest art thou,
And plead'st thy death for sinners now :

2 Thy off'ring still continues new :
Thy vesture keeps its bloody hue :
Thou stand'st the ever slaughtered Lamb :
Thy priesthood still remains the same :
Thy years, O God, can never fail :
Thy goodness is unchangeable.

3 O that our faith may never move,
But stand unshaken as thy love :
Sure evidence of things unseen,
Now let it pass the years between,
And view thee bleeding on the tree,
My God, who dies for me, for me !

*C. Wesley.*

**673 OLIVET. 6s & 4s.**

1. Come, Ho-ly Ghost! in love, Shed on us, from above,Thine own bright ray: Di-vine-ly

good thou art; Thy sacred gifts impart, To gladden each sad heart; Oh! come to - day!

---

*" Veni, Sancte, Spiritus !"*  6s & 4s.

1 Come, Holy Ghost! in love,
　Shed on us, from above,
　　Thine own bright ray:
　Divinely good thou art;
　Thy sacred gifts impart,
　To gladden each sad heart;
　　Oh! come to-day!

2 Come, tenderest Friend, and best,
　Our most delightful Guest!
　　With soothing power;
　Rest, which the weary know;
　Shade, 'mid the noontide glow;
　Peace, when deep griefs o'erflow;
　　Cheer us, this hour!

3 Come, Light serene! and still
　Our inmost bosoms fill;
　　Dwell in each breast:
　We know no dawn but thine;
　Send forth thy beams divine,
　On our dark souls to shine,
　　And make us blessed.

4 Exalt our low desires;
　Extinguish passion's fires;
　　Heal every wound;
　Our stubborn spirits bend;
　Our icy coldness end;
　Our devious steps attend,
　　While heavenward bound.

5 Come, all the faithful bless;
　Let all, who Christ confess,

His praise employ:
Give virtue's rich reward;
Victorious death accord.
And with our glorious Lord,
　Eternal joy!

　　Lat., *Robert II, of France*, 996.
　　　Tr. *Ray Palmer*, 1858.

**674**　　　　　　　　　6s & 4s.

1 Come, all ye saints of God,
　Through all the earth abroad,
　　Spread Jesus' fame:
　Tell what his love hath done;
　Trust in his name alone;
　Shout to his lofty throne,
　　"Worthy the Lamb!"

2 Hence, gloomy doubts and fears!
　Dry up your mournful tears;
　　Join our glad theme:
　Beauty for ashes bring;
　Strike each melodious string;
　Join heart and voice to sing,
　　"Worthy the Lamb!"

3 Hark! how the choirs above,
　Filled with the Saviour's love,
　　Dwell on his name!
　There, too, may we be found,
　With light and glory crowned,
　While all the heavens resound,
　　"Worthy the Lamb!"

　　　　*James Boden*, 1801.

SUPPLEMENT.

**675 MISSIONARY CHANT. L. M.** CHARLES ZEUNER, 1832.

1. Lord, on thy prom - ise I re - ly, That thou wilt hear a sin - ner's cry,

In ev - 'ry try - ing time of need, And show thy - self the friend in - deed.

---

*Trust in God.* L. M.

1 Lord, on thy promise I rely,
That thou wilt hear a sinner's cry,
In every trying time of need,
And show thyself the friend indeed.

2 To count thy mercies I begin,
When, lo, a voice comes from within—
Where shall the countless blessings end,
Which thou to me dost daily send?

3 Condemned by that most sacred law,
Which broken is each breath I draw?
Lord, only on thy grace I lean,
Thou canst the guilty soul make clean.

4 Lo, at thy feet I humbly fall,
And for thy mercy great I call,
O turn to me thy smiling face,
Send me the fulness of thy grace.
*Josie D. Heard.*

**676** *Opening of Conference.* L. M.

1 Lord, 'tis delightful, thus to meet,
Within these walls, in union sweet;
From varied fields, of plain and mount,
Our yearly labors to recount.

2 What hours of mingled joy and grief:
But Christ hath brought to us relief,
As daily, through the thorny ways,
We toiled, or rowed o'er stormy seas.

3 But, o'er the checkered paths did shine,
The guiding star, of Light divine :
Whose genial rays, caused fruit to bear,
And joy to crown the circling year.

4 Great God, do thou with us abide,
O'er every thought and step preside,
Let love, through every action run,
Unite, and perfect us in One.

5 Prepare, and send forth, in the field,
Men, thus prepared to do thy will,
With quickened ears, to 'tend thy voice,
And make the wilderness rejoice.

6 Then, shall the desert quickly bloom,
And fill the spheres, with sweet perfumes,
Rivers, and earth's far corners ring,
With praise to Zion's conquering King.
*Rev. James G. Sampson.*

337

677  MERIBAH.  C. P. M.                                     DR. L. MASON.

1. Thou great mys-ter-ious God un-known, Whose love hath gent-ly led me on    E'en

from my in-fant days; { Mine inmost soul ex-pose to view. } Thy just-i-fy-ing grace.
                      { And tell me if I ev-er knew }

*The inward witness.*    C. P. M.

1 Thou great mysterious God unknown,
  Whose love hath gently led me on
    E'en from my infant days;
  Mine inmost soul expose to view,
  And tell me if I ever knew
    Thy justifying grace.

2 If I have only known thy fear,
  And followed, with a heart sincere,
    Thy drawings from above;
  Now, now the further grace bestow,
  And let my sprinkled conscience know
    Thy sweet forgiving love.

3 Short of thy love I would not stop,
  A stranger to the gospel hope,
    The sense of sin forgiven;
  I would not, Lord, my soul deceive,
  Without the inward witness live,
    That antepast of heaven.

4 If now the witness were in me,
  Would he not testify of thee,
    In Jesus reconciled?
  And should I not with faith draw nigh,
  And boldly, "Abba, Father," cry,
    And know myself thy child?

5 Father, in me reveal thy Son,
  And to my inmost soul make known
    How merciful thou art;
  The secret of thy love reveal,
  And by thy hallowing Spirit dwell
    Forever in my heart.
                            *Charles Wesley.*

678        *The blessed hope.*        C. P. M.

1 But can it be that I should prove
  Forever faithful to thy love,
    From sin forever cease?
  I thank thee for the blessed hope;
  It lifts my drooping spirits up;
    It gives me back my peace.

2 In thee, O Lord, I put my trust,
  Mighty, and merciful, and just;
    Thy sacred word is passed;
  And I, who dare thy word believe,
  Without committing sin shall live,
    Shall live to God at last.

3 I rest in thine almighty power,
  The name of Jesus is my tower
    That hides my life above:
  Thou canst, thou wilt, my helper be,
  My confidence is all in thee,
    The faithful God of love.
                            *Charles Wesley.*

338

**679** **LANGRAN.** 10s.                                                J. LANGRAN.

1. From shore to shore shall Je - sus stretch his sway His bound-less

bless - ings flow to ev - 'ry sea! Lo! round his al - tar suppliant kings at -

tend; Be - fore his throne o - be - dient na - tions bend.

*Messiah's Triumph. Isai.* 11 : 9.        10s.

1 From shore to shore shall Jesus stretch his sway
  His boundless blessings flow to every sea!
  Lo! round his altar suppliant kings attend;
  Before his throne obedient nations bend.

2 Through him, the curse in boundless bliss shall end;
  From evil, good—from darkness, light ascend;
  Fresh springs of life, in thirsty deserts flow,
  And savage tribes th' immortal Saviour know.

3 Prostrate in dust his humbled foes shall lie,
  Or send their hymns of transport to the sky,
  And each blest land rehearse his praises o'er,
  Till moons shall walk their evening round no more.

                                         *Anderson's Col.*

339

SUPPLEMENT.

**680 EVENTIDE.**

WILLIAM HENRY MONK, 1861.

1. Go to the grave in all thy glo-rious prime, In full ac-tiv-i-ty of zeal and power; A Chris-tian can-not die be-fore his time; The Lord's ap-point-ment is the ser-vant's hour.

*Death of a Minister in his Prime.* 10s.

1 Go to the grave in all thy glorious prime,
   In full activity of zeal and power;
 A Christian cannot die before his time;
 The Lord's appointment is the servant's
   hour.

2 Go to the grave; at noon from labor cease;
   Rest on thy sheaves; thy harvest task is
     done;
 Come from the heat of battle, and in peace,
 Soldier, go home; with thee the fight is
   won.

3 Go to the grave; for there thy Saviour lay
   In death's embrace, ere he arose on
     high;
 And all the ransom'd, by that narrow way,
 Pass to eternal life beyond the sky.

4 Go to the grave:—no; take thy seat above;
   Be thy pure spirit present with the Lord,
 Where thou for faith and hope hast perfect
   love,
 And open vision for the written word.
                              *Montgomery.*

**681** *A present help in trouble.* C. P. M.
[Tune, Meribah, page 338. C. P. M.]

1 O God, thy faithfulness I plead,
   My present help in time of need,
     My great Deliverer, thou!
 Haste to mine aid, thine ear incline,
 And rescue this poor soul of mine:
     I claim the promise now.

2 One only way the erring mind
 Of man, short-sighted man, can find,
     From inbred sin to fly:
 Stronger than love, I fondly thought
 Death, only death, can cut the knot,
     Which love cannot untie.

3 But thou, O Lord, art full of grace;
 Thy love can find a thousand ways
     To foolish man unknown:
 My soul upon thy love I cast;
 I rest me, till the storm be past,
     Upon thy love alone.

4 Thy faithful, wise, almighty love
 Shall every stumbling-block remove,
     And make an open way:
 Thy love shall burst the shades of death,
 And bear me from the gulf beneath,
     To everlasting day.
                          *Charles Wesley.*

340

**682 LEONI.** 6s, 6s, 8s & 4s. HEBREW AIR. ADAPTED BY RABBI LEONI, 1770.

1. The God of A-brah'm praise, Who reigns en-throned a-bove,—
An-cient of ev-er-last-ing days, And God of love:
Je-ho-vah, great I Am! By earth and heaven con-fess'd;
I bow, and bless the sa-cred name For ev-er bless'd.

2    The God of Abrah'm praise,
At whose supreme command
From earth I rise—and seek the joys
At his right hand:
I all on earth forsake,
Its wisdom, fame, and power;
And him my only portion make,
My shield and tower.

3    The God of Abrah'm praise,
Whose all-sufficient grace,
Shall guide me all my happy days
In all his ways.

He calls a worm his friend!
He calls himself my God!
And he shall save me to the end,
Through Jesus' blood!

4    He by himself hath sworn;
I on his oath depend;
I shall, on eagles' wings upborne,
To heaven ascend:
I shall behold his face,
I shall his power adore.
And sing the wonders of his grace
For evermore.

*Olivers.*

341

**683** HOLLEY. 7s.

GEO. HEWS, 1835.

1. Ho-ly Spir-it, from on high, Bend o'er us a pity-ing eye;

Now re-fresh the droop-ing heart; Bid the pow'r of sin de-part.

*The teaching Spirit.*    7s.

1 Holy Spirit, from on high,
Bend o'er us a pitying eye;
Now refresh the drooping heart;
Bid the power of sin depart.

2 Light up every dark recess
Of our heart's ungodliness;
Show us every devious way
Where our steps have gone astray.

3 Teach us with repentant grief,
Humbly to implore relief;
Then the Saviour's blood reveal,
And our broken spirits heal.

4 May we daily grow in grace,
And pursue the heavenly race,
Trained in wisdom, led by love,
Till we reach our rest above.
*Bathurst.*

**684**    *Funeral of a Christian Sister.*    7s.

1 Lo! the pris'ner is releas'd,
Lighten'd of her fleshly load:
Where the weary are at rest,
She is gather'd into God!

2 Lo! the pain of life is past,
All her warfare now is o'er;
Death and hell behind are cast,
Grief and suff'ring are no more.

3 Yes, the Christian's course is run,
Ended is the glorious strife;
Fought the fight, the work is done,
Death is swallow'd up of life!

4 Borne by angels on their wings,
Far from earth the spirit flies,
Finds her God, and sits, and sings,
Triumphing in paradise.
*C. Wesley.*

**685**    *Christ in the Word.*    C. M.

1 Thou lovely Source of true delight,
Whom I unseen adore!
Unvail thy beauties to my sight,
That I may love thee more.

2 Thy glory o'er creation shines;—
But in thy sacred word
I read, in fairer, brighter lines,
My bleeding, dying Lord.

3 'Tis here, whene'er my comforts droop,
And sin and sorrow rise,
Thy love, with cheering beams of hope,
My fainting heart supplies.

4 Jesus, my Lord, my life, my light!
Oh, come with blissful ray;
Break radiant through the shades of night,
And chase my fears away.
*A. Steele.*

SUPPLEMENT.

## 686 HOW FIRM A FOUNDATION. 11s.

1. How firm a foun-da-tion, ye saints of the Lord, Is laid for your faith in his ex-cel-lent word! What more can he say than to you he hath said, You, who un-to Je-sus for ref-uge have fled?

2 In every condition—in sickness, in health;
In poverty's vale, or abounding in wealth;
At home and abroad; on the land, on the sea,—
"As thy days may demand, shall thy strength ever be.

3 "Fear not; I am with thee: O be not dismay'd!
I, I am thy God, and will still give thee aid:
I'll strengthen thee, help thee, and cause thee to stand
Upheld by my righteous, omnipotent hand.

4 "When through the deep waters I call thee to go,
The rivers of woe shall not thee overflow;
For I will be with thee, thy troubles to bless,
And sanctify to thee thy deepest distress.

5 "When through fiery trials thy pathway shall lie,
My grace, all-sufficient, shall be thy supply:
The flame shall not hurt thee: I only design
Thy dross to consume, and thy gold to refine.

6 "E'en down to old age, all my people shall prove
My sovereign, eternal, unchangeable love;
And when hoary hairs shall their temples adorn,
Like lambs they shall still in my bosom be borne.

7 "The soul that on Jesus still leans for repose,
I will not, I will not, desert to his foes;
That soul, though all hell should endeavor to shake,
I'll never, no, never, no, never, forsake."

*Kirkham.*

343

**687 ABRIDGE. C. M.**

ISAAC SMITH, 1770,

1. Ap - proach, my soul, the mer - cy seat, Where Je - sus an - swers pray'r; There hum - bly fall be - fore his feet, For none can per - ish there.

*The effort.*  C. M.

1 Approach, my soul, the mercy-seat,
  Where Jesus answers prayer;
  There humbly fall before his feet,
  For none can perish there.

2 Thy promise is my only plea,
  With this I venture nigh :
  Thou call'st the burdened soul to thee,
  And such, O Lord, am I.

3 Bowed down beneath a load of sin,
  By Satan sorely pressed,
  By wars without, and fears within,
  I come to thee for rest.

4 Be thou my shield and hiding place,
  That, sheltered near thy side,
  I may my fierce accuser face,
  And tell him thou hast died.

5 O, wondrous love, to bleed and die,
  To bear the cross and shame,
  That guilty sinners, such as I,
  Might plead his gracious name.

6 "Poor tempest-tossed soul, be still,
  My promised grace receive :"—
  'Tis Jesus speaks—I must, I will,
  I can, I do believe.

**688**          *Rest for the weary.*          11s & 10s.

[Tune, Hail to the Brightness, page 207.  11s & 10s.]

1 Come unto me, when shadows darkly gather,
  When the sad heart is weary and distressed,
  Seeking for comfort from your heavenly Father,
  Come unto me, and I will give you rest.

2 Large are the mansions in thy Father's dwelling,
  Glad are the homes that sorrows never dim :
  Sweet are the harps in holy music swelling,
  Soft are the tones which raise the heavenly hymn.

3 There, like an Eden blossoming in gladness,
  Bloom the fair flowers the earth too rudely pressed;
  Come unto me, all ye who droop in sadness,
  Come unto me, and I will give you rest.
                          *Unknown,*

344

# SUPPLEMENT.

## 689 METROPOLITAN. C. M.

J. T. LAYTON.

1. Let earth, with ev - 'ry isle and sea, Re - joice; the Sav - iour reigns:

His word, like fire, pre - pares his way, And moun-tains melt to plains.

### The Reign of Christ.     C. M.

1 Let earth, with every isle and sea,
Rejoice; the Saviour reigns:
His word, like fire, prepares his way,
And mountains melt to plains.

2 His presence sinks the proudest hills,
And makes the valleys rise;
The humble soul enjoys his smiles,
The haughty sinner dies.

3 Adoring angels, at his birth,
Made our Redeemer known;
Thus shall he come to judge the earth
And angels guard his throne.

4 His foes shall tremble at his sight,
And hills and seas retire;
His children take their upward flight
And leave the world on fire.

5 The seeds of joy and glory sown
For saints in darkness here,
Shall rise and spring in worlds unknown,
And a rich harvest bear.

*Watts.*

## 690     1 Thess. iv. 13, 14     C. M.

1 Take comfort, Christians, when your friends
In Jesus fall asleep:
Their better being never ends:
Then why dejected weep?

2 Why inconsolable, as those
To whom no hope is giv'n?
Death is the messenger of peace,
And calls the soul to heav'n.

3 As Jesus died, and rose again,
Victorious from the dead,
So his disciples rise and reign
With their triumphant Head.

4 The time draws nigh when, from the clouds,
Christ shall with shouts descend,
And the last trumpet's awful voice
The heavens and earth shall rend.

5 Then they who live shall changèd be
And they who sleep shall wake:
The graves shall yield their ancient charge,
And earth's foundation shake:

6 The saints of God, from death set free,
With joy shall mount on high:
The heavenly hosts, with praises loud,
Shall meet them in the sky.

*Anon.*

345

**691  TANNER. L. M. 6 lines.**

1. Lo! God is here! let us a - dore, And own how dreadful is this place!

Let all with-in us feel his power, And si-lent bow be-fore his face!

Who know his power, his grace who prove, Serve him with awe, with rev'rence, love.

*Opening Worship.* L. M. 6 lines.

[ From the German of Jan Van Segen.]

1 Lo! God is here! let us adore,
   And own how dreadful is this place!
   Let all within us feel his power,
   And silent bow before his face!
   Who know his power, his grace who prove,
   Serve him with awe, with rev'rence, love.

2 Lo! God is here! him day and night
   Th' united choirs of angels sing:
   To him enthroned above all height,
   Heaven's host their noblest praises bring:
   Disdain not, Lord, our meaner song,
   Who praise thee with a stamm'ring tongue.

3 Gladly the toys of earth we leave,
   Wealth, pleasure, fame, for thee alone:
   To thee our will, soul, flesh, we give:
   O take! O seal them for thine own!
   Thou art the God, thou art the Lord:
   Be thou by all thy works adored!

4 Being of beings, may our praise
   Thy courts with grateful fragrance fill:
   Still may we stand before thy face,
   Still hear and do thy sovereign will:
   To thee may all our thoughts arise,
   Ceaseless, accepted sacrifice.

5 As flowers their op'ning leaves display,
   And glad drink in the solar fire,
   So may we catch thy every ray,
   So may thy influence us inspire,
   Thou Beam of the eternal Beam!
   Thou purging Fire, thou quick'ning Flame!
                              *J. Wesley.*

**692**    *Praise to the Trinity.*  L. M. 6 lines.

1 Infinite God, to thee we raise
   Our hearts in solemn songs of praise :
   By all thy works on earth adored,
   We worship thee, the common Lord ;
   The everlasting Father own,
   And bow ourselves before thy throne.

2 Thee all the choir of angels sings,
   The Lord of hosts, the King of kings;
   Cherubs proclaim thy praise aloud,
   And seraphs shout the Triune God :
   And "holy, holy, holy," cry,
   "Thy glory fills both earth and sky!"

3 Father of endless majesty,
   All might and love they render thee ;
   Thy true and only Son adore,
   The same in dignity and power :
   And God the Holy Ghost declare,
   The saints' eternal Comforter.

**693 ALLEN. L. M.** DR. J. W. RANDOLPH.

*Moderato maestoso.*

1. My God, and is thy ta-ble spread? And does thy cup with love o'erflow?

Thith-er be all thy child-ren led, And let them all its sweetness know?

---

*The table prepared.* L. M.

1 My God, and is thy table spread?
   And does thy cup with love o'erflow?
   Thither be all thy children led,
   And let them all its sweetness know!

2 Hail, sacred feast, which Jesus makes!
   Rich banquet of his flesh and blood!
   Thrice happy he who here partakes
   That sacred stream, that heavenly food!

3 Why are its bounties all in vain
   Before unwilling hearts displayed?
   Was not for you the Victim slain?
   Are you forbid the children's bread?

4 O let thy table honored be,
   And furnished well with joyful guests!
   And may each soul salvation see,
   That here its sacred pledges tastes!

5 Let crowds approach with hearts prepared!
   With hearts inflamed let all attend;
   Nor, when we leave our Father's board,
   The pleasure or the profit end.
                                    *Doddridge.*

**694 The Transfiguration. L. M.**

1 When at this distance, Lord, we trace
   The various glories of thy face,
   What transport pours o'er all our breast,
   And charms our cares and woes to rest!

2 With thee, in the obscurest cell,
   On some bleak mountain would I dwell,
   Rather than pompous courts behold,
   And share their grandeur and their gold.

3 Away, ye dreams of mortal joy;
   Raptures divine my thoughts employ:
   I see the King of glory shine,
   And feel his love, and call him mine.

4 On Tabor thus his servants viewed
   His lustre, when transformed he stood;
   And, bidding earthly scenes farewell,
   Cried, " Lord, 'tis pleasant here to dwell!"

5 Yet still our elevated eyes
   To nobler visions long to rise:
   That grand assembly would we join,
   Where all thy saints around thee shine.

6 That mount, how bright! those forms, how
                                        fair!
   'Tis good to dwell for ever there!
   Come, death, dear envoy of my God,
   And bear me to that blest abode!
                                    *Doddridge.*

*Doxology.* C. M.

To Father, Son, and Holy Ghost,
   The God whom we adore,
Be glory, as it was, is now,
   And shall be evermore.
                              *Tate and Brady.*

**695 GOD BE WITH YOU.**

W. G. TOMER.

1. God be with you till we meet a - gain, By his counsels guide, uphold you,
2. God be with you till we meet a - gain, 'Neath his wings securely fold you,
3. God be with you till we meet a - gain, When life's perils thick confound you ;
4. God be with you till we meet a - gain, Keep love's banner floating o'er you ;

With his sheep securely fold you, God be with you till we meet a - gain.
Dai - ly man-na still pro-vide you, God be with you till we meet a - gain.
Put his arms unfailing round you, God be with you till we meet a - gain.
Smite death's threatening wave before you, God be with you till we meet a - gain.

CHORUS.

Till we meet......... till we meet, Till we meet at Je - sus' feet;
Till we meet, till we meet a-gain. till we meet;

Till we meet,......... till we meet, God be with you till we meet a - gain.
Till we meet, till we meet a-gain,

J. E. RANKIN.

348

**696** LISCHER. H. M.　　　　GERMAN. ARR. BY LOWELL MASON, 1841.

1. { Wel - come, de - light - ful morn, Thou day of sa - cred rest! }
   { I hail thy kind re - turn; Lord! make these mo-ments blessed; }
From the low train of mor - tal toys, I soar to reach im -
mor-tal joys; I soar to reach im - mor - tal joys.
I soar to reach im - mor - tal joys.

2 Now may the King descend,
　And fill his throne of grace!
Thy sceptre, Lord! extend,
　While saints address thy face:
Let sinners feel thy quickening word,
And learn to know and fear the Lord.

3 Descend, celestial Dove!
　With all thy quickening powers;
Disclose a Saviour's love,
　And bless these sacred hours;
Then shall my soul new life obtain,
Nor sabbath's e'er be spent in vain.
　　　　　　　　　　*Hayward*, 1806.

**697**　　　　　　　　　　H. M.
　"*They shall call his name Immanuel.*"

1 Let earth and heaven combine,
　Angels and men agree,
To praise, in songs divine,
　Th' incarnate Deity:
Our God contracted to a span,
Incomprehensibly made man.

2 He laid his glory by;
　He wrapped him in our clay:

Unmarked by human eye,
　The latent Godhead lay;
Infant of days he here became,
And bore the mild Immanuel's name.

3 Unsearchable the love
　That hath the Saviour brought;
The grace is far above
　Or man or angel's thought:
Suffice for us that God, we know,
Our God, is manifest below.

4 He deigns in flesh t' appear,
　Widest extremes to join:
To bring our vileness near,
　And make us all divine:
And we the life of God shall know;
For God is manifest below.

5 Made perfect first in love,
　And sanctified by grace,
We shall from earth remove,
　And see his glorious face:
Then shall his love be fully showed,
And man shall then be lost in God.
　　　　　　　　　　*C. Wesley.*

349

**698 DIADEMATA. S. M. D.** SIR G. J. ELVEY.

1. Crown him with man - y crowns, The Lamb up - on his throne;
Hark! how the heav'n-ly an - them drowns All mu - sic but its own!
A - wake, my soul, and sing Of him who died for thee;
And hail him as thy match-less King Thro' all e - ter - ni - ty.

2 Crown him the Virgin's Son!
The God incarnate born,
Whose arm those crimson trophies won
Which now his brow adorn.
Fruit of the Mystic Rose.
True Branch of Jesse's stem,
The Root whence mercy ever flows,
The Babe of Bethlehem!

3 Crown him the Lord of Love!
Behold his hands and side,—
Those wounds, yet visible above,
In beauty glorified:
No angel in the sky
Can fully bear that sight,
But downward bends his wondering eye
At mysteries so bright.

3 Crown Him the Lord of Peace!
Whose power a sceptre sways
In heaven and earth that wars may cease,
And all be prayer and praise.
His reign shall know no end;
And round his piercéd feet
Fair flowers of Paradise extend
Their fragrance ever sweet.

4 Crown him the Lord of heaven!
One with the Father known,—
And the blest Spirit, through him given
From yonder Triune throne!
All hail, Redeemer, hail!
For thou hast died for me:
Thy praise and glory shall not fail
Throughout eternity.

*Matthew Bridges, 1848.*

**699 EMBRY. H. M.**  J. T. LAYTON.

1. I give im-mor-tal praise To God the Father's love, For all my com-forts here, And bet-ter hopes a-bove: He sent his own e-ter-nal Son To die for sins that man had done..........

*The Trinity.*  H. M.

1 I give immortal praise
  To God the Father's love,
 For all my comforts here,
  And better hopes above:
 He sent his own eternal Son
 To die for sins that man had done.

2 To God the Son belongs
  Immortal glory, too;
 Who bought us with his blood
  From everlasting woe;
 And now he lives, and now he reigns,
 And sees the fruit of all his pains.

3 To God the Spirit's name
  Immortal worship give,
 Whose new-creating power
  Makes the dead sinner live:
 His work completes the great design,
 And fills the soul with joy divine.

4 Almighty God, to thee
  Be endless honors done,
 The undivided Three,
  And the mysterious One:
 Where reason fails, with all her powers,
 There faith prevails, and love adores.

*Watts.*

**700**  *Psalm lxxxiv.*  H. M.

1 Lord of the worlds above,
  How pleasant and how fair
 The dwellings of thy love,
  Thine earthly temples, are!
 To thine abode my heart aspires,
 With warm desires, to see my God.

2 O happy souls, that pray
  Where God appoints to hear!
 O happy men, that pay
  Their constant service there!
 They praise thee still; and happy they
 That love the way to Zion's hill.

3 They go from strength to strength
  Through this dark vale of tears,
 Till each arrives at length,
  Till each in heaven appears:
 O glorious seat, when God our King
 Shall thither bring our willing feet!

4 To spend one sacred day
  Where God and saints abide,
 Affords diviner joy
  Than thousand days beside:
 Where God resorts, I love it more
 To keep the door than shine in courts.

*Watts.*

351

# 701 SHALL WE FIND THEM AT THE PORTALS?

To the Memory of Walter N. Rankin.  PROF. O. H. EVANS, D. M.

*The first part may be used as a solo.*

1. Will  they meet us, cheer and greet  us,  Those  we
2. Hearts are brok-en for some tok - en,  That  they
3. And  we  oft-en, as days soft - en,  And  comes
4. Past  yon por-tals, our im - mor - tals,  Those who

*Organ.*

loved, who've gone be-fore ?  Shall  we find them at the por-tals,
live and love us  yet ;  And we ask, "Can those who've left us,
out the evening star,  Look-ing westward, sit and won-der,
walk with him in white,  Do they, 'mid their bliss, re-call us,

# SUPPLEMENT.

*rit.*

Find our beauti-fied im-mor-tals,    When we reach that ra-diant shore?
Of love's look and tone be-reft us,   Tho' in Heav'n, can they for-get?"
Whether when so far a-sun-der,        They still think how dear they are?
Know they what events be-fall us,     Will our com-ing wake de-light?

CHORUS.
They will meet us, cheer and greet us,

*a tempo.*
They will meet us, cheer and greet us, Those we've lov'd who've gone be-

We shall find them at the por - tals,

fore; We shall find them at the por-tals, Find our beau-ti-

fied im-mor-tals, When we reach, when we reach that ra-diant shore.

REV. J. E. RANKIN.

353

## 702 THE SONG OF THE EASTER ANGELS.

In Memory of Eames Birge Rankin.                    R. DeW. MALLARY, D. D.

1. On East er morn, when ho-ly chimes are ringing, God's breath of peace on all the
2. Assuaged our grief, we tread the path before us, Ful-fil the days of our ap-
3. Ye an-gels, bear love's cup of con-so - la - tion, Fly with the East - er sun round
4. Say that with him, shall come the dear depart-ed, Clothed in new beau - ty, they from

scene a round, I seem to hear de-scending an-gels sing-ing, Till they have
point-ed time; While each year brings a-gain the East-er cho - rus, And we look
the glad earth; Proclaim that death in Christ is but trans - la - tion, That at his
dust shall rise;—Sing of that land where are no broken heart-ed, Where God's own

CHORUS.

made the earth all hal-lowed ground.
for that last great change sub-lime.   } Rest, pilgrims, rest,    No more your hearts are
voice we rise to high - er birth.
hand wipes tears from weeping eyes.

ach-ing, No more ye burdens bear, or sor-rows weep; Rest, pil-grims, rest,

till life's glad morn be breaking, 'Tis God, who giv-eth his be - lov - ed sleep.

REV. J. E. RANKIN, D. D.

**703 GRANT. L. M. 6 Lines.**   THOMAS HASTINGS, 1847.

1. Sin - ners, be - lieve the gos - pel word, Je - sus is come, your souls to save! Je - sus is come, your com-mon Lord; Par - don ye all through him may have, May now be saved, who-ev - er will: This man re - ceiv -eth sin - ners still.

## The universal invitation. L. M. 6 lines.

1 Sinners, believe the gospel word,
  Jesus is come your souls to save !
 Jesus is come, your common Lord ;
 Pardon ye all through him may have,—
 May now be saved, whoever will :
 This man receiveth sinners still.

2 See where the lame, the halt, the blind,
  The deaf, the dumb, the sick, the poor,
 Flock to the Friend of human kind,
  And freely all accept their cure !
 To whom did he his help deny ?
 Whom, in his days of flesh, pass by ?

3 Did not his word the fiends expel,
  The lepers cleanse, and raise the dead ?
 Did he not all their sickness heal,
  And satisfy their every need ?
 Did he reject his helpless clay,
 Or send them sorrowful away ?

4 Nay, but his bowels yearned to see
  The people hungry, scattered, faint,
 Nay, but he uttered over thee,
  Jerusalem, a true complaint ;
 Jerusalem, who shedd'st his blood,
 That, with his tears, for thee hath flowed.

*C. Wesley.*

## 704    The mourner.   L. M.  6 lines.

1 Jesus, if still the same thou art,
  If all thy promises are sure,
 Set up thy kingdom in my heart,
  And make me rich, for I am poor:
 To me be all thy treasures given,
 The kingdom of an inward heaven.

2 Thou hast pronounced the mourners blest,
  And lo ! for thee I ever mourn ;
 I cannot, no, I will not rest,
  Till thou, my only rest, return ;
 Till thou, the Prince of peace, appear,
 And I receive the Comforter.

3 Where is the blessedness, bestowed
  On all that hunger after thee ?
 I hunger now, I thirst for God ;
  See the poor fainting sinner, see ;
 And satisfy with endless peace,
 And fill me with thy righteousness.

4 Shine on thy work, disperse the gloom ;
  Light in thy light I then shall see ;
 Say to my soul, " Thy light is come,
  Glory divine is risen on thee ;
 Thy warfare's past, thy morning's o'er ;
 Look up, for thou shalt weep no more."

*C. Wesley*

**705  NEARER HOME.  6s.**

JOHN M. EVANS, 1860.

1. One sweet-ly sol-emn thought Comes to me o'er and o'er;

I'm near-er home to-day Than e'er I've been be-fore:

CODA.

I'm near-er my home, near-er my home, Near-er my home to-day;

Yes, near-er my home in heaven to-day, Than ev-er I've been be-fore:

---

*Nearer Home.* 6s.

1 One sweetly solemn thought
  Comes to me o'er and o'er;
  I'm nearer home to-day
  Than e'er I've been before:

2 Nearer my Father's house,
  Where the blest mansions be;
  Nearer the great white throne,
  Nearer the crystal sea;

3 Nearer the bound where we
  Must lay our burdens down;
  Nearer to leave the cross,
  Nearer to gain the crown.

4 The waves of that deep sea
  Roll dark before my sight,
  But break, the other side,
  Upon a shore of light.

5 Oh! if my mortal feet
  Have almost gained the brink,
  If I am nearer home
  To-day than e'en I think:

6 Father! perfect my trust,
  That I may rest, in death,
  On Christ, my Lord. alone,
  And thus resign my breath.

*Phœbe Cary*, 1852, a.

---

**706**  S. M.

*"Lest there be an evil heart of unbelief, in departing from the living God." Heb.* 3 : 12.

[Tune, Dennis, page 296. S. M.]

1 Ye saints of God, awake,
  And hear the heavenly word:
  Depart not from the living God,
  He only is thy Lord.

2 What, if the finest gold,
  Be freely proffered thee?
  Depart not from the living God,
  Nor the temptation see.

3 What, if the foe arise,
  With threatenings false and loud?
  Depart not from the living God,
  Rather accept the cloud.

4 And what if friends beguile
  With softest, warmest love?
  Depart not from the living God,
  Who warns thee from above.

5 Depart, ye saints, depart
  Not from the living God,
  He will thy shield and buckler be,
  He will be, is thy rod.

*Bishop B. T. Tanner, D. D.*

356

SUPPLEMENT.

**707 I WILL NOT LET THEE GO.**

*mf*     *p*

1. I will not let thee go, Thou guest di - vine,
2. What though the day should break, The shad - ows flee,
3. What marks are these I see, Up - on thy brow?
4. The cross thou did'st en - dure, The cup, the shame;

Un - til thy name I know, By word or sign.
Thy leave thou shalt not take, I'll cleave to thee:
O Man of Cal - va - ry, I read thee now:
Ah, yes, I'm dou - bly sure Thou art the same:

Art thou the Man who died, Be - tween thieves cru - ci - fied?
Thy touch my pow'rs may numb, Till, halt - ing, I suc - cumb,
I read thy lin - eage well: Make Ja - cob, Is - ra - el!
The Rock, once riven for me, The Rod, that smote death's sea,

Un - til thy name I know, I will not let thee go.
But till thy name I know, I will not let thee go.
My suit till thou be - stow, I will not let thee go.
Thy bless - ing floods me so, O, Lord! I let thee go!

REV. J E. RANKIN, D. D.

Copyright, 1895, by Earnest Carter

657

## 708 TURNER.

MISS LILLIE M. FORRESTER.

Dedicated to the Ministers and Missionaries of the Arkansas Conferences.

1. On the shore be-yond the sea, Where the fields are bright and fair,
2. Just be - yond the roll-ing tide The up - lift - ed hand I see;
3. Fa-ther, moth - er, dar-ling child, I must bid you all a - dieu,
4. Bear me on, thou rest-less sea, Let the winds the can-vas swell,

There's a call, a plain-tive plea, I must hast - en to be there.
Lo! the gates are o - pen wide, And the lost are call-ing me.
Far a - way, in Af-ric's wild's, There's a work for me to do.
Af - ric's shores I long to see, Dear - est friend, fare-well, fare - well.

O, let me go,.............. I can - not stay,.............. It is the
O, let me go, I can not stay,

Mas - - - ter call-ing me;.......... Let me go........... I must o -
Master call-ing me, It is the Master calling me; Let me go,

bey,.............. My na-tive land................ fare-well to thee, farewell to thee.
I must o-bey, My na-tive land,

**709** ANVERN. L. M.

1. The Lord's an-noint-ed, O ye kings Touch not; no harm his prophets do. What if the wa-ter of your springs They drink? Your good-ly land pass thro'? They drink? Your good-ly land pass thro'?

2 The majesty, they represent
Of him who is enthroned on high,
Whose shimmering beams so widely sent
Are seen by all beneath the sky.

3 His purposes of peace and love
They represent to Adam's race,
God's angels they, sent from above,
The messengers of unsought grace.

4 The Lord's anointed, foolish kings
Touch not; no harm his prophets do.
What if the water of your springs
They drink? Your goodly land pass thro?

5 All are of God, the springs, the land,
The anointed, prophets, and kings, too,—
All, all the work of his own hand.
Give him ye all, the obeisance due.
*Bishop Tanner.*

**710** L. M.
" *In thy presence is fullness of joy.*"—
*Michtam of David.*

1 I sing the presence of my Lord,
The presence promised in his word
To all who will the door unlock,
To all who hear the heavenly knock.

2 Come in, come in, thou Guest divine,
And make my gloomy heart to shine

My cold and frozen heart to glow,
And waters from the rock to flow.

3 And yet, I've naught to offer thee,
As thou, dear Lord canst plainly see;
No milk, no honey and no wine,
Only an open door is mine.
*Bishop Tanner.*

**711** *Death no more a foe.* L. M.

1 Death is no more among our foes
Since Christ, the mighty Conqueror, rose;
Both power and sting the Saviour broke;
He died, and gave the finished stroke.

2 Soon shall the earth's remotest bound
Feel the archangel's trumpet sound:
Then shall the grave's dark cavern shake,
And joyful all the saints shall wake.

3 Bodies and souls shall then unite,
Arrayed in glory, strong and bright,
And all his saints will Jesus bring
His face to see, his love to sing.

4 Oh, may I live with Jesus nigh,
And sleep in Jesus when I die;
Then, joyful, when from death I wake,
I shall eternal bliss partake.
*Anon.*

# SUPPLEMENT.

**712  WELLS. L. M.**

ISRAEL HOLDROYD.

1. God of e - ter - ni - ty, from thee Did in - fant Time its be - ing draw;

Mo-ments, and days, and months, and years, Re-volve, by thine un - var - ied law.

L. M.

1 God of eternity, from thee
Did infant Time its being draw;
Moments, and days, and months, and years,
Revolve, by thine unvaried law.

2 Silent and slow, they glide away;
Steady and strong the current flows,
Lost in eternity's wide sea—
The boundless gulf from whence it rose.

3 With it the thoughtless sons of men
Before the rapid stream are borne
On to that everlasting home,
Whence not one soul can e'er return.

4 Great Source of wisdom, teach my heart
To know the price of every hour,
That time may bear me on to joys
Beyond its measure and its power.
*Doddridge.*

**713**                                    L. M.

1 God calling yet! shall I not hear?
Earth's pleasures shall I still hold dear?
Shall life's swift passing years all fly,
And still my soul in slumbers lie?

2 God calling yet! shall I not rise?
Can I his loving voice despise,
And basely his kind care repay?
He calls me still: can I delay?

3 God calling yet! and shall he knock,
And I my heart the closer lock?

He still is waiting to receive,
And shall I dare his Spirit grieve?

4 God calling yet! and shall I give
No heed, but still in bondage live?
I wait, but he does not forsake;
He calls me still; my heart, awake!

5 God calling yet! I cannot stay;
My heart I yield without delay:
Vain world, farewell! from thee I part;
The voice of God hath reached my heart.
*Tersteegen.*

**714**                                    L. M.

1 How vast the treasure we possess,
How rich thy bounty, King of grace!
This world is ours, and worlds to come;
Earth is our lodge, and heaven our home.

2 All things are ours, the gifts of God,
The purchase of a Saviour's blood;
While the good Spirit shows us how
To use and to improve them too.

3 If peace and plenty crown my days,
They help me, Lord, to speak thy praise;
If bread of sorrow be my food,
Those sorrows work my lasting good.

4 I would not change my blest estate
For all the world calls good or great;
And while my faith can keep her hold,
I envy not the sinner's gold.

**715  CLIFFORD.  C. M.**  GREATOREX COLL.

1. Daugh-ter of Zi - on, from the dust Ex - alt thy fall - en head;

A - gain in thy Re-deem - er trust; He calls thee from the dead.

---

*The Church Comforted.*  C. M.

1 Daughter of Zion, from the dust
Exalt thy fallen head;
Again in thy Redeemer trust;
He calls thee from the dead.

2 Awake, awake, put on thy strength,
Thy beautiful array;
The day of freedom dawns at length,
The Lord's appointed day.

3 Rebuild thy walls, thy bounds enlarge,
And send thy heralds forth;
Say to the south—"Give up thy charge,
And keep not back, O north!"

4 They come, they come;—thine exiled
bands,
Where'er they rest or roam,
Have heard thy voice in distant lands,
And hasten to their home.

5 Thus, though the universe shall burn,
And God his works destroy,
With songs thy ransomed shall return,
And everlasting joy.
*Montgomery.*

**716**  *Prayer for a Revival.*  C. M.

1 Come, Lord, in mercy come again,
With thy converting power;
The fields of Zion thirst for rain,
O send a gracious shower!

2 Our hearts are filled with sore distress,
While sinners all around
Are pressing on to endless death,
And no relief is found.

3 Dear Saviour, come with quickening pow'r,
Thy mourning people cry;
Salvation bring in mercy's hour,
Nor let the sinner die.

4 Once more let converts throng thy house,
And shouts of victory raise;
Then shall our griefs be turned to joy,
And sighs to songs of praise.
*Anon.*

**717**  *Let her rejoice.*  C. M.

1 Let Zion and her sons rejoice—
Behold the promised hour!
Her God hath heard her mourning voice,
And comes to exalt his power.

2 Her dust and ruins that remain
Are precious in our eyes;
Those ruins shall be built again,
And all that dust shall rise.

3 The Lord will raise Jerusalem,
And stand in glory there;
Nations shall bow before his name,
And kings attend with fear.

4 He frees the soul condemned to death,
Nor, when his saints complain,
Shall it be said that praying breath
Was ever spent in vain.

5 This shall be known when we are dead,
And left on long record,
That nations yet unborn may read,
And trust and praise the Lord.
*Watts.*

**718 GAYLORD. 8s & 7s. Double.**  ARR. BY. J. P. HOLBROOK.

1. Sa-viour, vis - it thy plan - ta - tion, Grant us, Lord, a gra - cious rain;
2. Keep no long - er at a dis - tance, Shine up - on us from on high,
3. Let our mut - ual love be fer - vent, Make us prev - a - lent in pray'rs;
4. Break the temp - ter's fa - tal pow - er Turn the ston - y heart to flesh;

S.                                                    FINE.

All will come to des - o - la - tion, Un - less thou re - turn a - gain.
Lest for want of thine as - sist - ance, Ev - ery plant should droop and die.
Let each one es-teemed thy ser - vant, Shun the world's be - witch - ing snares.
And be - gin from this good hour, To re - vive thy work a - fresh.

D.S.-Lord, re - vive us, Lord, re - vive us; All our help must come from thee.

D.S.

Lord, re - vive us, Lord, re - vive us; All our help must come from thee;

NEWTON.

**719 JUST NOW.**

1. Come to Je - sus, Come to Je - sus, Come to Je - sus just now,

Just now come to Je - sus, Come to Je - sus just now.

2 He will save you.
3 Oh, believe him.
4 He is able.
5 He is willing.
6 He'll receive you.

7 Call upon him.
8 He will hear you.
9 Look unto him.
10 He'll forgive you.
11 Flee to Jesus.

12 Only trust him.
13 Jesus loves you.
14 Don't reject him.
15 I believe him.
16 Hallelujah, Amen.

720 KENTUCKY. S. M.                                        JEREMIAH INGALLS.

1. Lord God, the Ho - ly Ghost! In this ac - cept - ed hour,

As on the day of Pen - te - cost, De-scend in all thy power.

---

720          *The day of Pentecost.*          S. M.

1 Lord God, the Holy Ghost!
   In this accepted hour,
   As on the day of Pentecost,
   Descend in all thy power.

2 We meet with one accord
   In our appointed place,
   And wait the promise of our Lord,—
   The Spirit of all grace.

3 Like mighty rushing wind
   Upon the waves beneath,
   Move with one impulse every mind;
   One soul, one feeling breathe.

4 The young, the old, inspire
   With wisdom from above;
   And give us hearts and tongues of fire,
   To pray, and praise, and love.

5 Spirit of light, explore,
   And chase our gloom away.—
   With lustre shining more and more
   Unto the perfect day.

6 Spirit of truth, be thou,
   In life and death, our guide;
   O Spirit of adoption, now
   May we be sanctified.

---

721          *All-sufficiency of His grace.*          S. M.

1 Jesus, my Lord, my God,
   Thy promise I embrace;
   And hail, beneath the Father's rod,
   Thy all-sufficient grace.

2 My oft-repeated prayer
   The kindest answer gains,
   When, by thy gracious aid, I bear
   Life's keen and varied pains.

3 Should dread of want oppress,
   And men or fiends assail,—
   Infirmities my frame oppress,
   And earthly comforts fail,—

4 Still may I trust in thee,
   And calm each rising fear;
   For none of these can injure me
   While thou, O Christ, art near.

5 My faith as gold refine;
   Each grace and virtue prove;
   That in my spotless life may shine
   The light of perfect love.

6 Thus shall thy mighty power
   Upon thy servant rest;
   Who glories in the trying hour,
   By thee upheld and blest.

**722  YOAKLEY. L. M. 6 lines.**

1. Thou, Lord, on whom I still de-pend, Shalt keep me faith-ful to the end:

I trust thy truth, and love, and pow'r, Shall save me till my lat-est hour;

And when I lay this bod-y down, Re-ward with an im-mor-tal crown.

L. M. 6 lines.

*The final conquest explains all mysteries.*

1 Thou, Lord, on whom I still depend,
  Shalt keep me faithful to the end :
  I trust thy truth, and love, and power,
  Shall save me till my latest hour;
  And when I lay this body down,
  Reward with an immortal crown.

2 Jesus, in thy great name I go,
  To conquer death, my final foe;
  And when I quit this cumbrous clay,
  And soar on angels' wings away,
  My soul the second death defies,
  And reigns eternal in the skies.

3 Eye hath not seen, nor ear hath heard,
  What Christ has for his saints prepared,
  Who conquer through their Saviour's might,
  Who sink into perfection's height,
  And trample death beneath their feet,
  And gladly die their Lord to meet.

4 Dost thou desire to know or see
  What thy mysterious name shall be ?
  Contending for thy heavenly home,
  Thy latest foe in death o'ercome;—
  Till then thou searchest out in vain,
  What only conquest can explain.

**723**  *Delight in the word.*  L. M. 6 lines.

1 When quiet in my house I sit,
  Thy book be my companion still ;
  My joy thy sayings to repeat,—
  Talk o'er the records of thy will.
  And search the oracles divine,
  Till every heartfelt word be mine.

2 O may the gracious words divine,
  Subject of all my converse be;
  So will the Lord his foll'wer join,
  And walk and talk himself with me :
  So shall my heart his presence prove,
  And burn with everlasting love.

3 Oft as I lay me down to rest,
  O may the reconciling word
  Sweetly compose my weary breast ;
  While on the bosom of the Lord
  I sink in blissful dreams away,
  And visions of eternal day.

4 Rising to sing my Saviour's praise,
  Thee may I publish all day long :
  And let thy precious word of grace
  Flow from my heart, and fill my tongue:
  Fill all my life with purest love,
  And join me to the church above.

**724 TRIUMPH. 8s & 7s.**

1. Cast thy bread up-on the wa-ters, Think-ing not 'tis thrown a-way; God him-self saith, thou shalt gather It a-gain some fu-ture day.

*Benevolent Efforts.* 8s & 7s.
*Eccl. xi: 1.*

1 Cast thy bread upon the waters,
Thinking not 'tis thrown away;
God himself saith, thou shalt gather
It again some future day.

2 Cast thy bread upon the waters,
Wildly though the billows roll,
They but aid thee as thou toilest
Truth to spread from pole to pole.

3 As the seed, by billows floated,
To some distant island lone,
So to human souls benighted,
That thou flingest may be borne.

4 Cast thy bread upon the waters;
Why wilt thou still doubting stand?
Bounteous shall God send the harvest,
If thou sow'st with liberal hand.

5 Give then freely of thy substance—
O'er this cause the Lord doth reign;
Cast thy bread, and toil with patience,
Thou shalt labor not in vain.

*Anon.*

**725** *"Brother's Keeper."* 8s & 7s.
*Gen. iv: 9.*

1 Blessed angels, high in heaven
O'er the penitent rejoice;
Hast thou for thy brother striven
With an importuning voice?

2 Art thou not thy brother's keeper?
Canst thou not his soul obtain?
He that wakes his brother sleeper
Double light himself shall gain.

3 Then, when ends this life's short fever,
They, who many turn to God,
Like the stars shall shine for ever,
In eternal brotherhood!

*Anon.*

**726** *Courage.* 8s & 7s.

1 Father, hear the prayer we offer!
Not for ease that prayer shall be,
But for strength that we may ever
Live our lives courageously.

2 Not forever by still waters
Would we idly quiet stay;
But would smite the living fountains
From the rocks along our way.

3 Be our strength in hours of weakness,
In our wanderings, be our guide;
Through endeavor, failure, danger,
Father, be thou at our side!

*Anon.*

**727** *Success from God.* 8s & 7s.
*1 Cor. iii: 6.*

1 Vain were all our toil and labor,
Did not God that labor bless;
Vain, without his grace and favor,
Every talent we possess.

2 Vainer still the hope of heaven,
That on human strength relies;
But to him shall help be given,
Who in humble faith applies.

3 Seek we, then, the Lord's Anointed;
He shall grant us peace and rest:
Ne'er was suppliant disappointed,
Who through Christ his prayer addressed.

*Lyte.*

365

SUPPLEMENT.

**728 DICKERSON.**

1. Oh, may the days of child-hood Be ev-er free from care,

Like song-sters in the wild-wood, Sing prais-es ev-'ry-where.

Let chil-dren sing the glo-ry Of God, the heav'n-ly King,

And tell the same "old sto-ry" Of Christ's own of-fer-ing.

*Ritard.* *Repeat pp.*

2 Let children feel they're wanted
To labor, love and pray,
To fight the foe undaunted
In childhood's early day.
Each child what e'er his station,
Can take an active part
To save a heathen nation,
To purify their heart.

3 Then children send the "story"
Across the mighty sea,
'Twill gain a crown of glory
For all eternity.
Then let the days of childhood
Be ever free from care,
Like songsters in the wildwood,
Sing praises everywhere.

*Rev. J. S. Thompson.*

366

# Selections for Educational, Festive, and Special Occasions.

**729 GAINES.**

MRS. M. E. MOSSELL, 1884.

*Moderato.*

1. Al-ma ma-ter, years have rolled Since we 'neath thy gentle rule,
2. Welcome, thrice I bid you come, Al - ma ma-ter calls to - day,

Asked that we, untaught, might hold Pla - ces in fair wis-dom's school,
Hast-en! hast-en! there is room, Why let fear your steps de - lay?

*tempo.*

Asked that we, untaught, might hold Pla - ces in fair wisdom's school.
Hast-en! hast-en! there is room, Why let fear your steps de - lay?

3 If in darkness or in doubt,
Seeking life's great end in vain,
||: Alma mater leads us out,
Makes the path of duty plain. :||

4 Have we ever friendless been?
Failure's foot-steps ever near?
||: Faithful Alma mater then,
Strengthens us in every fear. :||

5 Alma mater's voice we hear,
"Work in wisdom's school is done,
||: In the wide world, waste and drear,
Do the right and fear ye none." :||

6 Honor God and lift up man,
In the freedom of Christ's grace,
||: Preach the great salvation's plan
Unto kindred, tongue and race. :||

*A. H. Mevs.*

367

# SUPPLEMENT.

**730 LEE.**

Music composed by PROF. C. A. WHITE, of Wilberforce Concert Company.

*Andantino.* **p**

1. Soft - ly sing our part - ing lay, Vol - ume four we close to - day;

*f*     *rit.*     **p**

As - pi - ra - tion, cour - age, cheer, All are found re - cord - ed here.

TRIO. **p**     *f*

Lay this treas - ured book a - side, Oth - er vol - umes o - pen wide,

*f*     *rit.*

Rend we must our mu - tual bond, Grasp a - lone the more be - yond.

2 Grasping things to us now sealed,
Hidden truths will be revealed;
Myriad wonders meet our eyes,
Minds to higher levels rise.
We would lighten others' cares,
Lift them heavenward unawares;
Not for self alone would live,
Much received, would freely give.

3 Comrades, faint not, do not tire,
After nobler things aspire;
Ever onward, ne'er despond.
This our signal "More beyond."
Glorious race may each one run,
Priceless plaudits hear—"Well done,
Lay then every burden down,
Welcome, victor, wear thy crown."

— *Mrs. A. M. Adams.*

**731 OUR FATHERS' CHURCH.**

REV. L. J. COPPIN.

Respectfully Dedicated to the Children of the A. M. E. Church by the Author and Composer.

*Allegretto.*

1. We are the child - ren of the church, Our moth - ers reared by pray'r,
2. Strong are its mas - sive gates and wide, Its walls a tower - ing pile ;
3. Numerous its peo - ple as the stars, As pledged in days of old ;

The church our fa-thers for - ti - fied, By faith and man - ly care.
A - like im - preg - na - ble to all Who would its courts de - file.
And will be as the count - less sand, A num - ber yet un - told.

REFRAIN.

Our fath - ers' church,—our moth-ers' church— Is just the church for me ;

Our fa-thers' church—our moth-ers' church—Mine ev - er - more shall be.

4 And stirred it is by lofty aims,
  Of love toward man and God,
  And will be till the world accepts
  Messiah's staff and rod.

5 How glorious then this heritage,
  Burdened with storied wealth,
  Enriching us and all mankind
  With life, and peace, and health.

6 Already in our youthful days
  We children prize the gift
  That comes with gracious promises,
  Our trodden race t'-uplift.

7 As gathered on this Children's Day
  We at its altars vow,
  To mark its bulwarks, tell its towers,
  And hold our place as now.

*Rev. B. T. Tanner, D. D.*

**732 QUINN.**

MISS M. E. CHURCH.

1. Come, classmates, gath - er once a - gain, to sing our part - ing song,

Our school-days' sun is set - ting west, the shad - ows grow - ing long.

Our Al - ma Ma - ter's praise we sing, the pleas-ure and the joy,

The good re-ceived, the les - sons learned, that Time can ne'er de - stroy.

2 Life calls us forth to sterner tasks, bids each one dare and do,
   With heart and hand what Duty sets, her highest prize pursue.
   To teach and preach and live her Truth, to spread the Right abroad,
   To lift our erring human race, toward Truth and Right and God.

3 Courageous look ye forward then, from dangers never fly,
   Heed Duty's clarion trumpet call, and answer "Here am I,"
   Though leagues will soon divide our band, we're bound by friendship's spell:
   Friends, teachers, classmates, once again, a long, a last farewell.

*Miss A. H. Jones.*

370

**733 PAYNE.**

ARR. BY MRS. BERTHA B. COOK.

Sung at Jacksonville, Fla., Feb. 24th, 1891. Celebration of the Eightieth birthday of Bishop
Daniel A. Payne, D. D., LL. D.

*With feeling.*

1. Lord,  we  lift  our  hearts  to  thee,  Let  our

song  ac · cept · ed  be...........  We  would  thank  thee

for  this  day  Let  thy  pres · ence  with  us  stay.

1 Lord we lift our hearts to thee,
Let our song accepted be.
We would thank thee for this day,
Let thy presence with us stay.

2 As thou didst thy Samuel call,
Made on him thy Spirit fall;
So was called this righteous man,
For our leader in the van.

3 He a soldier, brave and strong,
Firmly stood against the wrong;
Fighting darkness with his might,
Striving for the truth and light.

4 Blooming like the almond tree,
His reveren'd head in whiteness see!

Worn and well spent in the race,
Ripened in God's love and grace.

5 All our blessings come from thee,
Help us this great gift to see.
He who doth thy law obey,
Casts a shadow o'er the way.

6 To encourage us to go,
On our journey here below,
Trusting in thy might alone,
Making thy blest will our own.

7 O, we praise thee for this day,
Gracious Lord, and we pray
That we consecrated be,
As this veteran was to thee.

*Mrs. M. E. Lee.*

371

# SUPPLEMENT.

## 734 HENDERSON.

The A. M. E. Church Rallying Song.

ROBERT LOWRY.

1. A song, I'll sing to you, of men both good and true, Who
2. 'Twas Rich-ard Al-len brave, a leg-a-cy who gave Of
3. The west-ern work be-gan, by Quinn a no-ble son, Who

la-bored, bat-tling for the right: With righteous-ness and truth, they
free-dom and of cour-age true: Then Brown and Wa-ters came, with
la-bored, preaching night and day; Then Naz-rey took the field, and

start-ed in their youth, And nev-er faint-ed in the fight.
heart and mind the same, And laid down work for us to do.
Payne, with might-y zeal, Did go forth light-ing up the way.

### CHORUS.

"Oh! the church is mov-ing on, the church is mov-ing on, From

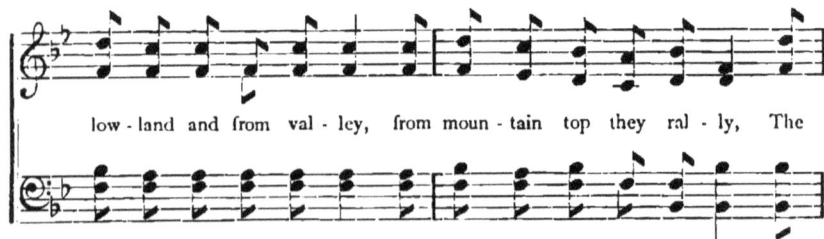

low-land and from val-ley, from moun-tain top they ral-ly, The

Used by Permission.

372

bat - tle bow is strung, the ban - ner is out - flung, And

gi - ant wrong no more is strong, for the church is . mov - ing on."

4 Then Wayman entered in, and Campbell did begin
To send forth words of truth and might;
And Shorter, Ward, and Brown, did labor for the crown,
And ceased not struggling for the right.—CHO.

5 Of Turner next we sing, a mighty host did bring
Of loyal men and women too,
And Dickerson and Cain, who did not long remain,
Are resting with the tried and true.—CHO.

6 Then Disney from afar, with mighty men of war,
Did cry out, from across the sea;
Our only daughter came, and we with heart aflame,
Will help her good and true to be.—CHO.

7 With Gains and Arnett's force, we'll keep our steady course,
And millions bring into the fold,
With Tanner and with Grant, we never will recant,
The landmarks set by men of old.—CHO.

8 And next we sing of Lee, and Salters like as he,
Will labor bringing souls to God:
And Handy, brave and true, a mighty work will do,
By trusting in his holy word.—CHO.

9 Of Derrick now we sing, and Armstrong, too, we bring,
And number with the royal band;
And Embry, gone before, to meet upon the shore,
The loved ones in the glory land.—CHO.

*L. J. Coppin.*

**735 SHORTER.**

REV. L. J. COPPIN.

1. My in fant, Lord, to thee I glad-ly bring, She is of earth, and
2. A bird-ling, I would teach its ti-ny wings To soar up, where each
3. But thou, and thou a-lone, canst give it might To spread her wings for
4. Then come, oh, come, my ba-by take and train For life's great work! She

yet a heav'n-ly thing; As the nude bird-ling in its moth-er's nest,
bright arch-an-gel sings, To join the songs of flam-ing ser-a-phim;
reg-ions out of sight; To nes-tle in the glo-ries of a throne;
must not live in vain; Of mun-dane birth, a more than mun-dane thing,

CHORUS.

So is this ba-by on my anx-ious breast.
And with the ran-somed sing th'e-ter-nal hymn.
Which none can reach but love, and love a-lone.
To thee, O Lord, my ba-by now I bring.

Oh, like an an-gel, may she ev-er be! And think, and speak, and act thro' life for thee!

5 To thee I consecrate my helpless child,
Whose nature may be rough, and crook'd,
and wild,
If thou dost not, with plastic power divine,
Remould her in thine image, yes, in thine.

6 Breathe in her soul the life—th' eternal
life,
Nor hatred, pride, nor lust be ever rife
Within her heart; but as an angel, she
May ever feel, and speak, and act for thee.

*Bishop D. A. Payne, D. D., LL. D.*

374

**736 GRANT.**

*Moderato.*

L. J. COPPIN.

1. On-ward! on-ward! on-ward christian soldiers, Hark, 'tis the watch-word to all,
2. On-ward! on-ward! see the foe ad-vanc-ing, Fast moves the Ar-my of Sin,
3. On-ward! on-ward! man-y are in dark-ness Wait-ing the Gos-pel to hear,

Work-ing for Je-sus 'gainst the foe u-nit-ed, Come to the Mas-ter's call.
Gird on your arm-or, Je-sus is our Cap-tain, Vic-t'ry we soon shall win.
Send forth the tid-ings, lift the Gos-pel ban-ner, Je-sus will an-swer prayer.

**CHORUS.**

We are march-ing, we are march-ing on, Till the vic-to-ry is won,

marching, marching, marching, marching

We are march-ing, we are march-ing, Marching, marching must be done.

L. J. COPPIN.

marching, marching, marching, marching,

737 ARMSTRONG.

Tempo di Marcia.

J. H. ELLIOT.

1. Shout, O shout we are com - ing! Al - len's youth-ful sons Fight-ing for the
2. Shout, O shout we are com - ing! walk - ing in the way That will lead us
3. Shout, O shout we are com - ing! though our foes as - sail, We will nev - er
4. Shout, O shout we are com - ing! filled with youth-ful zeal, Life to us is
5. Shout, O shout we are com - ing! ear - nest to de - clare, Might - y is our
6. Shout, O shout we are com - ing! just be-cause we can, Beat-ing last year's

bat - tles he so well nigh won, De - ter - mined to press for - ward,
on - ward, to a glo - rious day; At our head are march - ing;
cow - er nor be - fore them quail; For Camp - bell and Dis - ney,
ear - nest, as it's al - so real; On the heights of glo - ry
pur - pose, strong to do and dare; Hear our new com-mand - ers
rec - ord, though it was very grand. Hear the two com-mand - ers who

the work he be - gan, Hav - ing for its ba - sis the "Broth-er-hood of man."
Payne and Wayman grand, These, in part, the lead - ers of our glo - ri - ous band.
might - y in a fray, Will, with truth's two-edged sword, soon make clear the way.
we be - hold the crown, Which has oft been told us by Ward and Brown.
shout - ing o'er the plains! 'Tis the voice of Turn - er, Ar - nett and Gaines.
nev - er say "I can't!" One is Bis - hop Tan - ner, the o - ther Bis - hop Grant.

CHORUS.

mf

Shout! shout! we're coming, Al - len's sons, Shout! shout! we're coming, one by one;

f

p

Shout! shout! we're coming, hear our cry— Christ is our captain and vict - 'ry's nigh.

REV. C. S. SMITH.

376

## 738 WAYMAN.

REV. L. J. COPPIN.

1. The friends of Christian Education call, The friends of Missions too While darkness veils this

*rit.* *p* *tempo.*

sin-ful earthly ball, There's work for us to do, To educate aright th'immortal mind, Is

godlike, good, and grand: To give salvation to the heathen blind, Employ'd the Saviour's hand.

CHORUS. *Allegro.*

Come, chil-dren, join that ho-ly band, Who teach the hea-then what is truth,

*f* *p*

Come, chil-dren, join with heart and hand, To win from sin the err-ing youth.

2 Thrice blessed is the one who freely gives
His wealth to train the soul,
He shall be happy while on earth he lives,
And while the ages roll,
No jewel'd crown, that decks the royal brow
Of mighty queens and kings,
Shines so effulgent as the deathless fame
Of him who plans such things.

Copyright, 1892, by Theo. Gould.

3 Who trains th'immortal mind for its grand
Towards the throne of God; [flight!
Who makes it think and speak and act
As did the Christ, does good, [aright.
Th'angelic guard behind him ever walks,
Th'angelic guard before;
Wisdom inspires him as he grandly talks
And guides him evermore.

*Bishop D. A. Payne.*

**739 SALTERS.**

T. D. SCOTT.

1. "Scale the heights and take the ci - ty!" Means a strug - gle fierce and strong; But our ar - mor, wis - dom's teach - ing, We will gain by stu - dy long. Ig - nor - ance and acts im - mor - al, Call for sol - diers, val - iant,

2. Not the strength of bar, nor ram - part, Not the din of fran - tic war, Not the blaze of burn - ing ci - ty, Not the crash of mast nor spar, Not the blood of mar - tyred he - ro, Spilled like wa - ter through the

3. Sen - ti - ments in souls im - mor - tal Must be won on vir - tue's side; Minds per - verse and prone to e - vil Must be right - ed far and wide. With our eyes to heaven up - lift - ed, Bold - ly en - ter - ing the

378

tried; Schemes of dark - ness, deeds ap - pal - ling Must by
land; Not the voice of laws en - act - ed, Stays the
fight, "No steps back - ward," for - ward bat - tling, Con - qu'ring

**CHORUS.**

strength be put a - side.
wrong with i - ron hand. } Ours must be a peace - ful
wrong and strength'ning right.

strug - gle, Con - flict waged on men - tal strength, Win - ning

minds and souls to us - ward, Bolts and bars will fall at length.

**740  HANDY.**                                    ANNA LAURIA ARNETT.

*Moderato.*

1. Al - ma  Ma - ter, we are loath to  leave  thee;  Pleas - ures
2. Pa - tient - ly  we've wait - ed  for the  dawn - ing  Of this
3. Com - rades, take  this truth for grief's as - suag - ing—  Du - ty
4. Ties that bound  us firm - ly  soon must  sev - er,  Joys and

of  the past cling to us  still;  Pleasures decked by memory's hand with
day, so fraught with brilliant hope;  Yet re - luct - ant do  we greet the
will not compromise with tears:  Lend a  hand  till we, with pow'rs en -
woes un-numbered—who can tell;  We part with  you now, but  not for -

*ritard.*                          *tempo.*

beau - ty,  To en - trance a  faint-ing, falt'-ring will;  Pleas - ures
morn - ing  That dis - clos - es fields of broad - er  scope;  With re -
gag - ing,  Win for right those bound with er - ror's fears;  Lend a
ev - er;  Teachers, class-mates, all a  fond fare - well;  We part

*p*                          *dim.*          *pp*

decked by mem'ry's hand with beau-ty,  To entrance a  faint - ing, falt'-ring will.
luct-ance do we  greet the morn-ing  That disclos - es fields of broad-er scope.
hand till we, with pow'rs en - gag-ing,  Win for right those bound with error's fears.
with you now, but not  for - ev - er;  Teachers, classmates, all a fond fare-well.

H. P. JONES.

380

**741 DERRICK.**

"He is risen indeed." IDA M. YEOCUM.

1. Lo! the glo-rious dawn is break-ing, And the night of gloom is gone, All the earth from slum-ber wak-ing, Hails with joy the Eas-ter Morn! Lo! the sun's bright rays are peep-ing o-ver Cal-vary's crim-son height, Sol-dier guards who watch were keeping, Saw him rise in pow'r and might! rise in pow'r and might!

1 Lo! the glorious dawn is breaking,
  And the night of gloom is gone,
All the earth from slumber waking,
  Hails with joy the Easter Morn!
Lo! the sun's bright rays are peeping
  Over Calvary's crimson height,
Soldier guards who watch were keeping,
  Saw him rise in power and might!

2 Mary ran with footsteps fleeter,
  Than the other two that went—
Where an angel sat to greet her,
  And the grave a glory lent.
With their spices they were going,
  To the tomb where Jesus lay—
Faithful ones, without the knowing,
  Who should roll the stone away?

3 To the rich man's new sepulchre,
  Mary's eager feet drew near;
Lo, she saw the tomb was open,
  And her heart was filled with fear!

At the grave she stooped, and peeping,
  Angels saw in white arrayed,
Where her Lord was lately sleeping,
  "And the clothes aside were laid!"

4 Back she drew with fear and quaking,
  But the angel watcher said:
"Jesus is among the living,
  Seek him not among the dead."
"He is risen, he is risen,"
  Now dispel thy gloom and fear
From the grave's embrace and prison;
  Rose triumphant, "He is not here!"

5 Shout with gladdest acclamation,
  Raise with joy the gladsome sound,
And with great acceleration,
  Spread to earth's remotest bound.
He is risen! great in glory:
  Death is vanquished, lost its sting!
Vain the grave can boast of victory,
  He is risen Christ the King!

*Josie D. Heard.*

# SUPPLEMENT.

742 ARNETT.

Moderato.

H. Y. ARNETT.

1. We launch to - day on the voyage of life. The morn - ing winds are
2. We're freighted with les-sons of courage and truth, With mem'ries of pleas - ant
3. We dread not the dark and im - pet - u - ous tides, Tho' their dangers we cannot fore-

free: Our an - chors are weighed, and our sails are set; For our
hours: In the strength of our might we will stem the gales, Tho' the
tell. With God as our Cap-tain, his truth as our chart, We sig-

CHORUS.

ha - ven be - yond the sea.
an - gry tem - pest low - ers.
nal a Hail and Fare - well.

Thou - sands have launched from this

ad lib.

self - same shore, As they sailed, so must we, But we'll

drop our an - chors side by side, When our ships come in from sea.

MISS A. H. JONES.

382

**743  MITCHELL.**

MISS MATTIE F. ROBERTS.

1. Life's o-cean spreads a-way be-fore us, Our

boats are launched up-on the deep; We pray that he who is our

*rit.*

Pi - lot From dan - ger our frail barks will keep.

1 Life's ocean spreads away before us,
  Our boats are launched upon the deep,
  We pray that he who is our pilot,
  From danger our frail barks will keep.

2 The waters are now calm and peaceful
  But we know the billows soon will dash,
  Our barks upon the raging ocean,
  When gath'ring storms its bosom lash.

3 Dear Alma Mater now we leave thee
  But thy truths are stamped upon the heart.
  Our watchword " *Esse quam videri,*"
  Shall guide us as from thee we part.

4 Oh, Sacred Mother at our parting,
  Thy blessings grant to each and all;
  May grace divine forever keep us,
  Responsive to our duty's call.

*Miss E. L. Jackson.*

**744 JESUS, LOVER OF MY SOUL.**

Sop. Solo.

J. T. LAYTON.

1. Je - sus, lov - er of my soul, Let me to thy bos - om fly, While the near - er wa - ters roll, While the tem - pest still is high; Hide me, oh, my Sav - iour hide, Till the storm of life is past;

Safe in - to the ha - ven guide; Oh, re - ceive my

soul at last.

**CHORUS.**
*Allegretto.*

2. Oth - er ref - uge have I none, Hangs my help - less soul on
4. Plen-teous grace with thee is found, Grace to cov - er all my

*rit.* *p*

thee; Leave, oh, leave me not a - lone, Still sup - port and
sin: Let the heal - ing streams a - bound; Make me, keep me,

*tempo.*

com - fort me. All my trust on thee is stayed,
pure with - in. Thou, of life, the foun - tain art,

385

All my help from thee I bring;
Cov - er my de - fence - less
Free - ly let me take of thee;
Spring thou up with - in my

head With the shad - ow of thy wing.
heart; Rise to all e - ter - ni - ty.

BASS SOLO.
Andante sostenuto.

3. Thou, O Christ, art all I want; More than
Raise the fall - en, cheer the faint,

all in thee I find. Heal the sick and

DUET.—TENOR AND ALTO.
*Moderato.*

lead the blind. *mf* Just and ho - ly is thy

name, I am all un - right - eous - ness; Vile, and

full of sin I am, Thou art full of

truth and grace.

387

**745** *Enlisting Soldiers. Rev.* vi. 2. C. M.
[Tune, Metropolitan, page 242. C. M.]

1 Hark! listen to the trumpeters,
They call for volunteers;
On Zion's bright and flow'ry mount
Behold the officers :

2 Their horses white, their armor bright,
With courage bold they stand,
Enlisting soldiers for their King,
To march to Canaan's land.

3 It sets my heart quite in a flame
A soldier thus to be :
I will enlist, gird on my arms,
And fight for liberty.

4 We want no cowards in our band
That will their colors fly :
We call for valiant-hearted men
Who're not afraid to die.

5 To see our armies on parade,
How martial they appear!
All arm'd and dress'd in uniform,
They look like men of war.

6 They follow their great General
The great eternal Lamb,
His garments stain'd in his own blood
King Jesus is his name.

7 The trumpets sound, the armies shout,
They drive the hosts of hell ;
How dreadful is our God t' adore,
The great Immanuel !

**746** *Death of a Sister.* 8s & 7s.
[Tune, Rathbun, page 28. 8s & 7s.]

1 Sister, thou wast mild and lovely,
Gentle as the summer breeze,
Pleasant as the air of evening
When it floats among the trees.

2 Peaceful be thy silent slumber,
Peaceful in the grave so low ;
Thou no more will join our number,
Thou no more our songs shall know.

3 Dearest Sister, thou hast left us
Here thy loss we deeply feel,
But 'tis God that hath bereft us,
He can all our sorrows heal.

4 Yet again we hope to meet thee,
When the day of life is fled,
Then, in heaven, with joy to greet thee,
Where no farewell tear is shed.

**747** *Bereavement and Resignation.* 8s & 7s.
[Tune, Sicily, page 286. 8s & 7s.]

1 Jesus, while our hearts are bleeding
O'er the spoils that death has won,

We would at this solemn meeting,
Calmly say—thy will be done.

2 Though cast down, we're not forsaken ;
Though afflicted, not alone :
Thou didst give, and thou hast taken ;
Blessed Lord—thy will be done.

3 Though to-day we're filled with mourning,
Mercy still is on the throne ;
With thy smiles of love returning,
We can sing,—thy will be done.

4 By thy hands the boon was given ;
Thou hast taken but thine own ;
Lord of earth, and God of heaven,
Evermore,—thy will be done.

**748** *Death of the Christian.* 8s & 7s.
[Tune, Regent Square, page 263. 8s & 7s.]

1 Cease, ye mourners, cease to languish
O'er the grave of those you love;
Pain and death, and night and anguish
||: Enter not the world above. :||

2 While our silent steps are straying,
Lonely, thro' night's deepening shade,
Glory's brightest beams are playing
||: Round the happy Christian's head. :||

3 Light and peace at once deriving
From the hand of God most high,
In his glorious presence living,
||: They shall never, never die. :||

4 Endless pleasure, pain excluding,
Sickness, there, no more can come :
There, no fear of woe, intruding,
||: Sheds o'er heav'n a moment's gloom. :||

**749** *Death of the Righteous.* L. M.
[Tune, Federal Street, page 77. L. M.]

1 How blest the righteous when he dies !
When sinks a weary soul to rest,
How mildly beam the closing eyes !
How gently heaves th' expiring breast !

2 So fades a summer cloud away;
So sinks the gale when storms are o'er;
So gently shuts the eye of day;
So dies a wave along the shore.

3 Life's duty done, as sinks the clay,
Light from its load the spirit flies;
While heaven and earth combine to say,
" How blest the righteous when he dies !"
*Barbould.*

388

SELECTIONS FOR SPECIAL OCCASIONS.

**750** COME ALL YE PEOPLE.

Tune, Coronation.—"All hail the power of Jesus Name."

1 Come all ye people great and small
And praise the Lord, your King;
Who triumphed o'er the monster death,
And took away its sting.

2 With joyous step and happy heart
Into his courts repair;
And worship in his holy sight,
And make your offering there.

3 Come worship him, who came on earth
The lost to seek and save;
And bid them fix their hope beyond
The darkness of the grave.

4 Praise him with anthems rich and sweet,
And sounds of glad refrain;
For unto us he has made known
That now to die is gain.

5 Through love divine he's unto us
A new and living way;
And may the music of his name
Fill this glad Easter-day.

*Bishop T. M. D. Ward.*

**751** PRAISE HIM YE PEOPLE.

Tune.—"There is sweet rest in heaven."

1 Oh comfort ye my people!
All sadness put away;
The bells from many a steeple
Ring in the Easter-day!

CHORUS.

Then praise him ye people,
Then praise him ye people,
Then praise him ye people,
All people great and small.

2 To-day the lilies springing
From winter's gloom and cold,
Sweet bells of Easter, ringing,
Tell the glad song of old.—*Chorus.*

3 That Christ indeed is risen,
And all his saints shall rise,
Fair flowers from death's cold prison,
To bloom in Paradise.—*Chorus.*

*Rev. C. S. Smith.*

**752** EASTER HYMN. C. M.

[Tune, Metropolitan, page 217. C. M.]

1 From out the tomb the Saviour comes,
The first of all the dead.
From out the tomb the Saviour comes,
To be our living head.

2 What is the stone, his foes have placed
To make secure the grave?

And what the great Sanhedrim seal
The priests so freely gave?

3 He must awake, he must arise,
For have not prophets said,
God's Holy One shall never share
Corruption with the dead?

4 Now see in shimmering light, he leaves
The dead, no more to die.
Conqueror of sin, and death, and hell
He re-ascends the sky.

*Dr. B. T. Tanner.*

**753** ALL HAIL THE MORN.

[Tune, Antioch, page 43. C. M.]

1 All hail the morn! when from the skies,
At the first dawn of day,
An angel found the sepulchre,
And rolled the stone away.

2 All hail the morn! when Christ arose,
Triumphant from the tomb;
And shed a fragrance o'er the grave,
And scattered all its gloom.

3 All hail the morn! when to the tomb,
The women came with fear;
And heard the angels gladly say,
"He's risen, he's not here."

4 All hail the morn! no longer fear,
For now can all men sing,
O grave, where is thy victory?
And death, where is thy sting?

*Bishop W. F. Dickerson.*

**754** CHURCH EXTENSION. L. M.

[Tune, Ward, page 272. L. M.]

1 O Lord of hosts, we seek to raise,
Houses of worship, to thy praise;
Wilt thou thy people's hearts prepare,
Who meet this day for praise and prayer.

2 And Lord, let living souls be fed,
On this glad day, with heavenly bread;
That they in hope of glories blessed,
May hence prepare, thee, earthly rest.

3 That everywhere, throughout the land,
There may to thee a temple stand;
That there proclaimed, thy mercy sure,
Shall stand, while time and man endure.

4 Jehovah, here our hearts inspire,
Baptize our souls with hallowed fire;
Bless thou thy people's work for good,
And fill thy poor, with heavenly food.

5 That songs triumphant,—earth and sky,
May joyful to the sound reply;
And hallelujahs hence ascend,
With prayer and praise, 'till time shall end.

*Rev. C. T. Shaffer.*

389

# SUPPLEMENT.

## RICHMOND NOLLEY.

**755**                *He died at his Post.*                L. M.

1 Away from his home and the friends of his youth
   He hastened, the herald of mercy and truth,
   For the love of his Lord, and to seek for the lost;
   Soon, alas! was his fall—but he died at his post.

2 The stranger's eye wept, that in life's brightest bloom
   One gifted so highly should sink to the tomb;
   For in ardor he led in the van of the host,
   And he fell like a soldier—he died at his post.

3 He wept not himself that his warfare was done—
   The battle was fought, and the victory won;
   But he whispered of those whom his heart clung to most:
   "Tell my brethren for me that I died at my post."

4 He asked not a stone to be sculptured with verse,
   He asked not that fame should his merits rehearse;
   But he asked as a boon, when he gave up the ghost,
   That his brethren might know that he died at his post.

5 Victorious his fall—for he rose as he fell,
   With Jesus, his Master, in glory to dwell;
   He has passed o'er the stream and has reached the bright coast,
   For he fell like a martyr—he died at his post.

6 And can we the words of his exit forget?
   O no! they are fresh in our memory yet:
   An example so brilliant shall never be lost;
   We will fall in the work—we will die at our post.

                          *Hunter, Songs of Zion.*

**756** DENOMINATIONAL LOYALTY.  L. M.
   [ Tune, Federal Street, page 9.  L. M.]

1 My Saviour's name I'll gladly sing,
   He is my Captain and my King;
   Where'er I go his name I'll bless,
   And strive to live a Methodist.

2 The Devil's camp I'll bid adieu,
   And Zion's peaceful ways pursue;
   Come, sinners, join with me and list,
   And fight like valiant Methodists.

3 It is religion makes the man,
   The world may try to make it vain;
   But I would give the world for this,
   To be in heart a Methodist.

4 I am a soldier of the cross,
   All earthly things I count but dross,
   My soul is bound for endless rest,
   I'll never leave the Methodist.

5 Come now with me, and you shall know
   What a dear Saviour can bestow;
   His love to me I can't express,
   Although I'm call'd a Methodist.

6 A better church cannot be found,
   Their doctrine is both pure and sound,
   One reason which I give for this,
   The Devil hates the Methodists.

7 They're humble, loving, and sincere,
   They labor night and day in prayer;
   I hope the Lord will them increase,
   And turn the world to Methodists.

8 The world, the flesh, and Satan's crew,
   Are up in arms against us too;
   They can't prevail—the reason's this,
   The Lord defends the Methodists.

9 We shout too loud for sinners here;
   But when in heav'n we shall appear,
   Our shouts shall make the heavens ring,
   And all the saints in glory sing.

**757**     *Dismission.*    8s, 7s & 4s.

[ Tune, Zion, page 136.   8s, 7s & 4s.]

1 Lord, dismiss us with thy blessing,
Fill our hearts with joy and peace;
Let us each, thy love possessing,
Triumph in redeeming grace :
‖:Oh refresh us,
Travelling through this wilderness.:‖

2 Thanks we give, and adoration,
For thy gospel's joyful sound;
May the fruits of thy salvation
In our hearts and lives abound;
‖: May thy presence
With us evermore be found :‖

3 Then, whene'er the signal's given
Us from earth to call away,
Borne on angel's wings to heaven—
Glad the summons to obey—
‖: May we ever
Reign with Christ in endless day.:‖

*Burder.*

**758**     *Eternity in View.*    C. P. M.

[ Tune, Meribah, page 119.   C. P. M.]

1 Lo, on a narrow neck of land,
'Twixt two unbounded seas I stand;
Yet how insensible !
A point of time, a moment's space,
Removes me to yon heavenly place,
Or shuts me up in hell !

2 O God, my inmost soul convert,
And deeply on my thoughtless heart
Eternal things impress;
Give me to feel their solemn weight,
And save me ere it be too late :
Wake me to righteousness.

3 Before me place, in bright array,
The pomp of that tremendous day,
When thou with clouds shalt come
To judge the nations at thy bar;
And tell me, Lord, shall I be there,
To meet a joyful doom?

4 Be this my one great business here :
With holy trembling, holy fear,
To make my calling sure :
Thine utmost counsel to fulfill,
And suffer all thy righteous will,
And to the end endure.

5 Then, Saviour, then my soul receive,
Transported from this vale, to live
And reign with thee above ;
Where faith is sweetly lost in sight,
And hope in full, supreme delight,
And everlasting love.

*Wesley.*

**759**    *The Lord will provide.*   10,10,11,11.

1 Though troubles assail, and dangers affright,
Though friends should all fail, And foes all unite,
Yet one thing secures us, Whatever betide,
The promise assures us The Lord will provide.

2 The birds without barn Or storehouse are fed;
From them let us learn To trust for our bread:
His saints what is fitting Shall ne'er be denied,
So long as 'tis written, The Lord will provide.

3 We all may, like ships, By tempest be toss'd
On perilous deeps, But need not be lost ;
Though Satan enrages The wind and the tide,
Yet Scripture engages, The Lord will provide.

4 His call we obey, like Abrah'm of old ;
We know not the way, But faith makes us bold ;
For tho' we are strangers, We have a sure guide,
And trust in all dangers, The Lord will provide.

5 No strength of our own, Nor goodness we claim,
Our trust is all thrown On Jesus' name;
In this our strong tower For safety we hide :
The Lord is our power, The Lord will provide.

6 When life sinks apace, And death is in view,
The word of his grace Shall comfort us through :
Not fearing or doubting, With Christ on our side,
We hope to die shouting, The Lord will provide.

*Newton.*

**760**     *Departure.*    L. M.

[ Tune, Hamburg, page 280.   L. M.]

1 The hour of my departure's come,
I hear the voice that calls me home;
At last, O Lord, let trouble cease,
And let thy servant die in peace.

2 Not in mine innocence I trust;
I bow before thee in the dust;
And through my Saviour's blood alone,
I look for mercy at thy throne.

3 I leave the world without a tear,
Save for the friends I held so dear;
To heal their sorrows, Lord, descend,
And to the friendless prove a friend.

# Doxologies.

**1**     **L. M.**

Praise God, from whom all blessings flow;
Praise him, all creatures here below;
Praise him above, ye heavenly host;
Praise Father, Son, and Holy Ghost.

*T. Ken.*

**2**     **C. M.**

To Father, Son, and Holy Ghost,
  The God whom we adore,
Be glory, as it was, is now,
  And shall be evermore!

*Tate and Brady.*

**3**     **C. M. 8 lines.**

The God of mercy be adored,
  Who calls our souls from death,
Who saves by his redeeming word,
  And new-creating breath;
To praise the Father, and the Son,
  And Spirit all-divine,—
The One in Three, and Three in One,—
  Let saints and angels join.

*Isaac Watts.*

**4**     **S. M.**

To God, the Father, Son,
  And Spirit, One in Three,
Be glory, as it was, is now,
  And shall forever be.

*John Wesley.*

**5**     **L. M. 6 lines.**

Immortal honor, endless fame,
Attend the almighty Father's name,
The Saviour Son be glorified,
Who for lost man's redemption died,
And equal adoration be,
Eternal Comforter, to thee!

*John Dryden.*

**6**     **L. P. M.**

Now to the great and sacred Three,
The Father, Son, and Spirit, be
  Eternal praise and glory given,
Through all the world where God is known,
By all the angels near the throne,
  And all the saints in earth and heaven.

*Watts.*

**7**     **P. M.**

To God the Father's throne
  Your highest honors raise;
Glory to God the Son;
  To God the Spirit, praise;
With all our powers, eternal King,
Thy everlasting praise we sing.

*Isaac Watts, alt.*

**8**     **C. P. M.**

To Father, Son, and Holy Ghost,
The God whom heaven's triumphant host
  And saints on earth adore;
Be glory as in ages past,
And now it is, and so shall last,
  When time shall be no more.

*Tate and Brady.*

**9**     **7s.**

Sing we to our God above,
Praise eternal as his love;
Praise him, all ye heavenly host,
Father, Son, and Holy Ghost!

*C. Wesley.*

**10**     **7s. 6 lines.**

Praise the name of God most high;
Praise him, all below the sky;
Praise him, all ye heavenly host,
Father, Son, and Holy Ghost!
As through countless ages past,
Evermore his praise shall last.

*Unknown.*

**11**     **8s, 7s, 4s.**

Great Jehovah! we adore thee,
God the Father, God the Son,
God, the Spirit, joined in glory
  On the same eternal throne:
    Endless praises
To Jehovah, Three in One!

*William Goode.*

**12**     **8s, 7s.**

Praise the God of our salvation;
  Praise the Father's boundless love;
Praise the Lamb, our expiation;
  Praise the Spirit from above,
Author of the new creation,
  Him by whom our spirits live;
Undivided adoration
  To the one Jehovah give!

*Josiah Conder.*

# ORDER OF SERVICE.

### I.

1.—Doxology, or Prelude.

### II.

2.—*After announcing the Scripture Lesson and the Hymn, the Minister and Congregation, standing, shall read responsively the following:*

*Minister.* I was glad when they said unto me, let us go into the house of the Lord, our feet shall stand within thy gates, O Jerusalem.

*People.* For a day in thy courts is better than a thousand. I had rather be a doorkeeper in the house of my God than to dwell in the tents of wickedness.

*M.* Because of the house of the Lord our God I will seek thy good.

*P.* Those that be planted in the house of the Lord, shall flourish in the courts of our God.

*M.* Blessed are they that dwell in thy house. Lord, I have loved thy habitation, the place where thy honor dwelleth.

*P.* For the Lord is in his holy temple, let all the earth keep silence before him.

*M.* Let the words of my mouth, and the meditation of my heart, be acceptable in thy sight, O Lord, my strength and my Redeemer.

*P.* O sing unto the Lord a new song, for he has done marvelous things. Make a joyful noise unto the Lord, all the earth, and sing praises.

### III.

3.—Singing Opening Hymn. (*All sing.*)

### IV.

4.—Prayer. (*All kneeling.*)

### V.

5.—Organ Voluntary.

6.—Scripture Lessons. (*Pastor and Congregation responsively.*)

7.—Congregation arising, sing:

> "From all that dwell below the skies,
> Let the Creators's praise arise;" etc.—( *Hymn, No.* 10. )

8.—*The Congregation standing, repeating the Ten Commandments.*

And God spake all these words, saying:

### I.

*Minister.* I *am* the Lord thy God, who brought thee out of the land of Egypt, out of the house of bondage.

Thou shalt have no other gods before me.

*People.*

J. T. LAYTON.

Lord have mercy upon us, and incline our hearts to keep this law.

# ORDER OF SERVICE.

## II.

*M.* Thou shalt not make unto thee any graven image, or any likeness of *anything* that is in heaven above, or that *is* in the earth beneath, or that is in the water under the earth: thou shalt not bow down thyself to them. nor serve them: for I the LORD thy God *am* a jealous God, visiting the iniquity of the fathers upon the children unto the third and fourth *generation* of them that hate me; and showing mercy upon thousands of them that love me, and keep my commandments.

*P.* Lord have mercy upon us, and incline our hearts to keep this law.

## III.

*M.* Thou shalt not take the name of the Lord thy God in vain: for the Lord will not hold him guiltless that taketh his name in vain.

*P.* Lord have mercy upon us, and incline our hearts to keep this law.

## IV.

*M.* Remember the Sabbath day, to keep it holy. Six days shalt thou labor and do all thy work: but the seventh day is the Sabbath of the Lord thy God: *in it* thou shalt not do any work; thou, nor thy son, nor thy daughter, thy man-servant, nor thy maid-servant, nor thy cattle, nor thy stranger that is within thy gates. For in six days the Lord made heaven and earth. the sea, and all that in them *is*, and rested the seventh day: wherefore the Lord blessed the Sabbath day, and hallowed it.

*P.* Lord have mercy upon us, and incline our hearts to keep this law.

**THATCHER. S. M.**  HANDEL.

My soul be on thy guard, Ten thous - and foes a - rise; And
hosts of sin are press - ing hard, To draw thee from the skies.

## V.

*M.* Honor thy father and thy mother: that thy days may be long upon the land which the Lord thy God giveth thee.

*P.* Lord have mercy upon us, and incline our hearts to keep this law.

## VI.

*M.* Thou shalt not kill.

*P.* Lord have mercy upon us, and incline our hearts to keep this law.

## VII.

*M.* Thou shalt not commit adultery.

*P.* Lord have mercy upon us, and incline our hearts to keep this law.

VIII.

*M.* Thou shalt not steal.

*P.* Lord have mercy upon us, and incline our hearts to keep this law.

IX

*M.* Thou shalt not bear false witness against thy neighbor.

*P.* Lord have mercy upon us, and incline our hearts to keep this law.

X.

*M.* Thou shalt not covet thy neighbor's house; thou shalt not covet thy neighbor's wife, nor his man-servant, nor his maid-servant, nor his ox, nor his ass, nor anything that is thy neighbor's.

*People.*

J. T. LAYTON.

Lord have mercy upon us, and write these laws up - on our hearts.

**BETHANY. 6, 4, 6.**

LOWELL MASON.

Near - er, my God, to thee! Near - er to thee, E'en though it be a cross

*D. S.*—Near - er, my God, to thee,

FINE.

*D. S.*

That rais - eth me; Still all my song shall be, Near - er, my God, to thee,
Near - er to thee!

*M.* Hear what Christ our Saviour saith: Thou shalt love the Lord thy God with all thy heart, and with all thy soul, and with all thy mind. This is the first and great commandment. And the second is like unto it: Thou shalt love thy neighbor as thyself. On these two commandments hang all the law and the prophets.

# ORDER OF SERVICE.

9.—Gloria Patri.

**GLORY BE TO THE FATHER.**

Glory be to the Father, and to the Son, and to the Ho - ly Ghost.

As it was in the beginning, is now, and ev - er shall be, world with - out end. A - men.

10.—Notices.

11.—The 2d Hymn by Choir and Congregation.

12.—The Sermon.

13.—Prayer. (*Chanted, all kneeling.*)

**THE LORD'S PRAYER.**

{ Our Father, who } Hallow - ed be thy Name. { Thy kingdom come. }
{ art in heaven, } { Thy will be done on }

earth, As it is in heaven. Give us this day our dai - ly bread.

ORDER OF SERVICE.

{ And forgive us our tres- } those who trespass a · gainst us. { And lead us not into }
{ passes, as we forgive } { temptation; but de · }

liv · er us from evil: { For thine is the kingdom, and } ev · er. A · men.
{ the power, and the glory, for }

14.—Singing and Collection.

Give as the Lord has prospered you.   The Lord loveth a cheerful giver.

15.—Reception of those who wish to join the church.

16.—Closing Services.

*Then shall be said the Apostles' Creed, the people standing.*

I believe in God the Father Almighty, Maker of heaven and earth; and in Jesus Christ, his only Son, our Lord, who was conceived by the Holy Ghost, born of the Virgin Mary, suffered under Pontius Pilate, was crucified, dead and buried; he descended into hell; the third day he rose from the dead; he ascended into heaven, and sitteth on the right hand of God, the Father Almighty: from thence he shall come to judge the quick and the dead.   I believe in the Holy Ghost, the Holy Catholic Church, the communion of saints, the forgiveness of sins, the resurrection of the body, and the life everlasting.

17.—Doxology and Benediction.

*The following may be used at pleasure in lieu of the Decalogue, or even with it.*

TE DEUM.

*Minister.*   We praise thee, O God; we acknowledge thee to be the Lord.

*People.*   All the earth doth worship thee, the Father everlasting.

*M.*   To thee all angels cry aloud, the heavens, and all the powers therein.

*P.*   To thee Cherubim and Seraphim continually do cry.

*M.*   Holy, holy, holy Lord God of Sabaoth.

*P.*   Heaven and earth are full of the majesty of thy glory.

397

# ORDER OF SERVICE.

*M.*  The glorious company of the Apostles praise thee.

*P.*  The goodly fellowship of the Prophets praise thee.

*M.*  The noble army of martyrs praise thee.

*P.*  The holy church throughout all the world doth acknowledge thee.

*M.*  The Father of an infinite majesty.

*P.*  Thine adorable, true and only Son.

*M.*  Also the Holy Ghost, the Comforter.

*P.*  Thou art the King of Glory, O Christ.

*M.*  Thou art the everlasting Son of the Father.

*P.*  When thou tookest upon thee to deliver man, thou didst humble thyself to be born of a virgin.

*M.*  When thou hadst overcome the sharpness of death, thou didst open the kingdom of heaven to all believers.

*P.*  Thou sittest at the right hand of God, in the Glory of the Father.

*M.*  We believe that thou shalt come to be our judge.

*P.*  We therefore pray thee, help thy servants, whom thou hast redeemed with thy precious blood.

*M.*  Make them to be numbered with thy saints in glory everlasting.

*P.*  O Lord, save thy people and bless thine heritage.

*M.*  Govern them and lift them up forever.

*P.*  Day by day we magnify thee.

*M.*  And we worship thy name ever, world without end.

*P.*  Vouchsafe, O Lord, to keep us this day without sin.

*M.*  O Lord, have mercy upon us, have mercy upon us.

*P.*  O Lord, let thy mercy be upon us, as our trust is in thee.

*M.*  O Lord, in thee have I trusted; let me never be confounded.

*Choir Chant.*  Glory be to the Father, and to the Son, and to the Holy Ghost.  As it was in the beginning, is now, and ever shall be, world without end.  Amen.

## LITANY.

*The Litany may be used on prayer-meeting occasions and such other occasions as may be deemed necessary by the minister and people in devotional services, kneeling.*

*Minister.*  O God the Father of Heaven; have mercy upon us miserable sinners.

*People.*  O God the Father of Heaven; have mercy upon us miserable sinners.

*M.*  O God the Son, Redeemer of the world; have mercy upon us miserable sinners.

*P.*  O God the Son, Redeemer of the world; have mercy upon us miserable sinners.

*M.*  O God the Holy Ghost, proceeding from the Father and the Son; have mercy upon us miserable sinners.

*P.*  O God the Holy Ghost, proceeding from the Father and the Son; have mercy upon us miserable sinners.

# ORDER OF SERVICE.

*M.* O Holy, Blessed and Glorious Trinity, three Persons and one God; have mercy upon us miserable sinners.

*P.* O Holy, Blessed and Glorious Trinity, three Persons and one God; have mercy upon us miserable sinners.

*M.* Remember not, Lord, our offenses, nor the offenses of our fore-fathers; neither take thou vengeance of our sins. Spare us, good Lord, spare thy people, whom thou hast redeemed with thy most precious blood, and be not angry with us forever.

*P.* Spare us, good Lord.

*M.* From all evil and mischief; from sin; from the crafts and assaults of the devil; from thy wrath and from everlasting damnation,

*P.* Good Lord, deliver us.

*M.* From all blindness of heart; from pride's vain glory and hypocrisy; from envy, hatred and malice, and all uncharitableness,

*P.* Good Lord, deliver us.

*M.* From all inordinate and sinful affections; and from all the deceits of the world, the flesh and the devil,

*P.* Good Lord, deliver us.

*M.* From lightning and tempest; from plague, pestilence and famine; from battle and murder, and from sudden death,

*P.* Good Lord, deliver us.

*M.* From all sedition, privy conspiracy, and rebellion; from all false doctrine, heresy and schism; from hardness of heart, and contempt of thy word and commandment,

*P.* Good Lord, deliver us.

*M.* By the mystery of thy holy Incarnation; by thy holy Nativity and Circumcision; by thy Baptism, Fasting and Temptation,

*P.* Good Lord, deliver us.

*M.* By thine agony and bloody sweat; by thy cross and passion; by thy precious Death and Burial; by thy glorious Resurrection and Ascension; and by the coming of the Holy Ghost,

*P.* Good Lord, deliver us.

*M.* In all time of our tribulation; in all time of our prosperity; in the hour of death, and in the day of judgment,

*P.* Good Lord, deliver us.

*M.* We sinners do beseech thee to hear us, O Lord God, and that it may please thee to rule and govern thy holy church universal in the right way;

*P.* We beseech thee to hear us, good Lord.

*M.* That it may please thee to bless and preserve all Christian rulers; and magistrates; give them grace to execute justice, and to maintain truth;

*P.* We beseech thee to hear us, good Lord.

*M.* That it may please thee to illuminate all Bishops, Elders, and Deacons, with true knowledge and understanding of thy word; and that both by their preaching and their living they may set it forth, and show it accordingly;

*P.* We beseech thee to hear us, good Lord.

*M.* That it may please thee to bless and keep all thy people;

*P.* We beseech thee to hear us, good Lord.

# ORDER OF SERVICE.

*M.* That it may please thee to give all nations unity, peace and concord;

*P.* We beseech thee to hear us, good Lord.

*M.* That it may please thee to give us an heart to love and fear thee, and diligently to live after thy commandments;

*P.* We beseech thee to hear us, good Lord.

*M.* That it may please thee to give to all thy people increase of grace: to hear meekly thy word, and to receive it with pure affection, and to bring forth the fruits of the Spirit;

*P.* We beseech thee to hear us, good Lord.

*M.* That it may please thee to bring into the way of truth all such as have erred, and are deceived;

*P.* We beseech thee to hear us, good Lord.

*M.* That it may please thee to strengthen such as do stand, and to comfort and help the weak-hearted, and to raise up those who fall, and finally to break down Satan under our feet;

*P.* We beseech thee to hear us, good Lord.

*M.* That it may please thee to succor, help and comfort all who are in danger, necessity and tribulation;

*P.* We beseech thee to hear us, good Lord.

*M.* That it may please thee to preserve all who travel by land or by water, all women in the perils of childbirth, all sick persons and young children, and to show thy pity upon all prisoners and captives;

*P.* We beseech thee to hear us, good Lord.

*M.* That it may please thee to defend and provide for the fatherless children and widows, and all who are desolate and oppressed;

*P.* We beseech thee to hear us, good Lord,

*M.* That it may please thee to have mercy upon all men;

*P.* We beseech thee to hear us, good Lord,

*M.* That it may please thee to forgive our enemies, persecutors and slanderers, and to turn their hearts;

*P.* We beseech thee to hear us, good Lord.

*M.* That it may please thee to give and preserve to our use the kindly fruits of the earth, so that in due time we may enjoy them;

*P.* We beseech thee to hear us, good Lord.

*M.* That it may please thee to give us true repentance, and to forgive all our sins, negligences and ignorances, and to endue us with the grace of thy Holy Spirit, to amend our lives according to thy holy Word;

*P.* We beseech thee to hear us, good Lord.

*M.* Son of God, we beseech thee to hear us;

*P.* Son of God, we beseech thee to hear us.

*M.* O Lamb of God, who takest away the sins of the world;

*P.* Grant us peace.

*M.* O Lamb of God, who takest away the sins of the world;

*P.* Have mercy upon us.

*Choir chant.* Glory be to the Father, and to the Son, and to the Holy Ghost. As it was in the beginning, is now, and ever shall be, world without end. Amen.

# BAPTISM OF INFANTS.

1. Let every adult person, and the parents of every child to be baptized, have their choice either of immersion, sprinkling, or pouring. But in no case shall our ministers re-baptize any person. And if any knowingly violate this prohibition, he shall be subject to suspension or location as the Annual Conference may judge.

2. We will on no account whatever make a charge for administering baptism, or for burying the dead.

## EXHORTATION.

*The minister coming to the font, which is to be filled with pure water, shall use the following, or some other exhortation suitable to the sacred office.*

Dearly beloved, forasmuch as all men are conceived and born in sin, and that our Saviour Christ, saith, "None can enter into the kingdom of God, except he be regenerated and born anew of water and of the Holy Ghost," I beseech you to call upon God the Father, through our Lord Jesus Christ, that of his bounteous mercy he will grant to this child that thing which by nature it cannot have, that it may be baptized with water and the Holy Ghost, and received into Christ's holy church, and be made a *lively* member of the same.

## PRAYER OF SANCTIFICATION.

*Then shall the minister say:*

Let us pray.

Almighty and everlasting God, who of thy great mercy didst save Noah and his family in the ark, from perishing by water, and also didst safely lead the children of Israel, thy people, through the Red Sea, figuring thereby thy holy baptism; and by the baptism of thy well beloved Son, Jesus Christ, in the river of Jordan, didst sanctify water for this holy sacrament, we beseech thee of thine infinite mercies, that thou wouldst look upon this child; wash him, and sanctify him with the Holy Ghost, that he being received into the ark of Christ's Church, and being steadfast in faith, joyful through hope, and rooted in love, may so pass the waves of this troublesome world, that finally he may come to the land of everlasting life; there to reign with thee, world without end, through Jesus Christ our Lord. Amen.

O merciful God, grant that the old Adam in this child may be so buried, that the new man may be raised in him. Amen.

Grant that all carnal affections may die in him, and that all things belonging to the Spirit may live and grow in him. Amen.

Grant that he may have the power and strength to have victory, and to triumph against the devil, the world, and the flesh. Amen.

Grant that whosoever is dedicated to thee by our office and ministry, may also be endued with heavenly virtues, and everlastingly rewarded through thy mercy, O blessed Lord God, who dost live, and govern all things, world without end. Amen.

401

# BAPTISM OF INFANTS.

Almighty, everliving God, whose most dearly beloved Son, Jesus Christ, for the forgivness of our sins, didst shed out of his most precious side both water and blood, and gave commandment to his disciples that they should go teach all nations, and baptize them in the name of the Father, and of the Son, and of the Holy Ghost; regard, we beseech thee, the supplications of thy congregation, sanctify this water for this holy sacrament, and grant that this child, now to be baptized, may receive the fullness of thy grace, and ever remain in the number of thy faithful and elect children, through Jesus Christ our Lord. Amen.

## ADDRESS TO PARENTS OR GUARDIANS.

DEARLY BELOVED: Forasmuch as this child is now presented by you for Christian baptism, you must remember that it is your part and duty to see that *he* be taught, as soon as *he* shall be able to learn, the nature and end of this holy sacrament. And that *he* may know these things the better, you shall call upon *him* to give regular attendance upon the appointed means of grace, such as the ministry of the Word and the public and private worship of God; and further, you shall provide that *he* shall read the Holy Scriptures, and learn the Lord's Prayer, the Ten Commandments, the Apostles' Creed, the Catechism, and all other things which a Christian ought to know and believe to his soul's health, in order that *he* may be brought up to lead a virtuous and holy life, remembering always that baptism doth represent unto us that inward purity which disposeth us to follow the example of our Saviour Christ. That as he died and rose again for us, so should we, who are baptized, die unto sin and rise again unto righteousness, continually mortifying all corrupt affections and daily proceeding in all virtue and godliness. Do you therefore solemnly engage to fulfill these duties so far as it lieth in your power, the Lord being your helper?

*Answer.*—We do.

## THE CEREMONY.

*Then shall the people stand up, and the minister shall say:*

Hear the words of the Gospel written by St. Mark, in the tenth chapter, at the thirteenth verse:

"They brought young children to Christ, that he should touch them; and his disciples rebuked those that brought them; but when Jesus saw it, he was much displeased, and said unto them, Suffer little children to come unto me, and forbid them not, for of such is the kingdom of God. Verily I say unto you, whosoever shall not receive the kingdom of God as a little child, he shall not enter therein. And he took them up in his arms, put his hands upon them, and blessed them."

*And the minister shall take the child into his hands, and say to the friends of the child:*

Name this child.

*And then naming it after them, he shall sprinkle or pour water upon it, or, if desired, immerse it in water, saying:*

N., I baptize thee in the name of the Father, and of the Son, and of the Holy Ghost. Amen.

## THE LORD'S PRAYER.

*Then shall be said, all kneeling:*

Our Father which art in heaven, hallowed be thy name; thy kingdom come; thy will be done on earth, as it is in heaven; give us this day our daily bread; and forgive us our trespasses, as we forgive those that trespass against us; and lead us not into temptation, but, deliver us from evil. *Amen.*

*Then shall the minister conclude with an extemporaneous prayer.*

# BAPTISM OF ADULTS.

— ❖ —

## EXHORTATION.

*The minister shall use the following, or some other exhortation, suitable to this holy office:*

Dearly beloved, forasmuch as all men are conceived and born in sin, (and that which is born of the flesh is flesh, and they that are in the flesh cannot please God, but live in sin, committing many actual transgressions ) and that our Saviour Christ saith, None can enter into the kingdom of God, except he be regenerated and born anew of water and of the Holy Ghost, and received into Christ's holy Church, and be made lively members of the same: I therefore beseech you to call upon God the Father, through our Lord Jesus Christ, that of his bounteous goodness he will grant unto *these persons* that which by nature they cannot have, that they may be baptized with water and the Holy Ghost.

## FIRST PRAYER.

*Then shall the minister say:*

Almighty and immortal God, the aider of all that need, the helper of all that flee to thee for succor, the life of them that believe, and the resurrection of the dead, we call upon thee for these persons, that they, coming to thy holy baptism, may receive the remission of their sins by spiritual regeneration. Receive them, O Lord, as thou hast promised by thy well-beloved Son, saying, Ask, and ye shall receive; seek, and ye shall find; knock, and it shall be opened unto you: So give now unto those that ask; let us that seek, find; open the gate unto us that knock; that these persons may enjoy the everlasting benediction of thy heavenly washing, and may come to the eternal kingdom which thou hast promised by Christ our Lord. *Amen.*

## SECOND PRAYER.

*After which he shall say:*

Almighty and everlasting God, heavenly Father, we give thee humble thanks, for that thou hast vouchsafed to call us to the knowledge of thy grace, and faith in thee; increase this knowledge and confirm this faith in us evermore. Give thy Holy Spirit to these persons, that they may be born again, and made heirs of everlasting salvation, through our Lord Jesus Christ, who liveth and reigneth with thee and the Holy Spirit now and forever. *Amen.*

## SCRIPTURE LESSON.

*Then shall the people stand up, and the minister shall say:*

Hear the words of the gospel written by St. John in the third chapter, beginning at the first verse:

"There was a man of the Pharisees, named Nicodemus, a ruler of the Jews: the same came to Jesus by night, and said unto him, Rabbi, we know that thou art a teacher come from God; for no man can do the miracles that thou doest, except God be with him. Jesus answered and said unto him, Verily, verily, I say unto thee, except a man be born again, he cannot see the kingdom of God. Nicodemus saith unto him, How can a man be born when he is old? Can he enter the second time into his mother's womb, and be born? Jesus answered, Verily, verily, I say unto thee, except a man be born of water and of the Spirit he cannot enter into the kingdom of God. That which is born of the flesh is flesh; and that which is born of the Spirit, is spirit. Marvel not that I said unto thee, Ye must be born again. The wind bloweth where it listeth, and thou hearest the sound thereof, but canst not tell whence it cometh, and whither it goeth: so is every one that is born of the Spirit."

403

# BAPTISM OF ADULTS.

## ADDRESS TO THE CANDIDATE.

*Then shall the minister speak to the person to be baptized, on this wise:*

Well beloved, who are come hither desiring to receive holy baptism, ye have heard how the congregation hath prayed that our Lord Jesus Christ would vouchsafe to receive you, and bless you, to release you of your sins, to give you the kingdom of heaven and everlasting life. And our Lord Jesus Christ hath promised in his holy word, to grant all those things we have prayed for, which promise he, for his part, will most surely keep and perform.

Wherefore, after this promise made by Christ, you must also faithfully, on your part, promise, in the presence of this whole congregation, that you will renounce the devil and all his works, and constantly believe God's word, and obediently keep his commandments.

*Then shall the minister demand of each of the persons to be baptized:*

*Question.*—Dost thou renounce the devil and all his works, the vain pomp and glory of the world, with all covetous desires of the same, and the carnal desires of the flesh, and that thou wilt not follow, nor be led by them?

*Answer.*—I renounce them all.

*Question.*—Dost thou believe in God the Father Almighty, Maker of heaven and earth? And in Jesus Christ, his only-begotten Son, our Lord? And that he was conceived of the Holy Ghost, born of the Virgin Mary? That he suffered under Pontius Pilate, was crucified, dead and buried; that he arose again the third day; that he ascended into heaven, and sitteth at the right hand of God, the Father Almighty; and from thence shall come again at the end of the world, to judge the quick and the dead?

And dost thou believe in the Holy Ghost, the Holy Catholic Church,* the communion of saints, the remission of sins, the resurrection of the body, and everlasting life after death?

*Answer.*—All this I steadfastly believe.

*Question.*—Wilt thou be baptized in this faith?

*Answer.*—This is my desire.

*Question.*—Wilt thou then obediently keep God's holy will and commandments, and walk in the same all the days of thy life?

*Answer.*—I will endeavor to do so, God being my helper.

## THE COLLECTS.

*Then shall the minister say:*

O merciful God, grant that the old Adam in these persons may be so buried, that the new man may be raised in them. *Amen.*

Grant that all carnal affections may die in them, and that all things belonging to the Spirit may live and grow in them. *Amen.*

Grant that they may have power and strength to have victory, and triumph against the devil, the world, and the flesh. *Amen.*

Grant that they, being here dedicated to thee by our office and ministry, may also be endued with heavenly virtues, and everlastingly rewarded, through thy mercy, O blessed Lord God, who dost live, and govern all things, world without end. *Amen.*

* The Church Universal, and not the Papal Church of Rome.

## BAPTISM OF ADULTS.

Almighty, everliving God, whose most dearly beloved Son, Jesus Christ, for the forgiveness of our sins, didst shed out of his most precious side both water and blood; and gave commandment to his disciples, that they should go teach all nations, baptising them in the name of the Father, and of the Son, and of the Holy Ghost, regard, we beseech thee, the supplications of this congregation; and grant that the persons now to be baptized, may receive the fullness of thy grace, and ever remain in the number of thy faithful and elect children, through Jesus Christ our Lord. *Amen.*

## THE CEREMONY.

*Then shall the minister take each person to be baptized by the right hand, and placing them conveniently by the font, according to his discretion, shall ask the name: and then shall sprinkle or pour water upon him, (or if they desire, shall immerse them in water,) saying:*

*N.*, I baptize thee in the name of the Father, and of the Son, and of the Holy Ghost. *Amen.*

## THE LORD'S PRAYER.

*Then shall be said the Lord's Prayer, all kneeling.*

Our Father, who art in heaven, hallowed be thy name; Thy kingdom come; Thy will be done on earth as it is in heaven; give us this day our daily bread, and forgive us our trespasses as we forgive them that trespass against us; and lead us not into temptation, but deliver us from evil. *Amen.*

*Then let the minister conclude with an extemporary prayer.*

———————※※———————

# ᴿECEIVING ᴹEMBERS INTO ᶠULL ᶜONNECTION.

## ADDRESS TO THE CONGREGATION.

*Upon the day appointed, all that are to be received shall be called forward, and the minister addressing the congregation, shall say:*

DEARLY BELOVED BRETHREN: The Scriptures teach us that the Church is the household of God; the body, of which Christ is the Head, and that it is the design of the Gospel to bring together in one all who are Christ's. The fellowship of the Church is the communion that its members enjoy one with another. The end of this fellowship are, the maintenance of sound doctrine, and of the ordinances of Christian worship, and the exercise of that power of godly admonition and discipline which Christ has committed to his Church for the promotion of holiness. It is the duty of all men to unite in this fellowship, for it is only those that "be planted in the house of the Lord, that shall flourish in the courts of our God." Its more particular duties are, to promote peace and unity; to bear one another's burdens; to prevent each other's stumbling; to seek the intimacy of friendly society among themselves; to continue steadfast in the faith and worship of the Gospel; and to pray and sympathize with each other. Among its privileges are—peculiar incitements to holiness from the hearing of God's Word, and sharing Christ's ordinances: the being placed under the watchful care of Pastors, and the enjoyment of the blessings which are promised only to those which are of the household of faith. Into this holy fellowship the persons before you, who have already received the Sacrament of Baptism, and have been under the care of proper leaders for six months on trial, come seeking admission.

We now propose, in the fear of God, to question them as to their faith and purposes, that you may know that they are proper persons to be admitted into the Church.

# RECEIVING MEMBERS INTO FULL CONNECTION.

## ADDRESS TO THE APPLICANTS.

*Then addressing the applicants for admission, the minister shall say:*

DEARLY BELOVED: You are come hither seeking the great privilege of union with the Church our Saviour has purchased with his own blood. We rejoice in the grace of *God* vouchsafed unto you in that he has called you to be his followers, and that thus far you have run well. You have heard how blessed are the privileges and how solemn are the duties of membership in *Christ's Church*, and before you are fully admitted thereto, it is proper that you do here publicly renew your vows, confess your faith, and declare your purpose by answering the following questions:

*Question* 1.—Do you here in the presence of *God* and of this congregation, renew the solemn promise contained in the Baptismal Covenant, ratifying and confirming the same, and acknowledging yourselves bound faithfully to observe and keep that covenant, and all things contained therein?

*Answer.*—I do.

*Question* 2.—Have you saving faith in the *Lord Jesus Christ?*

*Answer.*—I trust I have.

*Question* 3.—Do yo entertain friendly feelings towards all the members of this Church?

*Answer.*—I do.

*Question* 4 —Do you believe in the doctrines of the Holy Scriptures as set forth in the articles of religion of the African Methodist Episcopal Church?

*Answea.*—I do.

*Question* 5.—Will you cheerfully be governed by the Discipline of the African Methodist Episcopel Church, hold sacred the ordinances of God, and endeavor, as much as in you lies, to promote the welfare of your brethren, and the advancement of the Redeemer's kingdom?

*Answer.*—I will.

*Question* 6.—Will you contribute of your earthly substance according to your ability, to the support of the Gospel, Church, and poor, and the various benevolent enterprises of the Church?

*Answer.*—I will.

## ADDRESS TO THE CHURCH.

*Then the minister, addressing the church, shall say.*

BRETHREN: You have heard the responses given to our inquiries. Have any of you any reason to allege why these persons should not be received into full membership in the Church?

## THE RECEPTION.

*No objection being alleged, the minister shall say to the candidates:*

We welcome you to the communion of the Church of God; and in testimony of our Christian affection and the cordiality with which we receive you, I hereby extend to you the right hand of fellowship; and may *God* grant that you may be a faithful and useful member of the Church militant till you are called to the fellowship of the Church triumphant, which is without fault before the presence of *God.*

*Then shall the minister offer an extemporary prayer.*

# ☞HE L̞ORD'S SUPPER.

——————»)■((——————

## PRELIMINARY.

Those persons who have scruples about kneeling to receive the Lord's Supper may be permitted to receive it whilst either sitting or standing. Let no person who is not a member of our society be admitted to the Supper without examination and some tokens given by an elder or a deacon. No person shall be admitted to the Supper among us who is guilty of any practice for which we would exclude a member from our church.

## SCRIPTURE SELECTIONS.

*The Elder shall say one or more of these sentences:*

"Let your light so shine before men that they may see your good works and glorify your Father which is in heaven." [ Matt. v. 16.]

"Lay not up for yourselves treasures upon earth, where moth and rust doth corrupt, and where thieves break through and steal; but lay up for yourselves treasures in heaven, where neither moth nor rust doth corrupt, and where thieves do not break through nor steal." [Matt. vi. 19, 20.]

"Whatsoever ye would that men should do to you, do ye even so to them: for this is the law and the prophets." [Matt. vii. 12.]

"Not every one that saith unto me, Lord, Lord, shall enter into the kingdom of heaven; but he that doeth the will of my Father which is in heaven. [Matt. vii. 21.]

"Zaccheus stood and said unto the Lord, Behold, Lord, the half of my goods I give to the poor; and if I have taken any thing from any man by false accusation, I restore him fourfold. [Luke xix. 8.]

"He which soweth sparingly shall reap also sparingly; and he which soweth bountifully shall reap also bountifully. Every man according as he purposeth in his own heart, so let him give; not grudgingly, nor of necessity, for God loveth a cheerful giver." [2 Cor. ix. 6, 7.]

"As we have therefore opportunity, let us do good unto all men, especially unto them who are of the household of faith." [Gal. vi. 10.]

"Godliness with contentment is great gain. For we brought nothing into this world, and it is certain we can carry nothing out." [1 Tim. vi. 6, 7.]

"Charge them that are rich in this world, that they be not high-minded, nor trust in uncertain riches, but in the living God; who giveth us richly all things to enjoy; that they do good; that they be rich in good works, ready to distribute, willing to communicate; laying up in store for themselves a good foundation against the time to come, that they may lay hold on eternal life." [1 Tim. vi. 17, 18, 19.]

"God is not unrighteous to forget your work and labor of love, which ye have showed toward his name, in that ye have ministered to the saints, and do minister." [Heb. vi. 10.]

"To do good and to communicate, forget not; for with such sacrifices God is well pleased." [Heb. xiii. 16.]

# THE LORD'S SUPPER.

"Whoso hath this world's good, and seeth his brother have need, and shutteth up his bowels of compassion from him, how dwelleth the love of God in him? [1 John iii. 17.]

"He that hath pity upon the poor, lendeth unto the Lord; and that which he hath given will he pay him again." [Prov. xix. 17.]

[While these sentences are in reading, some fit persons, appointed for that purpose, shall receive the alms for the poor, and other donations of the people, in a decent basin, to be provided for that purpose, and then bring it to the Elder, who shall place it upon the table.]

*After which the Elder shall say:*

## THE SOLICITATION.

Ye that do truly and earnestly repent of your sins, and are in love and charity with your neighbors, and intend to lead a new life, following the commandments of God, and walking from henceforth in his holy ways—draw near with faith and take this holy sacrament to your comfort; and make your humble confession to Almighty God, meekly kneeling upon your knees.

## THE GENERAL CONFESSION.

*Then shall this general confession be made by the minister in the name of all those that are minded to receive the Holy Communion, both he and all the people kneeling humbly upon their knees and saying, all together:*

Almighty God, Father of our Lord Jesus Christ, Maker of all things, Judge of all men: we acknowledge and bewail our manifold sins and wickedness, which we from time to time most grievously have committed, by thought, word, and deed, against thy Divine Majesty, provoking most justly thy wrath and indignation against us. We do earnestly repent, and are heartily sorry for these our misdoings; the remembrance of them is grievous unto us.

Have mercy upon us, have mercy upon us, most merciful Father; for thy Son, our Lord Jesus Christ's sake; forgive us all that is past, and grant that we may ever hereafter, serve and please thee, in newness of life, to the honor and glory of thy name, through Jesus Christ our Lord. Amen. (*Music No.* 1.)

J. T. LAYTON.

Music No. 1.   No. 2.   No. 3.

A - men.   A - men.   A - men.

Organ.

408

# THE LORD'S SUPPER.

## FIRST COLLECT.

*Then shall the Elder say:*

O, Almighty God, our heavenly Father, who of thy great mercy hast promised forgiveness of sins to all them that with hearty repentance and true faith turn unto thee, have mercy upon us; pardon and deliver us from all our sins; confirm and strengthen us in all goodness, and bring us to everlasting life, through Jesus Christ our Lord. Amen. (*Music No. 2.*)

## SECOND COLLECT.

Almighty God, unto whom all hearts are open, all desires known, and from whom no secrets are hid; cleanse the thoughts of our hearts by the inspiration of thy Holy Spirit, that we may perfectly love thee, and worthily magnify thy holy name through Jesus Christ our Lord. Amen. (*Music No. 3.*)

## PRAYER OF ADORATION.

*Then shall the Elder say:*

It is very meet, right, and our bounden duty, that we should at all times, and in all places, give thanks unto thee, O Lord, Holy Father, Almighty, Everlasting God.

Therefore, with angels and archangels, and with all the company of heaven, we laud and magnify thy holy name—evermore praising thee, and saying, Holy, holy, holy Lord God of hosts; heaven and earth are full of thy glory. Glory be to thee, O Lord most high. Amen.

## PRAYER OF HUMILIATION.

*Then shall the Elder say:*

We do not presume to come to this thy table, O merciful Lord, trusting in our own righteousness, but in thy manifold and great mercies. We are not worthy so much as to gather the crumbs under thy table. But thou art the same Lord, whose property is always to have mercy; Grant us, therefore, gracious Lord, so to eat the flesh of thy dear Son, Jesus Christ, and to drink his blood, that our sinful souls and bodies may be made clean by his death and washed through his blood; and, that we may evermore dwell in him, and he in us. Amen. (*Music No. 4.*)

## Music No. 4.

A - men, A - men, A - men, A - - men.

# THE LORD'S SUPPER.

## PRAYER OF CONSECRATION.

*Then the Elder shall say the prayer of consecration as followeth :*

Almighty God, our Heavenly Father, who of thy tender mercy didst give thine only Son, Jesus Christ, to suffer death on the cross for our redemption; who made there, by his oblation of himself once offered, a full, perfect, and sufficient sacrifice, oblation and satisfaction for the sins of the whole world; and did institute, and in his holy gospel command us to continue a perpetual memory of that, his precious death, until his coming again. Hear us, O Merciful Father, we most humbly beseech thee, and grant that we, receiving these thy creatures of bread and wine, according to thy Son, our Saviour Jesus Christ's holy institution, in remembrance of his death and passion, may be partakers of his most blessed body and blood, who in the same night that he was betrayed, took bread, [*here the Elder is to take the plate of bread into his hand*] and when he had given thanks, he brake it [*and here to break the bread*] and gave it to his disciples, saying, Take, eat, this [*and here to lay his hand upon all the bread*] is my body which is broken for you. This do in remembrance of me; likewise after supper he took [*here he is to take the cup into his hand*] the cup, and when he had given thanks, he gave it to them, saying, Drink ye all of it, for this [*and here to lay his hand upon all the vessels containing the wine*] is my blood of the New Testament, which is shed for you, and for many, for the remission of sins : do this, as often as ye shall drink it, in remembrance of me. Amen.

*Then shall the minister first receive the communion in both kinds himself, and then proceed to deliver the same to the other ministers in like manner, (if any be present,) and after that to the people in order into their hands. And when he delivereth the bread he shall say :*

The body of our Lord Jesus Christ, which was given for thee, preserve thy soul and body unto everlasting life. Take and eat this in remembrance that Christ died for thee, and feed on him in thy heart by faith, with thanksgiving.

*And the minister that delivereth the cup shall say :*

The blood of our Lord Jesus Christ, which was shed for thee, preserve thy soul and body unto everlasting life. Drink this in remembrance that Christ's blood was shed for thee, and be thankful.

[If the consecrated bread and wine be all spent before all have commemorated, the Elder may consecrate more by repeating the Prayer of Consecration.]

[When all have commemorated, the minister shall return to the Lord's table and place upon it what remaineth of the consecrated elements, covering the same with a clean linen cloth.]

## LORD'S PRAYER.

*Then shall the Elder say the Lord's prayer:*

Our Father, which art in heaven, hallowed be thy name, thy kingdom come, thy will be done on earth as it is in heaven, give us this day our daily bread, and forgive us our trespasses as we forgive those that trespass against us. And lead us not into temptation, but deliver us from evil, for thine is the kingdom, the power and the glory, forever. Amen.

## PRAYER OF THANKSGIVING.

*After which shall be said as follows :*

O Lord, our heavenly Father, we thy humble servants, desire thy fatherly goodness, mercifully to accept this our sacrifice of praise and thanksgiving; most humbly beseeching thee to grant, that by the merits and death of thy Son Jesus Christ, and through faith in his blood, we and thy whole church may obtain remission of our sins, and all other benefits of his passion. And here we offer and present unto thee, O Lord, ourselves, our souls and bodies, to be a reasonable, holy and lively sacrifice unto thee; humbly beseeching thee that all we who are partakers of this holy communion, may be filled with thy grace and heavenly benediction.

# THE LORD'S SUPPER.

And although we be unworthy, through our manifold sins, to offer unto thee any sacrifice, yet we beseech thee to accept this, our bounden duty and service: not weighing our merits, but pardoning our offences, through Jesus Christ our Lord, by whom, and with whom, in the unity of the Holy Ghost, all honor and glory be unto thee, O Father Almighty, world without end. Amen.

## PRAYER OF EXTOLLATION.

*Then shall be said:*

Glory be to God on high, and on earth peace, good-will towards men. We praise thee, we bless thee, we worship thee, we glorify thee, we give thanks to thee for thy great glory. O Lord God, Heavenly King, God, the Father Almighty.

O Lord, the only begotten Son, Jesus Christ; O Lord God, Lamb of God, Son of the Father, that takest away the sin of the world, have mercy upon us. Thou that takest away the sins of the world, have mercy upon us. Thou that takest away the sins of the world, receive our prayer. Thou that sittest at the right hand of God the Father have mercy upon us.

For thou only art holy, thou art the Lord, thou only, O Christ, with the Holy Ghost, art most high in the glory of God the Father. Amen.

*Then the Elder, if he see it expedient, may put up an extemporary prayer; and afterward shall let the people depart with this blessing:*

## BENEDICTION.

May the peace of God, which passeth all understanding, keep your hearts and minds in the knowledge and love of God, and his Son, Jesus Christ our Lord; and the blessings of God Almighty, the Father, the Son, and the Holy Ghost, be among you and remain with you always. Amen.

N. B.—If the Elder be straitened for time, he may omit any part of the service, except the prayer of consecration.

411

# THE BURIAL SERVICES.

## SCRIPTURE QUOTATIONS.

*N. B.— The following, or some other solemn service, shall be used.*

*The Minister meeting the corpse, and going before it, shall say:*

"I am the resurrection and the life, saith the Lord: he that believeth in me, though he were dead, yet shall he live; and whosoever liveth and believeth in me, shall never die." [John xi. 25, 26.]

"I know that my Redeemer liveth, and that he shall stand at the latter day upon the earth. And though after my skin, worms destroy this body, yet in my flesh shall I see God: whom I shall see for myself, and mine eyes shall behold, and not another." [Job xix. 25, 26, 27.]

"We brought nothing into this world, and it is certain we can carry nothing out. The Lord gave, and the Lord hath taken away; blessed be the name of the Lord." [1 Tim. vi. 7; Job i. 21.]

## SUPPLICATION AT THE GRAVE.

*At the grave, when the corpse is laid in the earth, the Minister shall say·*

"Man that is born of a woman hath but a short time to live, and is full of misery. He cometh up and is cut down like a flower; he fleeth as it were a shadow, and never continueth in one stay."

In the midst of life we are in death, of whom may we seek for succor, but of thee, O Lord, who for our sins art justly displeased?

Yet, O Lord God most holy, O Lord most mighty, O holy and merciful Saviour, deliver us not unto the bitter pains of eternal death.

Thou knowest, Lord the secrets of our hearts, shut not thy merciful ears to our prayers, but spare us, Lord most holy, O God most mighty, O holy and merciful Saviour, thou most worthy Judge eternal, suffer us not, at our last hour, for any pains of death, to fall from thee.

## THE COMMITMENT.

*Then, while the earth shall be cast upon the coffin by some person standing by, the Minister shall say·*

Forasmuch as it hath pleased Almighty God, in his wise providence, to take out of this world the soul of our deceased *brother*, we therefore commit *his* body to the ground, earth to earth, ashes to ashes, dust to dust, looking for the general resurrection in the last day, and the life of the world to come, through our Lord Jesus Christ; at whose second coming in glorious majesty to judge the world, the earth and the sea shall give up their dead, and the corruptible bodies of those who sleep in him shall be changed, and made like unto his own glorious body according to the mighty working whereby he is able to subdue all things unto himself.

*Then shall be said*

"I heard a voice from heaven, saying unto me, write—From henceforth, blessed are the dead who die in the Lord: even so, saith the spirit; for they rest from their labors."

*Then shall the Minister say·*

Lord, have mercy upon us.
Christ, have mercy upon us.
Lord, have mercy upon us.

Our Father who art in heaven, hallowed be thy name: thy kingdom come; thy will be done on earth as it is in heaven; give us this day our daily bread, and forgive us our tres·passes as we forgive them that trespass against us; and lead us not into temptation, but deliver us from evil. *Amen.*

## THE FINAL PRAYER.

*The Collect.*

O merciful God, the Father of our Lord Jesus Christ, who is the resurrection and the life, in whom whosoever believeth shall live, though he die; and whosoever liveth and believ·eth in him shall not die eternally. We meekly beseech thee, O Father, to raise us from the death of sin unto the life of righteousness, that when we shall depart this life, we may rest in him; and at the general resurrection at the last day, may be found acceptable in thy sight, and receive that blessing which thy well-beloved Son shall then pronounce to all that love and fear thee, saying, "Come ye blessed of my Father, receive the kingdom prepared for you from the beginning of the world." Grant this, we beseech thee, O merciful Father, through Jesus Christ, our Mediator and Redeemer. *Amen.*

## THE SOLEMN BENEDICTION.

The grace of our Lord Jesus Christ, and the love of God, and the fellowship of the Holy Ghost, be with us all evermore. *Amen.*

412

# INDEX OF FIRST LINES.

414

# INDEX OF FIRST LINES.

# INDEX OF FIRST LINES.

417

# INDEX OF FIRST LINES.

# INDEX OF FIRST LINES.

# METRICAL INDEX.

———■———

# METRICAL INDEX.

W. H. Keyser & Co., Phila., Pa.

www.ingramcontent.com/pod-product-compliance
Lightning Source LLC
Chambersburg PA
CBHW032259280326
41932CB00009B/624